Dialectics without Synthesis

The publisher and the University of California Press Foundation
gratefully acknowledge the generous support of the
Eric Papenfuse and Catherine Lawrence Endowment Fund
in Film and Media Studies.

Dialectics without Synthesis

Japanese Film Theory and Realism in a Global Frame

Naoki Yamamoto

UNIVERSITY OF CALIFORNIA PRESS

University of California Press
Oakland, California

© 2020 by Naoki Yamamoto

Library of Congress Cataloging-in-Publication Data

Names: Yamamoto, Naoki, 1977- author.
Title: Dialectics without synthesis : Japanese film theory and realism in a global frame / Naoki Yamamoto.
Description: Oakland, California : University of California Press, [2020] | Includes bibliographical references and index.
Identifiers: LCCN 2020010082 | ISBN 9780520351790 (cloth) | ISBN 9780520351806 (paperback) | ISBN 9780520975903 (epub)
Subjects: LCSH: Motion pictures—Japan—Philosophy—History—20th century. | Film criticism—Japan—History—20th century. | Motion pictures—Japan—Aesthetics—History—20th century.
Classification: LCC PN1993.5.J3 Y3736 2020 | DDC 791.430952—dc23
LC record available at https://lccn.loc.gov/2020010082

28 27 26 25 24 23 22 21 20
10 9 8 7 6 5 4 3 2 1

To my parents

CONTENTS

List of Illustrations — ix
Acknowledgments — xi

    Introduction: Realism, Film Theory, Japanese Cinema — 1
1. Naturalism and the Modernization of Japanese Cinema — 24
2. The Machine Aesthetic and Proletarian Realism — 52
3. Literary Adaptation and Textual Realism — 77
4. Documentary Film and Epistemological Realism — 103
5. Neglected Traditions of Bergsonism and Phenomenology — 133
    Epilogue: Hanada Kiyoteru and Postwar Debates — 166

Notes — 185
Selected Bibliography — 209
Index — 225

ILLUSTRATIONS

1. An example of Kabuki cinema featuring Onoe Matsunosuke   41
2. Kaeriyama Norimasa's *The Glow of Life*   42
3. The front cover of *Exchanges between Machine and Art*   55
4. Itagaki Takao and Horino Masao's "Characteristics of Greater Tokyo"   62
5. An ad for *The Woman That Night*   78
6. Uchida Tomu's *Unending Advance*   88
7. Kumagai Hisatora's *The Abe Family*   97
8. A chart in Nakai Masakazu's "Continuity of *In Spring*"   117
9. Taguchi Satoshi's *General, Staff, and Soldier*   131
10. Nishida Kitarō's philosophical worldview   155
11. A revised diagram of Nishida's philosophical worldview   156
12. Nagae's cinematic worldview   158
13. Hanada Kiyoteru's philosophical worldview   177
14. Hanada's cinematic worldview   178

ACKNOWLEDGMENTS

This book is a product of many unexpected, trans-Pacific encounters I have had during the past two decades. First of all, I want to express my deepest gratitude to Aaron Gerow, who has been my mentor since the late 1990s, when I was still an undergraduate student at Meiji Gakuin University, Tokyo. His lectures on Japanese cinema there were a life-changing experience because he taught me not only that studying film is more than being a cinephile but also that any successful historical research requires a solid theoretical foundation. Then, in 2005, I moved to Yale University to pursue my doctoral degree under his supervision, and through his guidance, I came to know and write about previously neglected works of Japanese film theorists. It is thus no exaggeration to say that I would never have written this book or even left Japan for graduate study if I had not met Aaron in the way I did. This book is based on my dissertation, and I would like to thank my professors at Yale as well. Dudley Andrew, John Treat, Francesco Casetti, Charles Musser, John Mackay, Katerina Clark, and Brigitte Peucker gave me rigorous trainings in both pedagogy and analytical methods. I am also grateful to Markus Nornes and Thomas Lamarre for having served as external commentators on this project from its inception to completion.

Over the past seven years, my colleagues at the University of California, Santa Barbara, have been a great source of inspiration and expansion. Peter Bloom and Glyn Salton-Cox carefully read my manuscript and always got back to me with well-conceived suggestions; Bhaskar Sarkar and Charles Wolfe helped me make my overall argument more accessible to the readers outside Japanese Studies; and Alenda Y. Chang, Michael Curtin, Mona Damluji, Anna Everett, Dick Hebdige, Jennifer Holt, Ross Melnick, Constance Penley, Patrice Petro, Cristina Venegas, Laila Shereen Sakr, Greg Siegel, and Janet Walker have all supported my project through their collegiality and friendship. At UCSB, I have also benefitted from conversations and collaborations with people outside of my home department, including Sabine Frühstück, Bishnupriya Ghosh, Fabio Rambelli, Katherine Saltzman-Li, ann-elise lewallen, Kate McDonald, and David Novak. I would also like to thank both the graduate and the undergraduate students who took my film theory courses and patiently spent hours with me in the classroom every week.

A number of scholars offered me invaluable assistance as I prepared my manuscript. In Japan, kudos go first to my former advisors at Meiji Gakuin University—Unami Akira, Yomota Inuhiko, Saitō Ayako, and Monma Takashi—who have all guided my initial foray into the world of critical thinking and provided me sustained support ever since. I am greatly indebted to Toba Kōji, who kindly served as a host professor during my one-year stay at Waseda University in 2018–2019. Joyous conversations with Toba-san helped me to maintain my sanity as I completed my manuscript in Tokyo last year. I equally appreciate Hirasawa Gō, Itō Kiyomi, Roland Domenig, Iwamoto Kenji, Senno Takumasa, Toeda Hirokazu, Takahashi Toshio, Munakata Kazushige, Mitsuyo Wada-Marciano, Kinoshita Chika, Niels van Steenpaal, Fujiki Hideaki, and Nakamura Hideyuki for sharing their time and insight with me. Outside Japan, Alexander Zahlten, Marc Steinberg, Yuriko Furuhata, Masha Salazkina, Victor Fan, Jane Gaines, Weihong Bao, Phil Rosen, Dan O'Neill, Alastair Phillips, Alice Lovejoy, Phil Kaffen, Diane Wei Lewis, Kim Jihoon, Stephen Teo, Kris Paulsen, and John Davidson all provided me the opportunity to present my work and inspiring feedback. I also thank Raina Polivka and Madison Wetzell, my editors at the University of California Press, and the two anonymous readers for their far-sighted direction and professionalism.

This book would have never been possible without the generous financial support from several organizations. The Prize Fellowship by the Council on East Asian Studies at Yale University enabled me to conduct one-year archival research in Japan. Film viewing at the Pacific Film Archive was supported by a summer grant from the Center for Japanese Studies at University of California, Berkeley. The Hellman Family Fellowship supported my two-week research trip to the Makino Collection at Columbia University. The Hakuhō Foundation Japanese Research Fellowship was especially generous in supporting my sabbatical leave and granting time to complete and polish my manuscript.

Finally, I wish to send my sincere thanks to my friends and family whose generosities have been the lifeblood for my endeavor. I acknowledge Che Sungwook, Asari Hiroyuki, Sawada Masayuki, Ahn Minhwa, Fujita Natsu, Ōmine Sawa, Kendall Heitzman, Arthur Mitchell, Brian Steininger, Ryan Cook, Tsunoda Takuya, Rea Amit, Pat Noonan, Ashton Lazarus, Sam Malissa, Erik Cronqvist, Akira Shimizu, Nora Gortcheva, Youn-mi Kim, Will Fleming, Kathy Lu, and John Graves for making my school years merrier and more rewarding. I thank my partner, Xiaowei Zheng, for her good spirit, love, and humor. She and her parents, Zhao

Jieping and Zheng Yisheng, have consistently supported me with love and patience, and I will forever be thankful for their unwavering trust in me. This book is dedicated to my parents, Mayumi and Shigetsune Yamamoto, who have distilled in me a lifelong desire to explore the uncertain possibilities in life. Unfortunately, my father passed away in 2018 and was unable to see the publication of this book. But I am certain that he would be happy with what I have written in the following pages. Indeed, he proudly told his best friends about my accomplishment—he even made up an imaginary story that I would be appearing on TV soon!—just a few weeks before his departure.

Several chapters in this book have been revised and expanded from earlier published versions: chapter 2 from "Eye of the Machine: Itagaki Takao and Debates on New Realism in 1920s Japan," *Framework* 56, no. 2 (Fall 2015): 368–387; chapter 5 from "Experiencing the World through Cinema: Nagae Michitarō and the Bergsonian Approach to Film in Wartime Japan," in *Dall'inizio, alla fine: Teorie del cinema in prospettiva*, edited by Francesco Casetti, Jane Gains, and Valentina Re (Udine, Italy: Forum Editrice Universitaria Udinese, 2010), 571–576; and the epilogue from "The Reception of Paul Rotha in Postwar Japan: On Hanada Kiyoteru's 'Sur-Documentary,'" in *The Creative Treatment of Grierson in Wartime Japan*, edited by Morita Noriko and Nakamura Daigo (Yamagata: Yamagata International Film Festival, 2019), 32–35.

Throughout this book Japanese names appear in the Eastern name order, with the family name first and the given name second, unless the person—including myself—deliberately adopts the Western name order, as in Yoko Ono.

Introduction

Realism, Film Theory, Japanese Cinema

In 2013, I was hired at a North American university to fill a position designated as assistant professor of "Theories of Film and Media." My primary task was to teach an intensive lecture course on the history of film theory, a course that all the film and media studies majors in our program must take and pass before their graduation. I learned a lot from teaching both classical and contemporary texts in film theory, but this teaching experience also put me in a difficult situation when I started thinking how I might improve the quality of this course by incorporating my own specialty: Japanese cinema. Because the English-language textbooks I used in that course—Leo Braudy and Marshall Cohen's *Film Theory and Criticism*, Bill Nichols's *Movies and Methods*, Dudley Andrew's *The Major Film Theories*, Toby Miller and Robert Stam's *A Companion to Film Theory*, and Marc Furstenau's *The Film Theory Reader*—cover only theoretical texts written in European languages (including Russian), I was only able to assign some well-known Japanese films by Ozu Yasujirō, Kurosawa Akira, and Mizoguchi Kenji to be analyzed by means of those canonical Western theories.[1]

After several occasions of teaching the course, I came to ask myself a series of questions regarding the discursive conditions that both inform and determine what we call "theory" in our discipline. Why, for instance, do we still distinguish between the West and the non-West in terms of knowledge production, always granting the former a privileged power to disseminate authentic accounts of cinema and its related phenomena? Is it valid to maintain such a rigid geographical divide, given that film was invented and then circulated as a modern medium to travel across the world? What do we really mean by the term *theory*, especially when we admit that a variety of nonacademic publications such as film reviews, short essays, and art and political manifestos comprise the basis of so-called classical film theory? Was there any qualitative or incommensurable difference between Western and non-Western critics in their adoptions of this particular mode of writing? If not, what might we gain by exposing hitherto neglected archives of non-Western film theories in an effort to redefine the very meaning of the global in twentieth-century modernity and its particular mode of cultural production?

This book offers my tentative answer to these pedagogical questions. It examines how generations of Japanese intellectuals from the early 1910s to the late 1950s—the period usually designated "classical" in film history—developed their theorizations of cinema in parallel with their Western counterparts. Of the many topics discussed during this time period, I have chosen realism to be the primary focus of my inquiry, partly because realism, whether treated positively or negatively, has always preoccupied the mind of film theorists. But a more specific reason lies in the ways in which Japanese cinema has been studied in the Anglo-American context. In his influential 1979 book *To the Distant Observer: Form and Meaning in the Japanese Cinema*, Noël Burch famously argued that Japanese cinema had long been immune to "the ideology of 'realism'" thanks to the visual languages it inherited from local traditional theaters such as Kabuki and Noh. Furthermore, to emphasize the alterity of Japanese film culture in general, Burch went so far as to declare that "the very notion of theory is alien to Japan: it is considered a property of Europe and the West."[2]

We should, of course, keep in mind that Burch strategically presented his argument as part of his ideological critique of Hollywood cinema's mesmerizing capitalist illusionism. And yet a critique of Burch's own illusion has also been long overdue, which is why I deliberately illuminate and scrutinize the existence of *Japanese theorizations of cinematic realism*. Even a glimpse at local film criticism in prewar and wartime Japan helps justify my revisionist approach. Beginning with the emergence of film journalism in the 1910s, Japanese filmmakers and critics had been eager to catch up with, discuss, and transform the latest ideas and techniques imported from abroad. As a consequence, major works in classical film theory, including that of Hugo Münsterberg, Béla Balázs, Jean Epstein, Rudolf Arnheim, and members of the Soviet montage school, had become available in Japanese by the mid-1930s.[3] Such timely translations of foreign texts, in turn, stimulated the continuous publication of theoretical books and articles written in Japanese, although these minor theories have yet to find their place in the current scholarship of both film theory and Japanese cinema. I hope to remedy this absence in the pages that follow. But in so doing, I also explicate the inherently hybrid, transnational nature of Japanese film culture.

NON-WESTERN THEORY AS PRAXIS

While several attempts were made to launch college-level film programs beginning in the 1920s, it is understood that film studies as we know it today is a product of the anti-establishment movement of 1968 and the years following. In fact, Burch, as well as the majority of film scholars during that period, strove to elevate the status of this newly established discipline by incorporating what seemed to be the most radical and iconoclastic ideas circulating in contemporary thought, namely, Althusserian Marxism and Lacanian psychoanalysis. These new approaches, often labeled as French poststructuralist theory, appeared as an alternative or the latest addition to preexisting analytical frameworks in other already established disciplines. But in film studies, they came to occupy the dominant place in its critical discourse and curricula, forming the foundation for what we call "theory" in our discipline. In addition, the history of film theory has equally privileged a particular lineage of the French intellectual tradition—including André Bazin, Christian Metz, and apparatus theory—with occasional or later additions of German, Russian, and Anglo-American inputs. Consequently, as Markus Nornes has observed, anyone attending introductory courses on film theory at North American universities would inevitably have the impression that "serious film criticism and theory are the exclusive domain of the West."[4]

Thus the exclusion of non-Western film theory was deeply embedded within the historical formation of film studies as an academic discipline, a problem that has been a subject of debate among scholars over the past decades. With the rise of postcolonial studies in the 1980s, scholars such as Teshome H. Gabriel, Homi K. Bhabha, and Mitsuhiro Yoshimoto took issue with the unilateral, indiscriminate application of Western canonical theory to non-Western film practices.[5] According to their criticism, the unabashed Eurocentrism that characterizes our critical discourse is not simply a matter of spatial segregation; it also has a temporal dimension. While the West tends to identify itself as an ahistorical and transcendental entity through its dedication to the creation of theory as a universal discourse, any critical or theoretical discourse produced in the non-West is always confined within its own spatial and temporal limitations, serving merely as an object for area-specific historical research.

Around the same time, David Bordwell and Noël Carroll similarly criticized the domination of contemporary film theory by what they called "Grand Theory" or "Big Theories of Everything" that originated in France.[6] Retrospectively, their inventions appear to us as attempts to increase the visibility of Anglo-American traditions in analytic philosophy by providing recourse to the fact-based interpretation of the viewer's normative cognitive behaviors. Nonetheless, they also suggested that scholars take part in "empirical studies of filmmakers, genres, and national cinemas" to prove that "an argument can be at once conceptually powerful and based in evidence without appeal to theoretical bricolage or association of ideas."[7] The 1990s and 2000s saw what one could call the "empirical turn," which was best represented in the upsurge of early cinema studies. This was also the case in the studies of Japanese cinema, where a new generation of scholars equipped with language skills produced a number of innovative works using a variety of primary sources excavated through extensive archival research. While these new studies were indispensable in proving the existence of a rich and long tradition of Japanese film criticism, they remained relatively silent as to how we assess those local writings in the broader, transnational context of the history of film theory.[8]

More recently, there have emerged monographs and edited volumes that pay special attention to previously underrepresented genealogies of non-Western film theory and criticism. Speaking only of those dealing with Japan and China, one could name works such as Aaron Gerow's "Decentering Theory: Reconsidering the History of Japanese Film Theory," Yuriko Furuhata's *Cinema of Actuality: Japanese Avant-Garde Filmmaking in the Season of Image Politics*, Victor Fan's *Cinema Approaching Reality: Locating Chinese Film Theory*, and Jessica Ka Yee Chan's *Chinese Revolutionary Cinema: Propaganda, Aesthetics, and Internationalism, 1949–1966*.[9] These publications, on the one hand, squarely respond to D. N. Rodowick's call for attaining "a more conceptual picture of how film became associated with theory in the early twentieth century, and how ideas of theory vary in different historical periods and national contexts."[10] But, on the other hand, they are equally motivated to address the shifting identity of what we call "cinema" in today's media environment. As nearly every aspect of film production, distribution, and exhibition becomes digitalized through the proliferation of new media platforms, it becomes imperative to revisit the question "What is cinema?" And precisely because the major film theories, premised on the ontological stability of the photographic image, have proved to be inadequate for addressing this question in earnest, film scholars in the twenty-first century have begun to explore different sets of discourses on the experience of moving images, focusing in particular on those developed either *before* or *outside* the institutionalization of film studies. The concomitant revival of classical film theory in the past decade must also be read in this light.[11]

The primary task for anyone working on non-Western film theory is to clarify how we could, or should, define the term *theory* in a given geopolitical context. In this respect, Marc Steinberg and Alexander Zahlten, editors of the recently published *Media Theory in Japan*, offer us a very useful insight.[12] To begin with, Steinberg and Zahlten problematize what they view as Western media scholars' obsession with Japan as one of the most influential sources of modern audiovisual media practice on the globe, a posture that in turn underscores their collective ignorance of the existence of local critical discourses regarding such practice. Media theory, to say the least, has equally been treated as the exclusive domain of the West. As a methodological guide for their own articulation of "media theory in Japan," the editors draw upon Shu-mei Shih and Françoise Lionnet's earlier commitment to the "creolization of theory." The objective of this project was to promote indigenous theoretical activities taking place in formerly colonized areas by consciously rejecting our commonplace understanding of (Western) theory as a universal discourse. In their attempt at deconstructing theory, creolization also means "pluralization." "Without being Theory with a capital *T*," argue Shih and Lionnet, "theory can engage with the objects of one's analysis in multiple ways and to different levels of intensity. When objects of analysis are not simple instances and illustrations of theory and are not made to conform to theory, theory as such performs a very different function."[13]

Steinberg and Zahlten refer to the "thought of the aughts" (*zeronendai no shisō*) group as an example of such non-Theoretical media theories in Japan. Represented by critics such as Ōtsuka Eiji and Azuma Hiroki, this loosely connected group of writers elaborates a series of theoretical and sometimes philosophical analyses of Japanese media culture, placing *anime* and subculture at its center. But the main agenda and the platform of the group are palpably different from those of media theorists in Europe and the United States. First, those associated with the group seldom use academic journals as the venue for their intellectual outputs but rely instead upon public forums generated through the internet. Second, they create discursive tools for interpretation through their active participation in the cultural phenomena or media events they analyze. The significance of this group is not limited to its ability to provide an alternative to "Theory" through their collective emphasis on local specificities and the vernacular. The group also blurs the categorical distinction between theory and practice, effectively making the role of both media producers and consumers the very act of theorizing.[14] Following this symptomatic mutation of the meaning and function of theory in the Japanese context, Steinberg and Zahlten declare that their volume of "essays proposes to make this shift from media theory as universal to media theory as a practice composed of local, medium-specific, and culture-inflected practices."[15]

I agree with Steinberg and Zahlten in that we need to provide a more nuanced and informed analysis of cultural, historical, and institutional aspects of theory production. However, I would also like to complicate their conception of Japanese media theory as a practice by taking into account the specific conditions surrounding classical film theory. Because their work appeared before the establishment of film studies as a discipline, most contributors of classical film theory were writing outside the traditional realm of academic institutions. In most cases, these theorists were also practitioners, as they often developed their ideas through actual filmmaking or constant viewing of films. This situation led to what Rodowick calls the "rarity of theory," meaning that the best theoretical insights during the classical period in film history were usually scattered across many different writing styles and publishing formats rather than neatly presented in monographs.[16] It is thus possible to say that film studies has already long engaged in pluralizing "theory," to the extent that it enshrines as its own canons a variety of non-Theoretical texts published in the form of poetic prose (Jean Epstein), written manifesto (Dziga Vertov), cultural criticism (Siegfried Kracauer), film review (Bazin) in addition to those akin to the more traditional sense of academic writing (Hugo Münsterberg, Belá Balázs, and Rudolf Arnheim).

This idiosyncratic status of classical film theory as both a vernacular and a practical discourse requires another level of reflection when it comes to Japanese theorizations of cinema. What should we do if the pluralization of "Theory" into "theories" is not sufficient enough to differentiate Japanese film theory from its Western counterpart? Does it mean that we have to come up with another alternative to the now common practice of treating the indigenous discourse building in historically understudied ethnic or sexuality groups as examples of the creolization of theory? How might we establish a reflexive and constructive comparative method to assess non-Western film and media theories that display not only divergence but also unmistakable proximity to Western canons?

TWO APPROACHES TO JAPANESE FILM THEORY

In recently published studies of Japanese film theory, two approaches address these methodological challenges. The first is what I call "interpretive comparison." This approach makes Japanese theoretical texts intelligible on a common and familar ground for comparison. It then confers upon some of the finest Japanese writings a full-fledged eligibility to be called a "theory" in the traditional sense. One example is Gavin Walker's reading of film essays by the Japanese Marxist thinker Tosaka Jun. At the beginning of his essay, Walker cautiously reminds us that his main objective is "to examine the development of the filmic moment in Tosaka's philosophy rather than to examine the specific historical circumstance and historical trajectory of film theory in Japan of the 1920s and 1930s."[17] Faithful to this opening remark, his argument makes frequent references to a cluster of contemporary philosophers including Walter Benjamin, Gilles Deleuze and Félix Guattari, Jacques Rancière, and Alain Badiou, as well as Paul Virilio, Susan Buck-Morss, and César Guimarães. Walker's interpretation of Tosaka goes like this: "Essentially, he [Tosaka] is drawing our attention to the fact that 'in the prosthetic cognition of the cinema, the difference between documentary and fiction is thus effaced....' In other words, what Tosaka argues essentially is that film constitutes 'a place of intrinsic indiscernability [sic] between art and non-art.'"[18]

In this passage, the first quotation comes from Buck-Morss's "The Cinema Screen as Prosthesis of Perception" and the second from Badiou's *Infinite Thought*.[19] The problem here is not simply that one could mistakenly take these quotations as Tosaka's own statement; it also makes us wonder whether Walker's interpretative comparison here helps to confirm Shih and Lionnet's concern that objects of analysis from the non-West—in this case, Tosaka's own theoretical writing—are more often than not used as "simple instances and illustrations of theory [with a capital T]."[20]

Like Walker, I will compare Japanese and Western theorists and sometimes eulogize the excellence and innovation of the former. Nevertheless, I also find it necessary to critically reflect on the very use of comparison as a method with the aid of recent discussions in the field of comparative literature. In her 2006 book *The Age of the World Target*, Rey Chow undertakes the difficult task of establishing "a fundamentally different set of terms for comparative literary studies" appropriate for the twenty-first century.[21] Although originally conceived in the late nineteenth century as a transnational project of disseminating the cosmopolitan ideal of "world literature," comparative literature as a discipline became ideologically problematic in its next hundred years of history, since it always placed literature as understood in Europe as a "grid of intelligibility," or the "common ground" for comparison.[22] The problem with this traditional comparative method is that it tends to render incongruous differences found in non-Western literary texts as mere examples of "chronologically more recent variations to be incorporated into a familiar grid of reference."[23]

A simple denial of this grid of intelligibility does not help us much here, for it inevitably brings studies of non-Western literature back to the nativist discourse of national or ethnic integrity. For this reason, Chow suggests that we instead treat both culturally and geographically specific formations of non-Western modernity as "full-fledged comparative projects." That is, even if a non-Western writer we study was completely monolingual and had never been abroad, her creative work was written and read in a discursive situation that required her to involve a self-reflexive comparison between herself (as well as her living situation) and the overwhelming presence of Europe and North America in modern world politics. This revised usage and understanding of the term *comparison* does not prevent us from comparing two or more writers from different parts of the world. It simply adds to our comparative method "a critique of *the uneven distribution of cultural capital among languages themselves*," as Chow explains.[24]

One could find a good example of this kind of internalized comparison in Aaron Gerow's concept of the "theory complex," which I refer to as the second approach to Japanese film theory. According to Gerow, the theory complex designates a "symptom of non-Western modernity" shared among Japanese intellectuals who, in the midst of their country's modernization project, expressed self-contradictory, or even schizophrenic, attitudes toward "theory" due to their full recognition of both the attractions and foreignness of this newly imported term.[25] In the discursive history of Japanese cinema, therefore, theory is at once needed and rejected because it has always been the subject of the constant comparison between the West and the rest, or between things (presumed to be) Japanese and non-Japanese.

Let us first see how the notion of theory has been rejected historically in the Japanese context. In 1941, the filmmaker Itami Mansaku expressed his total disagreement with the then popular belief that Soviet montage theory represents the sole essence of filmmaking. As a director specializing in the production of satires in the genre of period drama (*jidaigeki*), Itami was always critical of his fellow critics who blindly accepted and appreciated "theories of Western authorities" (*Seiyō no erai hito no riron*).[26] The main target of Itami's critique was Kurata Fumindo who, in his book *On Film Script* (*Shinarioron*), argued that all consecutive scenes in a film should be arranged in conflict with each other, as explained in Eisenstein's theory of dialectical montage.[27] As expected, Itami did not buy this argument because it was completely at odds with what he had learned from his firsthand experience as a film director: "To the degree that it is represented by its theory of collision ... the true nature of theoretical debates on film montage seems not far from mere speculation. As a result, I somehow came to have an impression that it [Soviet montage theory] was an illegitimate child in film theory who tried to take over the orthodox lineage of composition by taking its methodological tricks to the extreme."[28] Itami admitted that his counterargument went no further than repeating the basic principles of classical film editing. But he nonetheless added that "a theory can never have the power to convince people unless it grasps a truth applicable to most cases," and for this reason Itami refused to call Soviet montage theory a "theory" in its strict sense.[29]

The film historian Satō Tadao presents a similar view in his 1977 monograph *The History of Japanese Film Theory* (*Nihon eiga rironshi*). Despite the self-evident title of his study, Satō begins by provocatively asking, "Did film theory exist in Japan?" (*Nihon ni eiga riron wa attaka*). And his answer is "no," inasmuch as "individuals who have written in books on film theory in Japan have mainly authored translations introducing foreign film theory," and as a result, "in Japan, unfortunately, very few individuals can be called film theorists."[30] Satō's polemic here, however, does not really lament the total absence of "Japanese" film theory. Rather, he uses it to emphasize that we must employ an absolutely different conception of "theory" in order to illuminate the existence of a uniquely Japanese take on film theory. As Satō writes: "It is not that Japan has no original film theory. As I stated earlier, such an aesthetic tradition [of Japanese cinema] would not have been possible without its own film theory. . . . Unfortunately, however, Japanese film theory remains disorganized, buried in the word-of-mouth training at production studios, in the short essays and written interviews of directors and screenwriters, and in the film reviews written by critics."[31] According to Itami and Satō, then, only discourses born from the actual practice of domestic filmmaking can be genuinely called a "theory" in the Japanese context. This assertion, however, is not only historically inaccurate but to a large extent self-deceptive; both writers, in the end, mobilized another critical framework to *theorize* the non-*T*heoretical character of Japanese written or spoken accounts of cinema.

As I have already mentioned, the strong craving for film theory in Japan led to the translation of major classical film theories by the mid-1930s. But this translation fever also extended well into the work of minor theorists whose names were largely forgotten in the Anglo-American context, including V. O. Freeburg, Austin Lescarboura, Gilbert Seldes, Eric Elliot, and Fedor Stepun.[32] Besides these works, prewar and wartime Japan had many local film magazines—including *Kinema junpō* (*Movie Times*), *Eiga ōrai* (*Film Traffic*), *Eiga hyōron* (*Film Criticism*), *Eiga shūdan* (*Film Collective*), and *Nihon eiga* (*Japanese Cinema*)—that featured lengthy critical essays penned by local critics and thinkers. And these periodicals were followed by hundreds of film books dealing with auteur theory, film sociology, proletarian culture, the impact of sound revolution, documentary films, and many other relevant issues. This specific discursive situation also made film theory a highly profitable subject in Japanese print journalism. Imamura Taihei, dubbed as the "best film scholar of our times" by his fellow critics, was able to publish nine monographs composed entirely of his theoretical writings on cinema during the years between 1938 and 1943. Such a local demand for film theory did not change much even after Japan's defeat in World War II. In 1948, the editorial in the inaugural issue of *Eiga kikan* (*Film Quarterly*) declared the magazine's dedication to theory in this new era as follows: "Because of the poverty of 'theory,' [Japanese] film criticism had been easily and willingly exploited for the propaganda of imperialism and, again, is now about to give itself to fascism in many ways.... Cinema has fifty years of history in which it has developed itself through its association with capital and by being rendered either integrated or collective art. To establish our 'theory,' we expect the cooperation among many with good sense and brains rather than the emergence of a single genius."[33]

As these two conflicting attitudes testify, Gerow's concept of the theory complex signifies a self-reflexive comparative method intrinsic to Japanese local discourse on film theory. Rather than submissively accepting "Theory" as the sole and unchangeable grid of intelligibility, Japanese intellectuals frequently challenged the proclaimed universality of Western film theories without splitting themselves from the common task of theorizing cinema and its related culture as a global phenomenon in the twentieth century. In this sense, I will follow Gerow's conviction that any successful approach to the history of Japanese film theory must "consider at least partially how it performs theory at the same time that it is critical of the possibilities of theory itself."[34] Only on this condition, moreover, can we also reinvigorate classical comparativist aspirations to juxtapose Western and non-Western texts on the same "operating table." The goal of the following chapters, therefore, is to expand this new horizon of comparison by treating Japanese film theory as a variety of writings that were at once constructing and deconstructing the very act of theorization, or unfinished theories-in-the-making, through their constant and informed conversations with Western counterparts.

THE PARADOX OF REALISM

As shown in Burch's glorification of an anti-realist Japanese cinema, film scholars in the post-1968 period shared a strong antagonism toward realism under the banner of "political modernism."[35] These scholars, on the one hand, harshly criticized Bazin's earlier theorization of cinematic realism, condemning its "native" treatment of the existential bond between a sign and a referent in the photographic image as well as its ignorance of economic factors in both film production and consumption.[36] On the other hand, they also vilified the regressive character of mainstream Hollywood films, arguing how this highly commodified form of mass entertainment helped reproduce dominant capitalist ideologies by imposing on the viewer a false subject position and endlessly deferring the fulfillment of his or her own desire.[37] If, as Colin MacCabe asserted in 1974, the nineteenth-century realist novel succeeded in disseminating the value of bourgeois culture and society by means of its seemingly transparent narrative discourse, it is classical Hollywood cinema's unobtrusive, almost invisible camerawork and editing style that promulgate the American domination of modern capitalism under the guise of "verisimilitude," or more simply of "realism."[38]

Unsurprisingly, such a hasty disavowal of realism in the discourse of film studies became the subject of criticism in the decades that followed. Dudley Andrew and Philip Rosen, for instance, argued that Bazin's theorization of film's ability to generate an impression of reality was far from a simple matter, but rather was elaborated through his engagement in the contemporary philosophical discussion of existentialism and phenomenology.[39] By employing Sartre's famous motto "existence proceeds essence," Andrew, in particular, problematized the idealist attitude of poststructuralist film theory that aimed to deduce "what should be done from some abstract system" rather than observing and reflecting upon "what has been done in cinema."[40] Likewise, David Bordwell, in his study of the narratology of cinema, maintained that earlier attempts to liken Hollywood's classical mode of enunciation to the nineteenth-century realist novel were both theoretically and empirically unacceptable because they did not take into account the cognitive difference between fictional prose and film in their presentations of the development of a plot.[41]

Such revisionist calls for a more careful interpretation of realist film theory became more urgent with the rise of computer-generated imagery (CGI) and digital imaging in film production since the 1990s. Although we as viewers know that the images generated through digital devices no longer require actual objects existing in the world as their referents, why do we still perceive strong "reality effects" in watching them? In other words, how can we theorize the paradoxical ontology of digital imagery, which is at once referentially unreal but perceptually real? In addressing these new challenges, recent debates on cinematic realism have shifted their focus from the production to the reception of moving images, leading to the widespread popularity of phenomenological (also haptic and corporeal) approaches to the film experience.[42] Recently, Lúcia Nagib and Cecília Mello point out that in the twenty-first century, "film theory has been re-energized with a whole set of new concepts, all of which concern in varying degrees the physicality of the audiovisual experience."[43] Furthermore, insofar as ongoing processes of globalization intensify the possibility of more intimate encounters between people and customs from different classes, ethnicities, and cultures, that physicality in world cinema has "now become visceral, carnal, corporeal, sensate, in short, more real (and realist) than ever."[44]

This increasing visibility of what one may call a "realist" turn in recent scholarship has prevented the theoretical treatment of cinematic realism from being monolithic and outdated. Nevertheless, most historiographies of the intersection of film and realism in the past century still leave us room for critical consideration and refinement. Why in film history has realism often been discussed in rivalry with modernism, as exemplified in the schematic dichotomies between the so-called formative tradition (Georges Méliès, Josef von Sternberg, the Soviet montage school) and the realist tradition (the Lumière Brothers, Erich von Stroheim, Robert Flaherty), as well as between postwar realism and post-1968 political modernism?[45] How can we pin down the truly elusive nature of realism without losing its logical consistency as a concept? Should realism in film always be premised on the notion of medium specificity? Or is it necessary to take into consideration earlier and multiple definitions of realism developed in other art forms? Why have certain ideas of realism been associated with specific locales, such as French poetic realism and Italian neorealism? Finally, what makes it relevant, or even necessary, to recuperate Japanese contributions to the historical debates on cinematic realism?

To answer these questions within the context of film theory, I suggest first that we go back and see how Bazin originally defined realism in his seminal essay "The Ontology of the Photographic Image." In the section preceding his well-known account of the automatism of photography, Bazin states that there are at least two dominant notions of realism that developed in the realm of the visual and plastic arts. The first, which he calls "aesthetic (or true) realism," aims to offer the expression of spiritual reality through the symbol, an expression that is more true and meaningful to the idea, or the internal landscape of the mind; the second, "psychological (or pseudo-) realism," is achieved through the duplication of the external world, where the need for the illusions of visual semblance transcends its essence.[46] Drawing on this remark, moreover, Bazin cautions the reader that in every discussion of realism "we are faced with two different phenomena and these any objective critic must view separately if he is to understand the evolution of the pictorial."[47] Bazin attributes the coexistence of these two phenomena in the practice and discourse of realism to the conflict between style and likeness in realist painting, and in so doing he implies that his notion of cinematic realism is premised not on the simple extension or sophistication of one of these phenomena but rather on the dialectical relationship between the two.[48]

The paradox of realism that appeared in Bazin's "ontology" essay is given a further interrogation in Raymond Williams's *Keywords*. According to Williams, the earliest use of the term *realism* in English derived from the medieval philosophical school known as the Realists, whose doctrine had almost nothing to do with what we usually associate with the term in today's usage. In opposing the Nominalists' denial of transcendental universal Ideas and Forms and acceptance of the existence of individual objects, this school insisted that "these universal Forms and Ideas were held either to exist independently of the objects in which they were perceived, or to exist in such objects as their constituting properties."[49] Although this doctrine itself was marginalized over time, it nonetheless provided a conceptual basis for a major conceptualization of realism as indicating or revealing the "reality underlying appearances." On the other hand, since the fifteenth century, the term *realism*, and also its adjective form *real*, for that matter, came to signify an almost reverse phenomenon by adopting the meaning of the Latin word *res*, visible and tangible "things" as such. Consequently, Williams argues, "Real, from the beginning, has had this shifting double sense," which ultimately led to the coexistence of two contradictory definitions of realism still operative up to the present—that is, "in the sense of an underlying truth or quality" and "in the (often opposed) sense of *concrete* . . . existence."[50] Williams's etymological account of realism here is very useful in foregrounding this term's complicated relations with other related philosophical concepts: While in its earliest usage *realism* designated a position similar to that of *idealism*, the second and more recent usage of the term came to signify its undeniable affinity with *materialism*.

Like Bazin and Williams, Fredric Jameson also argues that the specificity of realism as a critical concept lies in its paradoxical claim, its seemingly impossible attempt to fulfill both aesthetic and epistemological vocations at one and the same time. Generally speaking, realism is understood as a slogan or attitude to achieve a "correct or true representation of the world." But such an epistemological demand must be delivered (or materialized) before us through some formal or technical artifices because otherwise it "ceases to be an aesthetic mode of representation and falls out of art altogether."[51] Jameson's account, however, is particularly instructive in that it helps us reconsider the troubled relationship between realism and modernism in twentieth-century art in general, and in film history in particular. On its most basic level, Jameson defines realism as a method or discourse that aims for the integration of epistemology in the realm of art and aesthetics. But he then suggests that we read this definition as also indicating the core mentality of modernism, strategically foregrounding the compatibility between the two. As a result of this practice, realism reemerges before us as "a form of demiurgic praxis" that restores "some active and even playful/experimental impulse to the inertia of its appearance as a copy or representation of things," and modernism, in turn, is relegated to "a passive-receptive activity, a discovery procedure like science, a process of attention no less demanding and disciplined than submission to free association."[52]

Jameson's intention here is not to deny the validity of realism and modernism as such. Rather, he deliberately shifts our attention from *what* to *when* these two art movements were. That both realism and modernism share a similar epistemological instinct—one is directed to grasp what we call reality in general, and the other to reveal the reality of the institution and making of art itself—attests their thrownness (*Geworfenheit*) into the world of nineteenth- and twentieth-century modernity. In this particular historical situation, the preexisting discursive condition of knowledge acquisition—or the "grid of intelligibility," to use Chow's term again—became totally destabilized and reimagined through numerous scientific discoveries and technological inventions. Having emerged as one such modern epistemological medium, film was able, or even destined, to enrich aesthetic possibilities of realism and modernism in the past century. Jameson argues, however, that film history has two peculiar sets of transitions—from realism to modernism and from modernism to postmodernism, divided into the silent and sound eras.[53] This statement itself requires a more rigorous historical verification, but it at least gives as some clues to think about the repetitive alternation of realism and modernism before and after World War II. Moreover, his reference to the paradoxical appearance of postmodernism before postwar realism seems relevant to the history of Japanese cinema, where not a few critics and filmmakers participated in or took inspiration from the notorious wartime debate known as "overcoming modernity" (*kindai no chōkoku*).[54]

The dialectic between form (essence, idealism) and matter (existence, materialism), the integration of epistemology into aesthetics, and the flexible or even amorphous relationship with modernism—these are the main features of realism I adopt and explore in my inquiry into the history of Japanese film theory. Then, one may ask, what does the specific locale of Japan and its local discourse contribute to our discussion of the paradox of realism?

REALISM WITHIN JAPANESE MODERNIZATION

First of all, we should take into account the accelerated process of modernization that frequently took place in the non-West. Marked by their belated or forced entries into the hegemony of Western modernity with the uneven distribution of cultural capital, people in non-Western countries confronted the increasing influx of foreign terms and concepts at an unprecedented pace and in overwhelming amounts. This was also the case in Japan, which officially declared its transition from a feudal society to a modern state only after the Meiji Restoration (1868). As a result, realism, or any other isms and schools of art that had emerged in Europe during the long nineteenth century and the early twentieth century, came to Japan less as a new visual or literary style to be added to the preexisting aesthetic norms than as a discourse for modernizing local practices of literature, painting, theater, and film. For instance, the premise of objective depiction brought to Japan at the turn of the twentieth century through the introduction of literary naturalism played a significant role in launching a criticism against the Kabuki-influenced, very formulaic acting style and narrative presentation dominant in 1910s Japanese cinema. Nevertheless, the dominance of naturalism in local film discourse became outdated by the early 1920s (though it made a comeback after the introduction of sound), as its main concern had already been shifted to adopt newer (or more modernized) trends in filmmaking such as German expressionism and French impressionism.

What I want to emphasize here, however, is the persistence of realism in Japanese local discourse even after the introduction of the art and cultural movements we usually associate with 1920s modernism. In the eyes of Japanese critics and practitioners at the time, the distinction between realism and modernism was not as obvious or decisive as we might think, because both seemed to pursue the same task of developing a better method to integrate the epistemological into the aesthetic, to better capture and grasp what they deemed to be true and authentic, in their multiple forms of expression. In his 1925 manifesto for the literary modernist group called New Sensation School (Shinkankakuha), the writer Yokomitsu Riichi declared that the group recognizes "futurism, cubism, expressionism, dada, symbolism, constructivism, and *some of the realists*" (emphasis added) as its constitutive elements.[55] Furthermore, the art historian Itagaki Takao and the literary critic Kurahara Korehito had a fierce debate over how to develop a new theory of realism around the turn of the 1930s, appropriating either the machine aesthetic or the proletarian art movement as the basis for their argumentation.

One could better understand this situation by looking at Roman Jakobson's 1921 essay "On Realism in Art" and what he called "the extreme relativity of the concept of 'realism.'"[56] According to Jakobson, "Classicists, sentimentalists, the romanticist to a certain extent, even the 'realists' of the nineteenth century, the modernists to a large degree, and finally futurists, expressionists, and their like, have more than once steadfastly proclaimed faithfulness to reality, maximum verisimilitude—in other words, realism—as the guiding motto of their artistic program."[57] With this overview Jakobson asserts that the idea of realism persists, but its contents and modes of expression vary over time. He also argues that isms or schools of art added to this list of *realisms* always yield an unusual or inauthentic impression at first glance, since "the artist-innovator must impose a new form upon our perception" by rewriting "the rules of composition canonized by his predecessors."[58] Although this essay was not translated into Japanese until 1971, a similar view of realism was commonly shared among Japanese intellectuals during the first half of the twentieth century.

The wide acceptance of the persistence of realism as a hallmark of modern art inevitably led to the maturation of Japanese local discourse on cinematic realism. In June 1936, the film magazine *Eiga hyōron* published a special issue entitled "Film and Realism" ("Eiga to riarizumu") featuring fourteen essays by the country's leading film critics. The result was somewhat chaotic: some argued that cinematic realism should always be premised on the camera's capacity to reproduce the impression of reality; others prioritized the film director's active intervention in addressing social problems; and still others attended to the viewer's lived experience of the world on and through screen. But equally important as these diverse approaches was the self-reflexive nature of their arguments. Tsuji Hisakazu, one of the contributors to the special issue, aptly summarized this point:

> Artists today no longer possess the same fortune that had allowed nineteenth-century writers to detect and depict reality under the name of *shajitsu shugi* [mimetic realism or more literally, "photocopying-the-truth-ism"] without casting doubts on their methods. The term "realism" becomes dependent on each individual's interpretation, and its contested meanings remain valid only among those sharing the same interpretation.... The singular principle of realism has disappeared. The twentieth century seemed to begin from here. Realism is not the problem restricted to either novel or theater. It is the problem that matters in all forms of art that intend to depict human truths. Newly born in the twentieth century, film art finally came to confront this problem in a serious manner.[59]

There was no exaggeration in Tsuji's self-observation. Readers will soon discover that the historical narrative I delineate throughout this book is loaded with countless disputes, disagreements, and miscommunications among a relatively small cohort of Japanese critics and filmmakers. But this does not attest to their failure to establish innovative theoretical accounts of cinematic realism. On the contrary, Japanese film criticism was remarkable for its persistent treatment of realism as the manifestation of a paradigm shift, always alert to cinema's aesthetic and technological potential to alter the very condition for our perception and understanding of the world. For this reason, I do not use the phrase *cinematic realism* as a signifier of certain film techniques or narrative patterns already registered as "realist" in general film history; I use it instead to encompass a larger (and undoubtedly transnational) discursive project that aims to articulate the lived experience of twentieth-century modernity with the aid of the film medium and its particular form of mediation. This last point necessitates a further clarification of the objective of my own approach, especially in comparison with the influential concept of "alternative modernities."

BEYOND ALTERNATIVE MODERNITIES

Originally proposed by scholars of subaltern studies, the concept of alternative modernities has been widely used and popularized for the past fifteen years as a practical tool for articulating diverse instances of modernity in non-Western contexts. Dilip Parameshwar Gaonkar, editor of the anthology *Alternative Modernities*, defines modernity as a specific mode of experience that "continues to 'arrive and emerge'" well into the twenty-first century.[60] This means that the concept of alternative modernities takes issue with the West's self-identification as the sole creator of the master-narrative of the modern, an attitude that was succinctly manifested in Western postmodernists' dissemination of the so-called "end of modernity" discourse in the last two decades of the twentieth century.[61] And yet Gaonkar intends neither to celebrate the increasing visibility of the non-West in today's global culture, nor to situate instances of non-Western modernities outside the reach of Western influences. Rather, he uses the concept of alternative modernities to open a site for questioning the dilemmas of Western modernity, consciously illuminating the neglected element of self-transformation in the historical processes of its replication and alternation in non-Western contexts.

To accomplish this task, Gaonkar suggests that we think of modernity as always being split between opposing movements, namely, convergence and divergence. He explains this opposition by associating it with the distinction between societal modernization and cultural modernity. As far as societal modernization is concerned, on the one hand, every process must take the form of convergence and sustain the centrality of the West as the singular model. Whether it was a result of colonization or voluntarism, non-Western countries have homogenously assimilated both institutional and cognitive frameworks developed in the West—republican states, industrial revolution, human rights, positivist thinking, and so on—to be modernized. On the other hand, assimilation is not always and necessarily the case when it comes to the realm of cultural modernity, where the production of cultural capital and products always hinges upon different sets of local traditions, individual tastes, and other contingent determinants—hence it orients itself toward divergence.

But a simple acknowledgment of divergence is not enough for the establishment of an alternative modernities approach, as it often ignores the geopolitical forces of totalization always implicit in actual instances of non-Western modernity. To put it simply, no cultural modernity is possible without societal modernization. For this reason, Gaonkar suggests that "we have to recognize and problematize the unavoidable dialectic of convergence and divergence" to "think productively along the line of alternative modernities." The main goal of alternative modernities is therefore to criticize "this neat dichotomy [between convergence and divergence] by foregrounding that narrow but critical band of variations consisting of site-specific 'critical adaptations' on the axis of convergence (societal modernization)."[62] While acknowledging the hegemonic presence of the West as the origin of the historical process known as modernization, Gaonkar encourages us to adopt what he calls a "site-based reading of modernities." The advantage of this approach, he continues, is that it helps us "provincialize Western modernity" through its marked emphasis on "a difference that would destabilize the universalist idioms, historicize the contexts, and pluralize the experience of modernity."[63] With this prospect in mind, Gaonkar then proceeds to define the thesis of alternative modernities as follows: "modernity is not one, but many."[64]

It is obvious that Gaonkar's concept of alternative modernities shares much in common with Shih and Lionnet's call for "the creolization of theory" in their mutual attempt at pluralizing the allegedly singular and universal existence of Western theory and modernity. However, this now common approach is not without problems. One such problem is the uncertainty about the condition under which the unity of a specific site and the pluralities of modernity are to coexist. In Gaonkar's account, the difference that is supposed to make modernity plural depends on the relative homogeneity of a given context—for example, local traditions, religious rituals, anti-colonialism sentiments—and, accordingly, all the differences initially mobilized to pluralize the experience of modernity become reintegrated under larger rubrics, especially that of a modern nation-state. This is exactly what Harry Harootunian finds problematic in his criticism of alternative modernities. As he writes: "What distinguishes this alternative modernity is its spatial location, a place that is not Euro-America, and thus its claim to an identity that is uniquely different.... Such appeals to cultural resources undisturbed by modernization—a folkloric fiction not worth keeping as Fanon also remarked—are made to offer the surety of an unmovable ground of authenticity on which to construct an identity capable of preserving the autonomy of genuine difference."[65]

It is important to note that Harootunian's counterargument is not only polemical but also historical. Indeed, Harootunian refers to the Japanese discourse formed around "Overcoming Modernity," the title of a symposium held in 1942 to discuss Japan's troubled relationship with Western modernity, as a genuine precursor of alternative modernities.[66] The main tenor of the symposium was that Japan must be a country that can lead world history exactly because Japan, after seventy years of enthusiastic assimilations of Western culture and technologies since the Meiji restoration, was now mature enough to provide an alternative vision of modernity with a difference. Moreover, the participants suggested more extensive use of cultural resources culled from Japan's folkloric, mythological, and premodern traditions to place Japan outside or beyond the reach of Western modernity. But given that the symposium was held amid Japan's ongoing transition toward a totalitarian state along with Nazi Germany and Fascist Italy, it is reasonable to see "Overcoming Modernity" not as proposing a promising alternative but as remaining within the discursive context of twentieth-century modernity. Since my inquiry into Japanese film theory deals with the same time period as the symposium, I must also take into account the negative outcome of the "site-specific reading" and its unabashed search for "indigenous" differences.

Another problem with alternative modernities is that they are incapable of solving what Thomas Lamarre calls the "problem of origins" in a productive way.[67] Although Gaonkar admits some originating acts on the side of non-Western modernities with his notion of "creative adoption," his model still presupposes the West as the unitary origin of both modernity and modernization. It is true that the possibility of pluralizing modernity lies in its incessant arrivals and emergences in different locales and in different temporalities, but at the same, this process of pluralization inevitably takes the form of outward diffusion, always moving away from the center to the periphery, and not vice versa. To put it bluntly, the concept of alternative modernities claims to deterritorialize certain site-specific instances of modern experiences in the non-West, but it does so only to recuperate the dominance of the West because all the local differences are judged by their deviations from the Western original. In this way, the status of the West as the genesis of alternative or all the other non-Western modernities is reaffirmed through the totalizing logic of reterritorialization.

To avoid this problem, Lamarre introduces Stuart Hall's deconstructive approach to Western modernity. Unlike Gaonkar's reaffirmation of the West as the unitary origin, Hall's approach "multiplies, transforms and thus problematizes the origins of modernity."[68] It is considered "deconstructive" precisely because it refuses to narrate the historical formation of Western modernity by means of the linear temporality of cause and effect, and instead sets up the "mutating existence of the origin" that changes its forms, positions, and meanings according to things or events that happen at later points in history. In other words, it is not our departure from A that determines our arrival at B; instead, "our arrival at B produces our point of departure from A." What, then, can we learn from this total negation of modernity as the epitome of a linear temporal progression? Here is Lamarre's explanation: "Simply put, it becomes difficult to say definitively when and where Western modernity is. It also becomes difficult to decide, once and for all, who is inside and who is outside. Once one speaks of modernity or of the West, one is paradoxically within it even while one claims to be without. It is impossible to locate and define a position of exteriority."[69]

With this remark, Lamarre offers us some useful tips for organizing our working agendas. First, what is needed is not a simple increase in the number of examples (pluralization) but a paradigm shift that propels us to question the relevance of the discursive framework under which we conduct our research. Second, any successful critique of modernity should always be made from within, and not from without. If one comes up with a plausible way of cracking or at least problematizing the confinement of the modern world system, it must be already inscribed in the very foundation and internal logic of Western modernity and its continuous reliance upon capitalism. Third, accepting the totalizing force of Western modernity does not always lead us to the practice of reterritorialization. In fact, considering Japanese modernization vis-à-vis the overwhelming presence of the West requires a reinscription of this specific locale in the same temporality as its Euro-American counterparts. This marked emphasis on the temporality (and not the spatiality) of non-Western modernity allows us to discuss local examples from Japan not as exterior or alternative to but as coextensive with or even constitutive of what we call "modernity" in retrospect. Taken together, these working agendas can be best summarized in a subtle but no less significant amendment that Lamarre adds to Gaonkar's dictum: "It may no longer be enough to say that 'modernity is not one *but* multiple,' but rather 'modernity is one *and* multiple.'"[70]

I adopt Lamarre's seemingly self-contradictory proposition—"modernity is one *and* multiple"—as a guide for my investigation into Japanese film theory. This is partly because Japanese film critics during the first half of the twentieth century collectively strove to reconcile mutually exclusive categories such as subject and object, essence and existence, mind and body, idealism and materialism, and aesthetics and epistemology under one and the same label of realism. But it is also because the majority of Japanese intellectuals have historically addressed twentieth-century modernity as an inherently schizophrenic or oxymoronic experience, always marked by the coexistence of the West and the non-West, the modern and the pre- or non-modern, the original and the deliberative, the spatial and the temporal, and the universal and the particular. Consequently, several Japanese thinkers and philosophers in the past century engaged in establishing a specific worldview that was based on the total denial of the law of identity (*jidōritsu*), namely, "A is at once A and not A" (*A wa A de ari katsu hi-A de aru*).

Among such thinkers was the Marxist critic Hanada Kiyoteru, who developed a concept called "the elliptical imagination" (*daen gensō*) in a series of essays published in the early 1940s. As a Marxist, Hanada properly understood the ellipse as a concept that was first used by Marx himself to explain the self-contradictory capitalist logic of exchange that makes possible the transformation of commodities into money. Marx wrote that "it is a contradiction to depict one body as constantly falling towards another, and as, at the same time, constantly flying away from it." However, the ellipse is a special geomatical figure that embodies this self-contradictory movement of the body, as it appears when the sum of distances from a point moving on a plane to the two foci located inside are equal and consistent. The shape (i.e., outer circumference) represented by this moving point can be seen as at once getting closer to and moving away from those two foci. Therefore, Marx referred to the ellipse as "a form of motion which, allowing this contradiction to go on, at the same time reconciles it" as in the metamorphosis of a concrete object (commodity or labor power) into an abstract idea (money).[71]

Similarly, Hanada defined the ellipse as embodying the coexistence of mutually exclusive elements in one and the same body, a situation in which "one is sleeping while being awake, crying while laughing, laughing while crying, believing while doubting, and doubting while believing."[72] Remarkable here are Hanada's steadfast resistance to the eclectic unity between those opposites with a single center (the circle or a synthesis) and his determined search for an inherent possibility of eternal transfiguration between two or more self-conflicting elements. Moreover, Hanada applies his concept of the elliptical imagination to reveal the actual function of modern capitalism. As Ōsawa Masachi points out, Hanada seemed to believe that capitalism had long sustained itself by disguising its inherently elliptical nature as a self-contained circle, by incessantly producing and exploiting differences to reclaim its purported totality.[73]

Developed as a product of this capitalist logic, the modern world system has inevitably necessitated the two opposing but deeply correlated foci, namely, the West and the rest, or the (exploitative) subject and the (exploited) object of the Enlightenment and its imperialist exploitation. In this geopolitical configuration, it is insufficient or even impossible to draw a perfect circle with a single center. It also becomes clear that diverse instances of modern experiences cannot be explained fully either by the teleological narrative of "modernization theory," which reduces everything to the alleged supremacy of the West, or by the nativist discourse of "alternative modernities," which tends to privilege "the autonomy of genuine differences" with its marked emphasis on cultural or spatial specificities of local activities.

Hanada often paraphrased his concept of the elliptical imagination in a deliberately self-contradictory formula of dialectics. Whereas Hanada's original phrase was "to integrate opposites as opposites" (*tairitsubutsu wo tairitsu no mama tōitsu suru*), I would rephrase it as a "dialectics without synthesis" for the sake of brevity.[74] Hanada admitted that this formula may seem illogical at first sight, but it in fact faithfully followed Lenin's observation of the laws of dialectics: "The unity (coincidence, identity, equal action) of opposites is conditional, temporary, transitory, relative. The struggle of mutually exclusive opposites is absolute, just as development and motion are absolute."[75] In addition, Hanada always stressed that the conflicting standpoints of a thesis and an antithesis—or the two foci of the ellipse—are not absolute but always relative and in motion. Seen from this perspective, proclaimed autonomies of the West and the non-West—or the homogeneity of a nation-state and other local communities—must also be put under investigation. As Hanada cautiously reminds us, "What is 'Japanese' is at once 'Western'" in the lived experience and discursive articulation of twentieth-century modernity.[76]

This is why the present study is entitled *Dialectics without Synthesis*. My research into the history of Japanese film theory, therefore, always illuminates the coexistence of two or more self-contradictory, mutually exclusive positions in the local debates on cinematic realism. As I have argued, the difficulty of realism as a concept always lies in its incessant vacillation between the two opposing claims that Bazin succinctly summarized as "aesthetic realism" and "psychological realism." My contribution will thus be to complicate these oppositions further by situating them within another set of opposing dyads consisting of the West and the non-West, the modern and the pre- or non-modern, and the universal and the particular. Previous studies of film theory, realism, and modernity usually end up presenting a series of concentric circles through their relentless search for a synthesis. By contrast, my own approach foregrounds internal struggles among Japanese film theorists in the form of self-mutating ellipses, dialectical processes with no end, that will in turn constitute a new constellation of transnational discursive exchanges in the course of the twentieth century. In other words, the goal of this book is to shift our attention from Hegelian difference to Derridean *différance*, to challenge the common root of all binary oppositions that continuously produce differences in order to defer the exposition of the non-existence of the original and transcendental unity of each contested term.

CHAPTER SUMMARIES

Chapter 1 examines how the introduction of literary naturalism at the turn of the twentieth century impacted the formation of the earliest examples of Japanese film theory in the 1910s. As a concept, naturalism in the Japanese context usually designates an attitude to depict a given object or phenomenon as it is, rather than the incorporation of scientific determinism and the theory of heredity. This seemingly simple call for objective or mimetic depiction, however, became a foundation for Japanese theoretical debates over the paradox of realism because it required the writer to provide a highly objective, empirical representation of subjective vision and experience. The aim of this chapter is to see how this localized notion of naturalism became intensified when it was brought into local debates on cinema and its potential to be a distinct form of art and mass entertainment. In so doing, it also illuminates the work of film theorists who criticized the dominance of naturalism in Japanese literary discourse in conjunction with the ongoing influx of more updated intellectual trends including pragmatism, the philosophy of Henri Bergson, and German expressionism.

Chapter 2 considers how Japanese intellectuals in the 1920s developed a new theory of realism through a particular mode of visual perception brought about by the camera's mechanical gaze. Throughout the chapter, I draw special attention to the work of the art historian Itagaki Takao, especially a series of essays compiled in his 1929 monograph *Exchanges between the Machine and Art* (*Kikai to geijutsu to no kōryū*). Itagaki deserves to be called a Japanese proponent of the machine aesthetic in that he celebrated the integration of the functional beauty of modern machinery in contemporary art and architecture, manifested in the work of Le Corbusier, László Moholy-Nagy, and Dziga Vertov. But the real innovation of Itagaki's writing rested in his creation of a new concept called "machine realism" (*kikai no riarizumu*). Why did he use the term *realism* to designate the art movement that is often labeled *modernism*? I answer this by resituating Itagaki within the discursive context of late 1920s Japan. Indeed, Itagaki presented his theory of machine realism as a critique of the then influential "proletarian realism" (*proretarian riarizumu*), a concept that was first proposed in 1928 by the Marxist critic Kurahara Korehiro. Looking closely at what was at stake in their prognostic call for a new realism, this chapter offers a geopolitical reading of the historical conjuncture between the machine aesthetic and the proletarian literary movement.

In chapter 3, I look into how the introduction of sound to film changed the direction of Japanese debates on realism in and of fiction film. In the late 1920s, Kurahara criticized Itagaki's machine realism for its underestimation of the role of human perception and imagination. Following this line of criticism, those involved in the production of sound film came to rely upon the language-based model of enunciation developed in literature as a plausible means for subjective expression. As a result, the 1930s saw the growing popularity of the new genre called "literary art film" (*bungei eiga*) which, through the adaptation of high-brow realistic novels, radically redefined the notion of the film auteur as someone in charge of both written scripts and completed films. However, this increased emphasis on written scripts also came to restrict the directorial freedom of film directors by the end of the 1930s. Because the 1939 Film Law ordered that all domestic film products be examined at the stage of written script, film directors were no longer allowed to alter any scenes or dialogues on the set unless they resubmitted those changes in written form. To examine these negative outcomes of literary adaptation, this chapter also examines the emergence of a subgenre called "historical film" (*rekishi eiga*) and its controversial promotion of what I call "textual realism."

Chapter 4 explores how the growing popularity of news films and other nonfiction genres after the outbreak of the second Sino-Japanese war (1937) helped develop a very different approach to the issue of cinematic realism. This chapter offers a comparative reading of three Japanese Marxist thinkers—Tosaka Jun, Nakai Masakazu, and Imamura Taihei—who shared a similar desire to conceptualize film viewing as a social practice by focusing on the medium's particular mode of mediation between the masses and their everyday lives. In particular, I refer to the realism at work in their written texts as "epistemological realism," following the title of Tosaka's 1937 essay "Epistemological Values of Cinema and Its Depictions of Social Customs." In some ways, these three theorists inherited the legacy of Itagaki's machine realism, as they argued that the camera's mechanical gaze could also reveal the hidden structure and mechanism of a given society. But my argument here also foregrounds how such a clichéd metaphor of "film as a mirror" became problematic when Japanese nonfiction filmmakers were given the quite controversial task of providing credible visions of the counterfeited political entity known as the Greater East Asia Co-Prosperity Sphere (*Dai-Tōa kyōeiken*).

Chapter 5 deals with an alternative, and overtly philosophical, approach that emerged on the eve and even after Japan's surprise attack on Pearl Harbor in December 1941. This approach was best represented by Sugiyama Heiichi and Nagae Michitarō. Both Sugiyama and Nagae were distinguished from other domestic theorists for their shared desire to establish a theory of cinematic realism by privileging their lived experiences of film as sensory and temporary phenomena. In elaborating their theories, Sugiyama and Nagae drew on two dominant schools in twentieth-century philosophy: Bergsonism and phenomenology. Sugiyama's recourse to Bergson was obvious as he, like Gonda in his earlier work in the 1910s, frequently referred to the French philosopher in his texts. The relationship between Nagae and phenomenology, on the other hand, requires a more careful contextualization because his surprisingly sophisticated argument on the ontology of the world experienced through cinema stemmed mostly from the work of the Japanese philosopher Nishida Kitarō. While explaining how Nishida and his colleagues at Kyoto University developed their own philosophies through their personal and intellectual ties with Edmund Husserl, Martin Heidegger, and other German phenomenologists, this chapter offers a new perspective to both historicize and globalize the relationship between classical film theory and twentieth-century philosophy.

In the epilogue, I conclude my inquiry by looking at the postwar development of Japanese theoretical debates on cinematic realism. Of many critics who participated in the debates, I choose to shed light on Hanada Kiyoteru, especially his concept of "sur-documentary" (*shuru-dokyumentarī*). Although Hanada is widely recognized as one of the most influential advocates of the 1950s Japanese avant-garde art movement, the significance of his theoretical contribution lies rather in his persistent call for the historicization of film theory on both domestic and international fronts. Indeed, he presented sur-documentary not simply as the application of his previous argument on the elliptical imagination to film practice but also as a meta-critique of existing interpretations of the Griersonian conception of documentary by his fellow Japanese critics. And because Hanada's intervention encompassed Marxism, the machine aesthetic and 1920s avant-garde art, and the Kyoto School of Philosophy, it allows us to reflect on how the legacy of prewar and wartime Japanese theorizations of cinema and its realism merged with postwar film practice and discourse in the form of the continuity of discontinuity.

1

Naturalism and the Modernization of Japanese Cinema

NIPPON REALISM

In an essay published in 1985, Satō Tadao coined the term "Nippon realism" (*Nippon riarizumu*) to designate the emergence of what he considered to be a uniquely Japanese school of realist filmmaking in the mid- to late 1930s.[1] Obviously, Satō was motivated to offer a counterargument to Burch's prior discussion of the antirealist character of Japanese cinema, and he strategically mobilized the already established fame of Ozu and Mizoguchi to advocate the high artistic standard of Nippon realism. However, Satō's deliberate use of the qualifier *Nippon/Japanese* immediately poses some reservations once we realize that the rise of realism as a plausible method or slogan for sound cinema was by no means unique to Japan. Starting with Hollywood films that squarely dealt with moral crises in the post-Depression era, a variety of realist film schools or movements appeared during the 1930s and 1940s, including the British Documentary Film Movement, French poetic realism, and Italian neorealism. What, then, makes Japan's contribution to this global trend unique and different from others? More specifically, what kind of realism is at work in Satō's conception of Nippon realism?

According to Satō, Nippon realism is not distinguished by certain techniques or narrative patterns that we can empirically detect in film texts. Rather, it is speculatively observed through the director's will or self-determination to "depict reality as it is without being manipulated by any ideological bias."[2] Consequently, Satō praises Ozu's famous obsession with low-angle shots as expressing this director's effort to depict the everyday life of the precariat from below, while at the same time appreciating Mizoguchi's innovative use of the long take as manifesting the latter's indictment of injustices among socially marginalized figures. Moreover, Satō tries to enhance the credibility of his undeniably "auteurist" approach by quoting the following words of Yoda Yoshikata, a screenwriter known for his long-term collaboration with Mizoguchi: "Mizoguchi always maintained a strongly realist point of view, which is usually called naturalism. One can observe this tendency in his portraits [of characters] in films such as *Mistress of a Foreigner* [*Tōjin Okichi*, 1930] and *And Yet They Go On* [*Shikamo karera wa yuku*, 1931]. In Mizoguchi's films, the naked truth of reality comes solely from the powerful effect of the duration of uninterrupted actions or facial expressions, and he intentionally made efforts to abandon anything artificial like the extensive use of the shot-reverse shot."[3] It is clear from this quotation that Satō defined his concept of Nippon realism as something equivalent to naturalism. But why did naturalism, despite its indisputable French origin, come to serve as a major point of reference for Satō's deliberate promotion of the distinctively "Japanese" branch of the realist film aesthetic?

This question gains more urgency as we notice that Satō is not alone in associating naturalism with the local tradition of realist filmmaking in Japan. For instance, Joseph L. Anderson and Donald Richie, in their *The Japanese Film: Art and Industry*, pay tribute to Tanaka Eizō's 1922 film *The Kyōya Collar Shop* (*Kyōya erimise*) precisely because the film, although no longer existent today, is said to depict a "realistic story of the lower class, a subject which other producers rarely touched upon, with the exception of films like Shōchiku's *Souls on the Road* [*Rojō no reikon*, dir. Murata Minoru, 1921]."[4] Following this remark, the film historian Chiba Nobuo maintains that *Souls on the Road* is representative of what he calls "naturalist realism" (*shizenshugiteki riarizumu*), a concept that the *shingeki* (new drama) playwright Osanai Kaoru brought to the world of Japanese cinema with his participation in the foundation of the film company Shōchiku in 1920.[5] Then, as the story goes, the later success of directors trained at Shōchiku's Kamata and Ōfuna studios—Ozu, Shimizu Hiroshi, Shimazu Yasujirō, Naruse Mikio, Yoshimura Kōzaburō, and Kinoshita Keisuke—further stabilized the enduring influence of naturalism on the historical development of Japanese film practice in general.

The aim of this chapter is to historicize and complicate Satō's discussion of Nippon realism by examining the degree to which the critical vocabulary of naturalism had impacted the formation of the earliest examples of Japanese film theory in the 1910s. In Satō's account, the qualifier *Nippon* signifies how the original premise of literary naturalism has been altered or even localized since it first traveled from France to Japan at the turn of the twentieth century. The term *naturalism* in the Japanese context is usually understood less as the incorporation of scientific determinism or the Darwinian theory of evolution than as an attitude to depict a given object or phenomenon *as it is* (*ari no mama*) in the form of "mimetic depiction" (*mosha* or *shajitsu*). In addition, it is widely believed that this revised notion of naturalism played an indispensable role in modernizing local practices of both literary and performing arts, marking a clear break from preexisting norms and conventions in representation. To put it briefly, there would be no *modern* Japanese literature, theater, or cinema as we know them today without the intervention of naturalism and its related discourse in the first two decades of the twentieth century.

But we should acknowledge that naturalism as a trope of modernization was far from an invariable principle and became subject to change over time. Therefore, while explicating the ways in which the first generation of Japanese film theorists adopted naturalist idioms in their work, I also want to illuminate how rapidly those theorists changed their perspective in conjunction with the ongoing appearance of more contemporary artistic and intellectual trends, including futurism, cubism, expressionism, pragmatism, and the philosophy of Henri Bergson. In other words, my intention in this chapter is not that of affirming the commonplace view that the film medium helped bring the naturalist premise of objective depiction to perfection due to its photographic nature. On the contrary, my focus goes primarily to theorists who were attentive to film's unprecedented potential to unsettle the traditional dichotomies between subject and object, intuition and intellect, and the real and the fantastic.

JAPANESE NATURALISM, OR THE AMBIVALENCE OF MIMETIC DEPICTION

As indicated in Satō's discussion of Nippon realism, Japanese debates on naturalism always revolved around the phrase "as it is." The first appearance of this phrase in Japanese literary discourse predates the arrival of naturalism, at a time when the literary scholar Tsubouchi Shōyō introduced the very notion of the modern novel through his essay "The Essence of the Novel" ("Shōsetsu shinzui," 1885–86). Of course, Japan had a long tradition of prose fiction that had already gone through the process of secularization during the Edo period (1603–1868). But prior to Shōyō's intervention, this literary genre was not called "novel" but was given different names such as "playful writings" (*gesaku*), "reading books" (*yomihon*), and "yellow covers" (*kibyōshi*).[6] More than a small change in terminology, Shōyō distinguished the novel/*shōsetsu* as a new literary enterprise first and foremost for its conscious attempt at separating itself from local writing conventions. As he writes: "The author of the novel should focus his thought on human psychology; even if fictional characters are nothing more than fictional creations of his own, he should treat them as living people once they appear in his own work. In describing their emotions, moreover, he should not dare generate an impression of didacticism through his own designs, but rather restrict himself to observing and depicting them as they are [*tada bōkan shite ari no mama ni mosha suru*]."[7] It should be noted that in this essay Shōyō gave more priority to the objective observation of human psychology (or subjectivity) than to the mimetic depiction of the external world. Indeed, Shōyō was aware of the fact that human beings are always involved with two distinct phenomena, namely, "the act that expresses itself externally" (*soto ni arawaruru gaibu no kōi*) and "the thought that hides itself internally" (*uchi ni kakuretaru shisō*).[8] The main purpose of the modern novel, therefore, would be inventing the best possible method to capture and express the complicated, and oftentimes invisible, relationship between these two phenomena. Shōyō also stressed that the creation of more credible characters with human feelings (*ninjō*) was crucial in liberating Japanese prose fiction from its former service in the dissemination of moralistic didacticism.[9]

A similar twist in early Japanese discourse on the modern novel can also be found in the concept of "mimetic depiction." In his 1886 essay "A General Account of the Novel" ("Shōsetsu sōron"), the writer Futabatei Shimei offered a perceptive account of this term by drawing on the vocabulary of Western philosophy. Like Shōyō, Futabatei argues that the world is composed of "the form" (*katachi*), a contingent and ever-changing phenomenon, and "the idea" (*i*), a universal and invariable essence. "The purpose of art," he contends, "is destined to capture the formless and hard-to-grasp idea through inspiration" and "to make that idea easily obtainable by the common people."[10] To accomplish this mission, writers must elaborate their work under the premise of "realism" (*shujitsu shugi*), consciously employing mimetic depiction as their method.[11] But, again, mimetic depiction in Futabatei's account designates the revelation of "the invisible essence [*kyosō*] through the concrete existence [*jissō*]," or an attitude to "present universal ideas explicitly in these contingent forms with the help of the writer's creative word choice and narrative composition."[12]

Futabatei then put his theory of mimetic depiction into practice through his own commitment to the composition of the modern novel. But we should keep in mind that this endeavor required a radical reform of the Japanese writing system itself as a medium for communication and artistic expression. Until the late 1880s, most Japanese fiction had been written in the traditional writing style known as *bungotai*. But because this style contained decorative and formulaic expressions borrowed from classical Chinese, and therefore differed considerably from the spoken language of the contemporary Japanese, cultural elites of the Meiji period (1868–1912) made tremendous efforts to establish the new writing style called *genbun itchi* (literally meaning, "the unification of speaking and writing") as one of the most urgent imperatives for their country's modernization. To initiate his own version of the *genbun itchi*, Futabatei first emulated the *rakugo* performer Sanyūtei Enchō's oral expression, which was recorded on paper by a stenographer; he then applied this new writing style to his translations of the Russian writer Ivan Turgenev's short stories "The Rendezvous" ("Aibiki," 1888) and "Three Encounters" ("Meguriai," 1888). As he later recalled in his memoir, Futabatei tried in these translations to "faithfully transpose the original writer's poetic imagination by becoming one with the original writer's mind and body."[13] Moreover, Futabatei imitated the ways in which Turgenev used commas and periods in the original texts so as to perfect his imaginary identification.

Although Futabatei himself admitted that his translations were not as successful as he had hoped, these early examples in modern Japanese literature nonetheless provide us a useful reference point for our inquiry into the complex, if not self-contradictory, nature of realism in the Japanese context. It cannot be denied that Futabatei considered realism to be one of the most important facets of the modern novel, but his was a realism that is more faithful to idea and mind than to matter and body. Similarly, his concept of mimetic depiction was applied exclusively to the depiction of the human mind, although he was very conscious of the fact that such an immediate capturing and expression of the invisible essence was only possible with the mediation of writing as both a medium and an institution.

The arrival of naturalism and its enduring impact on Japanese literary discourse should be understood in this context. According to the widely accepted account by naturalist playwright Shimamura Hōgestu, the process through which naturalism was adopted in Japan can be divided into two stages, with two different groups of writers having mutually opposed attitudes toward this single literary concept. The first stage, spanning from roughly 1900 to 1906, includes writers such as Kosugi Tengai, Oguri Fūyō, and Nagai Kafū, all of whom published stories in 1902 portraying a woman who miserably ruins her life at the end, following the plot of Émile Zola's *Nana*. While these so-called "first-generation naturalist writers" incorporated fictional elements that touched upon the issues of heredity and scientific determinism, their focus was rather on offering frank portrayals of the people at the margin, as part of their collective efforts to advance the *genbun itchi* style. In the oft-cited preface to his 1902 novel *Popular Song* (*Hayari uta*), Kosugi wrote: "When a painter is making a portrait, can he say to the subject, 'Your nose is too long,' and plane it down? The poet, when he is about to set down on paper what he has imagined, must not add even a particle of himself."[14]

This aspiration for more accurate and objective depictions of external reality became intensified when a group of literary critics began to participate in the local debates on naturalism. Among those critics was Hasegawa Tenkei, and his essays from the early 1900s concisely summarize the main tenet shared among the first-generation Japanese naturalists. To begin with, Hasegawa argues that old literary conventions premised on the romanticist ideal of art for art's sake had already collapsed due to the rapid and bewildering changes occurring in the modern world.[15] In one sense, Hasegawa's emphasis on a historical rupture reflects Japan's unexpected victory in the Russo-Japanese War (1904–5) and its newly acquired status as a member of the imperial powers. But more crucial to him was the emergence of a new mode of perception, or even a new modality of being in this world, engendered by the continuous flows of scientific discoveries and technological developments brought to Japan since the Meiji Restoration. It is this recognition of the impacts of modernity that led Hasegawa to stress the superiority of naturalism over other schools of art, given its purported allegiance to scientific methods. And his trust in the triumph of modern science was so profound that he went so far as to deny any subjective intervention in literary texts. In his view, naturalist writers must produce a novel that offers no value judgment. Here is Hasegawa's definition of naturalism: "Put briefly, naturalists must transcribe a truth as they observe it. They care little about whether this particular truth is universal, eternal, beautiful, or ugly. They do nothing more than depict it as it is. . . . Because naturalists describe nature only in the way they actually experience or observe it, they never present their compositions as offering the whole picture of nature, the ultimate truth, or any steadfast existence. For this reason, some people have even begun to adopt 'no solution' [as the motto of naturalism]."[16]

Undoubtedly, this was a radical claim that to some extent anticipated the emergence of anti-humanism in a later period. But for the same reason, it stimulated a number of disputes among his fellow Japanese writers and critics, and from these disputes emerged what Shimamura called the "second-generation naturalist writers." This generation, composed of writers such as Shimazaki Tōson, Tayama Katai, and Tokuda Shūsei, shared a tendency to foreground the protagonist's emotional development, deliberately incorporating in their novels the romanticist motif of *Sturm und Drang*.[17] Critics who supported these second-generation naturalist writers thus sought to revise the definition of naturalism. One such critic, Sōma Gyofū, wrote in 1907 that naturalism is a name given to "the self-awareness that has coincidently reached the integration of subjective and objective visions after long and tiring conflicts between knowledge and emotion." More precisely, continued Sōma, naturalism is a method to "reflect upon the internal [state of mind] with the intellectual attitude that had previously been applied to the phenomena of external nature."[18]

It is this particular understanding of naturalism as the integration of subjective and objective visions that informed the later development of modern Japanese fiction. Following the success of Katai's semi-autobiographical novella *The Quilt* (*Futon*, 1907), this localized form of naturalism eventually led to the emergence of the "I-novel" (*shi-* or *watakushi-shōsetsu*), a literary genre in which the first-person narrator, who is usually identified with the writer himself, offers a very detached and objective description of his own personal life. This new trend came to occupy the central place in the Japanese literary world from the late 1910s onward, following the success of writers associated with the White Burch School (Shirakabaha). It is thus possible to say that the enduring presence of naturalism in Japanese literary discourse was nothing but a result of this term's radical transformation from a method for observing external or physical reality to that of expressing internal or psychological reality.

In the meantime, this particular process of the localization—or the "personalization," if you prefer—of naturalism became the subject of criticism. As early as

1910, the poet Ishikawa Takuboku accused Japanese naturalist writers and critics of having been unable to provide a general definition of their "ism" about which they could all agree. In Takuboku's view, all the missteps made by his fellow Japanese writers derived from "their Roman Empire–like delusion to encompass every kind of modern tendency under the single name of naturalism."[19] A sympathizer of socialism and anarchism, Takuboku strongly demanded that Japanese naturalists recuperate the original premise of French naturalism and use literature as a practical tool for social reform, rather than restricting it to self-righteous indulgence in subjective expression. Put differently, Japanese naturalism, as he understood it, did succeed in reaching what Zola formulated as the stage of "observation," but it nonetheless failed to advance to the stage of "experiment," where writers were expected to offer a plausible solution for social problems with the help of modern scientific discourse.

Takuboku's critique of Japanese naturalism as an eclectic term to "encompass every kind of modern tendency," however, illuminates its potential to adapt to the burgeoning local theoretical discourse on cinema. The sociologist Gonda Yaunosuke (1887–1955) was among the first to offer a systematic account of the oxymoronic nature of both the mechanism and function of moving images. In his *Principles and Applications of the Moving Picture* (*Katsudō shashin no genri oyobi ōyo*, 1914, hereafter *Principles*), Gonda repeatedly stressed that film is able to integrate empiricism (*jikkan*) and intuition (*chokkan*) in the mind of the viewers. But since such a unity of subjective and objective visions already served as the main tenet of the second-generation naturalist writers, Gonda's film theory can also be read as an opportune commentary on naturalism in the Japanese context.

GONDA YASUNOSUKE: THEORIZING THE CINEMATIC INTUITION

Born in 1887, Gonda Yasunosuke was still in his late twenties when he published *Principles* just before his graduation from Tokyo University. In his adolescent years, Gonda expressed a sympathy with socialism and became acquainted with some of the most influential Japanese socialists and anarchists of the time, including Kōtoku Shūsui and Ōsugi Sakae. During his middle school years, moreover, he came under the tutelage of another socialist, Abe Isoo, who introduced him to Marx's *Capital* more than a decade before the appearance of the first Japanese translation (1919–1924). After graduating from college, Gonda worked closely with Takano Iwasaburō, a renowned sociologist who specialized in statistical research in various forms of popular entertainment (*minshū goraku*), including *yose* (vaudeville theater), cafés, and of course motion pictures. Gonda eventually became a full-time researcher at the Ohara Institute for Social Research and was widely recognized as a specialist of popular culture in general. But throughout his career Gonda intentionally avoided making one-sidedly negative judgments on both social and artistic values of popular entertainment. Indeed, Gonda's sociological stance was marked by his recognition that "popular entertainment has nothing to do with things one could interpret with the aid of dictionaries or in a research lab. Instead, it is only through immersion and breathing the air from within that one can apprehend it for the first time."[20]

Given this background, previous studies have discussed Gonda's *Principles* mostly in relation to the emergence of sociology as an academic discipline in Japan. For instance, Aaron Gerow writes that "much of his aesthetics is aligned with his film sociology, especially where he stresses the economic and technological basis of motion picture art."[21] It is true that Gonda, thanks to his earlier encounter with socialism and Marxism, never underestimated the significance of the commercial aspects of film practice, arguing that the particular beauty, attraction, and potential of film as a genuine form of popular entertainment stemmed from its conscious commitment to the mass production of big-budget spectacles, the saturation of duplicated (and thus inexpensive) prints for wider circulation, and the cultivation of customers from the lower and uneducated classes. In addition, Gonda devoted a considerable portion of this massive treatise—which amounts to 454 pages in total—to detailing not only the basic mechanisms and functions of the cinematic apparatus but also color, sound, 3D, and other new features that would be added to this medium in the future.

However, I suggest that Gonda's film theory be reinterpreted within the discursive framework of Japanese naturalism and other contemporary art and philosophical discourses. This is in part because Gonda intended his film writing to be a theory of a new aesthetic of the modern world, focusing on how the film medium and the viewer's lived experience of it had altered the basic condition of human perception. But this revisionist approach, I contend, also helps us remedy what seems to be a logical flaw in Gonda's film theory. Indeed, Gerow argues that Gonda's approach was marked by its "discursive ambivalence about the essence [of cinema]," and that this ambivalence was most clearly manifested in his discussion of cinematic realism.[22] Whereas Gonda anticipated the future development of film as the most adequate medium for the perfect replication of the external world through the addition of sound, color, and 3D imagery, he nonetheless expressed an equal or even greater interest in the same medium's current imperfect state, which required the viewer's subjective or mental effort to elicit "three-dimensional effects from flat images."[23] This seemingly paradoxical assessment appears paradoxical *only* when we read it in light of the general history of classical film theory, which privileges Hugo Münsterberg's rather traditional account of the purpose of art—that is, "The highest art may be furthest removed from reality"—as our benchmark for the period.[24] In contrast, Gonda found it mandatory to reinvent the very notion of art in light of film's own properties, consciously foregrounding this medium's ability to reconcile not only subjective and objective visions but also high and popular culture.

Gonda specifically addresses the philosophical trends of his times in the chapter entitled "The Philosophy of the Moving Picture, the Civilization of the Moving Picture" ("Katsudō shashin no tetsugaku, katsudō shahshin no bunmei"). Gonda points out that since the turn of the twentieth century, the earlier heritage of metaphysics, including Kant and Hegel's idealist philosophy as well as Hume and Locke's empiricism and skepticism, have been dethroned by the new form of philosophical thinking introduced by Henri Bergson, Rudolf Eucken, and William James. With the intervention of these contemporary philosophers, the increasing significance given to lived and sensual experience overturned Western philosophy's earlier emphasis on intellectual understanding or abstraction. As a result, Gonda writes, "today's philosophical thoughts are dominated by terms such as voluntary, pragmatic, intuitive, apperceptive, dynamic, the affirmation of actual life, and the improvement of content."[25] For Gonda, there is nothing more symptomatic and compelling than these ongoing shifts in twentieth-century philosophy that could better explain modern people's obsession with the overtly sensational and bodily attractions of the motion picture.

In particular, Gonda draws on the work of James and Bergson to formulate his own philosophy of film. For one, Gonda repeatedly uses the term *pragmatism* in his text to stress his belief that all kinds of things or phenomena in question must be interpreted through the practical effects they have on lived social situations. Moreover, the Japanese reception of pragmatism helps illuminate the specific discursive context surrounding Gonda's film writings. While the introduction of James as a psychologist had already begun at the end of the nineteenth century, his name became widely recognized by local readers when the Japanese translation of *Pragmatism: A New Name for Some Old Ways of Thinking* (1907) was published in October 1910, only two months after the author's death.[26]

Interestingly, the popularity of James and his theory of pragmatism among Japanese readers was also enhanced through the work of nonacademic popular writers. One such writer was the aforementioned Ōsugi Sakae, who, in essays such as "Labor Movements and Pragmatism" ("Rōdomondai to puragumatizumu," 1915), advocated certain affinities between pragmatism's championing of "free-will determinism" and anarcho-syndicalism's prioritization of the autonomous formation of a workers' union.[27] It would thus be possible to assume that Gonda came to know about pragmatism through Ōsugi's guidance. In any case, Gonda finds in pragmatism a potential for settling the chaotic disputes emerging around Japanese naturalism. Just as James considered pragmatism to be an antidote to the age-old conflict between theory and practice, the spiritual and the material, and rationalism and empiricism, so too Gonda anticipated that his pragmatic theory of film would reconcile similar sets of oppositions between essence and existence, subject and object, and idealism and materialism.[28]

Gonda states that all new technological inventions in modern society—including bicycles, automobiles, and cinema—must go through three consecutive stages of development. In the first stage, which Gonda calls the "era of luxury" (*zeitaku jidai*), such new technologies remain objects of luxurious consumption, just as automobiles were seen as a sign of affluence until Henry Ford introduced the Model T to the market in 1908. The next stage is what Gonda calls the "era of practical use" (*jitsuyō jidai*), where those technologies become more affordable through mass production. At this stage, everything should be assessed through its own utility. Or, as Gonda writes, "In order to attain perfect clearness in our thought of an object, we need only consider what conceivable effects of a practical kind the object may involve." The last stage in Gonda's historical account, which is named the "era of enjoyment" (*kyōraku jidai*), will come only when we clearly understand the full potential of the given object or technology through careful investigation of its utility and develop a particular form of beauty by "collecting and purifying the essence of its practicality."[29] Since he chooses film as his object of study, Gonda first examines how we might apply this medium to our everyday practices and then offers a more philosophical account of the particularity of the film experience.

Gonda argues that the practical utility of film as a new medium is best summarized in the following remark by Ernst Mach: "Cinematography opens up the possibility of changing the scale and direction of time to suit ourselves." Drawing on this remark, Gonda explains how film has great potential to change the direction of scientific inquiry:

> It is possible to say that this world in general is on the move, and that this world of movement equals the world of time.... Previous studies, however, have dealt mostly with immobile things, thus conducting research into "stillness." While such an approach has benefitted from two optical devices called the telescope and the microscope, I would argue that academic research of the future must take into account another direction called "movement." Needless to say, a proper device is needed for this to happen, and I believe the moving picture serves best in this regard. Let me then make my own maxim as follows: *The moving picture is both the microscope and telescope of movement.*[30]

Naturally, Gonda's argument at this point focuses on how this new optical device can be mobilized in fields such as botany, zoology, bacteriology, physics, physiology, and psychology. Celebrating the invention of techniques for the manipulation of time such as slow motion and time-lapse photography, Gonda also adds that these new techniques help us better observe and understand natural phenomena—the blossoming of a flower, the division of cells, and the trajectory of a bullet—whose movements are either too slow or too fast for our naked eyes to perceive correctly.

Gonda's film theory, however, is more complicated than a simple appreciation of technological determinism. He thus moves on to distinguish film as a distinct form of art in relation to ongoing local debates on naturalism. Like his fellow Japanese literary critics, Gonda never fails to recognize the significance of naturalism for the radical transformation of art since the late nineteenth century. As he writes, "Although it [naturalism] wasn't able to produce a great work of literature on its own, it nonetheless succeeded in the great achievement of overthrowing romanticism, symbolism, and classicism, which were all premised on old ideas such as association, inference, imagination, and syllogism."[31] Moreover, the impact of naturalism, as he understands it, lies in its objective exploration of subjective realities. As a result, continues Gonda, impressionism, cubism, and all the other schools of art that emerged after naturalism came to share the common purpose of capturing and expressing "people's empirical sense of reality, emotion, and even thought as they are."[32] Having appeared as the latest, and the most advanced enterprise to be added to this list of post-naturalist art, film must be involved with the creative integration or even the dialectic of empiricism and imagination in search for a higher truth.

It is for this reason that Gonda's account of the aesthetic potential of the film medium entails a seemingly inexplicable ambivalence. On the one hand, Gonda repeatedly calls for the return to nature, or for making good use of natural and life-like settings, as he sees this as indispensable to enhance the viewer's empirical sense of reality (*jikkan*) in their perceptual experience of the filmed world. Being dissatisfied with the then common practice of exploiting film as a cheaper substitute for theatrical plays, Gonda half-jokingly suggests that when popular historical figures such as Minamoto no Yoshitsune and Ōishi Kuranosuke appear in film, they ought to have not a top-knot (*chonmage*) but rather a crew cut (*kakugari*) just like people in modern times.[33]

On the other hand, Gonda equally stresses that the unprecedented advantage of the film medium also lies in its enhancement of the viewer's subjective imagination. Gonda often claims that the joy of film viewing comes from its lack of color, sound, and three-dimensionality. When perceiving the world on the flat surface of the screen, for instance, the viewer unconsciously commits to what Gonda calls the "sterotypification of a plane" (*heimen no rittaika*) so as to complement the information missing in filmic representation. With this almost unconscious, but no less subjective, function of our cognitive faculties, the experience of moving images becomes participatory, marked by the extraction or even embodiment of the viewer's own subjectivity. For this reason, he continues, "the beauty of content and emotion expressed by characters in the moving picture is, in effect, nothing more than the beauty of the viewer's subjective content and emotion."[34]

To better explain this contradictory situation, Gonda refers to Bergson's concept of "intuition" (*chokkan*). By intuition, Bergson designates "the kind of *intellectual sympathy* by which one places oneself within an object in order to coincide with what is unique in it and consequently inexpressible."[35] Although this concept, or rather attitude that prioritizes lived experience, is often contrasted with rational and more indirect modes of apprehension like abstraction and reasoning, Bergson, in a way similar to James, presents intuition as a plausible solution to the binary opposition between empiricism and rationalism—hence his famous dictum: "this true empiricism is the true metaphysics."[36] Similarly, Gonda uses the term *chokkan* not as antithetical to but correlative of *jikkan* (empiricism), another term that he applies to the specificity of filmic representation. Gonda's proposition here can be summarized as follows: The more film utilizes actual elements from nature and our everyday life to meet our empirical sense of reality (*jikkan*), the easier it becomes to mobilize our intuition (*chokkan*) to get closer to inexpressible truths of the world. Thus, for Gonda, the exhibition of motion pictures comprises an opportunity through which the viewers apprehend the essence of the given (or filmed) objects from within, the lived experience of intensified sympathy and identification.

Gonda further explicates this complementary relationship between empiricism and intuition by comparing different modes of reception in theater and film. In watching a stage play, says Gonda, viewers situate themselves in the position of "a sympathetic third-person" who, though emotionally moved by the events unfolding before his or her eyes, still draws a clear and conscious distinction between the world of the stage and the world of their own.[37] By contrast, film viewers can no longer have such a critical distance from what they see and experience because the world projected on screen is either part of or an extension of their own reality. This perceptual difference helps explain why the audience's reactions in the movie theater become more individual and subjective than those in the traditional theater. As Gonda writes:

> The stage has its own unique world, and tragedies are generated through the causal relations penetrating that world. The audience sympathizes with the tragedy of this world of stage, which is different from their own lives. This is why they feel sad simultaneously and no one fails to cry together with others. But in a motion picture drama, the self becomes energetic and moves around. It puts the drama into the causal relations of the world of subjectivity. In the meantime, the content of subjective vision differs from person to person because the experience of the self is individual. For this reason, the result [of interpreting moving pictures] also becomes individual and the ways people cry differ in type.[38]

Gonda also pays attention to the different viewing environments between the traditional theater and the movie theater. Sitting in a dimly lit auditorium at a distance from the stage, theatergoers can perceive whatever is taking place before and around themselves as a whole, noticing the integrity of their viewing experience, including eating snacks or lunch boxes, as a public event. Although similarly bound to their seats, moviegoers often forget about their spatial confinement, as their subjectivity begins to roam around the world on screen. In this imaginative separation between mind and body in the subjective experience of moving images, moreover, it becomes impossible to appreciate a dramatic event in its entirety. The presentation of the dramatic event itself is divided into many parts with different degrees of emphasis punctuated through the close-up, cutting, camera movements, and many other kinds of filming techniques.

At the end of his comparison between theater and film, Gonda mentions that while Japanese traditional theater such as Noh and Kabuki tends to foreground "the beauty of form" (*keishikibi*), the motion picture cultivates "the beauty of content" (*naiyōbi*) as its own exclusive domain. As he writes elsewhere in the book, the film experience "destroys our impression of the form and instead makes us feel the strength of *Inhalt* [content] or internal powers."[39] Here Gonda uses the term *form* as a synonym for the formulaic reification of ideas or emotions through symbolization (i.e., a female character holding bamboo grass in Noh plays always means that she has gone out of her mind). In this regard, Gonda's critique of the Japanese traditional theater appears akin to Shōyō's earlier denunciation of traditional *yomihon* literature, which, as we have seen, served to spread moralistic didacticism by drawing on highly conventionalized patterns of character building.

Writing almost thirty years later, Gonda adds that film's emphasis on content over form also receives support from the socioeconomic basis of this medium. Because most films in this formative period were targeted at customers with lower-class and uneducated backgrounds, film producers had to choose materials that appealed to the viewer's intuition or direct sensory apparatus, and obviously not "ones that are symbolic or in need of special preparation."[40] Here, too, Gonda highlights the importance of cinematic intuition, which can be realized only via the enhancement of the empirical sense of reality by means of the photographic image. And thanks to this shrewd insertion of class consciousness, Gonda's discussion of cinematic intuition now assumes a possibility to explicate the specific sensibility of modern capitalist society.

Thus, Gonda sees that the aesthetic potential of cinema lies in its mindful exploration of what he calls "the beauty of intuition" (*chokkanbi*). As long as it is premised on a unique property of the film medium, the fulfillment of this particular form of beauty will mark a substantial shift from the era of practical use to the era of enjoyment. As we have seen, Gonda's reference to intuition designates not a simple negation but a logical extension of Japanese debates on naturalism. It thus similarly aspires to go beyond the traditional oppositions between subject and object, mind and body, essence and existence without downgrading the empirical treatment of nature and everyday life. But because the reproduction of external reality in film is generated not by writing but through a mechanical process that involves the camera and the projector, Gonda no longer uses the term *naturalism* to refer to the new aesthetic experience brought by this medium. He argues instead that to properly grasp what is going on in this post-naturalist era, it is necessary to radically transform the concept of beauty as such in light of what film can provide us:

> As I have argued in detail, the moving picture, which is equipped with the power to universalize the culture of our society in general, has its own unique form of beauty that no other media can imitate. As this universalized culture is disseminated throughout society, the moving picture begins to establish itself as a new art based on that same culture. And only at this moment will modern civilization reach its full maturity, produce its unique flowers and fruits. This is a time when the concept of "beauty" transforms itself. Our present is a time when the concept of "beauty" is oscillating ... and new ideas of beauty about movement, splendor, spectacle, the principle of uniformity, and the pragmatic gradually begin to set in motion in our brains.... The transformation of the concept of beauty! Doesn't it mean a concomitant transformation of the concept of our life? Doesn't it speak of the creation of the value of our life?[41]

What Gonda denotes by the transformation of beauty via cinematic intuition provides more than a simple expedient to approve film as a distinct form of art. It exposes the ontological specificity of the film medium, designating its lived experience by the audience as the most relevant and updated modality of being in the modern world. This is why Gonda repeatedly claims that in writing his monograph he was actually motivated to develop a theory of modern civilization. And it is this ambitious resolution that gave him a rationale for his revolt against the conservative world of cultural elites, a reason to choose an ostensibly vulgar and inappropriate subject—the motion picture—as the object of his serious study.

Having said that, we should also admit that Gonda's vision of modernity as mediated through the experience of cinema is overtly positive and optimistic, if not thoroughly utopian. Beyond its indispensable contribution to the ongoing reform of art after naturalism, he deems motion pictures capable of abolishing both vertical and horizontal distinctions in this world.[42] It is obvious that the vertical distinction here means the apparent class divide in the consumption of art and entertainment, and therefore Gonda emphasizes that film excels at commingling people from different socioeconomic backgrounds not only by offering itself at a cheaper price but by utilizing its sensory appeal to intuition. In contrast, by the horizontal distinction Gonda refers to another cultural divide generated by geographical differences. Although there have been many attempts to introduce Western art and thought to Japan, he says, nothing is more effective and comprehensive than the moving picture in accomplishing this task. Given such remarkable power to unite such conflicting sectors of the world at large, Gonda goes so far as to declare in his conclusion that "the excellent virtue of the moving picture, we must say, lies in the universality of its culture."[43]

As indicated in Balázs's famous conception of silent cinema as the "first international language," it is not uncommon to encounter this sort of utopian sentiment in the texts of classical film theory.[44] However, Gonda's appraisal of the alleged universality of film culture is problematic for at least two reasons. First, while it should be remembered that Gonda was writing before Hollywood's hegemony of the global film market, his work does not consider the power relations that were already established between producers and consumers of internationally marketable film products. It is true that Gonda speaks highly of how film has made Western culture more easily accessible to the Japanese audience, but he talks little about the possibility of exporting Japanese or non-Western culture to the Western audience using the same medium. Consequently, despite his anticipation that film could abolish the cultural divide between the West and the non-West, Gonda's placement of the latter in the position of a passive receiver inevitably leads to the repartition of the world into the space of the universal (the West, modern, progressive, legible) and the particular (the non-West, premodern, regressive, illegible). This asymmetry in the guise of the universality of film culture became the subject of heated debates among Japanese film critics in the mid-1910s, when they confronted the blatantly exotic and disgraceful images of Japanese people and culture that European and American film companies disseminated worldwide by means of their international distribution networks.

Gonda was widely recognized as a powerful advocate of popular entertainment, but he was not always supportive of the tastes that grew spontaneously from and among the masses. This point provides us with the second critique of Gonda's utopian outlook. Compared to other domestic film reformers of the period, Gonda was certainly more sympathetic to burgeoning mass entertainment, and his strategic decision to speak from the side of the masses was most clearly manifested in his adoption of a playful writing style in the text, which seems to imitate the oral performance of the *benshi*, performers who provided live narration for silent films in Japanese movie theaters. Nevertheless, Gonda also made a number of imperative statements, especially when he addressed the popularity of the so-called "canned theater" among Japanese filmgoers. Indeed, Gonda confesses in his introduction that "I am dissatisfied with the current status of motion pictures and sometimes even running out of patience with their certain problems."[45]

No matter how popular it was among domestic film audiences of the period, this hybrid, overtly impure form of popular entertainment had to be eliminated because it, as Gonda believed, suppressed the unique aesthetic potential of the film medium and thereby prevented its healthy transformation into a site for experiencing the universality of modern culture. In the end, Gonda appears as a pedantic cultural elite, implicitly reaffirming the sociocultural divide between the upper- and lower-class people that he initially intended to abolish:

> If the moving picture gets down to lower and lower levels, it is partly because of the mercantile spirit of exhibitors or of the guilt of customers with vulgar tastes. But the main reason is that professional educators in our society have let it slide away from

their strange fastidiousness.... Measuring the true value of the moving picture, cultivating its real tastes, and displaying its intrinsic character—these are common and non-negligible problems in the present not only for those involved in education but also for those taking care of public morals and art in its broadest sense, and we must work out these common duties at all costs.[46]

Like his theorization of the oxymoronic nature of the film medium, this proposition ultimately left Gonda with another irresolvable ambiguity. To put it in Gerow's words, "Gonda was not immune to existing definitions of cinema as a problem, and so his conception of film study remains in the end crucially ambivalent, one that, in a transitional era on the cusp of pure film reform, envisions possible alternative cinemas while also helping justify discursive regimes to control the problem of cinema."[47]

It would, however, be too much to ask Gonda to be both theoretically and practically consistent on this point. Indeed, *Principles* was among the first works to offer a comprehensive theoretical analysis of cinema and its aesthetic potential, and it was only in 1914 that Gonda completed this massive tome as the culmination of his graduate research. Though potentially aware of his own shortcomings, Gonda continued to conduct research on popular entertainment, publishing a series of monographs including *Problems in Popular Entertainment* (*Minshū goraku mondai*, 1921), *Basic Conditions of Popular Entertainment* (*Minshū goraku no kichō*, 1922), and *A Crowd of Entertainment Providers* (*Goraku gyōsha no mure*, 1923).[48] While film still received considerable attention in these studies, Gonda's approach became more rigorously statistical, putting more emphasis on data analysis than on a philosophical interpretation of the unexplored potential of the film medium. Through his enduring commitment to the academic study of popular culture, he gradually shifted his position from that of an avid admirer to that of an informed observer of this particular form of mass entertainment.

Whether because of his idiosyncratic adaptation of Western philosophy or his later methodological shift toward sociology, Gonda's early theorization of cinema mostly failed to win recognition from contemporary readers. However, this does not mean that key theoretical issues addressed in *Principles*, especially those addressing the concept of realism, remained completely unnoticed among later generations of Japanese film theorists. Gonda's persistent calls for thinking beyond the premises of naturalism, for instance, set the tone for heated debates in the late 1920s on the Japanese reception of the machine aesthetic, which will be examined in the next chapter. Likewise, the concept of intuition as introduced via Bergson would also make an impressive comeback in the early 1940s, when theorists like Sugiyama Heiichi and Nagae Michitarō rekindled a philosophical approach to the film experience. In the discussion to follow, however, I survey how other local critics of the period adopted the critical vocabulary of naturalism in their commitment to the first major reform of domestic film practice known as the Pure Film Movement (jun'eigageki undō).

KERIYAMA NORIMASA: THE PURE FILM MOVEMENT

The Pure Film Movement was the collective efforts made by critics associated with the film magazine *Kinema rekōdo* (*Kinema Record*, 1913–17) to modernize Japanese film practice by consciously adopting the norms and techniques developed in Hollywood and European cinemas. Above all else, the pure film reformers demanded a more systematic and frequent use of the close-up, cross-cutting, location shooting, and most importantly, female actors, in order to eliminate the popular Kabuki cinema of that time, which was overtly dependent on local theatrical conventions including *onnagata* (male actors playing female roles), *kowairo* or *kagezerifu* (a group of *benshi* narrators providing the voices of characters on screen), *mie* (a distinctive posture struck by the actor who freezes his movement at a highlight of the play), stationary and distanced camera positions, and the extreme long takes that often lasted the entire duration of a whole sequence (see figure 1). In addition, the reformers called for a structural overhaul of the domestic film industry, in which exhibitors, whose revenue came largely from the popularity of their in-house *benshi* performers, had more power than film producers in deciding the format and content of their programs.

At the same time, the Pure Film Movement was indicative of the sea change occurring in local discourse on cinema during the second half of the 1910s. First of all, this period saw the emergence of a variety of film magazines, including *Katsudō shashin zasshi* (*Moving Picture Magazine*), *Katsudō no sekai* (*Moving Picture World*), *Katsudō gahō* (*Moving Picture Pictorial*), *Katsudō hyōron* (*Moving Picture Criticism*), and *Kinema junpō*, all of which provided lively public forums devoted to the discussion of cinema as a new form of art or popular entertainment. Second, a handful of established figures such as the playwright Osanai Kaoru and the novelist Tanizaki Jun'ichirō began to express keen interest in this new medium and soon became involved in film production on their own. Finally, government authorities also started to recognize the far-reaching and supposedly harmful effects of cinema on the mass public. In 1917, the Tokyo Metropolitan Police issued one of the first regulations to treat film independently of other sideshows.[49] As many scholars have noted, these radical changes were succinctly manifested in a shift in the very Japanese term used to signify this medium, from *katsudō shashin* (moving picture) to *eiga* (film).[50]

What is remarkable about the discourse of the Pure Film Movement, at least for the purpose of this chapter, is that its supporters generally agreed to promote the naturalist doctrine of objective or mimetic depiction as the foundation for their new conception of cinema. In their view, domestic film practice in its current state

FIGURE 1. An example of Kabuki cinema featuring Onoe Matsunosuke, with the *onnagata* actor Kataoka Chōsei in the role of the female character on the left (courtesy of the Kawakita Memorial Film Institute).

was destined to be impure and non-cinematic, not only for its reliance on extra-filmic devices like the live narration of the *benshi* but also for its lack of concerns about more natural (and realistic) presentations of actors, props, and dramatic events. The critic Nakagi Sadakazu provided a handy metaphor to summarize the point in question, arguing: "It is possible to think that everything in theater is artificial. In contrast, moving pictures can always be seen as natural. If one compares the theater to a bonsai [dwarf tree], motion pictures should be likened to beautiful landscapes in nature."[51] Another critic, Katano Hakuro, seconded this line of criticism by referring to the awkward experience he had when he saw male actors playing the roles of female characters in Japanese films: "It is truly regretful that we see close-ups of a rawboned (and expressionless) woman's face in Japanese films. The use of *onnagata* was in itself no more than a relic of the past around the time of the Meiji Restoration, when the status of women had not yet been recognized. It is thus nothing but awkward if *onnagata* still exists in our modern age where we have things like radiotelephones and airplanes, and even more so if it survives in film, which principally requires naturalistic depictions."[52]

It is not difficult to see that these statements were made in conjunction with the dominant presence of naturalism in Japanese literary discourse. But there were two other factors that informed the pure film reformers' discursive association of the cinematic with the naturalistic. The first was the rise of the *shingeki* (New

FIGURE 2. A still from Kaeriyama Norimasa's *The Glow of Life* (courtesy of the Kawakita Memorial Film Institute).

Drama) movement. Originally proposed in 1906 by Tsubouchi Shōyō, Shimamura Hōgetsu, and Osanai Kaoru, *shingeki* aimed at breaking from the preexisting norms of Japanese traditional theater by staging the work of European playwrights such as Henrik Ibsen, Gerhart Hauptmann, and Maurice Maeterlinck. While its direct adoption of Western methods and characters inevitably caused a sense of artificiality or exoticism among the local audience, the *shingeki* movement played a significant role in bringing less formulaic and unnatural elements into the Japanese performing arts. It is, indeed, this movement that opened the way for the first appearance of female actors on stage, beginning with Kawakami Sadayakko and Matsui Sumako.

The Pure Film Movement benefitted a lot from this concurrent reform of Japanese theater. *The Glow of Life* (*Sei no kagayaki*, dir. Kaeriyama Norimasa, 1918) (figure 2), often dubbed as a revolutionary film that embodied the idea of a more cinematic *eiga*, featured a group of *shingeki* actors including Murata Minoru, Kondō Iyokichi, and Hanayagi Harumi, the last of whom is believed to be the first female film actor in the history of Japanese cinema. Around the same time, the stage director Tanaka Eizō joined the oldest domestic film company Nikkatsu and began to recast the company's conservative repertoire by producing a series of *shingeki*-inspired films including *The Living Corpse* (*Ikeru shikabane*, 1918, adapted from Leo Tolstoy's play of the same title) and *One's Own Sin* (*Ono ga tsumi*, 1919, based on the novel by Kikuchi Yūhō). The incorporation of *shingeki* elements into the Japanese film world reached its apex in 1920, when the newly established film company Shōchiku hired the playwright Osanai Kaoru as the head of its subsidiary school of film acting. At Shōchiku, Osanai not only trained film actors using *shingeki* acting methods but also codirected Murata Minoru's naturalist masterpiece *Souls on the Road.*

The second factor behind the association of the cinematic with the naturalistic was the influx of Hollywood films during and after World War I. I have argued elsewhere that Japanese filmgoers initially expected Hollywood to be a temporary substitute for the then defunct European cinemas, favoring "quality" films released under Universal's subsidiary brand Bluebird Photoplays. Bluebird not only hired directors with distinctive artistic talents such as Lois Weber and Rex Ingram but also adopted Shakespeare's maxim "the play's the thing" as the brand's own slogan.[53] And yet as the number and variety of Hollywood films surpassed their European competitors, Japanese critics began to recognize the unique aesthetic qualities of this latest, and undoubtedly most powerful, addition to the foreign film market. One such quality was the manipulation of the viewer's emotional engagement through the use of close-ups, cross-cutting, and many other techniques that would later be considered the classical Hollywood style. Another, and sometimes overlooked, quality was early Hollywood's particular investment in location shooting. In *Visible Man*, Balázs spoke highly of "American realism," or "films that can have a powerful effect even though they are no more than the faithful copy of unframed nature 'in itself,'" stressing that the international success of Hollywood cinema in its formative years owed much to its collective efforts to present nature or natural settings with on-location shooting.[54] In the same manner, Japanese critics praised Hollywood directors' conscious "return to nature," treating it as an antidote to the highly "unnatural" nature of domestic film practice.

Nowhere was this admiration for Hollywood film aesthetics more evident than in the work of Kaeriyama Norimasa (1893–1964), arguably the most influential figure in the Pure Film Movement. Before making his own films, Kaeriyama had been very active in leading the movement as a cofounder of *Kinema Record*, and in 1917, he published a monograph titled *The Production and Photography of Moving Picture Drama* (*Katsudō shashingeki no sōsaku to satsueihō*, hereafter *Production*).[55] Though essentially written as a secondhand summary of English-language "how-to" books like E. W. Sargent's *The Technique of the Photoplay*, the monograph clearly tells us how Kaeriyama developed his own concept of "the pure film" through the incorporation of elements from contemporary Hollywood cinema. In the section on film acting, for instance, Kaeriyama quotes Thomas Ince's instruction that "the movements of actors must be natural," and he set the pursuit of naturalness in both the appearance and the gestures of actors as the foundation of the non-theatrical mode of filmmaking.[56] Nevertheless, because Kaeriyama already knew through experience how difficult it was for inexperienced actors to act naturally, he took a lesson from another giant of Hollywood cinema: D. W. Griffith.

Kaeriyama argues that Griffith's creative acumen resided in his ability to elicit very natural facial and bodily expressions from actors by means of his directorial skills. When Griffith needed a terrified face from young Mae Marsh, he secretly asked one of his crew members to fire a revolver just a few feet behind her so as to capture the exact expression he wanted regardless of the actress's acting skills.[57] Such a high demand for naturalistic acting also leads Kaeriyama to insist upon the use of location shooting. "The proper use of location," he writes, "is extremely important to moving picture dramas, and so one must make efforts to use both actual sceneries [*jikkei*] and actual objects [*jitsubutsu*] as much as possible."[58] Kaeriyama's articulation of Hollywood as a naturalistic cinema became influential among the supporters of the Pure Film Movement. As a result, the discursive association of the cinematic and the naturistic came to serve as the most feasible solution not only for demolishing the dominance of Kabuki cinema but also for modernizing local film practice in Japan.

The significance of the Pure Film Movement in the historical development of Japanese film practice and discourse is indisputable. However, we should keep in mind that the movement, and its recourse to the critical vocabulary of Japanese naturalism in particular, equally encompassed geopolitical issues surrounding the Japanese cinema world on a global level. When Kaeriyama and other film reformers made their commitment to the movement, they all agreed that both European and American film companies disseminated untruthful images of Japanese people and culture to pander to a colonial desire for appropriating the exotic life of the Oriental Other. As a contributor to *Kinema Record* wrote:

> In 1913, we saw two bizarre films—Ambrosio's *The Yellow Race* [*Ōshokujin*] and Bioscope's *The Japanese* [*Nihonjin*].... What did we feel most keenly when watching these two pictures? Was it an irritation at their maltreatment of the Japanese as an inferior race? Or was it a submission to the fact that anyhow the Japanese have gotten recognition from foreigners by becoming the object of their attention? No, it was completely different. We want to send our pictures to those countries as soon as possible, and to let them know what kinds of people we the Japanese are. We want to introduce them to a Japan that is filled with both beautiful people and scenery. It is these ardent hopes that came to our mind.[59]

Thus, the discursive association between the cinematic and the naturalistic in 1910 Japan must be understood in relation to an international politics of representation. If the reformers were so eager to abolish the local conventions of Kabuki cinema, it was precisely because they saw this impure and hybrid form of popular entertainment as incapable of authentically representing Japan in a way that was comprehensible to foreign spectators. In this sense, it can be said that the adoption of naturalistic elements from both *shingeki* theater and Hollywood cinema was also instrumental in making the film medium an effective tool for exporting unobtrusive and nonbiased representations of Japan and its culture to the outside world. Put differently, the naturalist doctrine of depicting things *as they are* helped transform local film practice not only into its modern form, but more specifically into a *Japanese* cinema that it shared with other national cinemas the same universal language of filmic expression. This observation ultimately leads us to understand why Satō and other Japanese film historians celebrated naturalism as the common denominator of *Nippon* realism.

TANIZAKI JUN'ICHIRŌ: CINEMATIZATION OF THE WORLD

Despite Kaeriyama's admiration, early Hollywood's attempt to offer a "faithful copy of unframed nature 'in itself'" did not remain the dominant approach in global film practice around and after the turn of the 1920s. As Kaeriyama's objective was less to promote naturalism as an unvarying foothold for his notion of "pure film" than to elevate the status of domestic film practice in general, he cautiously revised his main thesis when his *Production* was reprinted in 1921: "At present, the most accessible and democratic form of film practice is no doubt the one based on *shajitsu shugi* [mimetic realism].... Yet what is coming next is the one based on either symbolism or expressionism, and thus the purification of moving pictures now has to involve the symbolization of every form and action."[60] To minimize the impact of his theoretical conversion, Kaeriyama added to his reprint an abbreviated translation of Münsterberg's *Photoplay*, carefully choosing a section where Münsterberg argues the anti-mimetic nature of filmic representation as follows: "The photoplay tells us the human story by overcoming the forms of the outer world, namely, space, time, and causality, and by adjusting the events to the forms of the inner world, namely, attention, memory, imagination, and emotion."[61]

Kaeriyama's self-negation in 1921 did not create much surprise among his readers because by this time Japanese film and literary discourses had already made a transition from naturalism to anti-naturalism. One could better grasp this process by looking at the acclaimed novelist Tanizaki Jun'ichiro's (1886–1965) active involvement in both film production and criticism in the late 1910s. After writing occasionally on cinema, Tanizaki was hired in 1920 by the newly established film company Taikatsu as a literary consultant and soon became involved in making his own films in collaboration with the director Thomas Kurihara.[62] Tanizaki's intervention in domestic film practice had a crucial impact in elevating both the artistic and social status of cinema, causing a similar effect of Osanai's participation at Shōchiku in the same year.

Much has already been written about Tanizaki's involvement with film and its concomitant influence on his literary works such as *Naomi* (*Chijin no ai*, 1924).[63] I would therefore restrict my focus to his theorization of film as a medium that surpasses all other preexisting forms of art for its ability to be "very realistic" and "very fantastic" at the same time.[64] Tanizaki's assessment of cinema was very akin to that of the young Georg Lukács, especially the latter's 1913 essay "Thoughts toward an Aesthetic of the Cinema," in which Lukács maintained that film is genuinely to be called "fantastic" and "realistic" at once because it represents "a life without measure or order, without essence or value, a life without soul, of pure surface," while at the same time making that same world look "uncannily lifelike."[65] Though Tanizaki and Lukács were born around the same time—in 1886 and 1885, respectively—their own political or artistic credos contrast widely. Unlike Lukács, Tanizaki never became a member of the Communist Party and instead was known for his association with a romanticist literary group called Tanbiha (the Aesthetic School, or more literally, "the Indulgence-in-Beauty School"). Nevertheless, it is still possible to assert that their mutual fascination with cinema and its potential to alter our conception of the real was more than mere coincidence, indicating the historical significance of this medium as a manifestation of the lived experience of twentieth-century modernity.

In his 1917 essay "The Present and Future of Moving Pictures" ("Katsudō shashin no genzai to shōrai"), Tanizaki took a very similar position to the pure film reformers in his call for the abolition of *onnagata* and other theatrical elements still found in domestic film practice:

> [In film] actors cannot continue to use garish makeup for theatrical performances in order to camouflage their age, build, or features. For the role of a beautiful woman, a beautiful actress must by all means play the part, and an old man must without fail fill the role of an old man (as it is for the most part in Western pictures).... It is not that I insist that one make huge spectacles with trains colliding or steel bridges collapsing. First and foremost, I would ask for a return to naturalness. And I would ask that one try to depict Japanese customs and manners, simply and faithfully.[66]

Tanizaki's interest in film, however, surpassed its ability to provide a faithful reproduction of external reality. He equally stressed how profoundly this modern device had altered the way he looked at the world around him. For one, this new vision was made possible by newly invented cinematic techniques like the close-up, which allowed him to appreciate all the minute details of actors' faces or parts of their bodies, details that he had never been able to recognize with his naked eye. In addition, Tanizaki highlighted the durability, reproducibility, and transnationality of film products. This aspect—the mobility of the film medium—allowed him to appreciate previously unknown landscapes and customs of foreign countries recorded on the filmstrip more easily than before, making the entire world more attractive and accessible beyond any cultural or linguistic barriers.[67]

In short, Tanizaki's fascination with cinema was mostly derived from his conviction that film could represent things or phenomena in the world more realistically than the thing itself. Tanizaki delivered his own account of this undeniably modern instance of perceptual crisis through the following monologue by the protagonist of his 1923 novel *A Lump of Flesh* (*Nikkai*):

> To exaggerate a bit, the entire universe—all the phenomena of the world around us—is something like a film. Isn't it possible, then, that even though everything changes from moment to moment, the past remains wound up somewhere? Couldn't it be that we are all nothing but shadows that disappear quickly and without a trace, while our reality lives on in the film of the universe? Even the dreams we see and the things we imagine are films of the past projecting light on our minds. For this reason, they cannot be mere illusions.... Films are dreams that we see reflected on the screen instead of visualized in our minds. And, in fact, those dreams are the real world.[68]

Thomas Lamarre refers to what Tanizaki describes here as "the cinematization of the world," emphasizing how the appearance of the world itself, as well as people's perception and understanding of it, had been altered after the invention and global dissemination of the film medium.[69] Lamarre adds that it is with this concept that one can fruitfully compare Tanizaki with the likes of Béla Balázs, Jean Epstein, and Walter Benjamin, for they all "shared a sense of cinematic experience as one of the collapse of perceptual distance, an experience in which the heightened, too-real quality of the cinematic image forecloses the spectator's ability to see and contemplate the art object, allowing only for a shock to the body."[70]

However, Lamarre also reminds us that it is necessary to assess the writing of non-Western figures like Tanizaki in relation first to their own local discursive contexts, before treating them as proving the universality of the film experience. That is, if we are satisfied in inscribing Tanizaki into the canonical history of film theory based on his unmistakable affinity to his Western counterparts, we end up reaffirming, in the name of theory, the singularity of the West in the geopolitics of power, knowledge, and discourse formation. To avoid this pitfall, Lamarre pays attention to the racial dimension in Tanizaki's account of the cinematization of the world. While Tanizaki praised the Caucasian as always setting the universal criteria for beauty, pleasure, and cultural sophistication, he also treated the Orient as the source of exotic attraction to be exploited by *both* Westerners and the Japanese.

For my part, I argue that Tanizaki's fascination with the cinematization of the world can also be explained in light of his struggle against the dominance of naturalism in the Japanese literary world. Since his professional debut in the early 1910s, Tanizaki had always been discontent with the overconfidence of his fellow naturalist writers over the efficacy of their quasi-scientific methods. He wrote:

Inasmuch as art is not an imitation but a creation, how is it possible to delineate something without having recourse to the power of imagination? Even in the case of realist novels, no one can reproduce nature as it is; when they think they are able to accurately transcribe the actual world, the result is most likely no more than the world of their own imagination.... It was said that the so-called scientific attitude had frequently been discussed since Zola, but as far as I'm concerned, even scientists can make no discoveries without the power of imagination. Isn't it the case that what people call scientific truths are in effect based on speculation?[71]

Given this statement, no one would hesitate to categorize Tanizaki as an antinaturalist writer. In fact, when he started his career as a writer, the young Tanizaki was obsessed with writing blatantly fantastic and mesmerizing stories in which male protagonists became enthralled with their masochistic desire for majestically beautiful and dangerous women. In order to enhance the overtly artificial beauty of his imaginary world, Tanizaki employed a particular writing style that put more emphasis on "the visual and nonsignifying qualities of language over its verbal and semantic aspects," in sharp contrast to a decade-long effort by Japanese naturalists to polish the *genbun itchi* style as an unobtrusive, almost transparent means to faithfully transcribe both external and internal realities.[72]

It is obvious that Tanizaki developed his anti-naturalist rhetorical skills in order to foreground the materiality of the very medium of his creative expression—the written language. Thanks to his reflexive attitude toward the act of writing, Tanizaki is now regarded as one of the earliest examples of modernist writers in Japan. But what is more significant for the purposes of this chapter is that his media-specific approach also made him critically reflect on film's own significant property, its proclaimed ability to reproduce given things or phenomena as they are. Indeed, Tanizaki argued that in order for film to be "an art that is most suited to our times," it should first and foremost make a conscious "return to naturalness" and "try to depict Japanese customs and manners, simply and faithfully."[73] Nevertheless, because both the perceptual and emotional shock evoked in the mind of film viewers was so enchanting, Tanizaki came to a conclusion that "film is better suited than the stage for both realistic and fantastic plays" and suggested a handful of fantastic novels from the West and the non-West—including Dante's *Divine Comedy*, Edgar Allan Poe's *The Black Cat*, Wu Cheng'en's *Journey to the West*, and Izumi Kyōka's *The Holy Man of Kōya* (*Kōya hijiri*)—as potential sources for film adaptation.[74]

Tanizaki's identification of film as both a realistic and fantastic medium cast new light on the Japanese debates about realism in the first two decades of the twentieth century. Like naturalist writers' earlier attempts to reconcile subject and object, Tanizaki saw in film the possibility for invalidating the binary opposition between the fantastic and the realistic, the product of the conventional distinction between subjective imagination and objective representation. "In most cases," says Tanizaki, "imagination and nature contradict each other, and many people tend to think that imagination is false, whereas nature is true. But in their own truthfulness, imagination and nature are not as different as common sense tells us."⁷⁵ It is important to note that Tanizaki, despite his marked emphasis on imagination and the fantastic, made this claim as part of his critique of Japanese naturalism and did not raise it entirely against the premises of realism per se. That is to say, while attacking naturalism for its lack of attention to the power of imagination, he still specified the need for faithfully or even empirically depicting one's inner reality. As he wrote, "naturalist writers respect what they call experience. But for artists who live in imagination, the world of hallucination is also part of their own experience."⁷⁶ Therefore, a more holistic notion of realism must give the same thematic and stylistic weight to the subjective or imaginary side of reality. And if Tanizaki was fully preoccupied by the power of cinema, it was precisely because he considered it to be the best testing ground for developing this new realism through its seamless integration of nature and imagination, phenomenon and essence (noumenon), and the real and the fantastic.

Tanizaki, however, did not use the term *realism* to indicate what cinema could or should do with its new mode of visual presentation. He intentionally left it unnamed, inviting all kinds of contemporary artistic schools—including realism, romanticism, diabolism, naturalism, humanism, and classicism—to compete with one another to expose and realize the still-uncovered potential of this medium.⁷⁷ But one thing he made clear was that the new aesthetic experience and sensibility brought about by cinema must be far more complex and superior to what one could articulate with the critical vocabulary of naturalism alone.

As a result, the majority of Japanese filmmakers and critics after the turn of the 1920s began to separate themselves from the dominance of naturalism. Murata Minoru, director of the naturalist masterpiece *Souls on the Road*, wrote in 1922: "Because the photoplay is able to use natural scenery as a backdrop to the story, the viewers accordingly wanted everything in both acting and directing to be naturalistic. However, such an 'objective' attitude has no philosophical language behind it and is too weak to evoke any dramatic or emotional effects in the minds of the viewers."⁷⁸ The critic Midorikawa Harunosuke, who later became a scriptwriter for Ozu under the name of Noda Kōgo, also expressed his anti-realist sentiment in a similar manner: "If only realists deserve to be great filmmakers, we have to reject films based on symbolism or neo-romanticism. If this is the case, the photoplay must be confined to a position that is both too narrow and unnatural."⁷⁹ Then, in 1925, another critic named Mitsuse Sueo went so far as to pronounce the death of naturalism or any other old definitions of realism developed in the nineteenth century as a proper method for filmmaking:

> Both futurism and cubism appeared as a determined rebellion against the art of the past (for the most part, against realism). All rebellious movements are always filled with youthful zest as well as with a holy terror that burns down everything. It is thus

not surprising that some far-sighted people began to point to the crisis of realism. The crisis of realism? Yes. As long as it remains a habitual and thoughtless realism as is seen in the film world today, no one can deny the fact that realism is now no match for the dominance of the vibrant and rising expressionism.[80]

This passage does not merely indicate the periodic shift from one position to another in the history of Japanese film theory and practice. Rather, it shows that the very object of realism—reality—was also in the process of a radical transformation. As in other parts of the world, Japan experienced a sea change in every sector of social, cultural, and political life during the 1920s. Especially after the 1923 Great Kantō Earthquake completely destroyed the old landscapes of the country's capital, Japan witnessed the emergence of urban consumerist society, the growth of leftist activities and political turmoil, and the saturation of modern technologies and venues for mass communication. And because no one could deny the fact that the cinema came to play an increasingly central role in this undoubtedly modern mediascape, many began to call for a new concept of realism that could better articulate the ways in which film mediated or even determined the relationship between the masses and their everyday life.

Originally proposed in the late nineteenth century, naturalism was no longer competent in dealing with the vibrant and chaotic reality of the twentieth century. In the meantime, new and alternative forms of art practice appearing throughout the 1920s, marked by their collective effort to capture and illuminate the modern subject's experience of disintegration, fragmentation, and alienation, came to promote themselves as a total negation of Japanese naturalism and its basic premise of depicting things as they are. As Raymond Williams points out with regard to the history of modern literature, experimental writers working in the 1920s came to be "applauded for their denaturalizing of language, their break with the allegedly prior view that language is either a clear, transparent glass or a mirror, and for their making abruptly apparent in the texture of narrative the problematic status of the author and his authority."[81]

We should, however, keep in mind that Mitsuse, somewhat echoing Gonda's theorization of the cinematic intuition and Tanizaki's equal treatment of the realistic and the fantastic in filmic representation, presented his denial of naturalism not as a paradigm shift but as a continuation of the same demand for a truer realism. This is why, after the passage I quoted above, he added the following remark: "Here I declare the need for a renaissance of realism despite all possible hardships. The time has come for realism to awaken from its dormant state by putting a new passion and force into its old container.... Is there anyone who will stand at the forefront and sound the horn?"[82]

Mitsuse clearly declared that realism could or should be redeemed if one could come up with a new definition that is no longer premised on the old assumptions of naturalism. As we will see in the next chapter, it was in response to this widespread demand that critics like Itagaki Takao and Kurahara Korehito developed their own theories of a new realism toward the end of the 1920s. Their debates were inevitably colored with both a strong "anti-naturalist" sentiment and a newly emergent "modernist" sensibility, effectively blurring the alleged opposition between realism and modernism in our conventional historical accounts. In addition, Mitsuse's call for "a renaissance of realism" clearly tells us that in the context of Japanese intellectual discourse, realism remained a significant concept for anyone trying to articulate their lived experience of twentieth-century modernity. Rather than imposing a fixed way of looking at reality, this concept has radically altered its definition and function along with the ongoing transformations of modern Japanese society as such.

Some may attribute theoretical uncertainty about the concept of realism to the absence of an indigenous realist school in the history of Japanese art. Seen this way, Satō's discussion of Nippon realism would reappear before us as a deliberate attempt to cover up this perceived cultural deficiency, strategically mobilizing the "Japanized" definition of naturalism as the theoretical origin of realism. In contrast, I have tried in this chapter to abolish such a hierarchical dichotomy between the Western original and its non-Western imitation. Having no indigenous discourse to rely on, Japanese filmmakers and critics were better situated to more openly discuss "the crisis of realism," a problem closely connected with people's lived experience of twentieth-century modernity. Thus, if there is something that we could call "Nippon realism," I contend, it should be found somewhere between such unconcealed confusion and the remarkable creativity that a generation of Japanese intellectuals exhibited in their relentless search for a more plausible notion of cinematic realism in the decades to follow.

2

The Machine Aesthetic and Proletarian Realism

REALISM WITHIN MODERNISM

When Gonda and Tanizaki wrote about film in the 1910s, they were both fascinated by this medium's unique vision of the world containing two self-contradictory foci or standpoints at its center. More than anything, they agreed that film could not be defined as either a subjective or an objective medium, as it always forces us to renew our conventional understanding of the relationship between subject and object, essence and existence, and the external world and ourselves. It is within this line of philosophical inquiry that both Gonda and Tanizaki celebrated film's unprecedented potential to reconcile another set of conflicts—between empiricism and intuition (Gonda) and between the real and the fantastic (Tanizaki). To explain the point at issue here using Tanizaki's own formula, it is not simply that both realistic and fantastic elements can coexist in filmic representation; it is rather that in film things become fantastic because they are too real, and, in turn, things become real because they are too fantastic. And if Japanese film critics and theorists in the 1920s needed to develop a new definition of realism beyond the critical vocabulary of naturalism, it meant that they had to confront the complex nature of the film medium as it was, rather than borrowing ideas or practices developed elsewhere.

This brief overview may explain why German expressionism failed to provide a good model for a new realism in the discursive context of 1920s Japan. The introduction of German expressionist films to Japan started with the release of *The Cabinet of Dr. Caligari* in May 1921 at the Kinema Kurabu theater in Tokyo. Like the earlier discussion of naturalism, the Japanese reception of German expressionism went through the inevitable process of localization, for it treated this new school of art less as a modernist movement than as a feasible solution for the traditional conflict between subjective and objective visions in the cognition of the world. One such account can be found in the 1923 book *Expressionist Cinema* (*Hyōgenha no eiga*) by Kudō Shin'nosuke. According to Kudō, expressionism distinguishes itself from its precursors like naturalism for its marked emphasis on the subjective function of the ego, or more precisely, by consciously asserting that "the ego and the external world are mutually dependent" to the extent that the latter can never be accessible without being captured and expressed by the former in a reified form.[1] Consequently, where naturalists attempted to provide an objective or mimetic depiction of the world from a quasi-scientific and inhuman perspective, expressionists addressed the same world as a "totally subjectified being" (*hanahadashiku shutaika sareta sonzai*) by means of the human subject's creative power of free association and abstraction.[2]

This undeniably idealist account of expressionism, however, remained completely silent about how such creative function of the human subject would be altered when it began to compete or collaborate with another nonhuman viewing subject called the movie camera. Perhaps noticing this shortcoming, Tanizaki criticized *The Cabinet of Dr. Caligari* by arguing that although the film's ghastly storyline and deformed set designs did succeed in doing away with the conventions of the naturalistic theater, the acting style and appearance of the main characters still remained too "human" and not on a par with the mechanical nature of the film medium.[3]

In the meantime, the 1920s also witnessed the rise of filmmakers and theorists who tried to establish a new theory of cinema through the new mode of visual perception brought about by the camera's mechanical gaze. "This eye," said Jean Epstein in 1921, "sees waves invisible to us, and the screen's creative passion contains what no other has ever had before, its proper share of ultraviolet.... The Bell and Howell is a metal brain, standardized, manufactured, marketed in thousands of copies, which transforms the world outside it into art."[4] Béla Balázs also wrote that "the magnifying glass of the cinematograph brings us closer to the individual cells of life, it allows us to feel the texture and substance of life in its concrete detail.... Through its close-ups a good film will teach you to read the score of the polyphony of life, the individual voices of all things which go to make up the great symphony."[5] Most famously, Dziga Vertov summarized his commitment to filmmaking as follows:

> The main and essential thing is: The sensory exploration of the world through film. We therefore take as the point of departure the use of the camera as a kino-eye, more perfect than the human eye, for the exploration of the chaos of visual phenomena that fills space. The kino-eye lives and moves in time and space; it gathers and records impressions in a manner wholly different from that of the human eye. The position of our bodies while observing or our perception of a certain number of features of a visual phenomenon in a given instant are by no means obligatory limitations for the camera which, since it is perfected, perceives more and better.[6]

I use the term *machine aesthetic* to refer to what is at stake in these statements. It is, however, not that I see these theorists as simply eulogizing the newly discovered beauty of modern machinery. Rather, my contention is that they all understood aesthetics, following the term's Greek origin, as the study of the conditions of sensuous perception, and, from that perspective, addressed how these conditions had been radically transformed with the advent of cinema and its unique articulation of the world in motion. As Francesco Casetti points out, if the premise of this particular aesthetic—that cinema can teach us how to look at the world anew—became the dominant concern of 1920s film criticism, "it was not only because it embodied the gaze of the human eye, but because it embodied the gaze of the twentieth century."[7]

Since it offers a good reference point for assessing the close relationship between cinema and twentieth-century modernity, the critical discourse formed around the machine aesthetic has attracted much attention from scholars of film and avant-garde art. Among those scholars is Malcolm Turvey, who coined the term "the revelationist tradition" to discuss how a group of major film theorists from the classical period—including Epstein, Vertov, Balázs, and Kracauer—dealt with cinema's alleged ability to "uncover features of reality invisible to human vision."[8] While Turvey agrees that these theorists shared a growing skepticism about the alleged potency of human perception that was called into question by the recent development of modern science and technology, his main argument is dedicated rather to explicating the logical deficiencies of this critical tradition. In particular, he takes issue with this tradition's tendency to address metaphysical or irresolvable questions—such as whether cinema makes it possible to see the color of music—under the guise of scientism.[9]

Turvey then moves on to criticize this tradition's inappropriate application of positivist thinking by applying a more rigorous method of investigation developed by Ludwig Wittgenstein and other theorists of logical positivism. As he explains elsewhere, Turvey's critical inquiry is based on his desire to deal with classical film theory not only as the subject of historical research but also as a theoretical one.[10] By theoretical, he means that he is interested in demonstrating that "there might actually be some ideas and arguments in classical film theory that are true, or almost true in some way," and for this reason he has, in the end, attempted in the study cited above to argue that "Epstein and other early film theorists' notion of film as a revelatory medium is right, if reconstructed in a certain way."[11]

In the following, I will investigate the Japanese discourse formed around the machine aesthetic and what Turvey called the revelationist tradition. But my approach here is utterly antithetical to Turvey's presumption that theory must be—or at least intends to be—true and universal by transcending its historical and sociocultural constructedness. Rather than inquiring into the validity of the machine aesthetic as a universal account of the film medium, I shall examine how this dis-

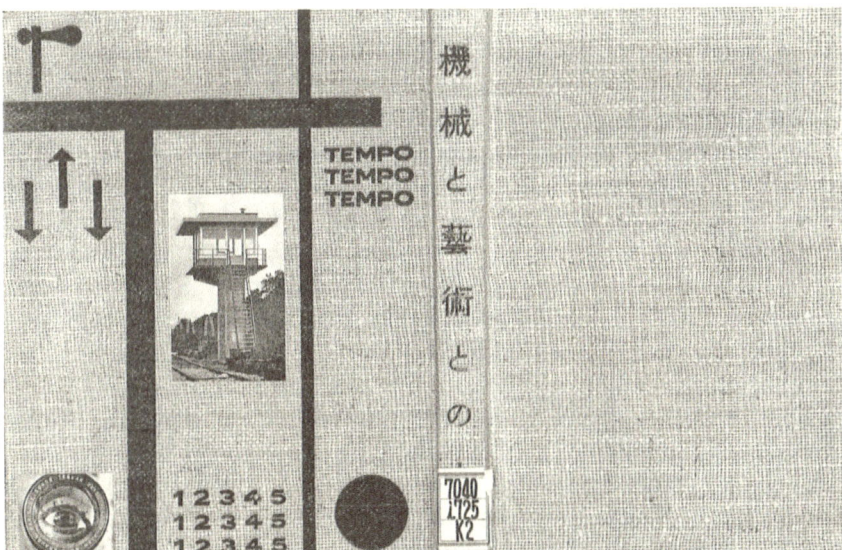

FIGURE 3. The front cover of *Exchanges between Machine and Art*.

course's problematic truth claims helped generate an actual site for local disputes and political conflicts when it traveled from Europe and the Soviet Union to Japan toward the end of the 1920s. To address this complex issue with precision, I look at the work of the art historian Itagaki Takao (1894–1966), especially a series of essays included in his monograph *Exchanges between Machine and Art* (*Kikai to geijutsu to no kōryū*, 1929) (see figure 3).[12] In his writings, Itagaki sought to discern the main characteristics of twentieth-century art by observing how it came to adopt the functional beauty of modern machinery—including airplanes, ocean liners, iron bridges, skyscrapers, and the cinema—as its main inspirational source. Itagaki's contribution therefore signals a synchronicity between the West and the non-West in terms of their mutual desire to give shape to social, cultural, and perceptual changes in everyday life engendered by the saturation of modern technologies.

But I should stress that I have chosen Itagaki as the subject of my inquiry in this chapter not for the novelty of his argument. Indeed, Itagaki was not the first among Japanese critics to introduce the discourse of the machine aesthetic. As early as 1924, the film critic Iijima Tadashi had already written about the new visibility of the objective world enabled by the camera's lens: "The lens is an eye, it is 'an eye that is given the characteristic of non-humanistic analysis,' as Epstein tells us. It is an eye that can see what our own eyes cannot see.... And in front of our eyes are undiscovered and unexcavated veins."[13] Moreover, as a participant in the global debates on the machine aesthetic, Itagaki's own contribution might appear minor and secondary because what he actually did through his writing was mostly limited to the informed annotation of the work of his contemporaries in Europe and the Soviet Union, including Le Corbusier, László Moholy-Nagy, and Dziga Vertov. Why, then, does he deserve our critical attention?

My answer is that Itagaki's innovation lies in the ways he presented his work to the local readers. Indeed, Itagaki was known domestically for the coinage of the neologism "machine realism" (*kikai no riarizumu*), and he used it to promote his fascination with the latest examples of the 1920s avant-garde art movement. Why did he employ the term *realism* to designate the cultural phenomena that are usually associated with *modernism*? To answer this, I must resituate Itagaki in the specific discursive context of late 1920s Japan. The fact is that Itagaki elaborated his theory of machine realism as a direct refutation of "proletarian realism" (*puroretaria rearizumu*), another new theory of realism proposed in 1928 by the Marxist literary critic Kurahara Korehito (1902–1991). Though sharing a similar desire to come up with a better definition of realism for the twentieth century, the difference between the two was unmistakable: while Itagaki suggested viewing the world through "the eye of the machine" (*kikai no me*) to grasp the spirit of the modern age, Kurahara found it necessary to be equipped with "the eye of the proletarian vanguard" (*puroretaria zen'ei no me*) to foresee the advent of a more advanced socialist society. Looking closely at what was at stake in their prognostic calls for new realism in the era of modernism, this chapter offers a geopolitical reading of the historical conjuncture between the machine aesthetic and the proletarian art movement in prewar Japan. Before examining the fierce disputes between Itagaki and Kurahara, however, it is necessary to look at how the ideas and practices of twentieth-century avant-garde art were introduced to Japan and its local discourse.

THE AVANT-GARDE ART MOVEMENT IN 1920S JAPAN

By the second half of the 1920s, Japanese artists and critics had already reached the point where they no longer felt any temporal lag in their knowledge about the latest trends in contemporary art imported from abroad. The beginning of this increased sense of synchronicity can be traced back to 1909, when the novelist Mori Ōgai published the first Japanese translation of F. T. Marinetti's futurist manifesto only three months after the original text appeared in the Italian newspaper *Gazzetta dell'Emilia* and the French newspaper *Le Figaro*.[14] The following decade accordingly saw the intermittent appearance of critics introducing the unceasing emergence of new isms and schools in European art, but it was in the 1920s that people in Japan began to witness in earnest the flourishing of local art forms directly influenced by those burgeoning avant-garde movements.[15]

The Japanese reception of avant-garde art in general was too rich and far-reaching to summarize here, as it took place in the diverse fields of poetry, literature, painting, theater, photography, and film. Indeed, even a brief glance at the chronology of Japanese art movements in the 1920s shows us a whirlwind of historically important events, including Hirato Renkichi's street demonstration in which he publicly displayed a leaflet on his "Japanese Futurist Manifesto Movement" ("Nihon Miraiha sengen undō," 1921), the foundation of dada-esque artist groups such as Action (1922) and Mavo (1923), the formation of the modernist literary group called the New Sensation School (Shinkankakuha, 1924), the publication of avant-garde poetry collections such as Hagiwara Kyōjirō's *Death Sentence* (*Shikei sengen*, 1925) and Nishiwaki Junzaburō's *O Fragrant Stoker* (*Fukuiku taru kafu yo*, 1927), and the production of Kinugasa Teinosuke's experimental films *A Page of Madness* (*Kurutta ichipeiji*, 1926) and *Crossroads* (*Jūjiro*, 1928).

A major factor behind the proliferation of Japanese avant-garde art was the emergence of the more direct liaisons between Japanese and European artists. During the first few years of the 1920s, Japan welcomed the visits of the likes of Russian Futurists David Burliuk and Victor Palmov who were traveling across the world to escape from the chaos of the Soviet Union. Moreover, the economic boom generated by Japan's "successful" participation in World War I facilitated individual visits of Japanese students and intellectuals to Europe. There had already existed a generation of Japanese writers and artists who studied in Europe during the Meiji period. But if the main purpose of these first-generation travelers was to report on Japan's cultural and socioeconomic backwardness, a new generation of travelers in the late Taishō (1912–1925) and early Shōwa (1925–1989) periods were able to witness the ongoing disappearance of both temporal and spatial distances between themselves and their Western counterparts.

Murayama Tomoyoshi (1901–1977), a multitalented artist and the founder of the Mavo group, provides us with the epitome of the transcontinental experience of such second-generation travelers. In February 1922, Murayama, still a freshman at Tokyo University, arrived in Berlin where he was supposed to study primitive Christianity. Although his stay there lasted less than a year and he learned nothing from the lectures at his college, Murayama avidly absorbed the emergence of the avant-garde art movement by roaming through cafés, theaters, and galleries. With the guidance of his Japanese friends such as Wadachi Tomoo and Iketani Shinzaburō, he soon became acquainted with the Russian sculptor Alexander Archipenko and the Italian futurist F. T. Marinetti. Meanwhile, in his spare time he quickly began creating his own artworks and successfully presented them at the International Futurist Exhibition in Berlin and the First International Art Exhibition in Düsseldorf.[16]

When he returned to Japan in 1923, Murayama soon distinguished himself as a central figure in Japanese avant-garde art, effortlessly crossing the boundaries between different genres of art production. Besides publishing theoretical works such as *The Art of Today and the Art of the Future* (*Genzai no geijutsu to mirai no geijutsu*, 1924) and *A Study of Constructivism* (*Kōseiha kenkyū*, 1926), Murayama wrote a number of short stories based on his turbulent experience in Berlin; organized street happenings or moving exhibitions with other Mavo members; and designed the constructivist set for Hijikata Yoshi's 1924 stage production of *From Morning 'til Midnight* (*Asa kara yonaka made*, based on a script by the German playwright Georg Kaiser). Murayama also made a foray into the world of film production as a set designer for Murata Minoru's *The Sun* (*Nichirin*, 1926).

In the Japanese local context, the Great Kantō Earthquake of 1923, a disaster that devastated much of Tokyo and adjacent areas and killed nearly one hundred thousand people, also played a significant role in demarcating the 1920s from the previous decades. The social impact of this disaster became more grave and intensified as it soon turned into a human atrocity: during the chaos immediately following the earthquake, dozens of leftist radicals and thousands of Korean and other immigrants from the expanding Japanese Empire were massacred by the police and local vigilantes due to groundless rumors that they had planned to plot against Japanese citizens. On a discursive level, people often likened the physical and emotional shocks generated by the earthquake and its aftermath to the crisis of human ethics that Europeans had experienced through the world war.[17] But on a practical level, the destruction of the nation's capital by this disaster offered a timely opportunity to bring new forms of art into the space of everyday life. As Gennifer Weisenfeld points out, a group of enterprising artists composed mostly of the members of Action and Mavo immediately began to decorate makeshift barracks appearing in the city with abstract and expressionistic designs.[18]

Besides these immediate impacts, the earthquake also prepared a more radical reshaping of the Japanese urban landscape with the introduction of new technologies for social infrastructure. Notable examples of this kind included the construction of the modern bridges and apartments made of steel and reinforced concrete, the opening of national radio broadcasting stations (1925), the establishment of personal telephone networks (1926), the opening of the first subway line in Tokyo (1927), the publication of mass-circulated weekly magazines such as *Kingu* (*King*, which sold 750,000 copies for its inaugural issue in 1924), and the mushrooming of new amusement sights including cafés, bars, dance halls, revue theaters, and department stores.

Given these rapid and perceptible changes, it is possible to say that the decade of the 1920s was a pivotal period that opened a new phase in the course of Japanese modernization. Perhaps more eager and determined than the advocates of naturalism, Japanese artists and intellectuals after the earthquake adopted the norms and idioms of the avant-garde aesthetic as a source for the continuing process of modernizing their own sensibilities and forms of expression. Thus, if there is something that we can call "Japanese modernism" in this period, it should encompass a wide range of discourse and cultural products that intended to articulate the impacts of twentieth-century modernity, rather than this or that concrete artwork that seemed to emulate the canons of European modernism. Indeed, the term *modernism* has at least two conflicting meanings in its usage in the Japanese language: Its transliteration, *modanizumu*, refers to things related to the divergence of cultural modernity and is tinged with a sense of emancipation, whereas its translation, *kindaishugi*, refers to things related to the convergence of societal modernization that always conforms to the supremacy of the West.

This nonrestrictive treatment of the term *modernism* in the Japanese context also helps clarify the idiosyncratic nature of the avant-garde art movement in 1920s Japan. Like their European counterparts, Japanese avant-gardists intended to attack the institutional norms of expression on which the very notion of art had been established. The founding manifesto of Mavo, for instance, passionately declared: "We are not enchained. We are radicals. We will carry out a revolution. We will advance. We will create. We will ceaselessly affirm, and ceaselessly deny."[19] At the same time, however, the Japanese avant-garde art movement often tended to pick up and incorporate random elements from different isms and schools in the European context. This tendency is most clearly expressed in the manifesto of the New Sensation School, which recognized "futurism, cubism, expressionism, dada, symbolism, constructivism, and some of the realists" as all belonging to this school."[20]

Needless to say, the most striking remark in this manifesto is the inclusion of "some of the realists." Usually regarded as the best example of literary modernism in 1920s Japan, the New Sensation School revolted against the prevailing view of language as a neutral and transparent medium for expression by consciously employing "unconventional grammatical structures and tropes, including fragmented sentences and montage constructions."[21] However, the school's founder, Yokomitsu Riichi, always considered his "modernist" work inseparable from his relentless search for a new form of writing that could best articulate his lived experience of the world as it appeared to him through perception. As a consequence, he went so far as to declare in another essay, "It is we [the New Sensationists] who deserve to be called 'realist' in its strictest sense."[22] In Yokomitsu's view, the opposition between realism and modernism did not prove self-evident because, at least in the context of Japanese critical discourse, both camps shared a similar desire to give shape to the ongoing transformation of the senses that required the constant and conscious renewals of modes of perception and expression.

In his study of literary modernism in prewar Japan, Gregory Golley offers an insightful observation regarding the conceptual compatibility between realism and modernism commonly found in this local context. Looking at the work of Tanizaki, Yokomitsu, and Miyazawa Kenji—all of whom have been labeled as modernist—Golley contends that these Japanese modernists always treated realism in a dialectical manner. All the literary texts examined in his study, he writes, "stand emphatically at odds with the thematic and stylistic conventions of *literary* realism; but none of these works opposes realism as an ontological or epistemological disposition."[23] Behind this seemingly self-contradictory attitude was the discovery of the new face of reality that began to reveal itself beyond the threshold of the human sensory apparatus, one that could be grasped only through a new aesthetic framework based either on recent scientific discoveries (Max Planck's quantum mechanics and Albert Einstein's theory of relativity) or on modern technologies (film, radio, airplane). Just as scientific facts discovered by modern physicists do not immediately elicit a strong reality effect in the eyes of the general public, aesthetic treatments of the reality of life experience in the twentieth century by modernist writers would inevitably seem anti-realistic at first glance. This perceptual detour, adds Golley, should not be understood at the level of its superficial appearance alone; it was in effect imbued with each writer's relentless search for a higher objectivity, "a new way of *knowing* and *depicting* the universe," as in the case of modern science.[24]

It is true that Golley's speculation places too much emphasis on the positivist tradition that had already been in vogue since the introduction of naturalism, and thus fails to offer a comprehensive account of the specifics of post-naturalist avant-garde art. Nevertheless, his reference to the "dialectic of realism" at work in the discourse of Japanese modernism is still very useful for the purpose of this chapter. As we will see shortly, the dispute between Itagaki and Kurahara emerged as a prime example of prewar Japanese debates on the dialectic of realism in that they presented opposing theories of realism—machine realism versus proletarian realism—as antitheses to naturalism or other preexisting definitions of realism proposed in the nineteenth century. On the level of their actual dialogues, Itagaki and Kurahara never came to an agreement, due to their conflicting political standpoints. But both theorists were equally motivated to theorize the new modes of sensory perception and knowledge acquisition made possible by two trans-human agents of the twentieth century, namely, cinema and communism.

ITAGAKI TAKAO: MACHINE REALISM

Itagaki Takao was born in 1894 to the family of a successful doctor. The only son in his family, Itagaki was initially expected to follow in his father's footsteps. But by the time of graduation from high school, Itagaki already developed a keen interest in Western painting and architecture, especially those from the Renaissance period, by constantly browsing the foreign book section at the Maruzen bookstore. After studying art history and aesthetics at Tokyo Imperial University under the guidance of the renowned aesthetician Ōtsuka Yasuji, Itagaki began teaching as a lecturer at the Tokyo School of Fine Arts, Nihon University, and Keiō University. In this early period of his career, Itagaki had no intention of straying beyond the confines of his academic discipline, diligently publishing works such as *A Sur-*

vey of Western Art History (*Seiyō bijutsushi gaisetsu*, 1922), *Historical Philosophy of the Neo-Kantian School* (*Shin-Kanto-ha no rekishi tetsugaku*, 1922), and *Major Currents in Western Art* (*Seiyō bijutsu shuchō*, 1923).

A critical shift in Itagaki's career occurred in 1924–25, when he took a one-year research trip to Western Europe (France, Italy, Germany) at the order of Japan's Ministry of Education. Unlike Murayama and other Japanese intellectuals who visited Europe around the same time, however, Itagaki was initially indifferent or even insensitive to the burgeoning avant-garde art movements. Indeed, so faithful was he to the official mission of his trip that Itagaki spent most of his time at museums and libraries collecting primary written documents and materials necessary for his academic writing. Yet as he delved deeper into archival research, Itagaki soon recognized that his scheduled return to Japan would inevitably mean the loss of his privileged access to those rare materials. It was this unavoidable dilemma over his position as a "distant observer" of classical Western art that caused him to turn his attention to what was happening in the contemporary art scene. In an autobiographical essay published in 1931, Itagaki refers retrospectively to the reason behind his conversion:

> For those living in the islands in the Far East, where one has no clue other than some insufficient documents collected with a limited budget or some vague impressions of the original work remaining in one's memory, it is totally hopeless and unrewarding to produce a work based on historical research. Even when I was working on the history of eighteenth- and nineteenth-century French paintings, I could not help but feel my geographical distance from Paris where the Bibliothèque nationale and the Musée du Louvre are located.... Once I entered the realm of contemporary art that emerged after the World War, however, I found the sun shining brightly. Here we can access as many primary materials as we need as long as we prepare ourselves properly.[25]

Upon his return to Japan, Itagaki began accumulating primary data and concrete examples of what he saw as constituting the art of the twentieth century. Traversing the diverse fields of painting, literature, architecture, photography, and film, this intensive "field research" eventually resulted in an astonishingly vibrant and prolific period of activity beginning in the late 1920s. First, in the years between 1929 and 1933 alone, Itagaki published fourteen monographs, including *Exchanges between the Machine and Art* (1929), *Acquisition of New Art* (*Atarashiki geijutsu no kakutoku*, 1930), *A Sociological Analysis of the Art of Superior Ships* (*Yūshūsen no geijutsu shakaigakuteki bunseki* 1930), *Aspects of the Artistic Modern* (*Geijutsuteki gendai no shosō*, 1931), and *Formal Construction of Architecture* (*Kenchiku no yōshikiteki kōsei*, 1931), to name but a few.

Second, Itagaki collaborated with the young photographer Horino Masao (1907–2000) to showcase his knowledge of the latest trends in contemporary art.

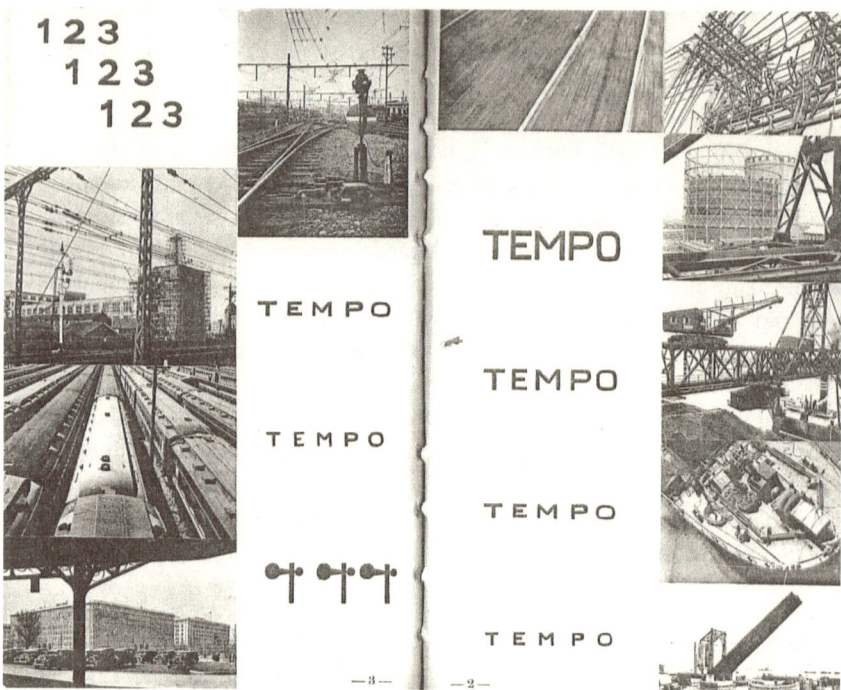

FIGURE 4. Photographs from Itagaki Takao and Horino Masao's "Characteristics of Greater Tokyo," *Chūō kōron* 46, no. 10 (October 1931): appendixes 2–3.

Under Itagaki's supervision, Horino soon became a leading figure in the New Photography (*shinkō shashin*) movement, skillfully adopting new techniques of photographic expression including photomontage, typo-photo, and constructivist compositions.[26] The collaboration between Itagaki and Horino can be seen in the latter's 1932 monograph *Camera, Eye × Steel, Composition* (*Kamera, me × Tetsu, kōsei*), which featured photographs of a transatlantic liner, an iron bridge, and a modern factory building, all taken from the constructivist perspective.[27] Equally important in their creative collaboration was the photo-essay "Characteristics of Greater Tokyo," ("Dai-Tokyo no seikaku," 1931) (see figure 4). This essay was remarkable in that it aimed to visualize the energy and dynamism of the nation's capital by emulating Moholy-Nagy's unrealized film script "Dynamics of the Metropolis."[28]

Third, and most importantly, Itagaki also took the initiative in creating sites for a public forum on the issues of the avant-garde by launching his own journal *Shinkō geijutsu* (*The New Art*, 1929–1930) and its short-lived successor *Shinkō geijutsu kenkyū* (*Studies of the New Art*, 1931). Coedited by leading critics of adjacent fields such as Iwasaki Akira (film), Sakakura Junzō (architecture), and Yoshikawa

Shizuo (music), *Shinkō geijutsu* assumed a truly interdisciplinary editorial policy. Indeed, through its coverage of a wide array of topics ranging from surrealist paintings, constructivist theater, industrial designs, International Style architecture, Soviet montage theory, and proletarian literature, it succeeded in capturing the expanded notion of the arts in the twentieth century. With such an enterprising spirit, *The New Art* was able to draw attention from a broad range of readers—including even those from outside Japan. For instance, Iwasaki Akira's article "Film as a Means of Agitprop ("Senden sendō shudan to shite no eiga"), published in the first and second issues of the journal, was widely read among Chinese readers through translation by the acclaimed writer Lu Xun.[29]

What made Itagaki distinct from other Japanese supporters of avant-garde art was the critical distance he had from the objects of his observation. In fact, Itagaki often referred to his stance as "contemplative" (*seikanteki*), stressing that he was not a practitioner but an "observer of contemporary art" (*gendai geijutsu kōsatsusha*). It is this ostensibly neutral—or some may call it empiricist—attitude that enabled him to investigate the rise of the proletarian literature movement without becoming fully embroiled in turbulent party politics. In one of the editorials for his own journal, Itagaki cautiously declared his noninterventionist standpoint in disgust at the commonplace disputes caused by each individual's political credo: "*Shinkō geijutsu kenkyū* is by no means an organ based on the demands of certain isms or claims. It is nothing but an experiment that aims to understand several aspects of the aesthetics of the modern times as accurately as possible from a purely contemplative perspective."[30]

However, it should be noted that such a pronounced apolitical statement more often than not had a strong political connotation in its original context. As the literary critic Hirano Ken points out, the period around the turn of the 1930s saw a three-sided struggle in the field of literature, involving naturalists (or "I-novelists"), modernists (the New Sensation School and a more commercially oriented group called the New Art school [*Shinkō geijutsuha*]), and proletarian writers.[31] Because they all took considerably different paths in approaching the contested relationships between art and politics, form and content, and subjective and objective descriptions, it became almost impossible to discuss and compare their texts on the same critical criteria. In attempting to break into this stagnant situation, Itagaki deliberately chose to promote the saturation of modern machinery as a way to disentangle the confusion and conflicts among those three groups. But his unabashed search for a universal norm for articulating the experience of twentieth-century modernity soon made him bear the brunt of attacks from the supporters of proletarian literature.

Itagaki's method of using the machine aesthetic as a universal account of twentieth-century modernity was best demonstrated in the two essays he published in 1929, "Machine Civilization and Contemporary Art" ("Kikai bunmei to gendai geijutsu") and "Exchanges between the Machine and Art" ("Kikai to geijutsu to no kōryū"). To begin with, Itagaki confirms the fact that a new sensibility that urges the viewer to see aesthetic values in modern machinery has appeared as a genuine phenomenon of the twentieth-century, disseminated first by the work and written manifestos of the Italian futurists.[32] For this reason, what is usually called the "machine aesthetic" in reference to this new sensibility can in itself serve as one of the most relevant cultural markers of the times. However, Itagaki also points out that there are at least two opposing standpoints regarding the integration of the machine into art in the early twentieth century. Earlier attempts made by the Italian futurists and the Russian constructivists before the turn of the 1920s, he argues, were generally marked by their romanticist tendencies, which mostly ended up fetishizing the external beauty of modern machinery, made of steel and displaying the power of masculinity.

On the other hand, the 1920s—especially the second half of the decade—had witnessed the rise of a group of other artists and architects sharing a different attitude that put more emphasis on the internal logic of the machine, a logic that can be summarized through a completely different set of terms, including *accuracy, rationality, progression, collectivity,* and *functionality*. Among those who promoted this renewed definition of the machine aesthetic were the Swiss-born French architect Le Corbusier, the Hungarian painter and photographer László Moholy-Nagy, and the Soviet filmmaker Dziga Vertov. As Itagaki observes, their "anti-romanticist" attitude toward modern machinery is most succinctly manifested in Le Corbusier's famous dictum: "The house is a machine for living in."[33]

Itagaki goes on to examine how and to what extent the rise of this second-generation, less romanticist machine aesthetic changed the traditional notion of the arts in general. It is in this inquiry that the significance of modern architecture comes to the fore because it not only benefits from recent technological and material innovations for construction—sheet glass for curtain walls, steel frames for structural supports, and reinforced concrete for both interior and exterior supports—but also embodies, in its own right, the internal logic of the machine—or its different approach to the division between subject and object. Unlike architects of the past centuries, says Itagaki, new architects of the 1920s including Le Corbusier, Walter Gropius, and Ludwig Mies van der Rohe do not follow or respect the existing norms of architectural beauty and decoration; instead, they now design buildings in search of the most rational and functional space to "live in" under the banner of the "International Style" or *Neue Sachlichkeit* (New Objectivity).[34]

Itagaki sees the emergence of this style as heralding an epistemological break in the history of Western art and architecture because, as opposed to his previous understanding of the arts, it privileges the materiality of given objects over and against the idea of beauty shared by individual artists. With this eye-opening discovery, Itagaki explores further examples of modern construction (e.g., factories, skyscrapers, iron bridges, airplanes, and battleships) designed by nameless industrial designers and architects to see how their collective commitment to functionalism could lead to the advent of a new concept of art and sensory perception—the machine aesthetic—that no longer presupposes or even requires the creative intervention of human imagination.

It is in this historical context that film emerges as the most promising medium, displaying its unique potential to spread the machine aesthetic among the mass public. For one, Itagaki argues, film is able to open the eyes of the general audience, still unaware of the attraction of functional beauty, by providing visually compelling illustrations of the mechanization of modern living spaces. A prime example here is Walter Ruttmann's *Berlin: Symphony of a Great City* (1927), which Itagaki praises as "depicting the social environment of machine civilization in the most intrinsic way."[35] However, more crucial to Itagaki is the fact that the cinematic apparatus is itself a genuine example of modern machinery par excellence: Not only can it easily disseminate this new form of beauty beyond any linguistic, geographical, and sociocultural boundaries through mechanical reproduction of the same prints, but the movie camera can also teach the viewer how to look at the world anew by showing us a more accurate and objective vision of natural phenomena seen through its own mechanical gaze. And just like Balázs and Epstein, Itagaki's fascination with this optical device derives mostly from its ability to reveal objective truths of natural phenomena that have heretofore been invisible to our naked eyes:

> In the past, no one clearly understood the movement of the legs of a galloping horse. Only after it became possible to take photographs in fast motion did factual errors in horse paintings begin to disappear. Microscopic, telescopic, and high-speed photography all complemented the limited ability of the naked eye, so much so that new forms of photographic expression have remodeled the ways we see the object. To put this in Moholy-Nagy's words, "We are now looking at the world with a completely new vision." One can also easily grasp film's rapid technological developments simply by noticing that the use of close-ups—which had already become a cliché—was indeed Griffith's innovation. Today, no one could deny that a machine called the "camera" possesses a more acute sensibility and subjectivity than those of naked human eyes.[36]

If, as Itagaki argues, the camera's mechanical gaze has altered the ways in which we perceive the world around us and, as a consequence, has also changed what we know as real, the next step is to establish a new theory of realism based on this new, nonhuman or object-oriented correlation between aesthetics and epistemology.

This is why Itagaki begins using the term *machine realism* in his subsequent essays, "The Road to Machine Realism" ("Kikai no riarizumu e no michi") and "Vertov's Film Theory" ("Verutofu no eigaron"). As the title of the second essay indicates, it is Vertov and his famous concept of "kino-eye" that informed Itagaki's attempt at reformulating his account of contemporary art and architecture under the aegis of realism. When he wrote these essays, however, Itagaki had not yet been able to watch any of Vertov's films himself. Moreover, while the introduction of Soviet montage theory to Japan began in 1928, the official release of major Soviet films including *Battleship Potemkin* (1925, dir. Sergei Eisenstein) and *Mother* (1926, dir. Vsevolod Pudovkin) was either forbidden or considerably delayed due to censorship.[37] Despite this, Itagaki was able to recognize the growing fame of Vertov through his daily reading of European art magazines and even retranslated from German the director's manifesto "From Kino-Eye to Radio-Eye" for the sake of Japanese readers.[38]

Though only eight pages long in its English translation, the manifesto clearly elucidates what Vertov was attempting with his cinematic experiments. "Kinoeye," wrote Vertov, "is the documentary cinematic decoding of both the visible world and that which is invisible to the naked eye"; it employs "every possible kind of shooting technique" as well as "every possible means in montage" in order to dialectically integrate the movie camera's penetrating gaze and the film director's (and editor's) intellectual decision; and, by so doing, it ultimately aims for a radical reconceptualization of the phrase "I see" in both perceptual and epistemological senses.[39] Introducing these statements with his own annotation, Itagaki considers Vertov's work to be a major point of reference for his concept of machine realism:

> *Man with a Movie Camera* is a depiction of everyday life. There is neither the actor who plays the lead nor a striking stage set. There is only the world reflected on an eye, and it is this "new eye" that observes the world as it sees it. This "new eye" is the "eye of the machine" which is more perceptive than our naked eye. Only through the eye of the machine shall a new realism be born. When used by American capitalists, this mechanical eye is forced to look at actors decorated with heavy make-up or to follow run-of-the-mill stories. Otherwise, it is being exploited by talkies and technicolor as the sign of the old-fashioned, nineteenth-century notion of "mimetic depiction" [*shajitsu*] or of a more banal expression of "verisimilitude" [*shinjitsu rashisa*]. However, here [in Vertov's work] the eye of the machine is freed from all kinds of constraints and in turn begins to construct a new "machine realism."[40]

It now seems obvious that Itagaki proposes his theory of machine realism as a radical critique of naturalism and any other past definitions of realism. Above all, machine realism begins with the total negation of the potency of the human sensory apparatus. According to Itagaki, recent developments in science and technology prove that people in the modern age have become less and less competent in and capable of discerning objective truths of physical or external reality on their own. The best possible way to cope with this irreversible process of the alienation of human perception from its living environment is to look at the world from the perspective of the kino-eye, fearlessly abandoning our imperfect way of seeing.

Thus, for Itagaki, machine realism does not mean a particular attitude or practice that aims for the creation of immediate reality effects. Like earlier practices of

1920s avant-garde art, machine realism must challenge naturalism's claim to depict things as they are by presenting completely new and unfamiliar visions of reality as seen through the camera's mechanical gaze. But for Itagaki such a modernist inclination toward the inclusion of the subjective experience of perceptual crises is a necessary step in the dialectic of realism, precisely because it designates the urgent demand for establishing a new way of knowing and depicting the world in motion more suitable to the modern subject's shifting relationship with the real as such.

In addition, Itagaki also stresses that machine realism helps envision a more rational, democratic form of society. Contrary to human perception, which can easily be distorted by each individual's personal concerns and politics, the camera's mechanical gaze is in principle indifferent to the hustle and bustle of any human activities. In fact, as long as an object is placed before the camera at a proper distance and with ample light, the object's exact shape and movement are automatically recorded on the surface of the filmstrip, regardless of the human operator's intention. Such a repudiation of the centrality of human subjectivity—or rather, the discovery of the camera's own nonhuman subjectivity—is the key to Itagaki's diagnosis of twentieth-century modernity. Drawing upon this diagnosis, he expects that people living in the twentieth century would begin reorganizing their living environment according to modern machinery's universal working principles, namely, "simplicity, hygiene, systematization, inexpensiveness, durability, and abundance."[41]

At the same time, Itagaki recognizes the negative effects of the mechanization of everyday life as well, rightfully citing Marx's warning that the machine can serve as a powerful means for the exploitation of human labor when it is wielded by capitalists.[42] But at this point in his career, Itagaki was largely preoccupied with glorifying the promise of twentieth-century machine civilization to enhance the quality and equality of life of the general public. And he even adopted another major principle of Marxist theory—dialectics—to justify or at least conceal his unwillingness to address the issues of class struggles: "Upon its discovery by humans, the 'machine' first appeared as a destroyer of our cultural values. But now it embarks upon a new task, taking the role of a constructor. From antithesis to synthesis—here we can also find the profound truth of history."[43] Naturally, this sort of nonchalant statement led to strong resentment among Japanese proletarian writers.

Reading Itagaki's discussion of machine realism, we are obliged to confront the question of how to assess his contribution to the general history of film theory. Certainly, Itagaki was one of the perceptive interpreters of Vertov and 1920s European avant-garde art and architecture in the non-West, and for this reason alone, his intervention becomes instrumental in tracking the translatability and global dissemination of the ideas and practices of the machine aesthetic. On the other hand, it is not difficult to criticize Itagaki for his lack of originality, since what he provided in his texts was nothing more than an arbitrary rearrangement of arguments imported from abroad. But before accepting this negative assessment, I want to illuminate the distinctive nature of classical film theory by treating it not as an accumulation of universal accounts of cinema but as a contingent collection of living discourses mobilized to articulate particular—and thus always local—instances of the varying experience of twentieth-century modernity. Indeed, as Hanada Kiyoteru retrospectively wrote in the 1950s, Itagaki's presence as the advocate of the machine aesthetic stimulated a number of debates among his readers, enabling his theory to assume historical significance that cannot be fully assessed in the global discussion of the machine aesthetic alone. To better understand this geopolitical tension between the global and the local, we now have to look at another set of critical discourses that equally informed Itagaki's theorization of machine realism.

KURAHARA KOREHITO: PROLETARIAN REALISM

As I have mentioned earlier, Itagaki presented his theory of machine realism in response to Kurahara Korehito's earlier discussion of proletarian realism. The relationship between the two is most visible in Itagaki's third essay on the topic, "The Road to Machine Realism" ("Kikai no riarizumu e no michi"), because it was named directly after Kurahara's 1928 essay "The Road to Proletarian Realism" ("Puroretarian rearizumu e no michi"). Appearing in the inaugural issue of *Senki* (*Battle Flag*, 1928–1931), the official organ of the All Japan Federation of Proletarian Arts (Zen Nihon Musansha Geijutsu Renmei, usually called NAPF based on its Esperanto notation Nippona Proleta Artista Federacio), Kurahara's essay provided one of the most powerful and systematic accounts of the burgeoning Japanese proletarian literature movement. As Mats Karlson points out, this essay was remarkable in that it "address[ed] the problems of creative method in concrete terms" and thereby made Kurahara "the leading theoretician of the movement and overall one of its most prominent figures."[44] But what kind of path did Kurahara pursue before achieving such high recognition as a Marxist literary critic?

Born in 1902 to the family of a renowned educator, Kurahara grew up in Azabu, one of the most upscale residential areas in Tokyo, and then studied Russian literature at the Tokyo University of Foreign Languages. His passion for the subject of his study—or more precisely, his growing interest in post-revolutionary Russia—was so profound that he moved to Moscow in 1925 and stayed there for about two years as a foreign correspondent for the Japanese newspaper *Miyako shinbun*. Kurahara made his initial foray into the world of criticism by contributing short articles covering what was happening in the art and politics of the Soviet Union. For instance, his 1927 article entitled "Recent Trends in the Soviet Film World" (*Saikin no Sowēto eigakai*) appeared as one of the earliest in-depth introductions of Soviet cinema to Japan, providing lengthy reviews of films such as *Battleship Potemkin*, *Mother*, and *The Bay of Death* (1926, dir. Abram Room).[45] Upon his return to Japan, Kurahara promoted himself as a specialist on Soviet literary theory and criticism by translating the work of Georgi Plekhanov, Nikolai Bukharin, and Joseph Stalin.

A turning point for Kurahara's career came in December 1927 when he published an abbreviated translation of the Comintern's thesis addressing "the Japan problem," adopted in July of the same year. The Japanese Communist Party (JCP) was initially founded in 1922 as a small illegal organization, but it collapsed within one and a half years due to the mass arrest of its core members. After this first attempt, Japanese leftists were largely divided into two opposing factions called Yamakawa-ism and the Fukumoto-ism named after the theoretical leaders of each faction, Yamakawa Hitoshi (1880–1958) and Fukumoto Kazuo (1894–1983). Though one of the founding members of the party, Yamakawa's political standpoint was more akin to that of the social democrats, as he sought to establish a legal political party based on a coalition of socialists, trade-unionists, and those associated with *rōnōha*, or the Workers and Farmers Faction. On the other hand, Fukumoto saw Yamakawa's call for a united front as inevitably leading to the dissolution of the Communist Party and its leadership in the Japanese leftist movement. Fukumoto therefore harshly criticized Yamakawa by calling him an "opportunist" and asked his followers to sort out party sympathizers based on Lenin's famous dictum, "before we can unite . . . we must first of all draw firm and definite lines of demarcation."[46]

This internal conflict ended with the victory of Fukumoto-ism, as the JCP adopted Fukumoto's demarcation strategy and appointed him a member of the standing committee when it was reestablished in December 1926. Nevertheless, Fukumoto's glory did not last long because he, together with other members of the standing committee, was called to visit the Soviet Union in early 1927 and became the target of Bukharin's harsh criticism for his too "theoretical" approach to the class struggle, an approach that he learned directly from Lukács's *History and Class Consciousness*. Following the earlier denouncement of Lukács himself, Fukumoto was also impeached in the Comintern's 1927 thesis and completely lost his influence among supporters of the JCP and leftist movements. Given his status as a translator of this thesis—which of course guaranteed his legitimate relationship with the Comintern—Kurahara soon became the next figure to advance the theory of art by and for the proletariat. From this moment on, Kurahara remained the chief advocate of Japanese proletarian literature until he was arrested by the police in 1932 and sentenced to seven years in prison for the violation of the Public Security Preservation Law (Chian ijihō).

Despite Kurahara's overtly political standing, he and Itagaki had much in common, not only in their privileged access to the latest art and intellectual trends imported from abroad but also in their own methods and terminology. In "The Road to Proletarian Realism" and other related essays, Kurahara, just like Itagaki, presents his notion of proletarian realism to be a fundamental critique of previous definitions of realism developed in the preceding century. Kurahara begins by admitting that nineteenth-century French writers, such as Gustave Flaubert, Edmond and Jules de Goncourt, and Guy de Maupassant, aimed to depict reality as objectively as possible, consciously excluding any arbitrary or judgmental treatment of social mores. But the realism at work in their fiction, he contends, had a "historical limitation" deriving from their general tendency to see the world from the perspective of bourgeois individualism. "The ways they recognize their life and reality," says Kurahara, "always remain unsocial and individualistic. There is no concern in their view about the control and oppression of the life of individuals by social structures. Not only was all emphasis placed on individuals, but their subject matter was also restricted to the individual life of human beings."[47] At the same time, Kurahara rightly points out that Zola and advocates of literary naturalism in the late nineteenth century strove to achieve a higher objectivity by having recourse to Social Darwinism and biological determinism. And yet even this new approach was not competent enough to grasp the foundation of modern society in its entirety, because "although they [naturalists] demanded of themselves the objectivity of natural scientists, they were lacking in the objectivity of social scientists."[48]

Kurahara's criticism of nineteenth-century literary realism is best represented in his ideological reading of Zola's 1885 novel *Germinal*. While acknowledging this work's vivid illustration of a miners' strike as a necessary step toward the socialization of literature as such, Kurahara is nonetheless fully discontent with the author's decision to depict the event "not from the perspective of the revolutionary proletariat but from the standpoint of class collaboration." In fact, in this novel Zola restricted himself to documenting the process through which the miners' initial excitement ultimately turned into their deep skepticism about the emancipation of the workers through direct action. But according to Kurahara, the conceptual limitation of naturalism and other previous definitions of realism revealed itself in their common inclination toward such a mimetic and observational treatment of given events and characters. In this regard, *Germinal* and other realist novels from the previous century were nothing but a passive mirror of society: although they told us of the existence of social problems and inequities, they remained completely silent as to how we could or should solve such problems by radically changing the modality of capitalist social formations themselves.

Consequently, Kurahara defines his notion of proletarian realism in the following manner: First, in contrast to nineteenth-century French realist writers' privatization of social problems, it aims to depict "all kinds of individual problems from a social perspective." Second, unlike naturalists' complicit reaffirmation of the status quo, it offers a more practical and dynamic articulation of reality by critiquing the capitalist logic of political economy that necessitates both the exploitation and alienation of human labor. Third, and most importantly, Kurahara insists that this dual task of proletarian realism can be realized only when writers come to look at the world anew through "the eye of the proletarian vanguard." Like Itagaki's "eye of the machine," this new eye helps reveal hidden truths of the world that have remained invisible to our normal perception. But this eye offers such a new vision of the world only through the lens of class struggle. As Kurahara writes:

> First of all, a proletarian writer must acquire a clear class perspective. To acquire a clear class perspective means that he must place himself in the position of the proletariat. To put it in the famous words of RAPP (the Russian Association of Proletarian Writers), he must see and depict the world through the eye of the proletarian vanguard. Only by acquiring and stressing this perspective can a proletarian writer become a true realist. I say this because at present no one other than the militant proletariat—or proletarian vanguards—can see the world in its truth, in its totality, and in its progress.[49]

The point here is unmistakable. Assuming that the success of the Russian Revolution would inevitably lead to the total demise of modern capitalist society at large, Kurahara finds it necessary to develop a new theory of realism that enables people to envision and participate in this ongoing transformation of the political reality of the times. As a result, the premise of proletarian realism must be antithetical to that of Japanese naturalism: rather than aiming to depict things as they are, it engages itself in the construction of "a reality beyond reality" (*genjitsu wo koeta genjitsu*) by consciously turning literature into a catalyst or even a weapon for social change.

One obvious problem with Kurahara's theorization of proletarian realism was that he did not provide invariable criteria with which one could judge whether this or that literary work was written with the eye of the proletarian vanguard. As the literary historian Sobue Shōji points out, Kurahara's argument was often marked by logical inconsistency, reflecting his tireless effort to keep up with the Comintern's shifting visions of art and its imputed missions. For instance, his earlier discussion of proletarian realism seemed to follow Engels's defense of Honoré de Balzac as a great realist, and Kurahara prioritized his fellow writers' discovery of typical characters living under typical circumstances as a necessary step toward the revelation of the exploitative nature of modern capitalist society. Nevertheless, in his later essays published under different pen names such as Satō Kōichi and Tanimoto Kiyoshi, Kurahara denied what he had written before—he even provided a peculiar form of self-criticism by openly denouncing the short-sightedness of "comrade Kurahara"— and redefined proletarian realism as a particular style or intention devoted to the optimistic depiction of the inevitable victory of the proletariat in the class struggle in accordance with Soviet leaders' adoption of socialist realism as its official doctrine.[50]

It seems, however, that Kurahara intentionally kept his theory variable because he was motivated less by the desire to offer a comprehensive account of ongoing cultural transformations than to hold sway over the proletarian art movement in

Japan by almost endlessly critiquing his fellow writers. As a result, the rhetoric Kurahara employed in his theoretical writings became fairly tautological. In his view, the majority of Japanese intellectuals were neither proletarian nor revolutionary enough, given their middle-class background and consciousness. But at the same time, the masses, or those from the working class, were equally problematic as long as they had yet to be enlightened enough to be a vanguard or true creator of new cultural values.

According to Kurahara and his followers, this dilemma could be solved only through the mediation of a newly emergent social apparatus: the Communist Party. In an essay entitled "The Current Stage of Proletarian Realism" ("Puroretaria rearizumu no gendaikai," 1930), the critic Komiyama Akitoshi argues that his fellow Japanese writers have continued to fail in realizing the premise of proletarian realism due to their reluctance to fully reconceptualize their creative commitment to prose fiction from the viewpoint of party politics. According to Komiyama, writers can obtain a more accurate and objective vision of reality "first by apprehending the dialectical materialist method of reality perception, and second by confronting reality with the recognition that their writing activities constitute one significant part of the party's strong chains [of command]."[51] When Komiyama proceeds to declare that "any deviation from the party line makes an accurate understanding of reality impossible," he succinctly elucidates what Kurahara sought to express with his notion of proletarian realism.[52] Like Itagaki's machine realism, Kurahara intended proletarian realism to be a plausible solution for the impasse of naturalism, for coming to terms with the more elusive and unpredictable reality of his times. But where Itagaki praised the camera's ability to recast our imperfect way of seeing, Kurahara counted on the Communist Party's potential to envision and enact a more advanced form of socialist society wherein both classes and the state were destined to wither away.

ANXIETY ABOUT THE KINO-EYE

Though similarly motivated to establish a new theory of realism, Itagaki found Kurahara's discussion of proletarian realism both ideologically too selective and conceptually too dogmatic. Consequently, Itagaki formulated his concept of machine realism in as neutral a way as possible, purposefully delineating a utopian vision of the future wherein people from different class or cultural backgrounds could unite under the dictatorship of the machine. However, Itagaki's highly political decision to depoliticize proletarian realism through the sweeping denial of the potency of human perception immediately came under attack from proletarian writers. Indeed, Kurahara was among the first to criticize machine realism from the proletarian perspective. In the first place, Kurahara admitted that the saturation of modern machinery and the concomitant shift in the very foundation of aesthetics had also come to constitute a significant facet of the life and art of the proletariat. But he soon rejected Itagaki's standpoint by arguing, "the machine can never be the protagonist of proletarian art. The main players of proletarian art are always *society* and *human beings*. We can appreciate the machine only as the most novel and most significant element in the material aspect of this society."[53] For proletarian realism, modern machinery must remain a practical means of production and never be treated as an object of fetishism.

The purpose of Kurahara's refutation was twofold: to confirm the subordination of the machine to human activities and to highlight the sociopolitical conditions surrounding the actual use of the machine in everyday life. Keeping these points in mind, the acclaimed proletarian writer Kobayashi Takiji provided a more trenchant criticism of Itagaki in an article aptly titled "On the 'Class Nature of the Machine'" ("'Kikai no kaikyūsei' ni tsuite," 1930). According to Kobayashi, what was missing in Itagaki's theory of machine realism was his own reflection on the ongoing struggle between the proletariat and capitalists over ownership of the machine. As he wrote: "Most of those interested in the machine only speak about its 'rationality' and 'dynamics' but never clarify their own positions. I don't know how these people solved their own 'romanticism' toward the machine. But as long as they continue to ignore 'class aspects,' their realism must remain a bourgeois or petit-bourgeois realism that is faithful only to the machine."[54] The critic Kimura Toshimi offered a similar line of criticism in his 1930 monograph *The Machine and the Revolution of Art* (*Kikai to geijutsu kakumei*): "'Exchanges between the machine and art'—if it ends up only addressing how certain characteristics of the machine are integrated into art, and in turn how this integration reflects back upon the transformation of the machine itself, nothing will be gained from this study.... From what kind of class perspective about reality can we properly appropriate the machine for the creation of truly new forms of art? This shall be our own methodological starting point."[55] It is clear from these statements that both Kobayashi and Kimura faithfully follow Kurahara's denunciation of machine realism, as he argues that the use-value of both artistic and intellectual activities must derive from each artist's and theorist's self-conscious commitment to the class struggle. Although it is still possible to explore the new mode of perception made possible by the camera's mechanical gaze, Kimura also stressed that anyone operating or commenting on this modern device must be equipped with the eye of the proletarian vanguard.

For the supporters of the proletarian literary movement, there was of course no exception to this fundamental principle. But for Itagaki, this insistent call for the repoliticization of his intervention was simply misleading. As we have seen, Itagaki's main purpose was not to change the world according to the agendas given by institutions like the Communist Party but to provide a holistic account of the present situation through firsthand observation of the latest trends in contemporary art. And if

Itagaki was reluctant to accept the political language of proletarian writers, it was precisely because he aimed to designate the saturation of modern machinery as a more universal symptom of twentieth-century modernity, a symptom that was equally observed not only in both capitalist and socialist societies but also in both Western and non-Western countries. In searching for a more versatile theory of realism that could dialectically reconcile this perceived conflict between capitalism and socialism, Itagaki remained open to inviting contributions to his own journals from proletarian writers and critics. But the result was not as fruitful as he had hoped: while his adversaries never changed the focus of their accusations and continued to criticize Itagaki's lack of proper class consciousness, Itagaki himself ended up justifying his own positivist, allegedly apolitical and objective, approach by saying that in order to understand the significance of his intervention, one has to "separate [his] 'document-oriented' historical science from any 'ideology-oriented' historical view."[56]

At the same time, one could also argue that Kurahara and his followers' persistent rejection of Itagaki's machine realism had to do with another core element of modern experience: estrangement or alienation. As most famously demonstrated in Charlie Chaplin's 1936 film *Modern Times*, the increasing intrusion of modern machinery into the space of everyday life and human labor did not always guarantee a bright and better future; it could also trigger both existential and perceptual crises of the ego, or the radical effacement of the harmonious unity between the body and the mind, or between individuals and their ancestral communities, by forcing people to endure the traumatic process of dislocation and fragmentation. Correspondingly, people in the twentieth century made tremendous efforts to regain or reinvent their lost totality, although these very attempts more often than not ended up calling forth more thorough and destructive processes of dehumanization, as evinced in the cases of Italian Fascism, German Nazism, and Japanese totalitarianism.

Seen in this historical context, it is not surprising that Itagaki's unabashed promotion of the transcendence of the ego by means of the superior gaze of the machine caused serious anxieties among his contemporaries. In fact, what Kurahara and his followers truly aimed to achieve in their rebuttals was not merely the victory of the proletariat over capitalists in the struggle for ownership of modern machinery but rather the self-affirmation of the supremacy of human beings over the machine. According to the aforementioned Kimura Toshimi, the collapse of the capitalist regime is the only plausible catalyst for the emancipation of human nature from the increasing mechanization of everyday life, because, as he said, "Only in the XXXX [communist] society can the machine fully exhibit its extraordinary power and creativity without oppressing human beings. Here the machine serves as a faithful slave of humans, and not vice versa."[57]

This strong antipathy toward the subordination of human perception to the camera's objective and superior mechanical gaze was also clearly manifested in the

Japanese reception of Vertov's *Man with a Movie Camera*. Originally made in 1929, the film was finally released in Japan in March 1932 under the title *Korega Roshia da* (*This Is Russia*). Though only a three-year difference, the gap between original and Japanese release dates turned out to be very decisive given radical shifts that occurred both in the cinematic apparatus (from silent to sound) and in the official Soviet discourse on art (from constructivism to socialist realism). As a result, the film received negative reviews from most Japanese critics. But as in the case of Itagaki's machine realism, this failure was also a result of the specific condition of Japanese local discourse.

First, perhaps deceived by its Japanese title, many Japanese viewers expected the film to be a faithful, if not officially approved, documentation of the ongoing progress of the Soviet Union as the first-ever socialist country. Thus, as one critic said, "Any portrayal of everyday life in the Soviet Union appears to be unnecessary rubbish at this time unless it is closely tied to the country's Five-Year Plan [1928–1932]."[58] Second, despite Vertov's own theorization of the kino-eye as the synthesis of the camera's superior gaze and the filmmaker's intellectual intervention, as well as despite his insertion in the film of a sequence portraying his editor Yelizaveta Svilova hard at work at her editing table, some other critics maintained that the film seemed to "remain one step short of the work completed fully by means of montage."[59]

The majority of critical comments by the Japanese, however, concentrated on Vertov's concept of the kino-eye as such, which they saw as rendering him an obedient and passive servant of the machine. Supporters of Kurahara's proletarian realism in particular made this type of accusation. In a review that appeared in *Purokino* (*Prokino*), the official organ for the Proletarian Film League in Japan, the critic Kamo Kyōji condemned Vertov for approaching reality from the perspective of the "technological intelligentsia" (*gijutsuteki interigencha*) and "anti-subjectivism" (*han-shukanshugi*): "Figures of art must not be mere documents of facts; they must be expression and have nothing to do with the 'facts as such' [*arinomama no jijitsu*] or with a theory of statistics. . . . There is no reason for us to deprive the cinematic realm of certain aspects of the artistic cognition, including various human thoughts and emotional processes, technologies and nature, individuals and the class struggle, and political life and relations of production."[60]

Tomioka Shō, a film director and scriptwriter also involved in the proletarian film movement, offered arguably the most controversial remark on the film. Tomioka was fully aware of the local specificity of his own intervention. Indeed, he purposely titled his own essay "The Road to Realism in Talkie Art" ("Tōkī geijutsu no rearizumu e no michi") under the direct influence of the previous debates between Itagaki and Kurahara. According to Tomioka, Vertov was nothing but a "slave of the cinema machine" (*eiga kikai no dorei*) who had completely sold his soul to this new *deus ex machina* in exchange for being able "to see things through the camera's *mechanical capabilities*." But for this very reason, continues Tomioka, "his film ended up showing a ghost-like imagery that was stripped of any *social facts* and in turn filled with the movement of empty figures accentuated by indiscriminate changes in both its speed and form."[61]

Tomioka then insists that any future attempts at achieving a higher and more authentic notion of realism must undergo the process of the rehumanization of filmmaking, diligently finding a way to reclaim the potency of human agency over the alterity of mechanically captured and reproduced photographic images. This urgent task of rehumanization, moreover, could only be possible with the introduction of sound to film because, unlike visual representation, both speech and writing still remained the exclusive domain of human expression and communication. Here lies the historical significance of the talkie as the latest technological addition to the cinematic apparatus. "Only with the advent of the talkie," declares Tomioka, "can human beings finally become able to reign over the cinema machine, and this will also move us forward to the direction of talkie realism!"[62]

In retrospect, this final remark appears to indicate not a single but two separate future directions of Japanese debates on cinematic realism. On the one hand, Tomioka's call for the rehumanization of filmmaking led to the emergence of the "Scenario Literature Movement" (*shinario bungaku undo*) in the mid-1930s. The premise of this new movement was to advocate for the efficacy of written or spoken words over images as a primary means of expression and communication in and through film. In doing so, it aimed to redefine the role of the filmmaker as someone in charge not only of mise-en-scène and other directorial duties but also of providing a blueprint for his or her own film project in the form of a written script. Of course, supporters of the Scenario Literature Movement were less politically motivated than proletarian writers. But they were still indebted to the legacy of Kurahara's proletarian realism for their insistence on the autonomy of human subjectivity and the dominance of literature as the most legitimate form of art.

On the other hand, the new visuality of the world revealed through the camera's mechanical gaze remained a key attraction for film viewers. Although Itagaki himself retreated from being a proponent of the machine aesthetic in the early 1930s and wrote mainly about Renaissance art afterward, his legacy was passed on to other local theorists such as Tosaka Jun, Nakai Masakazu, and Imamura Taihei. The incentive of these theorists was to uncover the utility of the film medium from the standpoint of epistemology, gauging the degree to which film and its related culture changed the very condition and meaning of knowledge acquisition through experience. Their main interest went to a newly emergent genre called documentary. But when it came to the theorization of this particular genre, the conflict, or even the dialectic, between subjective and objective visions reappeared. For, as we will see, Japanese debates on documentary always revolved around Paul Rotha's seemingly self-contradictory definition, namely, the creative *dramatization* of actuality.

3

Literary Adaptation and Textual Realism

1934: THE YEAR OF JAPANESE NEOREALISMO

In October 1934, Shimazu Yasujirō (1897–1945), a veteran director working at Shōchiku since its foundation in 1920, released the film *The Woman That Night* (*Sono yoru no onna*). Loosely based on King Vidor's pre-code sound film *Street Scene* (1931), the film depicts the mundane life of the lower-middle-class people living in Imakōji yokochō, a small shopping alley located in a suburb of Tokyo. Tanaka Kinuyo, one of the most popular Japanese female stars of the period, played the role of the heroine who comes up from the countryside to this alley to become a café waitress. Unfortunately, the print of *The Woman That Night* no longer exists, so I cannot go into further detail. One thing we know from its original reviews is that the film tried to enhance the verisimilitude of its diegetic space by building a life-size set of the real street corner adjacent to Shōchiku's Kamata studio.[1] But because the film failed to receive positive reviews from local critics, it soon faded into oblivion and is rarely mentioned today.

Despite such a minor presence in Japanese film history, *The Woman That Night* deserves critical attention. To our surprise, Shōchiku advertised the film with the catchphrase *neorealismo* (*neorearisumo*) (see figure 5), nearly a decade before people began using the same phrase to refer to films from post-Fascist Italy. As Anderson and Richie point out, however, this advertisement strategy designated less a radically new approach to cinematic realism than Japanese film producers' common practice of "searching for foreign words to describe their products and give them class."[2] In fact, it was not the first time that Shōchiku employed foreign words in promoting a film. Nomura Hōtei's all-star film *Constellations on the Earth* (*Chijō no seiza*, 1934) was advertised with a French phrase, *neo-film sans silence* (*neo firumu san shiransu*).

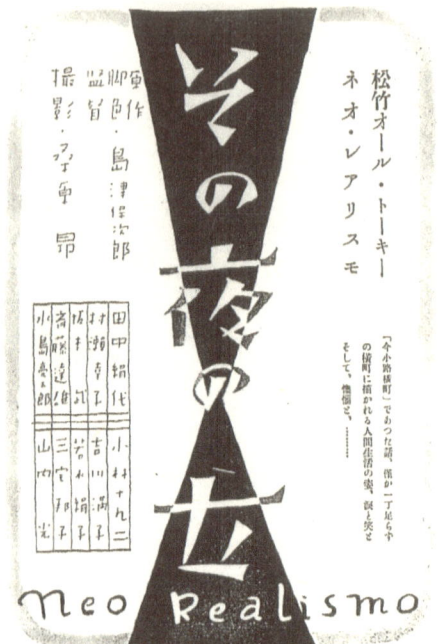

FIGURE 5. Advertisement for *The Woman That Night*, appearing in *Kinema junpō*, no. 520 (October 11, 1934): 96.

Shōchiku's use of this pretentious foreign phrase was largely deceptive since *Constellations on the Earth* was not a full talkie but a mixture of traditional *kagezerifu*, live orchestra, and some recorded sound tracks.[3] Nonetheless, the film still succeeded in earning the highest domestic box office revenue in that year thanks to the appearance of bankable stars.[4] It thus seems plausible that Shōchiku mobilized another foreign phrase *neorealismo* just to get the same benefit.

Even if this was the case, it is still worth considering why *The Woman That Night* called itself an example of neorealismo/new realism in the discursive context of mid-1930s Japan. As a director trained under Osanai Kaoru's *shingeki* method, Shimazu always gave the highest priority to adopting the norms and styles developed in Japanese literary and theatrical naturalism. Indeed, Shimazu was considered to be a director who had "the spirit of mimetic depiction" (*shajitsu seishin*), and his attentive documentation of trivial aspects of the everyday lives of people from the lower-middle class—such as young brothers playing catch while their mother repairs their socks—in his earlier films like *Maiden in the Storm* (*Arashi no naka no shojo*, 1932) and *Our Neighbor Miss Yae* (*Tonari no Yae-chan*, 1934) led him to earn a reputation as "being a realist in its most modest sense."[5] Shimazu also adopted a similar observational mode of mimetic depiction in *The Woman That*

Night. In particular, he made the heroine play the role of a curious but passive onlooker who, like actual viewers of the film, came to visit Imakōji yokochō from outside, happened to know a group of people living there, and left the alley after witnessing small human dramas being resolved without her active intervention.

What was remarkable in the original reception of *The Woman That Night*, however, is that most Japanese film critics unanimously rejected Shimazu's (and Shōchiku's) attempt to refurbish the legacy of Japanese naturalism as the basis for a new realism in the sound era. A contributor to *Kinema junpō* succinctly singled out the problem of Shimazu's approach as follows: "Just like the realism of the nineteenth century, the new realism in the film only had an artistic attitude that is no different than 'looking at reality as it is.' This film is thus no more than an old realism, and one would certainly find its display of *neorealismo* completely false and deceptive."[6] Another critic added that "the film's realism only randomly shows us a plausible reality of the small alley; it has no interpretation of or reflection on that reality and in turn gives its superficial observation an appearance of lively expression."[7] Lastly, Hazumi Tsuneo went on to express his profound doubt about the legitimacy of mimetic depiction as a method for cinematic realism: "The camera is able to record things as they are.... But because of this intrinsic condition of the camera, filmmakers today seem either naively or unconsciously to take the notion of mimetic depiction for granted. Doesn't this attitude stagnate our ongoing march toward cinematic realism, a promised land that we could reach only after getting past the stage of mimetic depiction?"[8]

One can see in these comments the effects of the previous debates between Itagaki and Kurahara. But unlike Kurahara's theory of proletarian realism, Japanese film critics of the mid-1930s were concerned less with each filmmaker's political perspective than with establishing a more practical method for inserting subjective visions of filmmakers into the process of filmmaking. As a result, local film practice in this period came to advocate the importance of the written script as a direct expression of the filmmaker's creative imagination or interpretation. Although the legacy of Japanese naturalism was rejected as a regressive return to old realism, producers of Japanese sound films nonetheless sought a new method for cinematic realism through literary adaptation.

This chapter examines how the increasing significance of written scripts in Japanese fiction films during the 1930s ultimately led to the formation of a controversial concept that I call "textual realism." By emulating the language-based mode of enunciation developed in literature, this realism radically redefined the role of the film auteur (*eiga sakka*) as someone in charge not only of mise-en-scène and editing, but also of the script prepared before the actual filming process began. But it equally functioned as a double-edged sword for both the emancipation and restriction of the filmmaker's intervention. More than anything, it made it easier for the censors to determine who should take responsibility for the end product of the intrinsically collective mode of filmmaking, effectively reducing the ambiguity of filmic signification. This prospect was soon appropriated by the state policy of domestic film practice under the war regime; when the government implemented the Film Law (*eigahō*) in April 1939, it became mandatory for all domestic films to be censored at the stage of written scripts. Accordingly, Japanese film directors after this period were no longer allowed to alter any scenes or dialogues on the set unless they resubmitted those changes in the form of scripts again.

In addition to such an overtly political connotation, the debates on textual realism also tell us how Japanese critics of the mid- to late 1930s strove to establish a theory of cinematic realism through the total denial of what film scholars after Bazin have conventionally called the indexicality of the photographic image. In other words, those Japanese critics evidently demonstrate the existence of a realist tendency *within* the so-called formative tradition, or among those who put their faith in "the plastics of the image" and "the resources of montage," as described in Bazin's historicization.[9] Because this formative tradition is often represented by Soviet montage theory, let us first look at how the Japanese reception of this influential theory seamlessly transformed into the dominance of scriptwriting practice after the introduction of sound cinema.

MONTAGE THEORY, SOUND CINEMA, SUBJECTIVE EXPRESSION

The first official screening of sound-on-film talkies in Japan took place in May 1929, when films made with Fox's Movietone were introduced at the Musashinokan and Denkikan theaters in Tokyo. Just like in other countries, the initial reactions of Japanese critics to sound cinema were negative, condemning its disruption of the further refinement of the silent film aesthetic and the concomitant return to the earlier days of the canned theater. And yet such negative assessments appear to have disappeared rather quickly, at least in the realm of local film criticism. Perhaps this shift was purposefully made to prompt a swifter transition of domestic film practice to the sound era. Indeed, the Japanese film industry's full conversion to the talkie was delayed until the late 1930s because small low-budget film companies like Daito continued to make silent films due to the popularity of the *benshi* and the inability of local theaters to install an expensive sound system.

The collapse of the cinematic Babel, paradoxically, helped increase the international synchronicity between Japanese cinema and its Western counterparts, in both film practice and discourse formation. Unlike earlier developments of silent cinema, the prospect of sound filmmaking and its theorization were equally open to those on both sides of the globe. This renewed sense of contemporaneity, on the one hand, led to the domestic invention of sound recording systems, including the Mina talkie, the Tsuchihashi system, and the Shigehara system. As is expected, these localized systems were called into being as a pragmatic solution to avoid the expensive patent fees of American systems. Such attempts to domesticate basic equipment for film production and exhibition, however, should be seen not only as Japan's revolt against the dominance of Western powers, but also as a result of Japan's militaristic expansion in Asia. For instance, all films made in Japan were not fully "Japanized" until 1934, when the company later known as Fujifilm succeeded in domesticating the production of positive and negative film stock. And yet this "successful" domestication of raw materials was only made possible by Japan's colonization of Taiwan, which served as the main supplier of camphor, a material indispensable for the making of celluloid.

On the other hand, the increasing synchronicity between Japan and the West can also be observed in the formation of the canons of the sound film aesthetic. Look, for instance, at the list of best foreign films chosen by *Kinema junpō* during the 1930s and it instantly becomes clear that highest acclaim was given to directors associated with the then burgeoning French poetic realism, including René Clair (*À nous la liberté*, 1931; *The Last Billionaire*, 1934), Julien Duvivier (*S.S. Tenacity*, 1934; *Christine*, 1937, and *Pépé le Moko*, 1937), and Jacques Feyder (*Pension Mimosas*, 1935; and *Carnival in Flanders*, 1935). In the meantime, 1930s Japan also saw the increasing popularity of documentary or nonfiction genres, as discussed fully in the next chapter. Amid increasing demands from domestic viewers to witness ongoing battles in China and beyond, both local critics and policy makers fiercely discussed the pros and cons of the British Documentary Film Movement and its state-funded mode of film production.

It seems possible to say that the introduction of sound to film helped sustain realism as the central concern of prewar and wartime Japanese discourse. But this does not mean that everyone addressing this issue treated the medium's expanded sound recording ability as the essential condition for cinematic realism. As Sekino Yoshio pointed out in 1930, the talkie was a scientific invention as well as an artistic discovery, and the fundamental task of this new form of expression was "to provide everyone with the true nature of reality that is not interrupted by superficial elements."[10] But this did not simply mean the reemployment of mimetic or objective depiction as the most legitimate method, given that Yoshino consciously employed the verb *reorganize* (*saisoshiki suru*) to stress the filmmaker's creative intervention. In this way, Japanese critical discourse in this early sound era came to privilege interpretation over observation, expression over perception, and the subjective intervention of filmmakers over the objective reproduction by the cinematic apparatus.

The automatism of the photographic image, however, had long been the subject of criticism for those who discussed the artistic potential of the film medium within the traditional (and idealistic) notion of art. As Thomas Elsaesser and Malte Hagener point out with reference to Rudolf Arnheim, behind this sort of criticism was the assumption that "if film were to affect the spectator in the same way as a complete sensory encounter with the world . . . then it could not be distinguished from reality itself and would amount to no more than its mechanical double. This duplication could not attain the status of art because art—this was the common argument of the time—presupposes active human involvement and cannot be generated by a machine."[11] This skepticism was also widely shared among the Japanese well before the introduction of Arnheim through translation (1933).[12] For instance, the aesthetician Nakagawa Shigeaki stated as early as 1911 that neither film nor photography could ever attain the status of art if they keep reducing the perceptual distance between their own visual representation and reality as such.[13]

Kawazoe Toshimoto, known as the translator of V. O. Freeburg's *Pictorial Beauty on the Screen*, also took a position similar to Arnheim and Nakagawa in his 1927 monograph *A Survey of Photoplay* (*Eigageki gairon*). In it, he argued that art is nothing but a reflection of the "spirit" of individual artists. He then saw the artistic value of filmic expression not in its capacity for mechanical reproduction but in its plasticity, or in the secondary reorganization of the images through directorial decisions made by the filmmaker. He wrote: "Seen objectively, a film is nothing more than an arbitrary arrangement of photographs. But we have learned that it can also have an enormous impact on us if the film director gives it a unity, a balance, accents, and rhythms, stimulating the viewer's memory and imagination. For this reason, it [film] is no longer a photographic copy of reality; rather, it creates a totally different world filtered by the spirit of the artist called 'film director,' a world that is far distant from our everyday life."[14] Kawazoe's statement here evinced a consensus among Japanese critics that editing could be the most concrete and visible means of the filmmaker's subjective expression. While films like Abel Gance's *La Roue* (1923) and Alexandre Volkoff's *Kean* (1924) were widely celebrated as embodying the promising potential of film to be a plastic art, it was the introduction of Soviet montage theory from the late 1920s on that led Japanese film critics to believe that film could also function like a language.

As in other parts of the world, Japanese filmmakers and critics welcomed Soviet montage theory with great excitement. But their critical involvement seemed to become more prolonged and profound than others precisely because Japan and its cultural traditions—ideograms, haiku poetry, woodblock prints, drawing textbooks, and Kabuki—played a central role in Sergei Eisenstein's influential theorization of dialectical montage.[15] As if to disavow Eisenstein's provocative statement that the idea of montage permeated Japanese culture except for its film products, Japanese critics continuously published numerous translations and annotations of theoretical texts by Vsevolod Pudovkin, Lev Kuleshov, Eisenstein, and other writers from the Soviet Union, well into the early 1940s. As I have argued elsewhere, montage as a method of creating a new meaning through the combination or collision of two or more elements also left its unmistakable mark on the broader field of Japanese cultural criticism, stimulating many to employ this theory as a catalyst to distill the spirit of twentieth-century modernity.[16]

The impact of Soviet montage theory on Japanese film criticism was so paramount that Satō Tadao even went so far as to write: "There was a time when, for people interested in film theory, Eisenstein's and Pudovkin's montage theory covered everything."[17] Satō's estimation here seems to be exaggerated, because as early as the mid-1930s, the major tenet of Japanese film discourse shifted to deny the proposition of montage as the sole essence of filmmaking. That being said, Satō was right in pointing out that the enduring dominance of Soviet montage theory in prewar and wartime Japanese film discourse derived less from its ideological implications than from its privileged emphasis on editing as a way to increase "the confidence of film critics who up until then had easily felt a sense of inferiority toward literature, theater, and other arts."[18]

Such an increased confidence can be found everywhere in Japanese film criticism around the turn of the 1930s. Shimizu Hikaru, one of the most devoted proponents of Soviet montage theory at the time, likened the impact of this theory to that of the Copernican (Kantian) turn in the history of Western philosophy. As he proclaimed:

> Although one can boldly assert that photography is totally inartistic compared to artificial artistic depictions in painting, film can still become art in its own right. I say this because it has already been proved [by Soviet montage theory] that film does not come into existence through mechanical arrangements of the photographic image, but it presupposes the intervention of an artist who creates a world in his own way by using those images as raw materials. So even if the photographic aspect of film is mechanical, this process guarantees the freedom of the artist, the realm of his pure and spiritual creation.[19]

Shimizu did not simply distinguish the photographic reproduction of reality from its filmic rearrangement, thereby assuming the former to be the work of the machine and the latter to be that of humans. He rather interpreted Soviet montage theory as an attempt to establish a new system of expression and communication comparable with verbal language, a system that was meant to enable filmmakers to express their subjective visions through the skillful composition of semantic components, just like the case of creative writers. Consequently, for Shimizu, any attempt to create meaning through montage became analogous to the process of literary composition in which writers "give words a literary life by structuring individual words into sentences."[20] To put it more succinctly, "A shot in film corresponds to a word in literature," as another critic asserted.[21]

The methodological affinity between sentence composition (writing) and montage (editing) eventually led Japanese filmmakers and critics to turn their eyes to literary adaptation. In the history of Japanese cinema, the boom in literary adaptation in the mid-1930s was no more than a transitory phenomenon, as it was soon replaced by a more urgent demand for original scripts prepared by filmmakers themselves. Nevertheless, the intimate relationship between film and literature in this period clearly designates a shifting relationship between word and image in the Japanese debates on cinematic realism. In 1937, Sawamura Tsutomu, who later worked as a scriptwriter himself, criticized the imperfections of montage, writing that "if it took three thousand years for letters to achieve their current expressive ability, it then must require several times longer in the case of montage." Accordingly, Sawamura came to reaffirm the efficacy of verbal language as a "means for the direct depiction of thoughts."[22] But for him and other supporters of literary adaptation, written scripts served not only as an expression of the creative intervention of human artists but as a means for exercising control over the contingency and uncertainty of filmic signification in general.

LITERARY ADAPTATION, OR THE REINVENTION OF THE FILM AUTEUR

Literary adaptation has a long tradition in Japanese film history if we define it simply as making films based on the stories that originate from literary works. Literary texts chosen for film adaptation in the 1910s and 1920s were mostly drawn from the genre of "popular literature" (*taishū bugaku*). Penned by writers such as Kikuchi Kan, Naoki Sanjūgo, Yoshiya Nobuko, Hasegawa Shin, and Hayashi Fubō, works in popular literature intended to provide readers with thrills and emotional catharsis in the forms of romance, mystery, comedy, swashbuckler, and historical fiction. One survey from March 1935 informs us that up until that moment, 156 films had been made based on novels by the five popular writers mentioned above, whereas only fourteen films were adapted from the works that were usually categorized as the more highbrow "pure literature" (*junbungaku*).[23]

From the mid-1930s onward, however, Japanese filmmakers began to adapt more stories from the genre of pure literature, giving their enterprise a new name called "literary art film" (*bungei eiga*). This shift yielded immediate success in the early sound period both at the box office and in critical terms. In fact, most domestic films ranked high among *Kinema Junpō*'s annual best films came from this new genre, including Kimura Sotoji's *Brother and Sister* (*Ani imōto*, 1936, written by Muroo Saisei), Kumagai Hisatora's *Common People* (*Sōbō*, 1937, written by Ishikawa Tasuzō), and Tasaka Tomotaka's *A Pebble by the Wayside* (*Robō no ishi*, 1938, written by Yamamoto Yūzō). The popularity of literary adaptation in sound cinema was not unique to Japan, as similar attempts were made in Hollywood, Germany, and France. But here I would like to draw attention to the local specificity of this phenomenon, addressing why the term *bungei* (literary art) became so dominant in Japanese critical discourse at the time.

The years around 1935, a period that immediately followed the demise of the proletarian literature movement, saw the emergence of "the renaissance of literary art" (*bungei fukkō*) in the world of Japanese print journalism. Initially used as a term to indicate the revival of once neglected naturalist or "I-novel" writers such as Nagai Kafū and Shiga Naoya, it soon became a nodal point at which long-standing conflicts between the left and right, machines and humans, and materialism and idealism were to be reconciled. As the Marxist critic Tosaka Jun rightly observed in 1935, the impetus behind this renaissance was Japanese intellectuals' blind acceptance of "literary liberalism," a particular form of liberalism that is conceived on the basis of literary consciousness. The followers of this liberalism, Tosaka continues, tend to "explain nature, history, and society only from the perspective of human beings and not vice versa, precisely because it seems more faithful to literature."[24] With this remark Tosaka criticizes *bungei fukkō* as an anachronistic revival of "idealist humanism" (*kan'nenteki ningengakushugi*) that sneakily emerged to fill the vacuum created by the Japanese government's violent and unceasing suppression of Marxism and other leftist standpoints.

Tosaka's criticism might seem odd, because it was Kurahara and supporters of his proletarian realism that called for the re-humanization of art and film production. However, what Tosaka problematizes here is not the centrality of human perception and expression per se but his fellow Japanese critics' lack of reflection on both historical and sociopolitical conditions surrounding the very existence of human beings in general and of Japanese citizens in particular. For this reason, he warns that any unconditional reliance on the proclaimed potency of a humanist perspective can easily fall into the trap of spiritualism (*seishin shugi*), an extreme form of idealism that he repeatedly condemns as the core mentality of wartime Japanese ideology. Moreover, Tosaka also denounces the literary consciousness fostered by the popularity of *bungei fukkō* as signaling an escapist tendency shared by Japanese intellectuals. Rather than trying to solve actual problems in society with the help of logical thinking, they indulge themselves in a pedantic and even metaphysical search for the universal meaning of human life to cover up their estranged situation on the verge of militaristic totalitarianism.

This shrewd observation helps us understand why Japanese filmmakers in the mid- to late 1930s found literary adaptation to be the most relevant method for the production of sound films. In addition to the alienation of the modern subject in the age of modern capitalism and Imperialism, filmmakers were simultaneously required to prove their subjective intervention in the process of filmmaking beyond the inherently nonhuman nature of the photographic image. The adoption of the literary consciousness into cinema therefore meant not only providing a handy template for enhancing the verisimilitude of newly introduced spoken dialogues, but it aspired to claim the potency of human cognition in the guise of universal and ahistorical idealist humanism.

Because literary art film was one of the most prolific genres in Japanese film practice throughout the second half of the 1930s, I try to keep my argument concise by focusing on the work of Uchida Tomu (1898–1970), arguably the most renowned director both in this specific genre and in cinematic realism in wartime Japan. Uchida belonged to the same generation as Shimazu and Mizoguchi, but his directorial debut did not happen until the late 1920s, as he had initially been trained as an actor at Tanizaki's Taikatsu studio. In his early career as a director, Uchida was a sympathizer of the proletarian art movement, earning his reputation as a forerunner of the so-called "tendency film" (*keikō eiga*) that, still funded by major studios, offered compassionate depictions of the plight of the lower class and socially marginalized people. In 1935, Uchida moved to Nikkatsu's Tamagawa studio, dedicated exclusively to the production of sound films set in the modern period. Not only were nearly all the films he directed at this studio during the 1930s adapted from the work of pure literature writers, he also helped establish the studio as a stronghold of realist filmmaking in collaboration with his peers such as Tasaka Tomotaka and Kumagai Hisatora.

The first film Uchida directed at Nikkatsu was *Theater of Life* (*Jinsei gekijō*, 1936), adapted from Ozaki Shirō's autobiographical novel of the same title. The film depicts the story of a young boy named Hyōkichi who, just like the author himself, went to Waseda University in Tokyo to study politics but was expelled from the school after taking part in a student strike to protest the school's corrupt administration. Then, as the story goes, Hyōkichi returned home at the news of his father's suicide and finally made up his mind to become a novelist. Uchida's choice of such an autobiographical novel, or the "I-novel," as it was called at the time, clearly illustrates people's collective search for a plausible method for subjective expression in and through film. If, as one critic mentioned, the purpose of an autobiographical novel like *Theater of Life* was to offer a "truthful document of human beings" (*shinjitsu naru ningen kiroku*), the primary task of the film director in charge of its screen adaptation would be to provide a faithful depiction of the author-protagonist's worldview by means of moving images and recorded sound.[25] However, this anticipation reveals another level of expectation: As an individual with artistic sensibility, the film director must also try to leave traces of his creative intervention by narrating the same story in his own way.

Uchida successfully accomplished this dual task by employing what Dudley Andrew calls the "fidelity-based" and "transformative" approaches to the screen adaptation of literary texts.[26] The fidelity of Uchida's adaptation is most clearly seen on the level of mise-en-scène, especially in his sympathetic treatment of the Hyōkichi character. Played by the acclaimed actor Kosugi Isamu, Uchida's longtime collaborator since his directorial debut, this character was highly praised for "exposing the abundance of the protagonist's human nature."[27] At the same time, Uchida won more accolades for his fearless intervention in narration, which is counted as the "transformative" side of adaptation. "Ozaki Shirō's I-novel writing style," as the critic Togata Sachio mentioned, "would be boring and unattractive if it were simply copied on the screen as it is." Thus Uchida garnered praise for successfully bringing "his own style" (*jikoryū no sutairu*) to the end product.

By *style* Togata did not simply mean Uchida's intervention on the visual level, including his frequent use of high-angle shots that metaphorically emulated Ozaki's intention to offer a panoramic view of his youth. The term *style* here also indicates Uchida's decision to abridge the plot structure of the original by omitting less important episodes and side characters. As a result, Uchida's retelling of the story came to revolve only around the troubled relationship between Hyōkichi and his father, adding a more serious dimension to Ozaki's original conception of *Theater of Life* as a sentimental, if not thoroughly melodramatic, coming-of-age story. In the end, Uchida succeeded in earning positive recognition even from the writer Ozaki himself. When asked about his thought on the film, Ozaki was quoted as saying: "This is no longer Ozaki Shirō's *Theater of Life* but Uchida Tomu's *Theater of Life*, and that's the way it should be."[28]

Following the success of *Theater of Life*, Uchida immediately directed two more films adapted from pure literature novels *The Crown of Life* (*Inochi no kanmuri*, 1936, written by Yamamoto Yūzō) and *A Naked Town* (*Hadaka no machi*, 1937, written by Mafune Yutaka). But it is *Unending Advance* (*Kagirinaki zenshin*, 1937), his fourth installment in the genre of literary art film, that offers us the most revealing example regarding the manifold nature of the incorporation of literary consciousness into the world of filmmaking. Chosen as the best domestic film at *Kinema junpō*'s annual poll, *Unending Advance* depicts a story about the life of the middle-aged *sararīman* (office worker) named Yasukichi, also played by Kosugi, who goes out of his mind upon hearing about the company's decision to dismiss him and other employees at the age of fifty-five or higher due to a financial recession. In facing the harsh reality of corporate restructuring, Yasukichi somehow sees himself appointed an executive board member and happily watches over the completion of his new house and the marriage of his daughter. But it turns out that everything he saw was a hallucination. Already living in a world of madness, Yasukichi invites his ex-coworkers to a Japanese-style restaurant and delivers an ostentatious retirement speech addressing his philosophy of "successful" life. In the end, he is taken to a sanatorium by his daughter's fiancé who, rather than feeling pity about his mentally impaired father-in-law, cruelly treats Yasukichi as a decrepit, down-and-out loser (figure 6).[29]

On its narrative level, *Unending Advance* appears as a kind of social realist film. It is clear that the film offers a critical commentary on the experience of alienation—a modern subject's complete loss of his or her own being—in capitalist society. But it is also important to note that the film can also be seen as a protest against the current state of the domestic film industry through its unconventional process of production.

FIGURE 6. The jobless father in hallucination: a still from Uchida Tomu's *Unending Advance* (courtesy of the Kawakita Memorial Film Institute).

It was Ozu Yasujirō who wrote the original story; then, Yagi Yasutarō, one of the most acclaimed screenwriters of the period, transformed it into a film script; and finally, Uchida adapted it into film, adding his own interpretation of Yagi's script. This threefold collaboration was remarkable for several reasons. First, it was rare in 1930s Japan for leading directors working at different film companies—Ozu at Shōchiku and Uchida at Nikkatsu—to make a film together, beyond the industry's self-serving policies that strictly prohibited such individual collaborations.[30] Second, Yagi's script, titled "What a Cheerful Guy, Mr. Yasukichi" ("Tanoshiki kana Yasukichi-kun"), was published in the August 1937 issue of the literary magazine *Shinchō* (*New Wave*), as if it were an original novel.[31] It already became a common practice within local film journalism to publish written scripts in printed form prior to the release of the completed film, but it was still very unusual for such scripts to appear in a literary magazine. With this pivotal acceptance by the literary world, *Unending Advance* heralded the maturity of Japanese filmmakers for their ability to produce a film with a developed literary consciousness without the help of professional novelists.

Thanks to the wide circulation of its original script, *Unending Advance* enabled contemporary viewers to distinguish different contributions made by Ozu, Yagi, and Uchida at different stages of film production. According to the critic Hazumi

Tsuneo, Ozu's original story contained a more humorous appearance similar to his own *shōshimin* (urban lower-middle-class) films like *I Was Born, But ...* (*Umarete wa mita keredo*, 1933). The protagonist in this original version, as Hazumi pointed out, was not seriously ill but playfully pretending to go insane to see how his family members and coworkers would react.[32] Yagi and Uchida, however, decided to transform the original into a more serious and severe social criticism by foregrounding the harsh reality surrounding precarious workers in the era of modern capitalism. Lastly, there is also a noticeable difference between Yagi's script and Uchida's completed film, and it is most clearly seen in the opposing endings they gave to their own versions. Written against public excitement about the outbreak of the Second Sino-Japanese War in July 1937, Yagi's script ends with an explicit affirmation of Japan's advancement to the war, which is denoted through the mouth of the daughter's fiancé: "By all means, living our life is a struggle.... It is an open warfare between different people, societies, nations, races, and even different periods. Though taking shape differently, these struggles are based on the same principle—survival. In order to survive, we must take part in all types of struggles.... In the world today, no one can stick to our lives passively. We must deal with everything aggressively. By fighting as aggressively as possible, we live through our lives."[33]

Here Yagi, using the fiancé character as his mouthpiece, justifies Japan's military aggression in Asia by self-righteously likening it to the evolutionist logic of the survival of the fittest. By contrast, Uchida was more cautious about the downside of this overtly ideological statement and, although he had already filmed all the scenes described in Yagi's script, he decided at the last minute to cut the last sequence that contained the lines quoted above. As a result, Uchida's film ends with a substitutional long shot of the three main characters—the father, the daughter, and her fiancé—walking side by side on a bridge crowded with cars, trolleys, and many other nameless people passing in the twilight. Contemporary reviewers of the film mostly praised Uchida's thoughtful decision. But this added final shot inevitably left an impression that the film took recourse in the expedient solution of social problems in the guise of idealist humanism.

Unending Advance also helps us detect the rise of the "auteurist" approach in Japanese film criticism. In addition to a series of special issues in local film magazines dedicated to individual film directors, this period saw the publication of a series of monographs such as Murakami Tadahisa's *On Japanese Film Authors* (*Nihon eiga sakkaron*) and Ōtsuka Kyōichi's *On Japanese Film Directors* (*Nihon eiga kantokuron*).[34] However, I do not mention these books to confirm that Uchida's particular engagement in literary adaptation served as a model for other directors to be called "film auteur." On the contrary, there was still little consensus among Japanese film critics as to how to define this concept on an equal basis, especially given each director's different commitment to scriptwriting.

Having started their careers as screenwriters, directors like Itō Daisuke and Itami Mansaku, for instance, always took full charge of their film scripts; Shōchiku directors including Shimazu, Ozu, and Shimizu Hiroshi often provided original stories by themselves but transformed them into scripts in collaboration with their in-house scriptwriters; still others like Uchida and Mizoguchi preferred working on the scripts prepared by external professional scriptwriters so that they could focus solely on their on-set directorial work. But the main current of the period gradually advanced to defining the film auteur as someone in charge of both scriptwriting and directorial work. As the 1939 Film Law clearly gave more authorial power to the person who prepared written scripts for preproduction censorship, younger directors making directorial debuts after this period—including Kurosawa Akira and Kinoshita Keisuke—had all received their initial trainings as a scriptwriter before directing their first film.

There was also an emphatic call among Japanese film critics for transferring authorial power to those in charge of original films scripts. In 1935, the poet and film critic Kitagawa Fuyuhiko wrote: "Film should always be based on an original script. But in reality, there remain certain problems with the quality of [domestic] scriptwriters, and this is why people have begun talking about the screen adaptation of pure literature."[35] To remedy such a problematic situation, Kitagawa moved on to launch the Scenario Literature Movement. Like other founders of art and cultural movements, Kitagawa edited his own magazine *Shinario kenkyū* (*Scenario Studies*, 1937–38) and made it a special venue dedicated for the publication and discussion of original film scripts. Given his personal background in poetry, Kitagawa always understood art as anchored in the creator's literary consciousness. Thus, in his view, everything in film production must be written and designed *before* the actual shooting process begins, even though it would radically reduce the freedom of the film director on the set.

In 1936–37, Kitagawa edited the six-volume *Anthology of Scenario Literature* (*Shinario bungaku zenshū*) with another film critic, Iijma Tadashi. Under the pompous slogan, "Make scripts a literature!" (*shinario o bungaku seyo!*), this anthology collected a number of scripts for critically acclaimed domestic and foreign sound films, as well as more than twenty previously unpublished scripts written by both filmmakers and novelists. Iijima stated in his introduction to the first volume, "The aspect that is most absent in Japanese talkie films is the literary element represented by the dialogue." Therefore, he continues, it becomes mandatory to stimulate the reform of domestic sound film production by showcasing good examples of dialogue composition.[36] Moreover, by collecting already released films in the form of printed scripts, Iijima also stresses the durability of written language as a medium for preservation and commemoration.[37] That is to say, Iijima considers scripts to be a credible substitute for 35 mm film prints that were easily scattered or even lost during their physical circulation among local movie theaters.

This argument is only tenable, however, in a specific historical circumstance in which those published scripts guaranteed an identical or even indexical relationship between what is written in the script and what is recorded on the surface of the filmstrip.

Interestingly, these collective efforts to preemptively control the function of filmic signification through written scripts can also be seen in the realm of documentary films, particularly in the work of Kamei Fumio. Kamei stayed in the Soviet Union from 1929 to 1931 and studied filmmaking under the tutelage of Grigori Kozintsev, Fridrikh Ermler, and Sergei Yutkevich.[38] He is widely remembered today for his fearless critique of Japan's militaristic actions in China in films such as *Shanghai* (*Shanhai*, 1938) and *Fighting Soldiers* (*Tatakau heitai*, 1939). Despite such a heroic presence in film history, Kamei was not immune to the ongoing growth of the literary consciousness in the process of filmmaking. In June 1938, Kamei published the script he wrote for another documentary film titled *Peking*. Prepared as a document of his directorial plan, Kamei's script was an odd mixture of poetical expressions and practical requests: "After a blast of wind, a small dark spot emerging in the sky grows bigger and bigger, and eventually the entire city becomes enveloped in the gathering gloom. . . . It would be great if you catch this particular wind around Qianmen Street."[39] Kawaguchi Masakazu, the cameraman whom Kamei was addressing here, was sent to Beijing after the publication of this written description and given no freedom to shoot things or events he actually saw there unless they had already been written in Kamei's original script.

This was surely a tough situation for a director like Uchida, who persistently refused to prepare scripts on his own. And yet he was still able to make contributions to the domestic development of realist film aesthetics, specifically with his acclaimed film *Earth* (*Tsuchi*, 1939). Adapted from Nagatsuka Takashi's naturalist novel published in 1910, the film was notable for its truthful depiction of the hard life of a family of poor tenant farmers living in the countryside. To enhance the visual verisimilitude of the film's diegetic space, Uchida built a life-size open set of the farmer's house, which was set on fire and completely destroyed at the film's climax. Uchida also took a full year for shooting so as to synchronize the development of the diegetic time to actual scenery changes of the four seasons.[40] As I have argued elsewhere, however, Uchida's obsession with "true-to-life" imaginaries was mobilized less to reveal the historical reality of wartime Japan than to make a compromise with it.[41] In fact, Yagi Ryūichrō and Kitamura Tsutomu, two screenwriters in charge of adaptation, eliminated many important episodes—including a labor dispute between the landowner and his tenants—in fear of possible rejection by the censors.

Judging from the criteria for a "fidelity-based" adaptation, such omissions were nothing but a disgraceful retreat. But instead of revising the script, Uchida chose to conceal narrative fissures by adopting cinematographic techniques often associated with documentary or nonfiction genres. Not only did he often use long takes that continued up to eighty-eight seconds at the longest, he also filmed the first segment of the film entirely on location in the village where the writer Nagatsuka actually grew up. Thanks to such an innovative film style, Uchida succeeded in maintaining his reputation as a realist filmmaker. But this accolade was given to him in exchange for the renunciation of his own authority over the content (narrative) of the film itself.

The practice of literary adaption and the Scenario Literature Movement did not herald the total victory of word over image, or of scriptwriters over directors, in the broader context of wartime Japanese film practice. This was in part because of the growing popularity of newsreel and nonfiction genres after the outbreak of the second Sino-Japanese war, which required a more dynamic and immediate representation of actuality than could be represented fully by written scripts alone. But I should add that there were also growing suspicions from the country's cultural elites about the ability of Japanese filmmakers to offer authentic and compelling visualizations of reality in film texts. It is true that this skepticism came mostly from the novelty of film as a medium. Yet it was also inseparable from the immaturity of the Japanese film industry at large, whose major practitioners were still in their thirties and early forties at a time when Japan entered into the full-fledged war against China and then the Allies. Those worried cultural elites therefore asked, in conjunction with Japan's irreversible advancement toward a totalitarian regime, not *how* but *who* had the right to offer proper interpretation of given historical events or political situations.

To address this other important issue, the rest of this chapter discusses the advent of another film genre, called "historical film" (*rekishi eiga*), which was originally proposed in 1937 by the film critic Tsumura Hideo (1907–1985) as a subcategory of literary art film. The critical discourse emerging around this genre took the local debates on cinematic realism to the next level by asking the following question: How and to what extent can film serve as a legitimate medium for both realistic and authentic depictions of the nation's past?

HISTORICAL FILM AND TEXTUAL REALISM

In March 1938, the director Kumagai Hisatora (1904–1986) released *The Abe Family* (*Abe ichizoku*). Adapted from Mori Ōgai's novel of the same title, the film dealt with the issue of ritual suicide (*junshi*), a custom in feudal Japan that obligated vassals to commit *seppuku* suicide upon the death of their lord. The original text was written in the wake of the suicide of General Nogi and his wife, who killed themselves on the day of the Meiji emperor's funeral ceremonies, September 13, 1912. Given this background information, Darrell W. Davis reads the film as a prime example of the spiritual glorification of the national past, a driving force behind wartime Japan's militaristic expansion.[42] What is missing in his reading, however, is a consideration of the fact that *The Abe Family* was produced as the very first film in the genre of historical film. Davis does refer to the emergence of historical film in the late 1930s, but his account is inaccurate in that it misidentifies another critic Hasegawa Nyozekan as the founder of this genre. As we will see, Hasegawa's contribution appeared much later, in 1941, adding a more complicated ideological twist to the concept. A careful reading of Tsumura's original argument prompts us to recognize the manifold nature of wartime Japanese film culture in general and of local debates on cinematic realism in particular.

It would be useful here to briefly look at the history of period films in Japan. At the beginning, domestic film products were schematically divided into two categories, the old school (*kyūha*) and the new school (*shinpa*). Originally borrowed from the vocabulary of traditional theater, these two categories distinguished films based on whether they were set in the periods before or after the Meiji Restoration. It was films of the old school that dominated the domestic film market throughout the 1910s thanks to the popularity of Onoe Matusunosuke, an ex-Kabuki player who became the first movie star in Japan. Not surprisingly, reformers of the Pure Film Movement like Kaeriyama specifically attacked such old school films and in turn called for adopting more cinematic and naturalistic elements from Hollywood films and the *shingeki* theater.

The first major reform of Japanese period films took place in the early 1920s, when filmmakers and scriptwriters at Shōchiku produced films such as *Shimizu Jirochō* (*Shimizu no jirochō*, dir. Nomura Hōtei, 1922) and *The Woman and the Pirate* (*Onna to kaizoku* dir. Nomura Hōtei, 1923) under the banner of *shin-jidaigeki eiga* (new period film). Just like the shift from "moving picture" to "film" in the late 1910s, this new term meant to signify the modernization of the genre of old school film through adopting female actors, close-ups, flashbacks and other editing skills, and well-prepared scripts.[43] After the Great Kantō Earthquake of 1923, most domestic studios for the production of period or *jidaigeki* films moved to Kyoto. Nevertheless, Japanese period films as a genre remained a testing ground for putting the latest film style and sociopolitical concerns in practice.

Kinugasa Teinosuke's *Before Dawn* (*Reimei izen*, 1931), for instance, is said to be the first Japanese film made under the direct influence of Soviet montage theory.[44] Itō Daisuke's *Man-Slashing, Horse-Piercing Sword* (*Zanjin zanba ken*, 1929) appeared to be a period drama version of a "tendency film" with its poignant exposure of social inequalities found in feudal Japan. And directors such as Itami Mansaku, Inagaki Hiroshi, and Makino Masahiro devoted themselves to developing a hybrid genre that is often dubbed the "contemporary drama with a topknot" (*mage o tsuketa gendaigeki*). Following the rise of the highly vernacular and sensual form of modernist sensibilities known as *ero guro nansensu* (erotic, grotesque, nonsense), this particular subgenre produced a number of comedies, love stories, and even musicals all set in the Edo period.[45]

The coming of sound around the turn of the 1930s equally stimulated a series of radical shifts in the production of Japanese period films. The first notable change was the increase in number of literary adaptations, although the majority of literary texts used in this genre still came mostly from the serialized work of popular literature, including Hayashi Fubō's *Tange Sazen* and Yoshikawa Eiji's *Miyamoto Musashi*. One exception in this regard was Itami Mansaku (1900–1946), whose first talkie *Capricious Young Man* (*Akanishi Kakita*, 1936) was adapted from the I-novel writer Shiga Naoya's short story of the same title. Itami's aspiration for using "pure literature" as the source of his filmmaking did not diminish until the end of his career, as his last film *The Tale of a Giant* (*Kyojinden*, 1938) was based on Victor Hugo's *Les Misérables*, drastically changing its setting to Japan's own "revolutionary" transition from the Edo to the Meiji periods.

Another remarkable shift occurring in the sound era was the addition of a more realistic treatment of fictional characters living in the historical past. This shift was most compellingly realized through the participation of the members of the Progressive Theater (Zenshinza) in the production of Japanese period films. Led by the two former Kabuki actors Kawarasaki Chōjūrō and Nakamura Kan'emon, the Progressive Theater and its long-term collaboration with the film company P.C.L. (which, with two other companies, were merged into Tōhō in 1937) succeeded in elevating the status of Japanese period films from popular entertainment for the young adolescent to one that could satisfy more adult and educated audiences. The realistic performance of the Progressive Theater was most vividly documented in the work of Yamanaka Sadao (1909–1938). Adapted from Kawatake Mokuami's modern Kabuki scripts, Yamanaka's late films such as *Kōchiyama Sōshun* (1936) and *Humanity and Paper Balloons* (*Ninjō kamifūsen*, 1937) won wide critical acclaim for their poignant depictions of the gloomy life of *rōnins*, or unemployed samurais.

The significance of Itami and Yamanaka in the history of Japanese period films is indisputable. As Anderson and Richie write, "They approached Japanese history as though it were contemporary, looking for values in it that they looked for in their own lives ... today, in the films by Mizoguchi, Kurosawa, and Yoshimura [Kōzaburō], the attitude of Yamanaka and Itami still exists."[46] However, history itself did not proceed straightforwardly. First, both Itami and Yamanaka stopped making films in 1938, with the former suffering from tuberculosis and the latter losing his life—Yamanaka died at the age of twenty-eight—during his military service in China. Second, despite their conscious effort to elevate the artistic status of period drama, the majority of directors working inside this genre continued making spectacular *chanbara* (sword fighting) films in response to the high demand of the general audience for popular entertainment. As an ardent opponent of these popular period films, Tsumura Hideo proposed his concept of "historical film" and called for a more serious and authentic treatment of the national past in film.

It can be said that Tsumura, like Itami and Yamanaka, found it necessary to bring realism into the production of period films. But Tsumura's contention was considerably different from a simple application of mimetic realism, given his very controversial argument about the proper treatment of historical facts with the film medium.

Tsumura delivered his concept of historical film in his 1937 essay entitled "A Letter to Mr. Kinugasa Teinosuke: A Proposal for Historical Film" ("Kinugasa Teinosuke-shi e no tegami: Rekishi eiga no teishō").[47] This public letter begins with Tsumura's confession that he had not seen any of Kinugasa's experimental period films in the silent era, including *The Sun* (*Nichirin*, 1925, based on Yokomitsu's modernist novel), *Crossroads* (shown in both Europe and the United States under the title *Shadows of Yoshiwara*), and *Before Dawn*. But Tsumura was still motivated to address this letter to Kinugasa because he saw in the latter's recent film *The Summer Battle of Osaka* (*Osaka natsu no jin*, 1937) a promising sign of what he considers to be the historical film. Ultimately, Tsumura admits that *The Summer Battle of Osaka* was a failure in terms of its artistic achievement, but it was still remarkable for its sincere approach to an actual historical event, a sincerity that had been long absent in popular period films.[48]

According to Tsumura, the major problem with the current Japanese period films lay in their "tendency to take pride in bringing in stories and themes more suitable to contemporary dramas, hunting after popular novelties by having the actors speak the modern language or, even worse, contemporary slang."[49] This perceived ignorance of historical accuracy, he added, was largely due to the director's lack of knowledge about the past, but Tsumura also ascribed it to the local convention in the domestic film industry, which schematically divided and trained newly joined candidates for director to be a specialist of either the period drama or the contemporary drama. Such a clear division of labor proved most dysfunctional when directors trained in the period drama section engaged in the production of contemporary films. Because they had long committed themselves to the creation of an imaginary world filled with fictional historical figures abstracted from modern sensibilities, most directors of the period drama failed to cultivate an ability to deal with any actual social events currently taking place. On the other hand, Tsumura argued that directors trained in the contemporary drama section were more versatile in their potential to depict given objects or phenomena faithfully. He then suggested that all future Japanese period films be made by contemporary film directors, or at least by veteran filmmakers like Kinugasa and Mizoguchi who already had ample experience in directing both genres.[50]

At first glance, Tsumura's call for a sincerer treatment of the historical past seems reasonable except for his blatant dislike for popular period films. However, Tsumura went on to declare that those who want to be involved in the genre of historical film must not make a film based on their own interpretation of the past;

instead, they have to refer to Ōgai's historical novels—including *The Abe Family*, *The Last Testament of Okitsu Yagoemon* (*Okitsu Yagoemon no isho*, 1915), and *Sanshō the Bailiff* (*Sanshō dayū*, 1915)—to learn how this great novelist has approached historical events and characters in his literary texts.

Born in 1862, Ōgai is known as a towering figure in the history of modern Japanese literature who wrote his novels while holding his official position as a surgeon general in the Imperial Japanese Army. While his earlier works, such as *The Dancing Girl* (*Maihime*, 1890) and *Foam on the Waves* (*Utakata no ki*, 1890), exhibit a strong influence from romanticism that he learned during his four-year stay in Germany (1884–1888), Ōgai spent the last ten years of his life mostly writing either historical novels or critical biographies of Japanese intellectuals of the past. These late writings are often praised for Ogai's obsession with historical accuracy, which he attained from extensive archival research into rare handwritten documents from the Edo period. But what is most striking to our inquiry into Japanese debates on cinematic realism is that Ōgai wrote those historical novels as his own response to the rise of Japanese naturalism in the first two decades of the twentieth century. As he wrote in 1915:

> First of all, by studying historical documents, I began to respect the reality found in them and became tired of making unnecessary changes. Second, seeing my contemporaries portray their lives as they are [*ari no mama*], I came to realize that if they could write about the present as it is, there should be no problem that I write about the past in the same manner.... Some of my friends told me that while others deal with things by means of their "emotion," I do this by using my "intellect." But this attitude applies to all of my writings and not merely to the ones that deal with historical figures.[51]

Needless to say, the key phrase here is "as it is," which, as we have seen, served as the principle of Japanese naturalism. But equally important here is Ōgai's intellectual treatment of actual people and events in the past, for this was exactly what Tsumura wanted his fellow Japanese filmmakers to adopt in their making of historical films. In other texts published around the same time, Ōgai also disclosed his desire to detach himself from historical facts because putting too much emphasis on factual accuracy would impede his own artistic freedom.[52] But Tsumura purposefully ignored this statement and instead likened Ōgai's writing method to Soviet montage theory. In Tsumura's view, both Ōgai's historical novel and Soviet montage theory exhibited the exemplary application of human intellect not by modifying the content of historical or photographic facts but by rearranging those facts into a consistent and compelling form of narrative.[53]

Tsumura's proposal for historical film failed to elicit any audible response from Kinugasa. However, it gave great inspiration to Kumagai Hisatora who, after spending several years as a specialist of contemporary drama, adopted *The Abe*

FIGURE 7. Osaki and Tasuke, two characters who opposed the *junshi* system in Kumagai Hisatora's *The Abe Family* (courtesy of the Kawakita Memorial Film Institute).

Family as his first foray into period films. Tsumura's overall reaction to the film was positive, but he nonetheless expressed his total disagreement with the director's "creative" decision to make unnecessary changes to Ōgai's original novel. Indeed, in preparing his film adaptation of *The Abe Family*, Kumagai publicly announced that his approach would be reminiscent of Jean Renoir's *The Lower Depths* (1936).[54] Just as Renoir drastically changed Maxim Gorky's original in accordance with the particular political situation of France in the Popular-Front era, Kumagai intended to insert his own subjective voice first by adding a pair of new characters—Osaki and Tasuke (figure 7)—and second by having them speak of the absurdity of the *junshi* system.

Like Uchida's transformative approach in *Theater of Life*, this conscious deviation from Ōgai's original led some local critics to praise the film as showing Kumagai's critical commitment to the reality of wartime Japan. As one critic pointed out, Kumagai asserted through his alteration of the original novel that under the current political situation, everyone in Japan must devote his or her precious life not to old and self-righteous ritual convention but to a more urgent and meaningful purpose like the construction of the new world order under the rule of Imperial Japan.[55] By contrast, Tsumura criticized this same deviation as a total abuse of Ōgai's respectful resolution to depict history "as it was" and gave the following warning to Kumagai and other future directors of historical film:

> It is inaccurate to judge Ōgai's spirit as trivial because this judgment stems from the reader's inability to apprehend his novel's "structure" through which each piece of the folds of reality [*genjitsu no hida*], or his depiction of fragments of a fate, comes to carry a meaning by surrounding and mobilizing people. In adapting Ōgai's literature, filmmakers must therefore begin by learning his way of looking at reality, its piety and preciseness. At the same time, they must notice that their adaptations would lose most of their meaning unless they make efforts to represent the astounding solemnity of the fate (i.e., reality) depicted by Ōgai.[56]

Given Tsumura's unflinching trust in Ōgai's acumen as a historiographer, one may assume that the original story of *the Abe Family* contains no factual errors or fictional treatment of the historical event it depicted. It is true that Ōgai made use of historical documents to provide a truthful account of the last days of the Abe family, whose lineage was completely cut off in March 1643 by the order of their former master Lord Hosokawa of the Kumamoto domain. However, as studies by Fujimoto Chizuko and Yamamoto Hirofumi have revealed, Ōgai's primary source text entitled *Tea Conversations about the Abe Family* (*Abe chajidan*) is far from a reliable document for rigorous historical research because it was written almost a century after the actual incident took place and relied upon a number of rumors and fictitious imagination. Moreover, both Fujimoto and Yamamoto also point out that Ōgai himself changed the plot or timeline of the incident for the sake of narrative economy.[57] For instance, Ōgai ascribes the miserable fate of the Abe family to Lord Hosokawa's enigmatic decision to refuse the petition of Abe Yaichiemon, the head of the Abe family, to commit *junshi* suicide upon the lord's death along with his colleagues. However, the official records of the Kumamoto domain tell us that Yaichiemon was one of the vassals who died together in 1641 through *junshi* suicide, and that the downfall of the Abe family had in fact nothing to do with the practice of *junshi* system. Needless to say, this kind of rigorous textual critique was not available when Tsumura presented his concept of historical film. But even if it were available, Tsumura would not have withdrawn his argument. For what was most valuable in Ōgai's historical novel was the strong reality effect that had preemptively been guaranteed not so much by the objective accuracy of its account as by the author's reputation as one of the most respected and matured intellectuals in the history of modern Japan.

The idea of using written texts to enhance the credibility of historical representation is not unique to Tsumura in the history of world cinema. For instance, the scriptwriter James Schamus coined the term "textual realism" in reference to the work of Carl Dreyer. Like late Ōgai, Dreyer is known for his obsession with factual accuracy; in making *The Passion of Joan of Arc* (1928) and *Day of Wrath* (1941) he is said to have composed his scripts based on actual documents of the trials of Joan of Arc and Anne Pedersdotter.[58] Nevertheless, Tsumura's conception of historical film still differs from Dreyer's textual realism in that it did not grant filmmakers—including both directors and scriptwriters—the right to interpret historical events according to their own research or artistic imagination. They were allowed only to provide a faithful filmic reproduction of the written accounts of the past already published in the form of historical novels. Such a strict restriction also distinguishes Tsumura from advocates of literary adaptation in 1930s Japan, whose main intent was to reinvent the notion of the film auteur by emulating the language-based expression developed in literature. In Tsumura's formula, words were used solely to prevent filmmakers from randomly inserting their inaccurate and untrustworthy interpretation of historical facts. If there is any trace of realism at work in Tsumura's conception of historical film, it is nothing but a more rigorous application of the idea of textual realism that is faithful only to Ōgai's "authentic" literary treatment of the nation's past.

Despite his marked distaste for popular period films, however, Tsumura was not a typical cultural elite who would completely deny both artistic and sociopolitical potentials of the film medium. In fact, Tsumura was one of the most influential—and also one of the most arrogant—film critics in Japan from the early 1930s through the end of World War II. Film reviews he wrote biweekly for the prestigious *Asahi* newspaper, written under the famous penname "Q," always supported the ongoing sophistication of sound film aesthetics, especially ones found in French poetic realist films. But as someone constantly watching and writing about films of all kinds, Tsumura was equally wary about the medium's enormous power to penetrate into the mind and knowledge formation of the mass audience. For this reason, he wrote a number of pedagogical essays on how to properly watch and evaluate films, or more precisely, how to discern good-quality films from harmful ones, at the request of high-brow literary magazines such as *Bungei shunjū* (*Literary Seasons*) and *Bungakukai* (*Literary World*). At the same time, Tsumura's specific concern about film reception also made him one of the most attentive Japanese critics to the fundamental ambiguity of filmic representation. As he wrote, "Mechanical aspects of the talkie made it possible to depict *how* the external world, consisting of both inevitable and contingent things, surrounds and affects the protagonist. With the aid of techniques such as *emphasis* or *concentration*, a talkie artist may portray *only what he needs*. Yet, as long as his creation is hinged upon the mechanical device called the camera, he can never eliminate *all the unnecessary things* from the world surrounding the protagonist. The camera somehow captures the residue of reality under any conditions."[59]

As an individual viewer of film, Tsumura was not hesitant to appreciate this increased sense of ambiguity, because it gave him enormous freedom to perceive and interpret things and phenomena appearing on the screen, just as when he confronted similar ambiguous situations in reality. Moreover, as if to foresee the advent of the French New Wave in the late 1950s, he even dreamed of a film in which no dramatic event would happen to the protagonist during its feature-length depiction of his usual morning walk, usual conversation with his friends, and usual return to his own house.⁶⁰ Yet, as a critic setting himself the task of enlightening the mass public, Tsumura could not help but problematize the same ambiguity of filmic representation. In this case, film reappeared before him as a dangerous medium, given its ability to seduce viewers into uncritically accepting or being deceived by the perceptual attraction of the events it depicts, regardless of the accuracy or sincerity of the film director's intention and articulation.

It is this internal split between his aesthetic taste and pedagogical mission that turned Tsumura to Ōgai's historical novel in his theorization of historical film. If, on the one hand, filmmakers remained cautious enough not to deviate from what Ōgai had already described in his literary texts, it would reduce the risk of letting the viewers get wrong or unfounded ideas about the national past. On the other hand, Tsumura emphasized the palpable affinity between Ōgai's "inhuman spirit" (*hininjō no seishin*) and the camera's mechanical gaze. As if to emulate the insistence of the first-generation naturalist writers on the idea of "literature with no solution," Ōgai always distanced himself from the historical events or situations or characters he described, strictly prohibiting himself from inserting personal commentaries. "While faithfully observing his protagonist from a historical and social perspective," said Tsumura, "Ōgai never intended to cast his own subjectivity upon his characters."⁶¹ Tsumura also added that Ōgai's historical novels tended to put too much emphasis on trivial matters. But this same attribute rendered Ōgai a perfect model to assimilate in his discussion of historical film, to the extent that its fundamental task was to test the film's ability to reify the absurdity of history's own being and progress.

Tsumura's concept of historical film might have appeared too restrictive to adopt in the production of Japanese period films in general. Indeed, after Kumagai's *the Abe Family*, screen adaptation of Ōgai's historical novel did not appear until Mizoguchi's postwar masterpiece *Sanshō the Bailiff* (1954). This, however, does not mean that the demand for a more authentic filmic treatment of the national past declined in wartime Japan. On the contrary, films such as Uchida's *History* (*Rekishi*, 1940), Inagaki Hiroshi's *The Last Days of Edo* (*Edo saigo no hi*, 1941), and Mizoguchi's *The 47 Ronin* (*Genroku chūshingura*, 1941–42) were all discussed under the rubric of historical film, though by this time a considerable conceptual shift had happened in the critical discourse of this genre. Hasegawa Nyozekan, the critic whom Davis misidentified as the originator of historical film, argued in 1941 that "our nation's historical film must be able to cultivate the emotional pattern and aesthetic sentiment unique to the Japanese."⁶² Similarly, in 1941, Mizoguchi explained his own approach as follows: "Aside from treating period film or historical film as its theme, I consider the existence of Japanese cinema to be standardized by a trans-individual nationalistic vision of the world, and not by a categorically imperative attitude toward art. I know one would criticize this as dogmatic, but we cannot move at all without our own foothold, whether it appears to be dogmatic or whatever. And the standard for the existence of Japanese cinema I explicate here is of course based on the historical reality of Japan today."[63]

It is in this particular discursive context that one could read historical film as "the most explicit articulation of nationalism in the cinema," as Davis denoted. Unlike Tsumura's initial proposal, this alternate usage of the term now required a different kind of realism, a realism that is faithful to essentially indefinable abstract ideas such as the Japanese spirit, Japanese historical traditions, and Japanese canons of beauty and ethics. Following this particular usage of the term, Mizoguchi maintained that if his foray into the genre of historical film turned out be successful, it should be praised not for "the depth and accuracy of historical investigation" (*shijiteki na kōshō no fukasa*) but rather for "the aptness of the nationalist view of history" (*kokka shikan no datō*) manifested in his films.[64]

Perhaps irritated by this deliberate distortion of his original concept, Tsumura stopped writing about historical film by the turn of the 1940s. However, it should be stressed that Tsumura was never left behind the currents of wartime Japanese discourse; from this moment on, he became one of the most ardent supporters of the state control of domestic film production, distribution, and exhibition. And in books with such disturbing titles as *On Film Policy* (*Eiga seisakuron*, 1943) and *Film War* (*Eigasen*, 1944) he sought a way to more actively exploit film's enormous power to make viewers believe whatever it presents as visual evidence for the construction of a counterfeit political entity called the Greater East Asia Co-Prosperity Sphere.[65] If this was the final outcome of the discursive formations of literary art film and historical film as genres, it clearly tells us about an important trait of Japanese film theory and its particular form of commitment to the historical reality of wartime Japan. That is, seemingly neutral and reasonable demands for active human intervention in the production of film texts effectively helped transform local debates on cinematic realism from a collective search for the legitimate method for subjective expression to an ideological tool for the construction of a new political reality commonly shared within the mind of Japanese war supporters.

That being said, what I have argued in this chapter is no more than one feasible option among many and various attempts that Japanese intellectuals have made to develop a more updated and suitable definition of realism in and for cinema. In the mid- to late 1930s, Japanese film critics and theorists also discussed a considerably different conception of cinematic realism in conjunction with the sudden rise of news film and nonfiction genres. The next chapter therefore examines a particular genealogy of documentary film theory in Japan, looking in particular at the Marxist critic Tosaka Jun's concept of "epistemological realism." In a sense, all the theorists discussed in the next chapter were taking a position closer to Itagaki's machine realism than to Kurahara's proletarian realism. But my argument there will also focus on how these seemingly self-conflicting approaches to cinematic realism eventually merged into one and the same horizon, following the radical dissolution of both conceptual and ontological gaps between fiction and nonfiction in the actual practice of wartime Japanese cinema.

4

Documentary Film and Epistemological Realism

UPSURGE OF NONFICTION FILMS

The 1930s, a period during which literary adaptation was at the height of its prosperity in the realm of fiction film, also witnessed a surge of public interest in newsreels and documentary films. Like the Russo-Japanese War of 1904–5, it was the outbreak of the Mukden Incident (also known as the Manchurian Incident), a political event staged by the Japanese army in 1931 to justify Japan's militaristic invasion of China, that provided the impetus for the growth and wider circulation of these nonfiction genres among domestic viewers. Newsreels, or a series of news films dealing with current affairs released on a weekly basis, became popular in Japan by 1935, when major newspaper companies such as Asahi, Yomiuri, Osaka Mainichi, Kokumin, and Dōmei tsūshin established their own film units. They began sending newsreels of the ongoing battles in China and related sociopolitical upheavals back to the home front. The demand for newsreels became more intensified in the years following the Marco Polo Bridge Incident (also known as the China Incident) of July 1937, as the incident signaled not only the beginning of the second Sino-Japanese War but eventually Japan's participation in the war against the Allies. In the first half of the 1930s, newsreels were usually shown either at outdoor screening sites near train stations in major cities or as appendages to the main program in traditional movie theaters. But by the end of the decade, there were twenty-three theaters specializing in the exhibition of newsreels in the Tokyo area alone.[1]

In this period of social unrest, the government authorities also began seeking a way to exploit nonfiction films as a tool for mass mobilization. Before the 1930s, the general policies of the Japanese government on film practice largely remained passive and restrictive. They sought to regulate the medium's allegedly harmful effects on the mass audiences through censorship and official recommendations. Yet, with the outbreak of the Mukden Incident, the Ministry of Education and the Imperial Japanese Army and Navy embarked on the production of propaganda films. This move soon resulted in a number of so-called current affairs (*jikyoku*) films that unabashedly supported Japan's militaristic invasions, including *Japan in Time of Crisis* (*Hijōji Nippon*, 1933, featuring Army Minister Araki Sadao speaking in front of the camera), *Lifeline of the Sea* (*Umi no seimeisen*, 1933, supervised by the naval officers Taketomi Kunishige and Shibata Zenjirō), and *Great Order* (*Daigōrei*, 1934, with Lieutenant Machida Keiji serving as a consultant).[2]

In the meantime, the Ministry of Home Affairs and some members of the National Diet began lobbying for a special law to grant the government control over domestic film production, distribution, and exhibition. The result was the implementation of the Film Law in 1939. This law, for one, introduced a compulsory government licensing system for all film industry professionals. But it also ordered that all fiction films shown at domestic movie theaters be accompanied by the screening of "a specific kind of film . . . films that contribute to the cultivation of the national spirit or to the development of the national intellectual faculties, recognized as such by the Minster of Education."[3] Because this specific kind of films included newsreels and a variety of documentary and propaganda films, both the making and viewing of nonfiction films came to assume a greater role in shaping screen culture in wartime Japan at large.

Despite such aggressive interventions by the government, the actual development of nonfiction filmmaking and its local theorization was always rife with conflicts and contradictions. The conceptual confusion surrounding nonfiction films in Japan can perhaps be best seen through the multitude of Japanese terms employed to designate this particular genre. Beginning with *jissha eiga* (actualities) produced by the Lumière Brothers and imported to Japan at the turn of the twentieth century, films that more or less featured nonfictional elements had been given various labels, including *kiroku eiga* (documentary film), *kyōiku eiga* (education film), *kagaku eiga* (science film), *nyūsu eiga* (news film), *senden eiga* (propaganda film), *senki eiga* (war record film), and *bunka eiga* (culture film). Moreover, John Grierson's concept of "documentary film" was widely shared among Japanese filmmakers and critics through the 1938 translation of Paul Rotha's *Documentary Film*. The term *documentary film* itself was also translated variably as *shiryō eiga*, *bunka eiga*, and *dokyumentari eiga*.[4]

To minimize terminological confusion, people in the mid- to late 1930s began to use the term *bunka eiga* to designate nonfiction films as a whole, but it only complicated matters further. First introduced as the Japanese translation of *Kulturfilm* by the German film company UFA (Universum Film-Aktien Gesellschasft), *bunka eiga* soon transformed itself into a very elusive, all-encompassing term when the 1939 Film Law used it to indicate a broad range of films considered beneficial in promoting national culture. It thus frequently crossed the conventional boundaries between art and science, documentary and propaganda, and even fiction and nonfiction. For this reason, nearly all local commentators writing about this newly emergent film genre in wartime Japan frequently asked the question, "what is *bunka eiga*?" (*bunka eiga to wa iitai nanika*).[5]

In addition, nonfiction films in Japan included a complex array of production personnel and supporters. In the late 1920s and early 1930s, it was members of the Proletarian Film League of Japan (known as Prokino for short) that initiated the making of nonfiction films. Sasa Genjū, leader of Prokino, authored a manifesto in which he called for using small gauge films, such as 16 mm and 9.5 mm, as a "weapon" to fight back against the capitalist mode of filmmaking. Prokino also produced newsreel and agitprop films featuring workers' strikes and mass demonstrations. In the aftermath of the Mukden Incident, such radical activities were outlawed and Prokino was forced to disband in 1934 along with many other leftist groups. After its dissolution, ex-Prokino members found employment in the domestic film industry, especially in its nonfiction film production sector. For example, Sasa participated in the establishment of a film unit at the Institution of Physical and Chemical Research (*Riken*) and then joined the newly established Geijutsu Eigasha (GES), where he became editor-in-chief of their film magazines, *Bunka eiga* (*Culture Film*) and *Bunka eiga kenkyū* (*Studies of Culture Film*). Increased demand for nonfiction films in wartime Japan therefore provided sanctuary for left-wing partisans during this time of social unrest. And if most of these "leftist" filmmakers eventually became enfolded into the ideology of Japanese totalitarianism, it was precisely because the emergence of the totalitarian state allowed them to put into practice an alternative to the capitalist mode of film production.

This chapter examines how this increased demand for newsreel and nonfiction films contributed to Japanese theoretical debates on cinematic realism. It is possible to tackle this issue by addressing the Japanese reception of the Griersonian concept of documentary, as I have done elsewhere.[6] However, here I will track another body of local discourse by looking at the work of Tosaka Jun, Nakai Masakazu, and Imamaura Taihei, all of whom had identified themselves as leftist when they published their essays from the mid- to late 1930s. Throughout this chapter, I refer to the realism at work in their writings as "epistemological realism," following the title of Tosaka's 1937 essay "Cinema's Epistemological Value and Its Depiction of Social Customs." The premise of this realism is that with the camera's revelatory capacity, film is able to teach us a new way of knowing about both natural and social realities. But my main concern is more with how the oft-cited metaphor of "film as a mirror" came to assume very ideological functions when Japanese "nonfiction" films began to assume the task of justifying Japan's ongoing military aggression and expansion within the terms of the Greater East Asia Co-Prosperity Sphere.

TOSAKA JUN: FILM AND SOCIAL EPISTEMOLOGY

The major suppliers of newsreels in 1930s Japan were not major film studios but newspaper companies. Similarly, intellectuals not directly connected to the film industry were among the first to claim its status as an attraction, or a new media form of visual journalism. Terada Torahiko (1878–1935), a renowned physicist and poet who was closely associated with the literary giant Natsume Sōseki, was a good example in this regard. From the late 1920s to the early 1930s, Terada frequently wrote essays on film from a scientific perspective, repeatedly stressing the ontological deviation of filmic representation from basic principles of the natural world including the persistence of space and time and the laws of causality and thermodynamics.[7] At the same time, Terada often criticized professional Japanese film critics for treating films only within the framework of modern art. He then paid special attention to the structural affinity between Soviet montage theory and the Eastern arts, including haiku and *waka* poetry, celadon pottery, and food arrangement. In so doing, he responded to Eisenstein's remark that Japanese culture is full of concrete examples of the montage aesthetic. Supported by his reputation as a public intellectual, Terada's film essays became a major source of inspiration for those arguing for the potential of nonfiction films to resolve the alleged opposition between art and science.

In his 1933 essay "News Film and the Newspaper Article" ("Nyūsu eiga to shinbun kiji"), Terada makes a lucid comparison between news film and newspaper as a tool of mass communication.[8] The purpose of newspaper articles, he says, is to provide factual information about the "five Ws" (who, what, where, when, and why) for social events. To avoid unnecessary confusion or misunderstanding, newspaper articles rely upon a variety of clichés developed in the world of print journalism. However effective, this writing convention makes the act of reading a dull and impassive exercise that does not stimulate the reader's intellectual curiosity. In contrast, Terada defines the news film as a medium of discovery, immune to such uninspiring conventions. "When watching a news film that deals with trivial things in our daily life," writes Terada, "all of us, adults and even children, often make an extraordinary 'discovery' in it.... In some sense, film is a concrete expression such that it contains a bottomless treasure box filled with hidden truths to be uncovered."[9] What makes this discovery possible is the ability of the movie camera and microphone to capture events as they occur in real time without prejudice or abstraction. Thus, for Terada, the attraction of the news film does not come from its supposed function of supplementing the latest news already covered in the newspaper. Rather, the news film is attractive because it serves as a "new organ of cognition" (*atarashii ninshiki no kikan*) that enables him to obtain a new and different body of knowledge about the external world.[10]

Terada's fascination with news films was as insightful as it was naive, given his emphasis on the semantic freedom granted to viewers. As Abé Mark Nornes points out, Terada's essay appeared prior to the hardening of stylistic and narratological norms in news films and other nonfiction genres.[11] Although Terada was aware of the possibility that some arbitrary formulas would sneak into the realm of nonfiction, he nonetheless failed to give it a more careful consideration, due to his death in 1935. With hindsight, we can say that such a "primitive" stage in the production of nonfiction films soon disappeared in the second half of the 1930s and became replaced with a more standardized use of voiceover narration and other editing skills for manipulating viewers' attention and understanding. That said, Terada's definition of the news film as a "new organ of cognition" foreshadowed subsequent local debates on documentary and its particular engagement with cinematic realism.

The idea of using film as a new cognitive faculty was taken up by Tosaka Jun (1900–1945), a Marxist philosopher known for his fearless critique of the cultural logic of Japanese fascism. Given his education in the Department of Philosophy at Kyoto University, Tosaka is often associated with the Kyoto School (*Kyōto gakuha*) of philosophy, formed by a group of leading Japanese philosophers working under the tutelage of Nishida Kitarō. However, Tosaka's own standpoint was clearly different from the dominant perspective of this school: Whereas most Kyoto School philosophers dealt with a metaphysics that could combine Western philosophy and Eastern religious thought, Tosaka consciously mobilized scientific methods and logical reasoning throughout his career.[12] In particular, Tosaka adopted Marxism as the theoretical basis for his own inquiries, always addressing social or cultural issues without bracketing out their material and historical conditions. Unlike proletarian writers who expressed nearly religious euphoria for communism, moreover, Tosaka was also cautious about the downside of party politics and direct action, and he developed a different strategy for protest after the demise of the proletarian literature movement.

In October 1932, Tosaka launched Yuibutsuron Kenkyūkai (Society for Materialism Studies, known as Yuiken for short) with the scientist Oka Kunio and the philosopher Saigusa Hiroto. The official mission of the society was to "study materialism in philosophy and natural and social sciences without being disengaged from actual problems."[13] But given the government's increasing oppression of the freedom of speech, it is also possible to say that the society aimed to retain a public sphere for Japanese leftists by adopting academic research as a shield for their political commitments. At first, Yuiken had as its official members nearly forty scholars from diverse academic fields, but it soon came under police scrutiny and many of those initial participants resigned their membership by the end of 1933. Nevertheless, Tosaka and other remaining members never lost their motivation during the six years of its existence. In addition to organizing lectures and workshops, Yuiken published its own journal *Yuibutsuron kenkyū* (*Journal of Materialism Studies*, 1932–1938) and a fifty-monograph series titled Compendiums of Materialism (Yuibutsuron zensho).

Iwasaki Akira, a leading Marxist film critic and a central member of Prokino, introduced Tosaka to writing about the film medium. After the dissolution of Prokino in 1934, Iwasaki joined Yuiken and invited its members to a weekly study group on the history of film theory. In May 1936, Iwasaki launched the film magazine *Eiga sōzō* (*Film Creation*) with other ex-Prokino members.[14] Consequently, members of Prokino and Yuiken met together and held debates over both social and philosophical values of film, making *Eiga sōzō* the final fortress of the Marxist approach in wartime Japanese film criticism.[15]

Tosaka published only a handful of film essays from 1934 to 1938, but they were nonetheless crucial in developing his own theory of social epistemology. For Tosaka, the term *epistemology* (*ninshikiron*) meant a process of critical thinking that enables us to articulate and understand things and phenomena in this world. And this reflexive process was essential to his philosophical treatment of the rise of mass culture and its impact on the formation of everyday life. As Harry Harootunian points out, "More than any other thinker of the age, he [Tosaka] viewed his present as a philosophical problem that needed to be interrogated, when others merely assumed its phenomenality as a given."[16] A mainstay of Tosaka's approach was a social and cultural phenomenon that he called "custom" (*fūzoku*). By this term he meant a broad range of everyday activities including the latest trends in fashion and hairstyle, new forms of leisure and amusement, and shifting patterns of behavior in the present time.

In the opening chapter of his 1936 monograph *Thought and Custom* (*Shisō to fūzoku*), Tosaka declares that he treats custom as a catalyst to distill major symptoms of the modern capitalist world.[17] However, he also reminds us that the major problem with making custom an object of research lies in its ephemeral quality. Both journalists and popular writers have tried to capture the currents of everyday life just as they emerge, but in most cases their attempts prove unsuccessful due to the inevitable process of abstraction through the written language. It is in this context that Tosaka realizes the great potential of film for providing concrete and recorded samples of customs. Thus, in his essay "Cinema's Realistic Property and Its Popularity" ("Eiga no shajitsuteki tokusei to taishūsei"), Tosaka prioritizes *jisshasei*, the photographic nature of filmic representation, as the most significant property of the film medium. As he writes:

> Of course, I have not forgotten that the artistic value of cinema contains theatrical or literary moments. But in order for these moments to be realized, we must first privilege *jisshasei*, the reproduction of actual reality. It is this *jisshasei* itself that has already granted film a particular artistic value.... Speaking of its treatment of natural phenomena, the screen teaches human beings about the *goodness of materiality*, the delight of the movement of worldly matters. These are the things we usually see in our daily life, but we haven't recognized their values until they appear on the screen.[18]

Perhaps some explanation is necessary to understand this passage. As a Marxist, Tosaka always treats the term *reality* (*genjitsu*) as inseparable from the material condition that determines the dominant mode of being and expression of any given object. When he talks about painting or theater, he therefore refers to the world (i.e., a distinct spatial and temporal configuration unique to a given object or phenomenon) delimited either by a flat and rectangular canvas or by the proscenium arch and drop curtains as the "realities" of these art forms. But these conditions are no more than what he calls "artistic reality" (*geijutsuteki riaritī*), and the very idea of art and artwork has been long held in the clear-cut distinction between this artificial reality of art and the "actual reality" (*genjiteki riaritī*) of everyday life. In Tosaka's view, the specificity of film and its realism lies in its radical unification of these two differing realities in one and the same visual representation. This is partly because the material condition of filmic representation—photography—embodies an indexical relationship between a sign (image) and its referent (the external world), proving the physical existence of whatever appears before the camera. But it is also because filmic representation enhances its credibility by enabling viewers to observe both dramatic and trivial events unfolding on screen in the same manner as they do in their everyday setting.[19] Thus, as Tosaka says, the unique attractions of films in general and of newsreels or nonfiction films in particular stem from their unprecedented ability to make "actual reality" a genuine object for the aesthetic experience.[20]

Tosaka's emphasis on the advantages of the photographic nature of filmic representation inevitably connects him to the advocates the machine aesthetic. But unlike Itagaki's earlier discussion of machine realism, Tosaka never took the position of technological determinism that tended to celebrate the superiority of the camera's mechanical gaze at the risk of nullifying the role of human onlookers. Rather, Tosaka was always attentive to the potential of film to expand and enrich the process of human cognition. As he stressed repeatedly, one could never apprehend the value of the film experience without considering its extraordinary power to make people *think*. This is why Tosaka, in his subsequent essays, came to define cinema as a "very modern means of cognition" (*ninshiki to iu mono no goku kindaiteki na ichi shudan*).[21] Tosaka did not undervalue the camera's revelatory capacity; he was just more cautious than others in claiming that any objective or scientific truths uncovered by this optical device could claim no epistemological value without the active and conscious involvement of the spectators.

Perhaps one could better grasp Tosaka's argument here by comparing it to Walter Benjamin's concept of the "optical unconsciousness," which appeared in the latter's seminal essay "The Work of Art in the Age of Its Technological Reproducibility."[22] What Benjamin aimed to clarify through this concept was not limited to the camera's revelatory capacity, but, as Thomas Y. Levin points out, extended to his conviction that film could be a *"materialization* of the new perceptual conditions of modernity."²³ But as in the case of the psychoanalytic unconsciousness, which requires the analyst's careful reading of the symptoms of his or her patients, the optical consciousness in film also necessitates a careful investigation. Some truth about given objects or phenomena is already captured there, but it is still waiting to be decoded by the viewers. Only through the proper articulation of sociocultural symptoms appearing in the form of the optical unconsciousness, can one grasp Benjamin's following remark on aesthetics: "The way in which human perception is organized—the medium in which it occurs—is conditioned not only by nature but by history."²⁴

Tosaka was equally aware of such diagnostic aspects of filmic representation. And he addressed this issue in his last film essay, "Film Art and Film: Toward the Operation of Abstraction" ("Eiga geijutsu to eiga: Abusutorakushon no sayō e"). We should keep in mind that the essay was published in December 1937, five months after the outbreak of the Second Sino-Japanese War. Accordingly, Tosaka begins his argument by referring to the rise of a nonfiction film practice that corresponds to the public demand at this particular historical moment: *bunka eiga*. For Tosaka, the term *bunka eiga* does not mean "films filled with 'cultural' content," but rather designates more specifically films that are "used as a tool for the government's cultural policy."²⁵ Needless to say, films made for this purpose are usually called "propaganda films," but *bunka eiga* tactfully conceals its ideological functions by giving itself the neutral look of educational or scientific films. Accordingly, Tosaka never trusts *bunka eiga* as a proper film genre, openly casting doubt upon its truth claims. Nevertheless, he also finds it important to critically reflect on *bunka eiga* as a cultural phenomenon supported by the government's apparent intervention in both promotion and regulation of this genre. A similar symptom can also be found in the sudden popularity of news films, especially those serving as war reportage. He argues that given the influx of visual spectacles peppered with nationalistic sentiments and the actuality of the battlefield, one can now see the advent of "some stupid people who insist that the war produces a new beauty, and that war news is transforming itself into a new art."²⁶ In these instances, nonfiction film begins to function as a mirror that inflects rather than reflects objective truths of reality. How, then, does Tosaka deal with this pressing problem?

At the very end of the essay, Tosaka poses a new concept called "abstraction" (*abusutorakushon*) to address the epistemological function of the film medium. This may seem strange at first sight, for both in this and other film-related essays Tosaka has prioritized the camera's mechanical ability to give concrete shape to the ephemerality of social customs. Nevertheless, abstraction serves as one of the most fundamental operations in Tosaka's theory of social epistemology, as it penetrates all kinds of cognitive processes. While people tend to think that abstraction is the property of science as manifested in chemical formulas and mathematical theorems, Tosaka claims that it is also at work in art because "without it, style in art would be meaningless and painting would never come into existence." He then continues:

> The difference in the degree of abstraction makes distinctions between science and art, between different genres of art. . . . However, abstraction is not simply beneficial in discerning differences between various modes of cultural production (or modes of cognition). This is to say that the operation of abstraction itself is grounded in the very method and function of cognition. Thus, cinema as a method and function of cognition—and not necessarily "cinema" as a mode of cultural production—must have its particular form of abstraction. And perhaps this will be the medium [*baikai*] through which we can correlate cinema and other methods of cognition.[27]

In the present essay, Tosaka does not give any further explanation of how abstraction works in filmic representation, except that he promises the reader that he will come back to this issue "at some other occasion." Despite such an open ending, it is still possible to apprehend what Tosaka tries to elucidate here with the concept of abstraction by looking at another statement he made around the same time. In an essay titled "What Is Epistemology?" ("Ninshikiron to wa nani ka"), Tosaka offers a hint as to why he changed his focus at the end of his last film essay: "The realization of mimetic depiction [*mosha*] is by no means the result of direct, natural, or unconditioned reflection, but always involves the process of exerting endless mediation [*kagirinai baikai no rōsaku no katei*]. Thus, in this case, mimetic depiction is never like what one thinks of as a passive and contemplative mirror; it is the actual relation that goes beyond such a metaphoric argument. This mirror metaphor is therefore nothing but a sign that indicates the goal of cognition gained through mimetic depiction."[28] What Tosaka calls "the process of exerting endless mediations" here indicates the operation of abstraction in the act of cognition. That is, in order for any sensible data or phenomena to be represented in people's minds as an object for cognition, they must transform themselves according to both material and discursive conditions that determine the substance of each representational medium. These representational media include written or spoken languages, icons or visual signs, and photographic or filmic images, and each of them has its own process of abstraction.

It is now clear why Tosaka was so attracted by film as a medium for social epistemology. His initial fascination came from film's ability to bypass or at least to radically reformulate the subjective process of abstraction, given its objective presentation of things or phenomena as they are. However, as he witnessed the Japanese government's appropriation of the factuality of filmic representation in the form of *bunka eiga*, Tosaka came to realize that cinema must have its own agenda for "the operation of abstraction," rather than serving as a passive and transparent mirror for society. Therefore, as Tosaka wrote, "The fundamental question is not whether or not film is art, or what kind of film could be an art. Rather, it should involve our actual analysis of the roles that cinema as a method of cognition plays in the history of human cognition."[29] After writing essays devoted to this philosophical issue, Tosaka now found it necessary to shift his focus from principle to praxis, to begin specifying the "rules" that govern cinema's particular form of expression. To put it in Bazin's famous remark, at this moment Tosaka became aware not only of the ontology of the photographic image, but also of the fact that, "On the other hand, of course, cinema is also a language."[30]

In reality, however, Tosaka never had a chance to develop his theory of cinematic abstraction because he was officially banned from writing by the end of 1937. A year later, Tosaka, along with other Yuiken members, was arrested for the violation of the Peace Preservation Law, just like Kurahara and his supporters in the proletarian literature movement. Tosaka was intermittently imprisoned between 1938 and 1945, and died of malnutrition on August 9, 1945, only a week prior to Japan's surrender to the Allies. Tosaka's theorization of cinema's epistemology could not develop fully, due to the disturbing political situation of wartime Japan, but his intervention in the field of film criticism still evoked what Japanese film historians later called the "film epistemology debate" (*eiga ninshiki ronsō*). Even though contemporary critics considered this debate to have been a false start, its emphasis on cognition had a significant future impact.

Ueno Kōzō, an ex-member of Prokino and the author of the book *Film Cognition* (*Eiga no ninshiki*), harshly criticized Tosaka for subjugating art to science. Ueno claimed that Tosaka's epistemology judged everything on the basis of scientific cognition, so much so that it completely underrated the role of artistic intuition or inspiration that was supposed to exist prior to or outside of such a cognitive process itself.[31] Obviously, this criticism missed the point. For Tosaka, as we have seen, stressed that in our experience of cognition, the operation of abstraction is inevitable whenever raw sensory materials move from the stage of impression and perception to that of expression and representation, and that this inevitable process of abstraction can be equally observed in both art and science.[32] And if Tosaka paid special attention to film as the most important cultural product of his times, it was precisely because film could help us expose ourselves to a radically new way of seeing and knowing about our reality beyond the traditional binary opposition between art and science.

In retrospect, the singularity of Tosaka's intellectual activities was in his resolution to go against the dominant patterns of behavior in his times. Unlike Japanese proletarian writers, Tosaka did not join the Communist Party and instead cultivated his ways of putting into practice what he learned from Marxism and its particular conceptions of dialectical materialism. Unlike his contemporary philosophers, he never fell for the lure of cultural hermeneutics that served as an ideological apparatus for Japanese fascism. And unlike his leftist colleagues, he did not commit himself to political conversion known as *tenkō*, even though it ultimately led to his premature death in prison. These episodes effectively granted Tosaka a legendary position in Japanese intellectual history, as one critic favorably called him "a robust leader climbing up a long and rugged path toward progress and freedom during the dark period."[33] However, if we situate Tosaka in the history of Japanese film theory, it becomes clear that his theoretical intervention had much in common with the major currents in wartime Japanese film discourse. Beyond his direct association with figures like Itagaki and Terada, Tosaka was not alone in rearticulating cinema's revelatory capacity in relation to the growing popularity of newsreel and nonfiction genres. Among these theorists was Nakai Masakazu (1900–1952), who, along with Tosaka, has been regarded by many as one of the most respected wartime thinkers for his persistent resistance to Japanese fascism.

NAKAI MASAKAZU: THE LOGIC OF COLLECTIVISM

Like Tosaka, Nakai graduated from the Department of Philosophy at Kyoto University, where he studied the neo-Kantian aesthetic under the guidance of the aesthetician Fukada Yasukazu. He was then appointed to the editorial staff of *Tetsugaku kenkyū* (*Journal of Philosophical Studies*), which featured essays by philosophers associated with the department. Through his editorial work, Nakai established a close relationship with members of the Kyoto School. At the same time, Nakai also became a close friend of Tosaka, with whom he had many intense arguments whenever they met on the street or at someone's house.[34] From the beginning, these two up-and-coming philosophers shared as many similarities as differences. Although they were both keenly aware of the necessity to adapt their philosophical trainings to the everyday life of the masses, they disagreed about how to put this shared agenda into practice. While Tosaka moved to Tokyo after graduation and radicalized his political stance under Marxian dialectical materialism, Nakai remained in Kyoto and became engaged with the consumer's union movement reflecting his sympathy with utopian socialism proposed by the likes of Henri de Saint-Simon, Charles Fourier, and Robert Owen. By the mid-1930s, however, Nakai developed a viable model for collective resistance against the rise of Japanese fascism. Just as Tosaka was active in organizing a public sphere through and around Yuiken, Nakai launched his own magazine *Sekai bunka* (*World Culture*, 1935–37) and the weekly newspaper *Doyōbi* (*Saturday*, 1936–37) named in recognition of the French Popular Front's periodical *Vendredi* (*Friday*). In establishing these publishing venues, Nakai hoped to cultivate solidarity between Japanese and European anti-Fascist movements.[35]

Nakai's engagement with film spanned from the early 1930s through the postwar years, and his fascination with this medium was so profound that he even tried his hand at amateur filmmaking.[36] Nakai sought to clarify both the properties and potentials of the film medium, employing the critical vocabularies he learned from

German philosophers ranging from Kant and Hegel to his contemporaries such as Ernst Cassirer, Hermann Cohen, and Martin Heidegger. And like Tosaka, Nakai gave the highest priority to the photographic nature of filmic representation:

> The greatest function of cinema is that it has an ability to capture the fact through the lens and then to reproduce it on film without losing its temporality. Of course, human beings can add many humanistic features in the process of reproduction. But this process itself still holds singularity because in it, things are passed from fact to film, from one physical matter to another physical matter. Thus, film has its own logic, and film art must have its own roots in this particular logic.... However, the so-called "cinema" that appears before us is mostly restricted to fiction films, especially to ones aimed at bringing laughter and tears to the masses.... In this sense, today's cinema is like a shallow and flattened theater. To be sure, cinema is something gigantic, but it has yet to realize its full potential.[37]

Nakai notes that documentary and other nonfiction genres indicate a promising future for this medium. At this point, the affinity between Tosaka and Nakai is unmistakable given their mutual interest in film's unprecedented ability to represent the physical or objective existence of the external world. Indeed, Nakai went so far as to declare that "in terms of its physical procedure, a black dot appearing [on the screen] as the figure of a soldier is directly connected from afar to the body of that soldier on the actual battlefield."[38] Nevertheless, the tangible similarity between Tosaka and Nakai stops there: while Tosaka integrated his film writing into social epistemology, Nakai defined cinema as a means of reconfiguring modern aesthetics from scratch, with a marked emphasis on both the dialectical and dialogical natures of the film experience.

Nakai's unique approach to film theory is derived from his careful treatment of the dual and self-contradictory structure of the cinematic apparatus. In his 1932 essay "The Wall" ("Kabe"), Nakai argues that the wall, as part of the human living environment, has been a site through which people in different areas and periods sought to grasp and preserve their differing visions of reality. From ancient to medieval times, people had created visual records of their everyday life upon walls, be they hand drawings of animals they hunted or colorful illustrations of figures in their own religious pantheons. Nakai then asks: "When machines, apartments, and co-ops begin to form the basis of people's life, what does the wall mean to us now?"[39] Following radical shifts in the materials used for the construction of modern buildings, walls in the twentieth century are now transparent architectural supports, consisting of glass, steel, and concrete. By looking at these "glass walls," people in the modern era discover pleasure in observing what Nakai calls "the picture of light" (*kōga*), which functions as "an animated wall painting, a painting scroll that unfolds itself with no limitation, and a revolving lantern that never repeats itself as time flows."[40] It is obvious that by this term Nakai implies twentieth-century people's daily experience of the world through film. But at least at this point, Nakai's comparison between film and the modern glass walls seems to follow the clichéd metaphor of film as a window opening onto reality, illuminating the passive character of the camera's mechanical gaze.

To address a more active side of filmic representation, Nakai immediately wrote a sequel entitled "To Project/Reflect" ("Utsusu") the following month. In this essay Nakai examines the self-contradictory nature of the cinematic apparatus by referring to multiple meanings attributed to the Japanese verb *utsusu*. In its everyday usage, the verb *utsusu* can signify "to reflect," "to project," "to copy," "to transfer," "to infect," "to transcribe," and "to photograph" while retaining the same pronunciation. Underlying such manifold meanings of the verb is a split between passive and active voices. Put briefly, the verb *utsusu* reveals its self-contradictory nature when it moves back and forth between the two opposing poles of meanings that are translatable in English as "to reflect" and "to project."

Nakai then argues that the cinematic apparatus is also marked by the same oxymoronic structure. Aside from the cinematographer's selection of angles, shot lengths, and the movement of the camera, the main function of the cinematic apparatus at this stage of production remains passive and reflective as long as it automatically records the traces of the light reflected from the object. But as soon as it moves to the stage of exhibition, however, the same apparatus radically transforms itself into a device for active expression, continuously throwing luminous moving images onto the screen through the projector.[41] Additionally, Nakai stresses that between these two poles of *utsusu* exists the possibility for inserting the human intellect by means of editing. This is why montage plays a critical role in Nakai's film theory, serving as a nodal point that unifies what he called the *geworfen* (thrown) and *entwerfen* (throwing) aspects of filmic representation.[42] However, it is still necessary to specify what Nakai actually meant by the term *montage* in his writing, because the way he adopted this concept was very different from our conventional usage and understanding of it.

Nearly all the major writings by members of the Soviet montage school were translated into Japanese by the time Nakai began writing about film in the early 1930s. Accordingly, Nakai expressed a keen interest in this new systematic account of film enunciation, following the guidance provided by other Kyoto-based critics such as Shimizu Hikaru and Nagae Michitarō.[43] Nevertheless, Nakai's fascination with montage did not come from accounts by Pudovkin and Eisenstein, which primarily revolved around the process of visual signification through associations of two or more successive shots. Instead, Nakai adapted what he imagined to be Vertov's approach to montage, though it was primarily of his own invention because of the limited availability of Vertov's writing.

Certainly, Vertov was very famous for his concept of the kino-eye, but his local reputation in Japan depended mostly on secondary sources. Léon Moussinac's *Le cinéma soviétique* (1928) was among the most influential, and its Japanese translation appeared in 1930.[44] According to Moussinac, Vertov was not only a pioneer in documentary filmmaking but also a formalist in terms of his experiments with what Eisenstein defined as "rhythmic" or "metric" montage. As a result, Vertov often presented his films as "a pictorial record of rhythm" (*rizumu no kiroku sareta e*) in which the length and form of individual shots are strictly arranged according to the film's entire structure.[45] It should be noted that Moussinac wrote this assessment before the release of *Man with a Movie Camera*. But it is this particular presentation of Vertov as a master of rhythmic montage that informed Nakai's film theory.

Nakai's fascination with Vertov is manifested in his 1931 essay "The Continuity of *In Spring*" ("*Haru* no kontinyuiti"). Having not yet been able to watch Vertov's own films, Nakai offers in this essay a close reading of *In Spring*, a film that was directed by Vertov's younger brother Mikhail Kaufman. In hoping to understand the entire structure of the film, Nakai measured the length of every single shot appearing one after another on screen with the help of his friend sitting next to him and holding a stopwatch. The result of this experiment was something akin to a mathematical table filled with numbers and letters, which visually testifies to the director's skillful orchestration of individual shots by quick edits (figure 8). This revelation, for one, led Nakai to celebrate *In Spring* as exemplary of a "mathematization of literature and poetry" (*bungaku no mata shi no sūgakuka*) following Moussinnac's prior argument. But Nakai's real discovery was that the film drew its main attraction from what he calls "a new composition of the senses" (*atarashiki kankakuteki kōsei*). *In Spring*, he says, collapsed a schematic division between seeing and hearing. When the rapid succession of moving images no longer allowed the viewer to grasp the meaning of individual shots, the viewer's perception of the film transformed itself from a spatial experience to a temporal one, as in the case of music. But while music remained invisible to us, *In Spring* made it possible for us to see "the beauty of time seen from the kino-eye ... by cultivating a special form of temporal perception."[46]

Nakai provides a more detailed account of this "special form of temporal perception" (*tokushu no jikanteki kankaku keishiki*) in his commentaries on an example of the UFA's educational *Kulturfilm*, *The Power of Plants* (*Kraftleistung der Pfanzen*, 1934, dir. Wolfram Junghans). Here, Nakai looks at how the film succeeded in combining the spectator's viewing experience of "plant time" (*shokubutsu no jikan*) and "human time" (*ningen no jikan*) through innovative use of time-lapse photography. In employing this particular technique, *The Power of Plants* liberated itself from the constraints of the human perception of time and successfully "penetrated into the plant's own time with the flexibility of the lens and film."[47] As a natural phenomenon, the sprouting of a bud—its visual representation in plant time—is too slow to perceive through the human sensory apparatus as a continuous movement. But it can still become visible to us by means of a three-stage process: capturing movement on a filmstrip through the camera, setting the

冷たい雪の中にして、遠い国の「春」の訪れを聴への思ひがある。
われわれはあの映画をいろいろの方面から分析してみる必要がある。今ここにかくんとす
るものは、ある映画のコンティニュイティーの時間的調子についての研究である。不完全なが
ら筆者がストップウォッチ、辻部政太郎君筆記でもただけの努力をもつて正確を期した。

春　60/100 秒標準　∴1＝0.6秒　日本数字は字幕、fはフラッシュバック、〰リズム
(京都松竹座にて)

I. 峠　三fff522223fffff43444ffff6571010154 3
2443224 6ff24410775444463ff5634131055555
105743432447766117103272210137744496372
11910710723645225七55520246238321026二2133 4
2五55

II. 春きたる　10 5 5 5 4 四 2 17 2 4 二 2 10 5 5 5 5 13 11 5 3 3 2 1 6 5 五 三 5
4 5 3 5 1 四 10 6 4 4 5 6 6 11 7 10 4 10 5 六 7 6 6 3 2 6 2 f f 3 6 3 2 2
3 6 12 6 3 3 3 3 10 2 3 1 六 2 3 3 11 10 6 6 5 3 4 6 7 4 7 7 20 10 4 4 4 4
4 4 4 10 4 7 6 2 f f f f 5 8 f f f f f 2 1 2 3 1 11 8 14 6 10 6 七 5 7 5
10 5 2 10 7 二 4 3 3 3 二 5 10 6 5 10 6 5 3 2 6 f f f f f 4 3 6 6 8 5 17
10 20 10 10

III. 春の営み　二三 4 5 4 3 2 5 f f 4 f f f f f 3 f f 1 1 f f f f 5 5 f 3 f 5
4 6 10 f f 7 f 6 f f f f f f f f f f f f f f f f 2 4 f f f f f f f
f 4 3 2 f f 20 2 10 3 f f f 3 3 5 f f f f f 7 5 4 (overrap) 10 (o) 12
(o) 14 3 3 2 4 5 f f 3 3 4 6 4 5 5 5 5 4 3 5 5 3 7 4 4 10 2 2 2 20 11 10 5
10 5 5 11 3 11 f f 5 f f f 6 2 4 4 (double print) 6 6 3 3 7 f f f 4 f f 4
7 4 3 f f f f f f 1 f f f 5 6 4 4 4 f f f f f f f f f f f 1 1 1 4 f
f f f f f f f f f f 4 4 4 四 4 3 3 4 4 4 4 4 10 f 6 6 10 (double) 5 5 3
7 5 三 5 五 2 三 3 (〰) 6 (〰) 7 6 3 15 五 f f 11 10 f f 7 (〰) 10 5
f f

IV. 春の生物学　4 6 12 4 4 10 11 6 11 f f 6 3 6 2 6 5 3 3 4 f f 3 f f 10 3 5 10 3
4 3 2 7 6 6 5 7 8 4 4 10 4 5 2 2 1 7 3 3 10 15 f f f 3 3 4 5 5 f f 2 二 二
3 3 2 f f 4 10 5 三 15 5 f f f 8 1 1 1 f f 7 f f 9 11 4 5 3 2 3 5 f 3 3 5
9 10 4 4 6 7 f f f 5 5 f 5 1 4 f f 6 3 4 4 4 f f f f 3 3 7 6 10 5 7 7 4
4 5 三 10 5 5

V. 二つの人生　9 4 4 4 4 3 2 f f f 5 5 3 4 4 7 7 4 6 5 四 3 15 6 — 1 —— f 10
——— 6 7 f 15 5 f 7 5 f 7 (〰) 15 f f f 6 (〰) 10 4 14 4 6 6 5 f f f
f f f f f f f f f f f f (字幕ヲマジウ) 6 8 8 1 1 4 f f f f f f 4 9 9 7 6

FIGURE 8. Shot lengths and patterns visualized in Nakai Masakazu's "Continuity of *In Spring*," in *Nakai Masakazu zenshū*, ed. Kuno Osamu (Tokyo: Bijutsu Shuppansha, 1981), 3:146–147.

shutter speed, and projecting these images on a screen at the right speed. In so doing, this film taught Nakai how to perceive and understand what Tosaka called "the goodness of materiality," a new perceptual experience that is not bounded by our normal vision.

Nakai deploys the term *montage* to indicate the formation of a new aesthetic based on this specific encounter between human and nonhuman modes of visual perception. As he writes:

> The regulation of the humanistic aesthetic is that sense perception must always mediate and pass through our psychological subjectivity. And yet in film, raw materials for such sensory representation now regulate themselves in the realm of physical objectivity. In this instance, the logic of natural phenomena—i.e., natural dialectics—and the logic of human phenomena—i.e., social dialectics—come to wrestle with each other without *Medium* and in turn by becoming *Mittel* in themselves.... *Montieren* is by no means an operation through acetone and a pair of scissors. It must designate the process through which both the logic of natural phenomena and the logic of human phenomena wrestle, imitate, see through, and come across each other within physical objectivity.... The purpose of true film art must be the realization of montage in this specific sense.[48]

This passage is not easy to apprehend because of the German terms used here. *Montieren* is a transitive verb with the meaning of "to mount" or "to assemble" something, and, just like its French equivalent *monter*, it came to signify "to create a montage" when adopted in the critical vocabulary of film theory. But more important for us here is the distinction between *Medium* and *Mittel*. Although the latter is often used as the German translation of the former, Nakai gives them two discrete meanings as indicated in the different Japanese terms he employed, *baizai* and *baikai*. On the one hand, *Medium/baizai* means the normal process of mediation by something external or substitutive, including the way in which we understand a given object with the aid of language or other secondary media for *re*-presentation. Thus, *Medium/baizai* presupposes knowledge acquisition through reason or intelligence as in the case of abstraction. On the other hand, *Mittel/baikai* indicates what Nakai calls the "mediation without medium" (*mubaikai no baikai*), a self-contradictory form of mediation that enables us to apprehend a given object in itself without the intervention of secondary media.[49] Therefore, *Mittel/baikai* anticipates knowledge acquisition through experience or sympathy as in the case of intuition.

Nakai came up with his concept of *Mittel/baizai* to indicate a specific mode of mediation at work in our viewing of film. With its ability to mechanically reproduce the visual impression of the world through the photochemical process, film can evade the normal process of human cognition/abstraction without losing the concrete objectivity of the things or phenomena it presents us. Moreover, we as the viewers should apprehend the epistemological value of this new mode of visual perception not by contemplating the meaning of film texts in abstract terms, but by experiencing the emotionally attractive, but at the same time mathematically and physically accurate, representation of the world-in-motion with our own eyes. At this moment, Nakai treated the viewer's fixation on visual pleasure as a radically new form of knowledge acquisition. In this sense, his stance was analogous to Kracauer and Benjamin's positive treatment of the concept of "distraction." Nonetheless, Nakai's emphasis on "montage" as a sign of the dialectic between human (subjective) and nonhuman (objective) perspectives still deserves our critical investigation, especially when coupled with "collectivism" (*shūdanshugi*), another key term in his film theory.

According to Nakai, collectivism marks the dominant mode of cultural production and consumption not only in the twentieth century but also in the ancient Greek period. In this remote past, the work of art was always premised on *techne* (*gijutsu*) and *mimesis* (*mohō*), as it aimed to be a faithful imitation or representation of the universal existence of transcendental categories comprised of truth, goodness, and beauty.[50] With the rise of romanticism in the nineteenth century, however, *techne* and *mimesis* were replaced with *genius* (*tensai*) and *creation* (*sozō*). The work of art in this period has thus become the expression of the alleged supremacy of human creativity, as manifested in Oscar Wilde's famous dictum: "Art does not imitate nature, but nature imitates art."[51] This marked emphasis on the genius and creativity of individual artists, Nakai explains, was inseparable from the rise of civil society and the associated petit-bourgeois class consciousness in the formative period of modern capitalism. However, just as contemporary forms of monopoly including cartels and trusts contradict capitalism's initial support of the idea of free trade, the work of art produced in this new era of modernity cannot help but contradict the ethos of individualism. Hence the resurgence of the Greek model of collectivism in the twentieth century. This is partly because of the increasing penetration of modern technologies (*techne*) for mechanical reproduction (*mimesis*) into the space of everyday life. But an equally important reason is that the machine itself can serve as an antidote to the impasse of individualism by reorganizing the behavioral patterns of modern individuals under the new working ethics of modern collectivism including *standardization* (*tōitsu*), *discipline* (*kiritsu*), and the *universal* (*fuhen*).[52]

Nakai often refers to the popularity of team sports such as rugby and regatta as an example of this modern collectivism. As he writes, "The attraction of modern sports lies in this aesthetic sense of organization. . . . Its greatest pleasure must stem from the beauty of uniformity that underlies each player's own experience." What is important here is that people in the twentieth century came to perceive and appreciate "this aesthetic sense of organization" not as passive observers but as active participants of these collective sports. In Nakai's view, this *Mittel*-based, intuitive form of mediation is equally informed by recent group activities, from the formation of institutions such as factories, co-ops, and political societies, to the mass consumption of newspapers, radio, and film. The machine aesthetic in Nakai's writing therefore comes to signify the observable omnipresence of collectivism in addition to its glorification of the functional beauty of modern machinery: "When we look at the machine, we are not confronting the machine as individuals. Rather, we gaze into ourselves as an element of a bigger collective—that is, as its tissue cell—under the control of the *organization* of the machine. The *sense of organization* at work here becomes a new protoplasm for our pleasure. By incorporating the concept of the machine into the realm of aesthetics, we must set up this sense of organization as the basis of a functional sense of beauty that could *reveal* equivalent relations toward the multiple layers of [today's] phenomena."[53]

Nakai designates film as the most relevant example to expound his concept of collectivism. First, making a film requires a series of collaborations between a number of specialized personnel in the film industry as a modern institution. Professional film directors are unable to assert full authorial control, no matter how competent, over any production unless they work in the field of amateur or experimental film. Second, the consumption of film was counted as a group activity until the introduction of consumer-level recording and playback devices such as VHS, DVD, and online streaming services. Given its mechanical reproducibility, a film can deliver the same content not only to individual audience members gathered in a movie theater, but also countless viewers around the world and in different time periods. Third, and most importantly, a film is composed of a series of shots whose meaning is not always self-contained but contingent upon what comes before or after. Thus, it can be said that filmic signification stems from this continuous and complicated process of organization. And Nakai uses the term *montage* again to indicate this organizing process itself.

Nakai believes that montage as a signifier of the collective mode of film production and consumption can exert its strongest impact on society when it is used in nonfiction genres. In film, Nakai argues, "documentation can achieve its best results less by the hands of art specialists than through the committee's [dedication to] correct and responsible editing of the reports culled by mass technicians. The future of the so-called documentary film could be meaningful and plentiful in this collective structure alone."[54] In the days of individualism, the factuality of historical events was confined within people's limited ability for commemoration. As a result, any historical accounts preserved in the form of written texts or paintings could seldom achieve the status of an "objective" record in its strict sense. But the situation becomes totally different when people begin using film as a means of historical documentation. Beyond the increased sense of factuality given by the photographic nature of the film medium, the collective process of filmmaking can also anticipate a more impersonal and comprehensive documentation of the given event by reflecting consensus among a variety of the people involved. As Nakai writes:

> At the basis of this *factuality* lies the dialectical system through which history—or more precisely, the fact—becomes a more objective cosmos at its most fundamental level. And as a great shadow of its operation, this factuality must contain in itself a haptic sense that everything in the world is grasped there.... This is a sense that makes us feel the heavy hand of history behind scattered incidents taking place all over the world. Taking the form of reportage and montage, this [new] sense of factuality is now descending to the deepest level [of reality] which no other art could ever reach before.[55]

Thus, for Nakai, the task of documentary film is not restricted to offering credible audiovisual recordings of actual events alone. It should also serve as a guiding principle for people's active and reflexive participation in the irreversible flow of history, a movement that he sees as leading to the formation of a more advanced, anti-capitalist society based on the idea of the cooperative ownership of the means of production, expression, and communication.

Nakai's film theory was so obviously based on an optimistic foundation that it cannot help but lead us to ask one remaining question: In what kind of political system could Nakai's idea of collectivism be successfully realized? Nakai seemed to anticipate the advent of a socialist society in which the production of noncommercial documentary films provides the best reification of the idea of modern collectivism. However, he remained absolutely silent as to how people should put this idea into practice, as if this radical shift from capitalism to socialism were already predetermined in the course of history without the intervention of the Communist Party or other political entities. This seemingly passive stance explains less about Nakai's personal detachment from Marxism than his ambivalent relationship with the sociopolitical milieu of wartime Japan. Indeed, when Nakai published another essay titled "The Logic of the Committee" ("Iinkai no ronri") in 1936, his own standpoint was vacillating between utopian socialism and vulgar totalitarianism.[56] Following the outbreak of the Second Sino-Japanese war in the following year, the Japanese government began calling for mass mobilization for the war effort; it was also a pivotal period for the consolidation and restructuring of the Japanese film industry from an anti-capitalist perspective.

Proposed within this particular historical dynamic, Nakai's seemingly progressive idea of collectivism came to coincide with the official discourse of wartime Japan. Both collectivism and totalitarianism celebrated the genius of a system that could effectively exploit individual members of local communities or organizations for the benefit of a larger society and the state apparatus. The effects of this coincidence cannot be overemphasized. Nakai was arrested in late 1937 for the violation of the Peace Preservation Law, but unlike Tosaka, Nakai was released in a few months and able to survive the war. And in his wartime writings, Nakai celebrated the emperor-centered structure of Japanese national polity (*kokutai*) as the most admirable example of "the dissolution of individuals into the massive structure of the state."⁵⁷

In sum, Nakai's writings have a tendency to reduce everything to the bare essentials, while lacking or intentionally avoiding reflexive investigation into actual political conditions that informed his object of speculation. Consequently, his film theory also appears to be more idealist than empirical, more inward looking than outward, and more conformist than reformist, when compared to Tosaka's inquiry into the ideological implication of the growing popularity of nonfiction genres in late-1930s Japan. But this does not mean that Nakai was less influential than Tosaka among their contemporaries. For instance, Imamura Taihei (1911–1986), arguably the most influential theorist of documentary film in wartime Japan, openly expressed his intellectual indebtedness to Nakai. In one of his postwar essays, Imamura went so far as to praise Nakai as "the person who possesses a true thought" (*hontō no shisō no mochinushi*).⁵⁸ But, as we will see shortly, Imamura's own wartime writings inherited more of Nakai's conversion from socialism to Japanese totalitarianism than of a theoretical inquiry into the oxymoronic nature of the cinematic apparatus.

IMAMURA TAIHEI: DOCUMENTING THE WAR EFFORT

In the history of Japanese cinema, Imamura Taihei has been recognized as one of the nation's most preeminent film theorists. As early as 1938, when his first monograph *The Form of Film Art* (*Eiga geijutsu no keishiki*) was published, Imamura had already earned a reputation as someone who "has most beautifully proved the theoretical character of Japanese [film criticism]."⁵⁹ A similar assessment can also be found in Satō Tadao's *The History of Japanese Film Theory*: "In Japan, unfortunately, very few individuals can be called film theorists. Imamura Taihei ... is about the only person who has consistently worked as a film theorist, writing several theoretical books on film."⁶⁰ In fact, Imamura displayed an astonishingly prolific and systematic mode of writing in his early career. From 1938 to 1945 alone, he published ten monographs, including *The Form of Film Art*, *Film and Culture* (*Eiga to bunka*, 1940), *On Documentary Film* (*Kiroku eigaron*, 1940), *On Animated Film* (*Manga eigaron*, 1941), and *War and Film* (*Sensō to eiga*, 1942).⁶¹ Imamura's privileged presence in Japanese film history was also validated by international recognition for his work. For instance, his essay "Japanese Art and the Animated Cartoon" appeared in the September 1953 issue of *The Quarterly Review of Film, Radio, and Television*, making him one of the first Japanese theorists introduced to the West.⁶² As if to revitalize this long-forgotten encounter, North American scholars including Mark Driscol, Yuriko Furuhata, and Thomas Lamarre have recently written about Imamura's film theory.⁶³

Unlike the majority of Japanese intellectuals discussed throughout this book, Imamura was a self-taught critic with no special academic training. After leaving junior high school due to his father's unexpected death, he held a variety of jobs to make his living. While working at a postal insurance company, he first became involved in leftist activism through participating in the labor union movement. Imamura was arrested in 1932 on suspicion of being a sympathizer of the Japanese Communist Party, and it was during the time of his probation that he began watching films seriously. But because he was always a little short of money to spend for this activity, he chose to go to second- or third-rate theaters, where he could watch newsreels and animated films with a lower ticket price. This atypical exposure to film culture was decisive for Imamura because it was these two marginalized genres—animation and documentary—that constituted the central concerns of his film theory.

In 1935, he entered the world of film criticism by sending essays to the film magazine *Kinema junpō*. In this early period, Imamura set himself the task of "clarifying the reciprocal relationship between a certain form of society and a certain form of art," following Russian literary critic V. M. Friche's 1926 book *The Sociology of Art*.[64] Although his Marx-infused contributions were well received by both editors and readers of the magazine, Imamura needed more space to elaborate his thought on film culture at large. Thus, he soon launched his own magazine *Eiga shūdan* (*Film Collective*) with other non-professional contributors to *Kinema junpō* and members of college film societies in the Tokyo area. Like Tosaka's Yuiken and Nakai's *World Culture* group, Imamura and his *Film Collective* fellows organized a number of lectures, study groups, and roundtables. Though their collective activities also came under police scrutiny, the magazine survived until 1940 by changing its name to the less controversial *Eigakai* (*Film World*).

Like Tosaka and Nakai, Imamura aimed to single out film's properties and potentials, privileging certain genres and forms of expression unique to this medium. It is in this context that animation and documentary emerged as the most relevant genres, given their capacity to most effectively reveal how the very notion and practice of art could change according to cinema. For this reason, Imamura's theory of animation had less to do with its deviation from the laws of physical reality than with the mechanical aspects of its image production. At times he celebrated Disney and Max Fleischer's innovative use of rotoscoping, a technique in which animators trace over a live-action film frame by frame, as it substantially transformed the animated image from mere imagination to "a mechanical analysis of the secret of movement by the lens."[65] On the other hand, if one turns the same visual capacity of the camera to social phenomena, it then begins to serve as the basis for the attraction of documentary films. Drawing upon Tosaka's earlier essays on film's epistemological value, Imamura maintained that the greatest task of nonfiction genres is to encourage the viewer to know the social fabrication of the world. It is, he explains, through the act of direct observation of people, landscapes, languages, appearances, fashions, habits, and manners from all over the globe that we come to understand them. From these diverse contexts for film technique and epistemological value, Imamura defines film as "a form of art based on documentary and reportage."[66]

Another important factor for Imamura's investigation into the specificity of the film medium is its total negation of the individual mode of production and consumption. Having developed at the height of industrial capitalist production, cinema is undeniably "collectivist" in character, a view that Imamura borrowed from Nakai's earlier writings. According to Imamura, nowhere was this shift from individualism to collectivism more apparent than in the production of Hollywood's animated films. He wrote in 1939: "The impetus to animate pictures necessitated the division of labor at studios like Disney with over fifty artists. This marked the industrialization of art. Drawings now grow into a large-scale industrial collective project involving several hundred people."[67] At this point, however, the product remains a series of still frames composed of motionless images; it is the active participation of the viewers that animates these images for two reasons. First, the optical illusion of the continuous movement of the animated image can only emerge with the help of the bodily phenomenon known as the persistence of vision. Second, as long as these films are produced under the capitalist regime, it is also the viewers' persistent desire to consume new products that effectively keeps the industry moving forward. In this respect, what one calls "animated" films could never appear as the finished work of an individual artist as in the case of literature or painting. They exist as the product of continuous collaboration between the cinematic apparatus, a group of industrial personnel, and viewers.

What is striking in Imamura's film theory is that he extends the idea of collectivism to illuminate the potential of film as a means of mass communication. Anticipating the work of scholars like Benedict Anderson and Marshall McLuhan, Imamura argues that the main purpose of newspaper, radio, and film is to generate the sense of connectedness, through which people in the twentieth century are assured of their imagined belonging to their own times and communities. Thus, modern mass media take on particular importance when they circulate the latest news from all over the world. As Imamura writes, "In feudalistic societies consisting of small and dispersed self-contained communities, there was no need for these forms [of mass communication]. As individuals became integrated into an international division of labor, all forms of production became totally socialized, and we began to realize that we are always and invariably connected to the world."[68]

It is in this undeniably modern, twentieth-century mediascape that news films began to assume their importance in mediating between the masses and their everyday lives. For one, news films offered universally legible images of ongoing events beyond national and linguistic boundaries. However, Imamura's promotion of news film as a medium of mass communication was more radical and progressive. As if to reverse Benjamin's famous remark, "*Any person today can lay claim to being filmed,*" he dreamed of a world in which everyone became a producer of news film with the dissemination of small and portable movie cameras.[69] He explains this in his 1940 book *On Documentary Film*:

> When documentary film makes full-scale progress, everyone will carry a movie camera like a pen and keep records with film just as they do with writing. Of course, this means the individualization of cinema, but such individualization would never be possible without a far-reaching socialization of cinema. . . . Truly objective news films will be premised on this socialization of the camera. Increased manufacturing capacity will spread the cinematic apparatus more thoroughly than today's radio or still cameras. . . . As the [movie] camera becomes popularized, a multitude of people will shoot the same incident, inevitably adding more diversity and objectivity to its coverage. What is implied here is that we are no longer outside of news films; we are now participating in the production of the news.[70]

Beyond its unmistakable affinity with Alexandre Astruc's postwar concept of "caméra-stylo," this idea continues to resonate with our own electronically saturated landscape of cell phones, tablets, and other portable devices, all equipped with video cameras.[71] Yet just as our daily experience of mass media remains within the logic of late capitalism, it is necessary to uncover the historical dynamics and political implications at work in Imamura's assertion. On the one hand, Imamura's stance here seems very akin to the "do-it-yourself" spirit of the Prokino leader Sasa Genjū, who argued that small-gauge films could be a "weapon" to disseminate news by and for proletarian workers. On the other hand, it can also be read as an extension of Nakai's discussion of the future of documentary filmmaking, in which all films would be edited by the collective opinion of the committee. In either case, we should ask again: In what kind of society can this utopian vision of mass communication be possible? And who could hold sway over the multiple visions and voices informing the highly collaborative nature of film production? Imamura's answers for these questions became more and more problematic in parallel with the progress of Japan's war against China and the Allies.

AESTHETICIZATION OF THE DOCUMENTARY METHOD

At the beginning of his career, Imamura championed cinema's revelatory capacity, which he saw as able to expose some objective truths about reality regardless of the filmmaker's intention. "Despite its pursuit of commercial fiction," he wrote in 1936, "the cinematic expression [developed in Hollywood cinema] is the self-revelation of American culture."[72] However, as he witnessed the growing popularity of news films following Japan's military expansion in China and other parts of Asia, Imamura began to expect nonfiction films to become a more active agent in the creation of a new reality beyond its previous function as a passive mirror reflecting the logic of a modern capitalist society alone. Seen in this light, he wrote, Hollywood-made newsreels like Paramount News and Fox Movietone News were irrelevant and incompetent. While they gave the viewers a glimpse of the world in motion through their immediate coverage of the latest news, their random arrangement of historical events often ended up presenting a world full of ambiguity. As a method of overcoming such passivity in the nonfiction genre, Imamura suggested a more innovative use of montage, considering it the best film technique to put things in order, to support and promote the irreversible march of history in the making.

In Imamura's view, the term *montage* does not simply mean the editing process that takes place only after the shooting is done. It designates all kinds of subjective, aesthetic, and ideological interventions that filmmakers insert at any stage of their interpretation of given historical events. For this reason, Imamura likens the operation of montage with that of human cognition, thereby proposing an oft-cited dictum of his film theory: "To document is at once to recognize" (*kiroku suru koto wa dōji ni ninshiki suru koto demo aru*).[73] There is no doubt that Imamura came to this phrase under the influence of Tosaka's theorization of film as "a modern method of cognition." Indeed, in the above-mentioned book on documentary, he also emphasized the novelty of cinematic cognition by foregrounding the collaboration between human and nonhuman sensory apparatuses: "To document on film means to express only through film, to think through film."[74] But contrary to Tosaka, Imamura defines the epistemological value of cinema as contingent upon the cognitive activity of the filmmaker, and not that of the viewer. Instead of asking how cinema has changed the ways we the viewers see and think about the world, he transforms the film medium into an internal mirror that projects outward how filmmakers interpret reality through their sensory organs and intellectual faculties:

> The idea that something is already expressed in documentation makes everyone involved in the production of news films and documentaries more conscious and responsible. It is no longer possible to produce dull and thoughtless documentaries like the ones that make a carbon copy [of reality]. It is also wrong to assume that news films are always boring and conventional. They are by no means mere documents; they can fully express how the documentarist recognizes the situation. If we find differences in news films reporting the same incident, it is exactly because they express (document) the personality of each news filmmaker. . . . Documentary is not a mere document of the external world but must be a document and expression of human cognition.[75]

This passage tells us that the objective accuracy of the camera's mechanical gaze was no longer central to Imamura's concerns. Instead, it was replaced with the subjective authenticity of human cognition and interpretation. This move, for one, gets Imamura closer to the discourse of literary adaptation and scenario literature, which, as I have discussed in the previous chapter, also prioritized the filmmaker's subjective interpretation of reality by using written texts as a primary means of expression. It is, however, important to note that Imamura never dispensed with the idea that film can represent the object "as it is." He privileged the indexical quality of the photographic image because he saw it as constituting the foundation of realism at work in nonfiction genres. Nevertheless, he also shifted the object to be captured by the camera's objective gaze from the external world to the internal vision of the filmmaker so that documentary film can also become a distinct (idealist) form of art. "It is entirely possible," he writes, "that documentary as a record of facts transforms it into various artistic genres. This is not an expectation; it has already become reality."[76]

For Imamura, Leni Riefenstahl's 1938 film *Olympia* offered a prime example of his concept of aestheticized documentary film. Like many Japanese critics of the era, Imamura favorably received this famous Nazi propaganda. Yet his fascination came not so much from its overt ideological message as from its potential to be a model for his idea of collective filmmaking: "Although its entire progression is based on a real event, elements that constitute the film form an entirely new objectivity that no single subject has ever seen before, an objectivity achieved only through the collaboration of many subjectivities. To look at one event from a variety of perspectives like this is not yet available in other art forms. In integrating diverse observations culled from dozens of cameras, *Olympia* proves again the supremacy of cinema's cooperative vision over a solitary vision."[77] Imamura's statement here no longer presupposed the Hollywood model of the mass production of film. Instead, he was more enthralled by the possibility of perfecting cinematic collectivism outside the reach of modern capitalism. His earlier writings drew upon the socialist model of production developed in the Soviet Union. But he now discovered a promising alternative in Germany's national socialist model, which could be a more appropriate and achievable template for the reform of Japanese documentary films in conjunction with the country's own shift toward a totalitarian regime. In particular, Imamura applauded Nazi Germany's decision to nationalize all the sectors in its domestic film industry: "Nationalized and socialized with no concerns for profit making, documentary could surpass today's fiction films.... This is what we learned from the particular attraction of *Olympia*."[78]

When Imamura wrote this review, the Japanese government was making a steady move toward the state control of the domestic film industry with the implementation of the 1939 Film Law. Unlike in Germany, however, Japanese film companies were not entirely nationalized, although from 1941 onward the government forced the industry to consolidate ten feature film companies into three, more than two hundred news and short film companies into four, and a dozen distributors into one. Put in this context, Imamura's admiration of *Olympia* serves as evidence of his confirmation of the official discourse and film policies of the wartime government. In Imamura's mind, there was virtually no contradiction between his support of total mobilization for the war effort and his seemingly progressive assertion that every member in society should become a *prosumer* of news films.

This is how Imamura survived the war without losing his idea of cinematic collectivism. Furthermore, he was even able to promote himself as one of the most reliable commentators on the increased attentions and importance given to nonfiction genres under the wartime regime. This conversion from a left-wing activist to a right-wing nationalist, from a critical observer to an ardent supporter of Japan's military aggression, was made so seamlessly that Imamura himself might have failed to recognize its decisive impact on his film theory. But if we look carefully at his writings published after Japan's sudden attack on Pearl Harbor in December 1941, we can clearly detect and discern a critical shift occurring in his writings. In fact, what we see there is one of the most disturbing examples of how fiction and nonfiction became integrated in the making of Japanese propaganda films.

INTEGRATION OF FICTION AND NONFICTION

Imamura's 1942 monograph *War and Cinema* suggests the integration of fictional elements into the realm of nonfiction films as a necessary step for the reform of domestic film practice. As Nornes points out, Imamura had, in some way or another, intended to "bring fiction and documentary into increasingly close contact" from the beginning of his career.[79] While his earlier writing was largely motivated to subvert the conventional hierarchy between fiction and nonfiction genres by highlighting cinema's own distinctive representational properties, in this period Imamura enlisted the use of fictional elements in nonfiction in support of the construction of the Greater East Asian Co-Prosperity Sphere, which went into full swing after Pearl Harbor. At this point, the neglected metaphor of the "film as a mirror" seemed to make a comeback with a vengeance: rather than mystifying the counterfeit idea of liberating non-Western countries from the hands of Western colonizers, it now clearly reflected the sinister face of Japan invading Asia and beyond for its own survival.

Imamura argues that the most urgent task of producers of nonfiction films after Pearl Harbor is to visualize the irreversible progress of world history from the Japanese perspective. However, Imamura is totally dissatisfied with the current status of domestic news films because they often produce monotonous and unimaginative recordings of important historical events for the immediacy of their coverage. He thus suggests a radical transformation of the task and meaning of news films. Imamura's conviction is that any news films produced from this moment on must remain inspiring sources of aesthetic contemplation even after they lose their initial news values. And in order for news films to attain such an enduring status, "[they] must present those singular and precious moments as more real than reality, more compelling than hundreds of spoken words."[80]

Imamura's suggestion here stems directly from his viewing of a news film covering the Fall of Singapore in February 1942. Due to the shortage of portable sound equipment, the film was shot silent and missed the opportunity to record in full the moment in which the British lietenant-general Arthur Percival officially declared, "I surrender." Imamura ascribes this "misfortune" to the limited budget and lack of attention to the aesthetics of news film production. Considering the increasing importance of news films, he goes on to demand the abolition of any distinctions between news and fiction films: "Thinking this way, we find no necessity to distinguish news film from fiction film. In covering all kinds of incidents, news film can also observe a variety of people and depict their human feelings. From this perspective, we demand that news film should be made under the same condition as fiction film. If we make news film using the same camera, microphone, lighting, and, most importantly, well-planned découpage as fiction film, it will be possible to elevate these documents of facts to the level of art."[81] For Imamura, the improvement of the aesthetic quality of news and other nonfiction genres is contingent upon the incorporation of basic techniques in the making of fiction films including editing, mise-en-scène, synchronized sound, variable shot sizes and durations, changes in angles, and, if necessary, detailed storyboards prepared in advance. This was obviously a violation of the autonomy of nonfiction genres that had long informed Imamura's film theory. What, then, drove him to make such a radical concession to fiction or narrative cinema?

Briefly stated, the main impetus behind Imamura's proposal was the pressing need to export Japanese cinema to the newly occupied areas in Southeast Asia, including Hong Kong, Singapore, Burma, Malaysia, Indonesia, and the Philippines. Historically, people in these areas had been familiar with Hollywood films. Yet as the emperor's army marched into their territories, the Japanese film industry began to make enormous efforts to expand its sphere of influence, aiming to replace Hollywood's domination with its own. In the meantime, both Japanese film critics and government authorities engaged in ongoing debates about the successful export of Japanese film products, which never came to fruition until the 1950s. Imamura participated in this debate in his capacity as a nonfiction film expert. For instance, he strongly believed that the mechanical reproducibility and universal legibility of the filmic image could be the best means to "enlighten" a vast population now enclosed within the expanded territory of the Japanese Empire. But he also warned that current Japanese news films were conceived as visual illustrations of the news already covered and circulated in print and would not be able to gain significant international appeal. Imamura thus stressed the need to enhance the efficiency of visual storytelling and suggested adopting fiction films' conventions.

Moreover, he added that politicians, military officers, or anyone who made frequent appearances on these news films should be more conscious of how they look on screen, noting how Hitler and Stalin succeeded in creating their public persona on film.[82] For Imamura, reality must be constructed like a film, and accordingly, people must behave like film actors in Japanese nonfiction films to achieve significant international success.

Imamura's suggestion for using fictional elements in nonfiction films was in parallel with the increasing influx of documentary elements into the realm of fiction film. A series of Japanese war films from this period, including *Five Scouts* (*Gonin no sekkōhei*, dir. Tasaka Tomotaka, 1938), *Naval Brigade at Shanghai* (*Shanhai rikusentai*, dir. Kumagai Hisatora, 1939), *Legend of Tank Commander Nishizumi* (*Nishizumi senshachō den*, dir. Yoshimura Kōzaburō, 1940), *Flaming Sky* (*Moyuru ōzora*, dir. Abe Yutaka, 1940), and *The War at Sea from Hawai'i to Malaya* (*Hawai Marē oki kaisen*, dir. Yamamoto Kajirō, 1942), made extensive use of both pre- and post-filmic conventions borrowed from documentary filmmaking. These conventions include location shooting, handheld camera techniques, long shots, long takes, non-professional actors, non-Japanese extras, and the use of voiceover narration.

This sweeping shift in film style was equally evident in films dealing with the everyday life on the home front. In talking about *Spring on Leper's Island* (*Kojima no haru*, dir. Toyoda Shirō, 1940), which was based on a real story of a female doctor who dedicated her life to the treatment of quarantined leprosy patients, the critic Aikawa Haruki remarked, "This film was born out of the impasse of fiction filmmaking. The poverty of fiction film directly leads to the poverty of theater, as they both are grounded on the naivete of everyday life as inseparable from the trivial decadence of theatrical realism. However, the film skillfully redeemed its fundamental shortcomings as a fiction film by foregrounding its documentary aspects. This was a risky enterprise, and many of us witnessed the severe confrontation between fictional and nonfictional elements."[83] Aikawa did not praise *Spring on Leper's Island* as a success. Rather, he took it as evidence of the final victory of nonfiction over fiction as the dominant genre of Japanese filmmaking at large. In the end, Aikawa also found it more effective to work in the confluence of fiction and nonfiction from the latter's perspective, suggesting the need to categorize such fictionalized nonfiction films under the all-encompassing term *bunka eiga*.[84]

The confluence of fiction and nonfiction film in early 1940s Japan was not restricted to matters of film style or genre. More than anything, it constituted an ethical problem. I am not simply referring to the phenomenon of the so-called fake or reenacted documentary films, which had been practiced since the days of the Russo-Japanese War. Instead, I am speaking of a Japanese war film that even crossed a final taboo in fiction filmmaking—that is, killing people in front of the camera to enhance its reality effect. The film in question here is *General, Staff, and Soldiers* (*Shōgun to sanbō to hei*, dir. Taguchi Satoshi, 1942). The director Taguchi

FIGURE 9. Chinese soldiers running away from a merciless bombardment in Taguchi Satoshi's *General, Staff, and Soldier* (courtesy of the Kawakita Memorial Film Institute).

and his crew members were allowed not only to follow a Japanese army brigade deployed in China's Shaanxi Province, but also to use Chinese prisoners of war as extras.[85] The climax of the film comes in a twenty-minute segment filled with discharges of artillery fire and explosives. The spectacle of the battle looks so real because Japanese soldiers mercilessly bombarded a Chinese fortress with its soldiers still inside and then killed a crowd of unarmed Chinese soldiers running from their attacks (figure 9).

The viewer might assume that the scene was composed entirely of footage taken from actual military actions on the battlefield, given the excess of nonfictional elements. However, it seems likely that Taguchi set up the scene using Chinese POWs and turned them into living targets to be shot to death before the camera's objective gaze. There is no historical document that can prove this speculation, but Imamura himself referred to two more Japanese fiction films—*War Comrade's Song* (*Senyū no uta*, dir. Richard Angst, 1939) and *Yangtze River Fleet* (*Yōsukō kantai*, dir. Kimura Sotoji, 1938)—that used Chinese POWs as extras without questioning the ethical basis of this disturbing practice. If these films actually killed Chinese POWs for the sake of a higher realism in Japanese war propaganda, I argue, it is imperative to investigate wartime Japanese discourse on cinematic realism for complicity in Japan's war crimes, including the unethical human experiments perpetrated by Unit 731 that resulted in the unforgivable death of thousands of Chinese people.

In his 1977 book *A Contemporary History of Japanese Cinema* (*Nihon eiga gendaishi*), the film historian Fujita Motohiko harshly criticizes the confluence of fiction and nonfiction elements in Japanese wartime film practice by calling it "the process by which documentary techniques and methods became integrated into the structure of the political system as such." And at the end of this process, he continues, there was nothing but "the total collapse of Japanese cinema."[86] Fujita's poignant criticism impels us to critically reflect upon the complex, and often disturbing, relationship between theory and history in the Japanese context. At first, Imamura's film theory appeared as an emancipation of the collective mode of documentary filmmaking, but it soon and seamlessly transformed into a discursive tool for both supporting and justifying Japan's military aggression and the concomitant construction of the Greater East Asia Co-Prosperity Sphere. Given its adherence to the political reality of the given historical moment, film theory in Japan cannot be interrogated fully as a transcendental and ahistorical search for some universal truths about the film medium and its related phenomena. As Tosaka reminded us with his theory of social epistemology, the meaning and value of modern cultural products are always imbricated in a web of social discourse and practices. It is thus our responsibility to both carefully historicize the theoretical texts in question and inventively theorize our own approach to history as such.

5

Neglected Traditions of Bergsonism and Phenomenology

THEORIZING CINEMA THROUGH EXPERIENCE

In 1938, the Japanese government promulgated the National Mobilization Law (*kokka sōdōin hō*) in an attempt to transform the country into a more genuine totalitarian state. The law not only made it easier to mobilize both natural and personal resources for the war effort but also stimulated the forced consolidation or nationalization of strategic and other domestic industries beyond the capitalist logic of the market economy. The film industry soon followed this directive with the enforcement of the 1939 Film Law and the subsequent mergers of production companies and distributors. To understand how this top-down social restructuring impacted wartime Japanese film theory, however, we should also look at a similar shift occurring in the publishing industry. In 1940, the Cabinet Intelligence Bureau (naikaku jōhōkyoku) established the Japanese Cultural Publication Association (Nippon shuppan bunka kyōkai) which regulated the official distribution of printing paper; in the year to follow, 240 domestic paper distributors were merged into the single state-owned company named the Japan Paper Distributing Company (Nippon shuppan haikyū gaisha). From then on, all publishers in Japan had to go through the two-step process of inspection, since the association was given the power to approve the publication of the submitted manuscripts in addition to normal press censorship. The advent of such assertive state intervention inevitably led to the suspension and discontinuation of many local film magazines by the early 1940s. Consequently, writing about film under these circumstances became limited mainly to an address to the contingencies of war propaganda and mass mobilization, as manifested in the writings of Tsumura Hideo and Imamura Taihei.[1]

However, the period around 1940 also saw the emergence of an alternative mode of film writing, which may be called the last stand of Japanese film theory before 1945. This approach was best represented by Sugiyama Heiichi (1914–2012) and Nagae Michitarō (1905–1984), who were both poets and film critics throughout their careers. Sugiyama and Nagae published their monographs, *Essays on Film* (*Eiga hyōronshū*) and *Cinema, Expression, Formation* (*Eiga, hyōgen, keisei*), on the eve of and after Japan's attack on Pearl Harbor.[2] Nonetheless, their writings did not refer to the ongoing war or the Japanese government's increasing intervention in film practice. Rather than taking an overtly political approach, both Sugiyama and Nagae addressed cinema as an object for philosophical investigation. More specifically, they discussed film and its particular form of realism by reflecting upon their experience of moving images and recorded sounds as sensible and temporary phenomena. In other words, these two theorists focused on the role of the viewers as the synthesis of the oppositions between subject and object, essence and existence, mind and body, expression and perception, and the human and nonhuman gaze.

The viewing experience has become a significant theoretical topic in recent film and media studies, especially in relation to a surge of fan and reception studies. Its rhizomatic expansions in new forms of commodified spectacle and play, even as forms of intentional misinterpretation, have since given way to studies of fandom and participatory culture. Nevertheless, I contend that there is also an underlying philosophical context shared by these seemingly very different approaches to the film experience. Whereas Sugiyama drew on the work of Henri Bergson, Nagae used phenomenology as his theoretical framework. Their informed adoption of Western philosophical strands also permits us to consider yet another historical inflection to the question of "what is cinema?" in the discursive context of wartime Japan.

The return to Bergson in film theory owes much to Gilles Deleuze's two-volume *Cinema 1* and *2*. In *Creative Evolution*, Bergson famously argued that movement occurs only in a concrete duration that is both indivisible and untranslatable to the space covered. He then used the phrase *cinematic illusion* to refer to the false or imaginary reconstruction of movement by "immobile sections + abstract time."[3] This argument, says Deleuze, is rather odd for two reasons. First, what we as viewers perceive in and through film are not photograms—sixteen to twenty-four immobile images captured on the filmstrip—but "movement-images" that are in themselves as mobile as they appear on the screen. Second, Bergson himself had already described the movement-image in *Matter and Memory*, published ten years prior to *Creative Evolution*. But if this aspect disappeared in later commentary on the medium, it was because films produced around 1906 had not yet stabilized as an intuitional form, and lacked basic techniques such as "montage, the mobile camera and the emancipation of the viewpoints" that made the shot not only a "spatial category" but a "temporal one." Thus, as Deleuze maintains, it is possible to say that "cinema would rediscover that very movement-image of the first chapter of *Matter and Memory*" in its own historical self-transformation.[4]

Deleuze's reapplication of Bergson to film theory has been significant. However, there were much earlier adoptions of Bergsonian themes in the history of French film criticism. Jean Epstein, for instance, corrected Bergson's misrecognition of cinema as a false reconstruction of movement in *The Intelligence of the Machine* (*L'intelligence d'une machine*) by revisiting Zeno's paradox of the arrow. As Epstein explains, "the cinematograph seems to be a mysterious mechanism intended to assess the false accuracy of Zeno's famous argument about the arrow, intended for the analysis of the subtle metamorphosis of stasis into mobility, of emptiness into solid, of continuous into discontinuous, a transformation as stupefying as the generation of life from inanimate elements." In cinema, he continued, "the discontinuity becomes continuity only after it has made its way in the [mind of the] spectator."[5] In 1956, André Bazin also wrote an essay entitled "A Bergsonian Film: *The Picasso Mystery*" and discussed how the presentation of Picasso's drawing process succeeded in revealing "the painting itself, in other words, a work that exists in time, that has its own duration, its own life, and sometimes—as at the end of the film—a death that precedes the extinction of the artist."[6] Born four years before Bazin, Sugiyama belonged to a generation of Japanese intellectuals who sought to specify the film experience through Bergson's philosophical legacy. Sugiyama's wartime film writing, therefore, stood aligned with the theoretical approach of his French counterparts.

As Dudley Andrew reminds us, there has also been a long tradition of phenomenology in French film theory, beginning in the immediate postwar period with the work of Bazin, Henri Agel, Amedee Ayfre, Maurice Merleau-Ponty, and those associated with Gilbert Cohen-Séat's *Revue internationale de filmologie* (1947–1960).[7] In the meantime, Vivian Sobchack's 1992 monograph *The Address of the Eye: A Phenomenology of Film Experience* made a decisive contribution to the revival of phenomenology in recent Anglo-American film studies.[8] Drawing on Merleau-Ponty's existential phenomenology, Sobchack illuminates the potential of this philosophical branch as a countercurrent with film theory, one that no longer reduces actual works of cinema to their material condition or ideological surroundings. Schematically divided into formalist (idealist) and realist (materialist) traditions, classical film theory tended to presuppose a binary opposition that "has argumentatively and analytically severed expression from perception in its inquiries into the 'true nature' or ontology of the cinema."[9] The formalists, she argued, have defined film as a medium of "expression" by foregrounding the artist's creative ability to frame the world according to an internal vision. The realists are then described as having defined film as a medium of "perception" by privileging the camera's mechanical ability to reflect the world without losing its unknowability. By contrast, the phenomenologists foreground the act of viewing, their own experience of the filmed world as it is lived on and through the screen. The primary task of phenomenological film theory is therefore "to describe the origin, locus, and existential significance of cinematic vision and the film experience."[10] It is through this process of self-reflection that Sobchack asserts cinema to be "an expression of experience by experience."[11]

Nagae's purchase on what one would call a phenomenological film theory derived from a very different historical path, although his approach itself resonates much with Sobchack's theorization of the film experience. Nagae's monograph predates Merleau-Ponty's *Phenomenology of Perception* (1945), and Nagae himself never used the term *phenomenology* (*genshōgaku*) in his own writing. Does this mean that my use of *phenomenology* here is a mere working hypothesis? I hope this is not the case. Indeed, Nagae developed his film theory under the strong influence of the Japanese philosopher Nishida Kitarō. Nishida is remembered today as the founder of the Kyoto School. Although Nishida himself did not travel abroad in his lifetime, members of the school, composed of his colleagues and students at Kyoto University, frequently visited Germany beginning in the 1920s and closely studied with Edmund Husserl and Martin Heidegger. Just as Merleau-Ponty's work came under the influence of the work of these German phenomenologists, Nishida's work also incorporated Husserl's critical vocabularies into his larger system of thought.

In the Japanese context, Nishida was often criticized by Tosaka Jun and other Marxist critics as a *transcendental* phenomenologist for his "hermeneutic, transhistorical, formalist, and romanticist" treatment of philosophical categories.[12] At first glance, Nagae's film theory might appear as similarly transhistorical and apolitical. Nevertheless, Nagae's seemingly detached, transcendental gesture came to attain a very political connotation within the register of "anti-politics," especially when all local film criticism was subject to the conspiracy of the war machine. Therefore, my use of the term *genshōgaku* as an appropriation of *phenomenology* becomes very apt to describe the philosophical and political nature of Nagae's film writing. Both Sugiyma and Nagae's theoretical writings, however, require careful contextualization within the history of modern Japanese philosophy, which developed almost simultaneously with the history of Japanese film theory.

ANTI-DUALISM IN MODERN JAPANESE PHILOSOPHY

Although there was a long lineage of intellectual traditions informed by Buddhism, Confucianism, and Shinto or Nativist (*kokugaku*) schools, it was after the Meiji Restoration that philosophy as a distinct mode of thinking and academic discipline began to take root in Japan. Indeed, the Japanese term for philosophy, *tetsugaku* (meaning the "study of wisdom"), did not exist until 1877, when the enlightenment scholar Nishi Aamane (1829–1897) coined that neologism along with a series of Japanese words for concepts newly imported from the West. Thus, "learning to philosophize meant learning a foreign idiom" in this formative period, as editors of *Japanese Philosophy: A Source Book* point out.[13] In fact, the first professors of philosophy in Japan, including Ludwig Busse (1862–1907), Raphael von

Koeber (1848–1923), and Ernest Fenollosa (1853–1908), were all visiting from abroad and teaching their courses in German or English at the University of Tokyo, established in 1877. Their contributions were indispensable in introducing philosophy as "the universal science" that aims to give "a comprehensive and satisfactory view of the Essence and Significance of all Reality."[14] But their own presence and mediations inevitably gave students the impression that philosophy is an exclusive domain of the Greco-Roman tradition.

Despite—or rather because of—this initial exposure, the first generation of modern Japanese philosophers tended to test the virtues and limitations of Western philosophy by applying it to traditional Japanese and Eastern systems of thought. In 1886, Inoue Enryō (1858–1919), a reformer of Pure Land Buddhism and the very first student majoring in philosophy at the University of Tokyo, argued that philosophy differs from natural science (*rigaku*) in that where the latter deals only with "material things," the former studies "the formless matters of mind" and thereby "inquires into the axioms of truth and the foundations of the [different kinds of] disciplines."[15] With this relatively simple definition of philosophy in mind, Enryō contended that Buddhist scriptures should be best understood in light of (Western) philosophical inquiries, given their metaphysical search for the underlying truths of the world and human destinies. "Inasmuch as Kant and Hegel believed their theories represented eternal and unchanging truth," as he writes, "their position does not differ at all from faith in religion. . . . Buddhism's connection to both philosophy and religion are especially close. Indeed, the link Buddhism has with philosophy has no parallel as yet among the many other religions."[16]

Similarly, Inoue Tetsujirō (1855–1944), the first Japanese professor of philosophy at the University of Tokyo, shed light on Buddhism to claim the existence of a uniquely Eastern philosophical tradition. But Tetsujirō's main focus was more about clarifying the limitations of Western philosophy since Descartes and Kant, and of the split between subject and object, mind and body, idea and matter. In an essay published in 1894, Tetsujirō defined his philosophical perspective as based on what he calls the "phenomena-as-reality theory" (*genshō soku jitsuzairon*). This theory was conceived as a negative dialectic of idealism and materialism. It accepts the existence of an objective world as distinct and independent of subjective sensory perceptions, and yet it encompasses phenomena that have no material existence, such as space, time, and causality. He then proceeded to claim that "although it is possible to distinguish phenomena from reality on a theoretical level, the two are, in fact, inseparable and of the same substance, a unity in duality."[17] Unlike Enryō, Tetsujirō also criticized Indian philosophical traditions, including the Upanishads and the Vedānta, as idealist. But it is still possible to read his phenomena-as-reality theory as a purposeful retelling of the basic Buddhist doctrine known as *shiki soku zekū*, usually translated as "a form is emptiness" or "matter is void," which explains the fundamental unity of the two opposing positions.

It is no exaggeration to say that both Enryō and Tetsujirō established the future direction and development of modern Japanese philosophy. Their attempts at reconciling the East-West and subject-object divides constituted the central concern of anyone involved with this intellectual venture in the first half of the twentieth century. But as many scholars have pointed out, their writings did little more than acknowledge the coexistence of two differing positions, without fully deconstructing or integrating these dichotomies. This challenge was passed on to the second generation of Japanese philosophers, of which Nishida Kitarō (1870–1945) was the most original and influential contributor.

Nishida was born in 1870 and studied philosophy as a credited auditor at Tokyo University. In 1911, Nishida published his first major work, *An Inquiry into the Good* (*Zen no kenkyū*), just after he had secured his tenure as a philosophy professor at Kyoto University.[18] In this book, Nishida aimed to elucidate the spiritual or religious awakening he had experienced in his earlier life through the discursive framework of Western philosophy. He thus paid special attention to the existence of a pure or direct state of experience that transcends the divisions of subject and object, mind and body, perception and expression. Today, *An Inquiry into the Good* is widely celebrated as "the first true work of Japanese philosophy" and remains Nishida's most famous work.[19] But this does not mean that this work succeeded in solving the problem first proposed by Enryō and Testujirō. Rather, it only marked the beginning of Nishida's lifelong commitment to developing his own philosophy of the "self-identity of absolute contradiction" (*zettai mujunteki jikodōitsu*). It is a position that rejects any form of dualism in the search for a universal account of totality in the world and its self-transformation. Indeed, Nishida's maturation as a philosopher came at a late stage in his career, especially after he retired from teaching in 1928 at the age of fifty-eight. In the last ten years of his life, Nishida solidified his continuous struggle against dualistic thinking by employing a series of self-contradictory expressions including "active intuition" (*kōiteki chokkan*), "the continuity of discontinuity" (*hi-renzoku no renzoku*), "interior qua exterior" (*uchi soku soto*), "inverse correlation" (*gyaku taiō*), and "the eternal present" (*eien no ima*).

In the meantime, *An Inquiry into the Good* also marked a shift in the way Japanese philosophers dealt with their Western counterparts. No longer a simple application of already established foreign idioms imported into the Japanese school of thought, this book intended to have a more active and reciprocal conversation with contemporary philosophers from Europe and North America. It is said that Nishida set up his inquiry into the primordial state of experience through his discovery of William James's concept of "pure experience" and Bergson's concept of "intuition." But what Nishida found most valuable in his encounter with these two philosophers was less the universality of their concepts than the contemporaneity of their mutual attempts at overcoming conventional dichotomies. In a series of public lectures given from 1906 to 1907, James presented his theory of pragmatism as a reconciliation of rationalist (idealist) and empiricist (materialist) temperaments.[20] Likewise, by and around that time Bergson had designated the goal of his philosophical endeavor to be the achievement of "a true metaphysics" by way of "a true empiricism."[21] But precisely because Nishida appreciated both James and Bergson for their intentions and not for their methods, he soon began criticizing their penchant toward psychologism. As a consequence, he radically shifted his focus from the particularity of a subjective experience to the universality of the environment or context that makes all kinds of subject-object relations possible. Nishida called this new perspective "the logic of place" (*basho no ronri*).

Throughout the 1910s, modern Japanese philosophy was dominated by neo-Kantianism. But the situation became completely altered during the interwar period, when a group of scholars who later became affiliated with the Kyoto School of Philosophy—Tanabe Hajime (1885–1962), Watsuji Tetsurō (1889–1960), Mutai Risaku (1890–1974), Miki Kiyoshi (1897–1945), Nishitani Keiji (1900–1990), and so on—visited Germany and studied closely with Edmund Husserl, Martin Heidegger, and other leading German phenomenologists.

For instance, Tanabe spent two years (1922–23) as a government-sponsored scholar studying first at the University of Berlin and then the University of Freiberg. At Freiberg, Tanabe was under the tutelage of Husserl and Heidegger, with the latter serving as his personal tutor. Upon his return to Japan, Tanabe immediately wrote articles disclosing what he had learned in Germany. Most notably, in 1924, he published one of the earliest introductions to Heidegger, an essay titled "A New Turn in Phenomenology: Heidegger's Phenomenology of Life" ("Genshōgaku ni okeru atrashiki tenkō: Haidegā no sei no genshōgaku"), three years prior to the publication of *Being and Time*.[22] For Tanabe, the problem with neo-Kantianism rested in its futile pursuit of lifeless and formalistic abstractions detached from actual life and experience. He then discovered Heidegger's phenomenology as a promising academic doctrine that could bring philosophy back to "the things themselves." But Tanabe was cautious enough to distinguish Heidegger's "existentialist" standpoint from Husserl's "transcendental" one, arguing that phenomenological inquiry should be more meaningful when it stops bracketing its analysis from questions about the actual existence of the external world and instead intends to directly apprehend "reality as such" (*genjitsu sono mono*) through the examination of *Dasein*, or "being-in-the-world."[23] This remark contributed to sustaining the popularity of Heidegger among Japanese intellectuals. Nevertheless, it did not limit their interest in adopting Husserl's methodological rigor. In fact, the number of Japanese students taking his courses at Freiberg was so large and consistent that Husserl was quoted as saying: "In this world, Japan is the second country after Germany to bring about the prosperity of phenomenology."[24]

Another, and perhaps the most notable, figure in this direct liaison was Kuki Shūzō (1888–1941), one of Tanabe's colleagues at Kyoto University. Kuki stayed in

Europe for more than seven years (1922–1929) and both attended and gave lectures at Heidelberg, Freiberg, Marburg, and the University of Paris. During his extended stay, Kuki became acquainted with Bergson, Heidegger, Husserl, and the young Jean-Paul Sartre, the last of whom served as his private tutor.[25] Although Kuki wrote a very detailed annotation of Heidegger's *Being and Time* in a book titled *Existentialist Philosophy (Jitsuzon no tetsugaku)*, his sympathy with Heidegger stemmed more from the latter's attempt to combine phenomenology with hermeneutics.[26] While in Europe, Kuki was often asked to explain the essence of Japanese cultural traditions. Conceived as a response to that enquiry, his monograph *The Structure of "Iki" (Iki no kōzō)*, published in 1930, offers a hermeneutic interpretation of particular aesthetic sensibilities widely shared by townspeople of Edo Japan.[27]

But for the purpose of this chapter, Kuki's significance lies more in his expedient summary of Japan's particular engagement with major trends in modern Western philosophy. In his article "Bergson au Japon," which was originally presented in French, Kuki argues that the era of neo-Kantianism in Japan started to fade away not in the early 1920s but already in 1910, when the first Japanese translations of Bergson's major works became available. Among other things, Bergson taught Japanese philosophy students that "to philosophize means to place oneself, through an effort of intuition, right in the center of concrete reality."[28] Needless to say, what Bergson meant by "reality" was restricted to an inner, subjective reality that could be seized only from within, in the mind of perceptive philosophers. And yet Bergson's effort to reinstate the authenticity of one's lived experience as a concrete object of self-reflexive descriptions inevitably placed him as a forerunner of phenomenology. Or to put it in Kuki's own words, "In any case, we in Japan had been led from neo-Kantianism to 'phenomenology' by way of Bergsonian philosophy."[29] Given this firsthand account, it can be said that at least in Japanese critical discourse, Bergson and phenomenologists were seen as forming a coalition against the traditional split of things into subject and object *in parallel with* Nishida's ongoing refinement of his own philosophy. If Nishida's popularity seemed to surpass those of his Western counterparts after 1935, it was precisely because many local readers came to believe that by that time Nishida had finally succeeded in elaborating a more compelling account of the issues in question.

Recently, Naoki Sakai has argued that we have to detach ourselves from a dualistic thinking when addressing the work of Nishida and other contributors to modern Japanese philosophy: "*As far as the internal formation of its disciplinarity is concerned, the dichotomy of the West and the Rest or Asia is utterly irrelevant to the comprehension, apprehension or critical evaluation of Japanese philosophy in general and of Kyoto School philosophy in particular.*"[30] Sakai offers this remark in part because the domestic evaluations of Kyoto School philosophy, especially those made by postwar commentators, have advocated the alleged "Japanese" origins of the school, stressing its members' personal ties with or training in Asian intellectual traditions and Oriental religion. But a more profound reason is that Nishida and his colleagues shared the idea of philosophy as a discipline dedicated to the production of universal knowledge, consciously internalizing the discursive and geopolitical superiority of the West as the source for their own intellectual activities. This situation, for one, requires us to read the Kyoto School philosophy as a legitimate branch of modern *Western* philosophy. Ultimately it presents us with "the project of changing and creating a means of knowing about humanity and the world" under the rule of capitalism.[31] Yet, it also compels us to consider how adherence to universality in the name of philosophical discourse was appropriated in the political sphere of wartime Japan. Indeed, Nishida's lifelong attempt at elaborating a universal account of the self-identity of absolute contradiction served as a philosophical justification of Japan's militaristic process of becoming the sole colonial power in the non-West.

While the complicity of philosophical themes with the discourse of totalitarianism has been part of an ongoing debate, I would like to directly relate it to the history of Japanese film theory. As we have seen in chapter 1, Gonda's theorization of the cinematic intuition in 1914 was based on the philosophical inquiries of James and Bergson, as in Nishida's *An Inquiry into the Good*. Then, in 1941, Sugiyama's *Essays on Film* appeared as an updated application of Bergson's concept of intuition to the Japanese theoretical debate on cinematic realism after the introduction of sound. Meanwhile, Nagae's *Cinema, Expression, Formation* appeared in the following year to testify to the growing popularity of Nishida's philosophy among Japanese intellectuals from the mid-1930s on. Indeed, the two special terms used in the title of Nagae's book, *expression* (*hyogen*) and *formation* (*keisei*), were borrowed directly from Nishida's own terminology, and they also appeared in works such as Mutai Risaku's *The Logic of Expression* (*Hyōgen no ronri*, 1938) and Kimura Motomori's *Formative Self-Awareness* (*Keiseiteki jikaku*, 1941).[32] Tracking these intriguing but largely neglected interactions between philosophy and film theory in wartime Japan inevitably impel us to reconsider the historical reality of wartime Japan from a different perspective.

SUGIYAMA HEIICHI: A BAZINIAN BEFORE BAZIN

Throughout his life, Sugiyama maintained his reputation as a reputable poet and film critic for whom these idioms of writing were closely aligned. As a poet, Sugiyama belonged to the Four Seasons School (*Shikiha*) founded in the early 1930s by the poets Miyoshi Tatsuji and Hori Tatsuo. His first poetry collection, *A Night Student* (*Yagakusei*), published in 1943, was awarded the Bungei Hanron poetry prize the following year.[33] As a film critic, Sugiyama started his career in 1934 by contributing reviews to *Kinema junpō*, while still a student of aesthetics at Tokyo University.[34] In 1935, Sugiyama became a founding member of Imamura's *Film Collective* group. Thereafter, Sugiyama became a close friend of Imamura, and in 1990 he wrote Imamura's posthumous biography in commemoration of their lifelong friendship. That said, their theoretical approaches to cinema and realism were markedly different. Whereas Imamura praised the factuality of the photographic image as a means of transforming the actual political condition, Sugiyama saw film as a concrete expression of the world itself, an expression that gently invites us to experience its representational events through our senses.

When Sugiyama began publishing in the mid-1930s, Japanese film criticism was rife with countless discussions about the popularity of literary adaptation in sound filmmaking. Having a dual interest in film and poetry, he soon joined the debate, though his motivation was to criticize the hasty integration of these two distinct forms of expression by contrasting the perceptual differences between viewing and reading. For Sugiyama, film and literature share the same task of delivering stories and abstract ideas, but they also require completely different modes of reception. The pleasure of reading a novel, he said, comes from the fact that it gradually discloses situations that the author has already conceived in advance, thus imposing a form of anticipation in the mind of the reader. In watching a film, on the contrary, the viewer is immersed in a concrete reality displayed on the screen, and only retrospectively can reflect upon the original intent of the author. Given the abundance of signification in the projection of the moving image, its richness and ambiguity often overcome what is described or inferred through the written text. As Sugiyama writes, "Film viewers not only participate in the creation of the author's spiritual life but also live their own [lives]."[35] With this observation, Sugiyama moves to criticize the advocates of literary adaptation and scenario literature. "Interestingly," he says, "these people are speaking only about written scripts; they never look at what appears on screen."[36] He then sarcastically concludes: "If there exist film producers who want to make a great literary film using the same method they have already developed, I could only recommend that they film the [original] book page by page."[37]

Similarly, Sugiyama attacked those who spoke of cinematic realism by resorting to ready-made definitions of realism first developed in literature. Here, again, Sugiyama makes a handy comparison between literature as a language-based medium and film as an image-based medium, foregrounding their conflicting registers of perception. In both cases, the primary task of realism is to reproduce the world as faithfully as possible. The difference lies in the ways in which both literature and film achieve their own reality effects. While literature composes credible characters and episodes through the writer's imagination and life experience, film projects a "mechanically accurate reflection of reality" (*kikaiteki ni seikaku na genjitsusei no han'ei*) that precedes the creative intervention of the film author.[38] Sugiyama argues that in making a film, too, filmmakers should use written scripts as a blueprint of the world they intend to depict. However, once the shooting process begins, they must negotiate with the actual presence of the external world that always speaks back to their imaginary conceptions of reality.

At first glance, this remark on film as a medium for mechanical reproduction might seem ordinary and unimaginative. But Sugiyama was considerably different from his contemporaries in that he inquired into the psychological effects that both the moving image and recorded sound imposed on the viewer's mind. To explain the specificity of this psychological effect, Sugiyama employed the term "atmosphere" (*fun'iki*). In his account, the principal purpose of filmmaking is the construction of "an atmosphere that is grounded on our sensory perception." If seemingly unimportant or even unnecessary scenes in a film often leave us a strong and unforgettable impression (e.g., scenes in which a main character in Ozu's *Passing Fancy* [*Dekigokoro*, 1933] repeatedly puts on and takes off his pants), it is because these scenes are indispensable for cultivating the film's own atmosphere. This example also helps us understand that the pleasure in watching a film is based less on a flawless narration of the story than on sensory and emotional stimuli generated through the viewing experience.[39]

More importantly, Sugiyama used his notion of the cinematic atmosphere to consider the revival of fantasy or horror films in the early sound era. He maintained that the significance of films such as G. W. Pabst's *L'Atlantide* (1932) and Carl Dreyer's *Vampyr* (1932) was not restricted to their skillful displays of the marvelous or uncanny atmospheres inherent in those genres. These films were important precisely because they succeeded in revealing the paradoxical nature of filmic representation. He wrote: "The more the science underlying cinema becomes intensified, the more cinema becomes able to perfectly depict the imagination that runs counter to science."[40] Here, Sugiyama stood very close to Tanizaki inasmuch as he rediscovered the coexistence of the real and the fantastic in sound film.

Sugiyama's film writings culminated in *Essays on Film*, published in November 1941. Despite its modest title, it is a comprehensive account of cinema's role and function as a distinct mode of expression. Indeed, the topics covered in this volume include frame, editing, screen, narration, sound, color, close-up, actors, props, and self-referentiality ("film-in-a-film"), which are followed by short film reviews he had written since 1934. As he explains in the preface, he was fully aware of the task he imposed on himself: "These [essays] were written as a result of my painstaking attempt to clarify the essence of film art. Accordingly, I could have simply given each essay a number, like 1, 2, 3, and 4; but being ashamed that they are not yet systematic enough, I just attached suitable titles instead."[41] Sugiyama's humbleness is not an exaggeration; some sections remain brief commentaries of a few pages. In the discussion to follow, I confine my focus to several key concepts that are related to his conceptualization of the film experience.

Sugiyama mobilizes two commonplace metaphors, namely, "film as a mirror" and "film as a window." Technological developments of the cinematic apparatus in the past fifty years, he says, have always come into being with the collective and persistent desire to make this medium a modern equivalent to a mirror, reflecting our everyday life as faithfully as possible.[42] While this impulse should be the foundation of all film art, he also adds that it should remain a starting point and never be treated as its final goal. Therefore, the main objective of film art is not to create a perfect duplication of reality but to make use of reality as the basis of its own expression. To clarify his point, Sugiyama brings to light the significance of "framing" in filmmaking. By framing, however, he does not mean the filmmaker's formative manipulation of the viewer's semantic or emotional comprehension through montage. Rather, he considers framing to be the process of providing adequate points of view or reference that stimulate the viewer's inborn curiosity about the world around us. He writes:

> When riding a bicycle or walking down the street, children do not pay much attention to the landscape surrounding them. Yet once on a train, they compete with each other to look out the window. The only difference is whether there is a simple and rectangular window frame. Framing by the window, the landscape, as well as its movement and transformation, can impress those young minds.... If we are to liken film to that train widow, this train must be running through the world, from cities and the countryside, mountains and valleys, skies and oceans, to inside the houses of the rich and the poor. With the same impetus that propels children to crawl up to the window, millions of people now go to movie theaters.[43]

Beyond its allusion to the primordial attractions of phantom ride films at the turn of the twentieth century, this passage explicates Sugiyama's approach to the film experience. First, unlike the still frames of a painting or photograph, the cinematic frame relies upon multiple frames that mark the world in motion by delimiting the ungraspable expansion of space and the continuous flow of time. Second, for Sugiyama, there is no ontological difference between the external world and cinematic images. The latter is a physical extension of the former but is still able to take a form of expression when it is articulated by spatial, temporal, and semantic frames provided by the filmmaker. Lastly, film is a medium that makes us reevaluate the actual existence of the world as the source of attractions. Thus, the primary task of filmmakers in Sugiyama's film-as-a-train-window metaphor is not to set up illusions outside the window, but instead to keep the train running so that its passengers-as-viewers can make new discoveries about the world through their lived experience.

Sugiyama makes this last point clear by disclosing his profound discontent with Soviet montage theory, particularly Pudovkin's *Film Technique*.[44] In this monograph, Pudovkin proudly refers to his experiment with montage through which he claims to have created the best filmic expression of an explosion using three consecutive shots of dynamite, flashes of magnesium flares, and rapids of a river.

Another example is what Pudovkin calls the scene of "a motor-car accident—a man being run over."[45] Since it was impossible to actually kill a man in front of the camera, Pudovkin divided the scene into a series of shots of brief duration, composed of a close-up of the face of the startled chauffeur, the face of the victim opening his mouth wide, and the braking wheels of the car. Having read this famous argument through translation, Sugiyama sees these examples as Pudovkin's escape from reality, decidedly rejecting the commonplace attitude that treats montage as the essence of filmmaking:

> That Pudovkin was unable to achieve a satisfactory result by plainly filming the explosion of dynamite is not a definitive phenomenon applicable to all cases. The foundation [of filmmaking] should be grounded in the intent to record an actual explosion. It should be better if one could plainly film a real huge explosion. There is no reason to escape from it and rely instead on creation by montage. Because it was impossible to film a real scene of a man killed by a car accident, Pudovkin created an editing technique based on flash cuttings. In every case, these were nothing more than escapist tactics.[46]

Sugiyama was not the first among Japanese film critics to challenge the premise of Soviet montage theory. Still, his critique was remarkable in that he discovered promising alternatives to this technique in recent sound films. The first is the "long take," which became dominant in Japanese filmmaking during the late 1930s and early 1940s, frequently used by directors like Mizoguchi and Uchida.[47] In anticipation of Christian Metz's postwar development of film semiotics, Sugiyama explains his preference for the long take to montage by using the metaphor of sentence composition: "The Kuleshov School's idea of treating a shot as a word has already been proven false because the shot in today's films began to contain rich meanings comparable with a short story and no longer with a word."[48] With the proliferation of the long take as a more suitable technique for sound cinema, he continues, filmmakers now tend to insert a cut only when the shot reaches its limit in holding as much temporal and semantic tension as possible. In this instance, consecutive shots should be spliced not by the semantic collision between them but by both spatial and temporal continuities of the filmed event so that the following shot only functions to receive what is about to overflow from the previous shot.[49]

Equally important for Sugiyama's critique of montage theory is what he calls "the shot in depth" (*okuyuki no aru gamen*), also known as "deep focus."[50] In general film history, this technique is often ascribed to the innovation of the Hollywood cinematographer Gregg Toland and his camerawork in films like *Citizen Kane* (dir. Orson Welles, 1941) and *The Best Years of Our Lives* (dir. William Wyler, 1946). But remember that Sugiyama was writing at a time when *Citizen Kane* was just released in the United States and that it was not officially released in Japan until the 1960s due to Japan's attack on Pearl Harbor. Despite this historical rupture, Sugiyama was still able to acknowledge the emergence of this particular technique in the mid- to late 1930s. He refers to Jean Renoir and Yamanaka Sadao as pioneers of "putting actions and human relations in both the foreground and background" of a single shot.[51] For Sugiyama, deep focus, or the shot-in-depth technique, is preferable for more than just its potential to satisfy the viewer's desire to "see everything at once in a single shot." Used in combination with the long take, it also enables the cinematographer to capture "the internal and temporal development of the [filmed] object" (taishō no naiteki jikanteki tenkai) by changing the zoom or moving the camera position within a single shot.[52]

Given these remarks, one could immediately notice a striking similarity between Sugiyama and Bazin. In a series of essays later compiled in his four-volume Qu'est-ce que le cinema? Bazin frequently made arguments and used metaphors akin to Sugiyama's. They include the following: that the photographic image has an existential bond with the object it captures and represents without the intervention of man;[53] that a frame in cinema is by nature "centrifugal" and not "centripetal" as in painting;[54] that montage is no longer the foundation of filmmaking and it must be prohibited when it obstructs the viewer's sense of the "homogeneity of space";[55] and that as alternatives to montage, both the long take and the so-called "shot in depth" technique became dominant in the sound period through the work of Renoir, Wells, and Wyler.[56] Like Sugiyama, moreover, Bazin always, as Andrew has pointed out, "begins with the most particular facts available, the film before his eyes, and through a process of logical and imaginative reflection, he arrives at a general theory."[57]

These tangible similarities between Sugiyama and Bazin were not by accident but historically grounded in their mutual interest in Bergson and other trends in Western philosophy. Sugiyama's reference to Bergson appears in the chapter entitled "eye" (me), which he wrote upon hearing of the death of this French philosopher in January 1941. Sugiyama's application of Bergsonian philosophy to his film theory begins with the following statement:

> The existence of the concrete immediacy given to us, or what Bergson calls the pure duration (creative evolution), is a living thing that is in a constant and evolutional state of flux and never stops any time. This duration is a kind of tension. As a sincere form of existence, our life represents the point at which this tension hits the limit; on the contrary, the point at which this tension comes loose is seen as the world of matters. When I saw in a movie theater a still frame projected on the screen due to the abrupt breakage of the film print, I arbitrarily thought this was exactly what Bergson calls the material world (inorganic matter), as it gave me an uncanny sense of desolation, unlike in the case of a mere static image (landscape and still life). Then I also thought that I should consider film not a thing that is simply moving but rather a thing that is living.[58]

Sugiyama does not argue that film can represent the Bergsonian concept of pure duration in its well-known capacity for animating immobile things or frames. For him, pure duration is a phenomenon that can only be achieved in and through human perception. As he claims, "Only when it rests on the organic relations of human vision, can it be said that film is alive and in flux."[59]

In the meantime, Sugiyama argues that the cinematic apparatus can provide us with what Kant calls "the transcendental schema."[60] This schema, according to Kant, indicates a special form of representation that "must stand in homogeneity with the category [or pure concept of the understanding] on the one hand and appearances [or sensible entities of the objects] on the other, and makes possible the application of the former to the latter."[61] Again, what is important in Sugiyama's recourse to Kantian philosophy here is that film does not offer either a pure concept or a concrete object as such. Rather he insists that film represents something in between, something that can connect the understanding (*Verstand*) and sensibility (*Sinnlichkeit*) for the sake of the viewer's speculative cognition of reality or even the thing-in-itself. As Sugiyama points out, film as a medium of the transcendental scheme becomes most meaningful when it provides the viewers "an opportunity to expand their imaginations to a stage that is unattainable with such concepts (words) alone."[62]

It seems clear that Sugiyama specifies the difference between human vision (empirical) and cinematic vision (transcendental). But how do these two distinct modes of seeing interact with each other in the experience of film? Here Sugiyama turned to "intuition," another key concept for Bergson, claiming that science and art have developed two different ways of seeing truths in the world. The former, usually called the "objective" or "rational" gaze, looks at things from the outside so that one can grasp the *substance* of the object (matter) in question on the level of concrete and accountable data such as shape, color, materiality, and other physical features. The latter is what one calls the "subjective" or "intuitive" gaze, seizing the *essence* of the given object from inside, by becoming one with that object through sympathy. Sugiyama then moves on to apply these descriptions of the gaze to account for the substantial difference between the eye of the camera and that of human beings:

> The eye of the camera is the first gaze. It is the purification of this objective gaze with its single perspective, rectangular frames, and monotonous vision. There is no other way to grasp the shape of things. But even if the camera presents us with different and multiple perspectives, it is still unable to reach the essence of the things themselves. As a spectator, however, I am able to feel the life of the things already captured on the screen by the lens. These things still lack color, smell, and sense of touch, but I can freely know them by intuition.[63]

Sugiyama also extends this distinction to the ontological difference between photography and film. Photography, on the one hand, emerged as a technology to demonstrate causality or other general laws of natural science (as it generates an image as the result of chemical reactions occurring on the filmstrip caused by light and other electromagnetic radiation coming through the lens). But film, on the other, turns a series of the same photographic images into a temporal experience by means of the viewer's physiological misrecognition of them as one continuous movement. For this reason, he argues, it is possible to say that "what we call film tells us about something that deviates from the law of causality" and in turn "composes itself according to the internal order of [the viewer's] direct experience."[64]

Sugiyama's film theory is remarkable when read as an account of the viewer's lived experience of the moving image. And yet it becomes problematic when describing film as a form of art. As someone trained in aesthetics, Sugiyama believed that the main purpose of art is to achieve the absolute unity of subject and object and of form and matter. But like Nishida's early account of his religious awakening, Sugiyama tends to prioritize subject over object in the dyad, inevitably getting him closer to the position of psychologism. Indeed, he often puts too much emphasis on the role of the filmmaker in the creation of film art. As he writes, "Although the foundation of film art should be located in the lens, any footage filmed without human intervention cannot be a film. Realistic aspects of film do not immediately yield artistic value."[65] Of course, Sugiyama admits that in the production of a film, two distinct agents of seeing—that is, the camera and the filmmaker—coexist with each other. But in order for film to be art, the human gaze must always take control of the camera's mechanical gaze. In other words, only when film is composed in a way that is compatible with what human artists see through their intuitive eyes can it transform itself from a mere illustration of natural phenomena to a concrete expression of the filmmaker's artistic imagination.

Sugiyama's overemphasis on the supremacy of the human vision is controversial for at least two reasons. First, Sugiyama seldom addresses what kinds of visual language or other means of communication are used in the delivery and expression of the filmmakers' active and subjective interventions in filmmaking. Consequently, the communication between the film author and the viewer in Sugiyama's model becomes either purely esoteric or absolutely deterministic. As he argues, "When the author grasps a totality based on his naked eye, the moving image begins to harmonize with the viewer's mental picture and creates an artistic moment that unifies matter and mind."[66] In addition, he writes, "However spontaneous they seem, characters, wind, and props appearing on the screen all move and develop themselves according to the director's rules."[67] What is missing in these statements is a recognition that the legibility of moving images is not always self-evident but conveyed through a system of signs shared by both the producers and viewers of given film texts. Unless we take into account both the ideological and organizational functions of this system, we are likely to end up confusing what Bazin calls "the genius of the system" (i.e., conventions developed in the studio system) with the intent of individual filmmakers.

Another problem with Sugiyama's film theory is its lack of concern with the prevailing political reality and its relation to film practice. It is not that he simply puts aside or even brackets many contemporary instances that use film for non-artistic or propagandistic purposes. More importantly, Sugiyama, unlike his predecessors such as Gonda, Tanizaki, and Itagaki, does not address how the very notion of art had been transformed after the introduction of photography and film, among other technologies of mechanical reproduction. As a result, even when he briefly talks about news film, he judges the value of films produced within this particular genre not by what they actually present to us as media coverage of ongoing events, but by the personal character thematized through the eyes of the individual news film producers.[68] In so doing, Sugiyama ultimately reduces the experience of all kinds of films to the intuitive and imaginary conversation between the filmmaker and viewer. Put differently, what is really implied in Sugiyama's "film-as-a-window" metaphor is the window that opens only inward, or that protects him from facing the brutal reality of wartime Japan.

In his commentary on the 2003 reprint of *Essays on Film*, the film historian Tanaka Masasumi points to the ambivalence of Sugiyama's film writing. While it is easy to criticize Sugiyama for his romantic "art for art's sake" attitude toward the film experience, we should acknowledge that he was writing in a particular discursive context in which all the leftist and liberal thinkers had already been suppressed. Read against this backdrop, Tanaka suggests, Sugiyama's decision to focus on the pure experience of film and to exclude all external factors constituting the larger picture of film culture had "a historical necessity to emerge in the late 1930s" as the only way to keep writing about cinema without overtly conforming to ultranationalism and other official ideologies of wartime Japan.[69] And thanks to this active and conscious escape from the political currents of the period, Sugiyama was able to survive the war and continued his dual career as a poet and film critic until his death in 2012. Writing within the same political milieu, Nagae also adopted a similar strategy in his *Cinema, Form, and Expression*. But unlike Sugiyama's aesthetic treatment of the film experience, Nagae set himself the task of answering the question "what is cinema?" (*eiga to wa ittai nande aru no ka*) from a more rigorously philosophical and ontological perspective.

NAGAE MICHITARŌ: A THEORIST IN OBLIVION

Despite its originality and theoretical rigor, Nagae's *Cinema, Formation, Expression* has long been forgotten even among historians of Japanese cinema.[70] This is in part because the book was originally published by a local publisher based in Kyoto. Thereafter, it remained out of print for more than sixty years, until it was finally reprinted in 2003.[71] But a more plausible reason for this neglect was his self-effacing commitment to the world of film criticism. It is true that Nagae's presence was quite visible in the 1930s, when he was a regular contributor to the film magazine *Eiga hyōron*. Although he kept sending articles to the magazine until the 1950s, his contributions became less and less frequent over time.

Moreover, from the beginning of his career, Nagae preferred to develop his own system of thought, rather than actively participating in the discussion of the most topical and urgent issues, such as the increasing intervention of the state in the domestic film industry. He seemed to have consciously withdrawn himself from the center stage of film writing after he elaborated his own film theory with his 1942 monograph. Nagae then decided to put more emphasis on his career as a poet throughout the postwar period, while working as a specialized judge for Eirin, the Japanese film industry's in-house organization for rating and self-censorship. Because no study has yet been published about Nagae's career as a film theorist, I begin by providing a brief overview of his earlier activities.

Born in 1905, Nagae studied literature at Kyoto University. After graduation, he launched the film magazine *Eiga geijutsu* (*Film Art*) with his college friend Shimizu Hikaru. By that time Shimizu had already established his fame as a specialist of montage theory and the machine aesthetic, whereas Nagae was said to be involved with the then-illegal Japanese Communist Party and was once arrested for organizing people working at film studios in Kyoto. Given Shimizu and Nagae's mutual interest in the art and politics of the Soviet Union, the magazine was filled with excitement about the revolutionary work of Soviet filmmakers, as manifested in Nagae's own translations of some of Vertov's writing under the title "The Kino-Eye and Its Theory" (*Kino-ki to sono riron*).[72] Though circulated only in and around the Kyoto area, this article led him to become acquainted with Nakai Masakazu, an alumnus of the same college and enthusiastic devotee of Vertov. This friendly encounter had a decisive impact on Nagae's later theorization of the ontology of cinema, which was informed by Nakai's observation of the cinematic gaze as a dialectical integration of the binary opposition between the projective and reflective, transitive and intransitive, and human and nonhuman visions.

While still in Kyoto and working at Shōchiku's Shimokamo studio as a planner, Nagar became a regular contributor to *Eiga hyōron*, the theory-oriented film magazine originally established in 1926.[73] Like Sugiyama, Nagae started his career in the 1930s as an opponent of literary adaptation and the Scenario Literature Movement, especially treating Murayama Tomoyoshi's 1934 essay "The Limitation of Cinema" ("Eiga no genkaisei") as the target of his criticism.[74] In this essay, Murayama dismisses film as an insignificant artistic medium because of its persistent dependence on visuality even after the introduction of sound. "In this world," says Murayama, "there is a truth that can never be represented with visual expression. The more it touches on a profound and inner truth, the further it goes beyond the reach of visual methods."[75] Nagae interprets this statement as an idealization of literary adaptation, since it eulogizes the superiority of the word over the image as a medium to express human creativity. In short, Murayama believes that verbal language is a creation of man and a legitimate form of human expression, whereas moving images are a mere product of the mechanical process.[76]

Nagae agrees with Murayama that film is a form of visual expression, but he does so only to expand this basic presumption further. To make his point clear, Nagae quotes Béla Balázs's famous admiration of silent cinema as the "first international language" that is legible to people from different linguistic and cultural backgrounds.[77] In spite of the advent of sound cinema, Nagae insists that Balázs's argument remains a legitimate historical assessment of the film medium, provided that verbal expression and cinematic expression are given differing or even opposing functions:

> What film has tried to do so far is not to make an expression out of written sentences but to directly express something that exists before language. The task of language is to signify this something, to translate it into words as signs based on certain rules. It is thus unlikely that words can become a direct expression of vague and unstable feelings in the mind, or of some ideas floating inside this emotional ambience. Against someone saying that "literature can directly delve into these feelings or ideas," we must declare that film, especially film art, has been offering us better and more direct expressions of those things with a new language that is no longer the language [of verbal expression].[78]

Film presents us with "a direct expression of the things that precede the word" (*kotoba izen no mono no chokusetsuteki hyōgen*). By contrast, verbal language can only provide us with a reification of those prelinguistic objects or phenomena through abstraction. Nagae claims that Murayama is insensitive to this fundamental difference between verbal and cinematic expressions and thus appears before him as an "illiterate who can only read the old language."[79]

In other essays published around the same time, Nagae looks further into the substantial difference between verbal and cinematic expressions by connecting it to ongoing debates about cinematic realism. For Nagae, there are at least three different modes of address. The first is to make claims about what is reflected on screen, focusing on the camera's ability to reproduce objective impressions of things or phenomena in the external world. The second is to illuminate the filmmaker's subjective interpretation of the current state of society and people's everyday life. This is usually expressed either in the form of written scripts or montage and other filming techniques. These two approaches may be likened to the conventional separation between the "realist" and "formative" traditions in film history. The third approach, which Nagae takes as his own perspective, investigates the shifting relationship between what we perceive (and then believe) as the real and its expressions.[80] Nagae adopts this approach partly because it allows him to situate the discussion of cinema and its particular form of realism within a specific historical context of twentieth-century modernity. But equally important to him is that it also enables him to look at the dyad of perception and expression not as mutually exclusive but as dependent and interchangeable.

Nagae refers to the emergence of modernist fiction in 1920s Japan to support his own approach to realism. Nagae reminds us that the writing experiments of Yokomitsu Riichi and his New Sensation School should not be assessed within the simple divide between realism and anti-realism. Rather, he suggests that we treat them as a conscious attempt at creating a new language to embrace and articulate the ongoing transformation of what is counted as "real" in the post-WWI period. As a stylistic innovation in literature, the New Sensation School clearly captured and foregrounded the impasse of the then dominant *genbun itchi* style.[81] Similarly, Nagae refers to visual expressions developed in cinema as another evidence for twentieth-century people's increased distrust of traditional verbal languages. As he writes:

> I do not say that this literary phenomenon [the emergence of modernist fiction] can be applicable to cinema as it is. In some cases, the situation might be opposite. If we are to be honest, we must take into account moments at which we lost ourselves facing a cinematic expression that was irreconcilable with the logic of thinking. Like verbal expression, cinematic expression must have its own rhetoric. But what is implied in our bewildered experience of cinematic expression is that its logic or rhetoric contains something new, something that differs from our conventional way of thinking and the logic of [verbal] language.[82]

Significant in this statement is the phrase "the situation might be opposite." While literary experiments found in Japanese modernist fiction present us with the effect of the perceptual crisis that broadly struck the writers of the 1920s, cinematic expression can embody in itself the very cause of that crisis. In other words, if we as the viewers often encounter things that are unintelligible or uncanny in film, it is precisely because cinema bases itself on a new logic of expression that transcends our normal perception and cognition. Nagae then concludes that anyone involved in contemporary debates on cinema and its realism must aim at clarifying this particular logic of cinematic expression.

This is how Nagae tried to establish his own approach to film theory in his early writings. But his argument at that time remained largely speculative and lacked a theoretical rigor. Toward the end of the 1930s, however, Nagae was able to devote significant time to writing *Cinema, Expression, Formation* while recuperating from illness. It is likely that in this period Nagae studied Nishida Kitarō's philosophy carefully. By this time, Nishida had already unified his system of thought under the concept of "the self-identity of absolute contradiction." And it is Nishida's philosophical account of the fundamental unities between subject and object, perception and expression, and being and nonbeing that informed Nagae's philosophical approach to the film experience.

NISHIDA'S THEORY OF THE SELF-IDENTITY OF ABSOLUTE CONTRADICTION

Throughout his career Nishida devoted himself to establishing a philosophical system that could overcome a series of binary oppositions inherent in Western philosophy since Plato, including subject and object, form and matter, mind and body, time and space, man and nature, noumenon and phenomenon, and essence and existence. Thus, Nishida's primary mission was to prove that these opponents are indeed identical in the form of self-negation, and he often explicated this contradictory relationship by using Husserl's concepts of "noesis" and "noema."

By means of example, Nishida applies the pair of noesis and noema in his account of the correlation between human beings and their environment. Ecologically speaking, the environment serves as the noesis (subject) because it creates and determines the existence of human beings and other species in this world as the noemata (objects). However, human beings can also serve as the noesis if we adopt the contemporary assertion of the Anthropocene that draws attention to social, historical, and infrastructural impacts cast upon the life-world of the environment. In this correlation, human beings as the object created by the environment become the subject that is making, and in turn, the environment as the object transformed by human beings, can also become the subject that is making. Unlike traditional Western metaphysics, which separates these two categories, Nishida contends that human beings are always being surrounded—or more precisely, "environed"—by the world and acting upon it from within; at the same time, the world itself also radically changes its meaning, appearance, and mode of being in reaction to the active intervention of human beings.[83]

This correlation between noesis and noema, says Nishida, can also be observed in the very existence of human beings. In essays published after the mid-1930s, Nishida proposes a concept called "active intuition" (*kōiteki chokkan*) to specify how such bilateral orientations function and reconcile each other in ourselves.[84] Usually, the term *action* indicates our attempt to make meaning of or to have influence upon an object from without, keeping some measurable distance from that object. In contrast, the term *intuition* means a process through which to directly grasp an object from within, becoming one with or being influenced by that object. Nishida, in fact, rejects the view that intuition, or immediate or direct perception, is passive and precedes the intervention of reason and understanding. Instead, he stresses the importance of our body as the nodal point at which both perception and cognition are dialectically unified. He goes on to write:

> There is no intentional action, no praxis, that is not productive. Anything that is not production is no more than abstract will. This is to say, it is necessarily corporeal. Intuition does not imply that the self is merely passive. The self is subsumed dialectically within the world of things; the subjective is subsumed within the objective.

Therefore, intuition is always active intuition. From the standpoint of abstract logic, action and intuition are considered merely a mutual opposition; something like "active intuition" might even be thought to be a contradictory concept.... [But] To speak of intuition is to say that the self, as the self-negation of the world of things, is born of the world of things; the thing provokes our action.[85]

Nishida suggests that both human beings and the external world (or the world of things) share the same ontological contradictions in their own structures. Normally, we tend to think that the world is the passive object of our subjective activities. But just as our physical body functions as the nodal point of noetic (active and subjective) and noematic (passive and objective) orientations, Nishida also pushes us to see the subjective aspects of the world's own activities. However, it is not simply that the world has its own existence independent of our consciousness. More importantly, we are always placed and go about our daily lives within the world as an integral part of it. Thus, it is possible to say that the existence of a species called human beings is nothing more than the objective expression of the world's own ecology. However, we are still allowed to stimulate the ongoing and subjective formation of the world from within by consciously transforming our own being as well as our living environment through subjective self-transformation.[86] As Nishida describes, "While the thing and the self are utterly opposed and utterly contradict each other, the thing affects the self and self affects the thing; as contradictory self-identity, the world itself forms itself, moving in active intuition from the made to the making."[87]

In addition, we should also acknowledge that Nishida specifically uses the terms "expression" (*hyōgen*) and "formation" (*keisei*) to indicate the same process of self-negation through which both human beings and the world transform themselves from the made to the making, from the object of passive expression to the subject of active formation. Nishida explains the reciprocal relationship between expression and formation as follows: "The individual becomes the individual by forming itself through the operation of expression. But this means that the individual possesses itself in its self-negation, as part of the world that forms itself. The world forms itself as the negative integration of unlimited individual things that go through the same operation of expression. When we say that in this world the individual carries the self-formation of the world, the individual becomes insatiable with no limit."[88] As the title of his book indicates, Nagae borrowed this particular pair of Nishida's terms (*expression* and *formation*) to capture and define the oxymoronic nature of the cinematic apparatus.

In 1939, Nishida coined the phrase "the self-identity of absolute contradiction" to succinctly indicate his rather complicated philosophical worldview. A diagram might best explain the main points of his argument (see figure 10). Nishida always argues that things or phenomena in this world consist of mutually exclusive orientations,

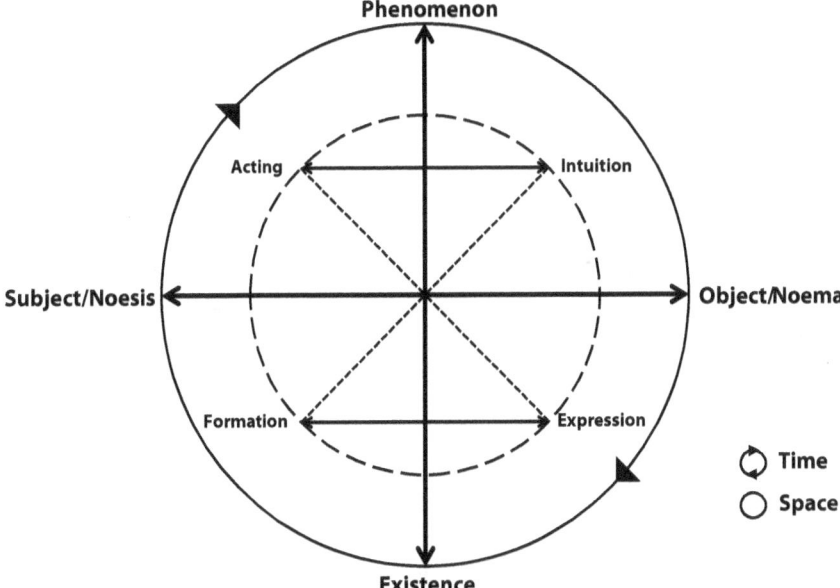

FIGURE 10. Nishida Kitarō's philosophical worldview.

namely, the noetic/subjective and the noematic/objective as well as the phenomenal/sensible and the existential/physical, as indicated by vertical and horizontal axes in the diagram. Although Nishida's philosophy is all about proving the fundamental unity of these contradictions, he does not propose that they simply coexist with each other. On the contrary, he insists that they can, or are forced to, extend to the other sides of the axes by continuously negating their given statuses, thereby inducing a series of qualitative leaps and self-transformations of themselves.

For this reason, Nishida suggests that we consider his concept of "the self-identity of absolute contradiction" as a temporal category. Like Bergson, Nishida considers our life to be the most legitimate modality for experiencing time. But Nishida's understanding of time considerably differs in that it negates the concept of pure duration. "The true life," says Nishida, "should not simply be a continuous and internal development as described in Bergson's *Creative Evolution*. It should rather be seen as 'the continuity of discontinuity' [*hi-renzoku no renzoku*], as that which is born out of its own death.... There is no true death in Bergson's life, and so it is not clear where in his philosophy the spatial limitation of [life] is grounded."[89] Therefore, in Nishida's view, time must be divisible and consciously transform or translate itself into the space it covers in order to negate its given property. Moreover, time must also redefine itself not as the expression of a linear movement predetermined by

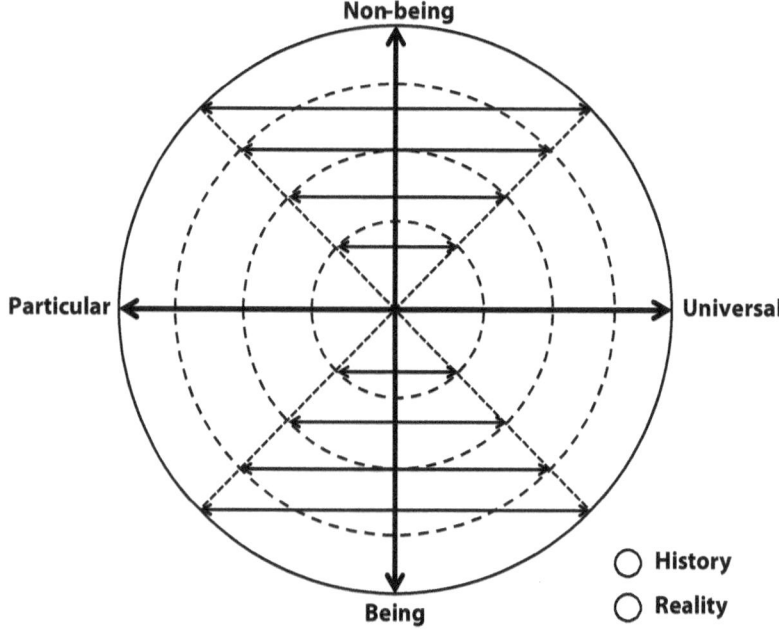

FIGURE 11. A revised diagram of Nishida's philosophical worldview.

causality, but as a circular movement that allows us to experience time as embodying "the eternal present" (*eien no ima*), or the dialectical unity of the past (necessity) and the future (possibility) at every given moment. Thus, the circle appearing in the diagram represents the temporal transgression of each of the categories into their opposing states, whereas the area enclosed by this circular movement indicates the spatial limitation of any given objects.

Lastly, Nishida argues that the whole universe is a series of concentric circles, each of which designates different instances of the self-identity of absolute contradiction (see figure 11). This outward expansion ultimately reaches and stops at the total resolution of ontological dualism, which Nishida explains with formulas like "being qua non-being" (*yū soku mu*) and "the particular qua the universal" (*tokushu soku ippan*). Nishida's emphasis on the oneness of the whole universe inevitably leads him to adopt Leibnizian monism. Indeed, Nishida sometimes called his worldview "creative monadology" (*sōzōteki monadoroji*), arguing that while parts can reflect themselves inside the whole, the whole can reveal its entirety in its parts. More importantly, Nishida adopts Leibniz's concept of "pre-established harmony" to explain his understanding of history as a temporal form of reality, as well as reality as a spatial form of history-in-the-making. According to this logic, any actual events or phenomena taking place in reality are always and already programmed by the will of the transcendental being—whether it be God or the emperor or the world's own destiny. Therefore, human beings in Nishida's philosophy are always destined to accept, embrace, and conform to whatever is happening in this world as a given.

It is for this passive acceptance of the totality of historical reality that Nishida's late philosophy became an effective discursive tool to support Japan's military aggression in Asia and beyond. Although Nishida's own contribution to the war effort was limited, his disciples such as Kōsaka Masaaki (1900–1969) and Takayama Iwao (1905–1993) became vocal and fanatic ideologues of Japanese fascism. From their politically authoritarian perspective, Japan represents a nodal point at which the number of self-contradictory entities—the West and the East, modern and premodern, physics and metaphysics, materialism and spiritualism, individual and collective—dialectically synthesize themselves through the continuity of discontinuity. For this reason, they repeatedly claimed that Japan was now required to provide a new vision of world history that would come after the demise of the singularity of Western modernity, by becoming "a creator of the new world by defeating the 'ABCD encirclement [the alliance of America, Britain, China, and the Dutch/Netherlands]."[90] Predictably, these ideologues also praised the counterfeit idea of the Greater-East Asia Co-Prosperity Sphere as evidence of Japan's active contribution to the construction of a new world order.

My contention is that Nagae applied Nishida's theory of the self-identity of absolute contradiction in his ontological response to the question "what is cinema?" However, this does not mean that Nagae blindly accepted Nishida's transhistorical discussion or that he became an ardent supporter of Japan's military expansion. Alternatively, Nagae presented his writing as a corrective to Nishida's ahistorical stance. For instance, Tosaka Jun harshly criticized Nishida for promoting the most advanced form of bourgeois idealist philosophy under the guise of Husserlian "bracketing" of actuality or of phenomenological reduction. Besides its subjectivist attitude, which tried to explain everything only from the noetic side of given phenomena, Nishida's philosophy was very problematic to Tosaka because it never took into account the actual sociopolitical condition of twentieth-century modernity. By describing history as a circular and repetitive movement, as Tosaka contends, Nishida's philosophy makes the concept of time at once a sacred and a vulgar category, stripped of the very possibility for progressive change. Moreover, although Nishida considered dialectics to be the principle of the movement of things, his own usage of the term always prioritized the transcendental or predetermined synthesis of a thesis and antithesis without examining how and under what conditions these opposing positions could or should be reconciled.[91]

Nagae evaded this sort of criticism by restricting his adaptation of Nishida's philosophy to an explanation of our lived experience of the world through cinema. Rather than aiming to offer a universal and holistic account of our own being in this

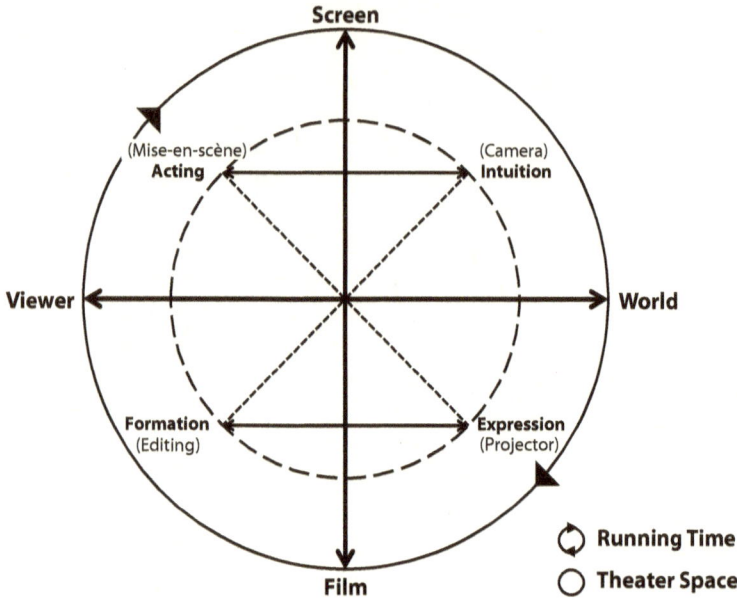

FIGURE 12. Nagae Michitarō's cinematic worldview.

world, he decided to focus on one special form of our life experience, which is always delimited by the finitude of the running time of film and the closed space of a movie theater. As shown in this third diagram (figure 12), the cinematic apparatus exhibits both passive (the camera) and active (the projector) gaze, which Nagae explained by following Nakai's earlier argument on the dual meaning of the Japanese verb *utsusu* ("to reflect" and "to project"). Likewise, humans may also be positioned as the noema and noesis, taking either a position of actors and objects to be looked at, or that of filmmakers and viewers to be onlookers. Moreover, whatever we see on the screen is brought into being through the collaboration between the human and nonhuman gaze, inevitably offering a new way of sensing and knowing the world in excess of our normal perceptual and cognitive processes. Lastly, the outer circle and the area enclosed signify the temporal (running time) and spatial (theater) limitations of film screening. Unlike Nishida's eternal universe, this artificial universe vanishes before our eyes as soon as the projector stops moving.

With this subtle but no less significant alternation, Nagae succeeded in reframing Nishida's critique of Western dualism as a legitimate twentieth-century philosophical problem. In addition, he also reinserted a certain materialist perspective into Nishida's undeniably idealist argument, addressing how film as a medium effaces its own physical existence when it is projected on screen and then perceived by the viewer as a series of flat moving images. How, then, did Nagae elaborate his unique theorization of cinema and its realism in his 1942 monograph?

CINEMA, EXPRESSION, FORMATION

Nagae begins his monograph by criticizing nearly all the major film theorists before him—including Münsterberg, Arnheim, and Balázs—for their attempt to focus on the artistic value of the film medium.[92] The problem of this dominant approach, he says, is its tendency to limit our scope to one aspect of the medium before our eyes, judging its essence with standards borrowed from outside. Similarly, it is also misleading to foreground the medium's social or political function, because what is needed is a standpoint from which to describe the full potential of cinema in its totality. Nagae goes on to define cinema as a genuine form of expression and communication comparable with sign, sound, and drawing. For this reason, Nagae places the origin of cinema not in the late nineteenth century when figures such as Eadweard Muybridge, Étienne-Jules Marey, and Thomas Edison experimented with proto-cinematographic devices, but, curiously, in the Paleolithic era, when early people living in the caves of Altamira first attempted to depict the shape and movement of wild animals.[93] While positing visual representation as part of a human genealogy of invention, Nagae distinguishes cinema from all preceding means and forms of expression in two ways: the camera's mechanical gaze, on the one hand, and, on the other hand, the capacity of cinema to provide visual recordings of time.[94] Consequently, to clarify the basic functions of these two features becomes the first mission of Nagae's inquiry.

At first, Nagae asks what film shares with photography. Like his contemporaries, Nagae affirms that they both rely on the same mechanism of photographic reproduction that compels us to believe that any filmed or photographed objects "must have at least once existed in front of the camera."[95] Thus, the specificity of film is grounded in its photographic nature, yet this does not mean that "the sum total of photographs can be cinema."[96] One essential difference is that film can give those objects an impression of "being alive." This is in part because film can represent the uninterrupted development of a motion within a single shot, especially when it makes use of the long take. But the invention of cutting or montage is of equal importance to Nagae. With these editing techniques, the viewer is able to look at the same object from multiple points of view. And if the viewer recognizes the procession of shots as showing the identical object rather than different ones, it is then possible to argue that the spatial and temporal consistency of that filmed object is further enhanced and concretized through the "continuity of discontinuity."[97]

Given his earlier interest in Soviet film theory, it is not surprising that Nagae employs Vertov's concept of "kino-eye" as his point of reference in clarifying the specificity of the camera's function. The advantage of Vertov's theory, says Nagae, lies in its full recognition of the camera's own corporeality (*shintaisei*) and personality (*kosei*), which is an autonomous noetic subject of seeing. As we have seen, the camera's mechanical gaze is not identical with that of human beings; instead, it has its own logic and capacity to look at the world more accurately and objectively than our normal vision. With this famous definition in mind, Nagae makes a remark that seems to resonate with Sugiyama's earlier discussion:

> It would be unnecessary to repeat here how the eye of the camera in photography and film has made possible our new discovery of the world.... This revelation used to be the property of the "eye of art." But what opens our eyes today is not the human eye but the eye of that new being. At stake in the eye of art was how it could symbolize nature, or in some sense, how it could get away from reality. On the contrary, the task of this new eye is to reconcile us with reality, to bring our eyes back to nature once again.[98]

Unlike Sugiyama, however, Nagae does not prioritize the alleged superiority of human intuition. More essential is the dialectical unity of the human and nonhuman visions in the experience and production of moving images. While film invites us to see the world from its own perspective, we as human beings can still express how we interpret or make meaning of the world through editing in the course of filmmaking or semantic and affective associations in the viewing experience of the moving image. Therefore, as Nagae stresses, what we should really explore is not how we can retain our own identity in confronting the alterity of the cinematic gaze, but rather what we could achieve by consciously trying to become one with film through self-negation.

Nagae expands on this dialectical unity of film and human beings by examining the actual condition under which these two independent "viewers" meet and work together. The question he asks at this point is: "What makes cinema a concrete thing?" or more simply, "Where is cinema?" His answer is neither the materialistic (filmstrip) nor the idealistic (the filmmaker's mind) one. Rather, he defines cinema as a phenomenon that manifests itself through the viewer's sensory experience of the moving images projected on the screen.[99] Here, Nagae speaks specifically of the dissolution of strict spatial distinctions in our viewing of films. On its material level, the screen exists before us as a white rectangular plane, just like a canvas standing before a painter. But in order for it to play its given role, Nagae asserts, the cinema screen has to deny its own physical existence, or more simply "to stop being the screen."[100]

The disappearance of the screen in the darkness of the movie theater helps cinema break with the tradition of the plastic arts (*zōkei geijutsu*). The autonomy of the plastic arts has long been premised either on the ontological stability of the medium, or on a clear-cut division between the subject seeing and the object being seen. When we look at a painting or sculpture, we always presuppose some physical distance from the artwork to recognize what is represented there. But in watching a film, we are obliged to replace the perceived distance from the screen with the psychological intimacy of its ever-changing contents. Freed from its spatial constraints, cinema now defines itself as an amorphous, non-ontological being, destined to remain in a state of flux.[101]

What, then, does the viewer share with film by using the screen as their meeting point? Nagae's answer is time. It is here that Nagae discloses his indebtedness to Bergson, even though he does not mention the name of this philosopher throughout the monograph. Like his French counterparts such as Jean Epstein and Germaine Dulac, Nagae defines film as a temporal medium that lends itself to a perception of the fourth dimension.[102] Moreover, by taking *The Power of Plants* as an example, the UFA film previously discussed by Nakai, Nagae refers to the time-lapse photography used in this film as a handy example of the new temporality brought by the camera's mechanical gaze:

> Filmed in the continual movement of time, the shots must be considered in the form of continuity.... Each time it is projected on screen, the picture inscribed on the filmstrip as a mold always comes into being as the moving image of the present. This is to say, the moving image can only exist here and now.... And if we perceive a flower depicted in film as more characteristic and beautiful than ones we find in nature, it is precisely because there is no difference between the time *lived* by the moving image and the time *lived* by our visual experience.... By using our visual experience as a means of mediation, that filmed flower is no longer an alien object to us. In this instance, a new life is born between the flower and us. We can thus even say that the flower is living inside us in its true sense.[103]

No doubt this is Nagae's own account of the cinematic intuition. But Nagae, unlike Sugiyama and Bergson, does not treat intuition as a genuinely subjective or humanistic mode of seizing the essence of a given object through the perceiver's intellectual sympathy or artistic imagination. Instead, Nagae foregrounds the active intervention of the film medium as precondition for human intuition. As he reminds us, only when the viewer sees mechanically reproduced images of a flower in motion can the life or vital force of that flower be intuited through lived experience.

Nagae then goes on to describe the paradox of cinematic realism in response to the dichotomy of the so-called formative and realist traditions that have prioritized the role of either expression (editing) or perception (the camera). The common problem with these traditions is their tendency to draw a clear-cut division between subjective and objective visions of the world that exists "out there," whether inside or outside of the human mind. The advantage of cinema, according to Nagae, is that it allows the viewer to live and experience the world "from within," by making itself a special place or environment in which both human beings and the world itself can meet up and interact. That said, Nagae does not maintain that film provides us with a replica or simulacra of the outside world. Rather, filmic representation can transform itself from a mere reflection of preexisting objects to a genuine expression of realism by consciously divorcing itself from reality. "If certain films seem very realistic," Nagae contends, "it is rather because they are not the representation of *reality as it is*. Reality in film is composed and ordered according to its new structure in the world of expression."[104]

Therefore, Nagae employs a form of dialectical reasoning.[105] Just as the duration of time became visible by dividing its indivisible whole into the rapid succession of immobile frames, the objective existence of the world becomes visible and accessible to us by means of the cinematic translation of its three-dimensional space and natural color into flat black-and-white images. In the meantime, we should remember that human beings are also an integral part of the world, as repeatedly emphasized in Nishida's philosophy. Thus, to look at the world represented on screen means to look at our own being as both the viewers viewing and the viewers viewed, along with the dual (passive-active) function of the camera and the projector. Nagae elaborates on these multilayered reciprocal relationships by examining how human beings and the world interact with each other in the movie theater, a special spatiotemporal "environment" (*kankyō*) that enfolds these two distinct forms of being:

> The world of filmic expression cannot exist on the same ground as nature, unlike the case of the plastic arts. . . . Rather, nature has already been negated in this "environment." But through this negation, film can enclose the reality of nature as such within its "world" of expression. As a result, we feel that the space of this sensible "world" fills the emptiness of our space of consciousness, so much so that we witness that the once-negated reality [of nature] revitalizes itself as a new reality of the world of expression. This new expressive reality serves as the mainstay of our existence in this viewing "environment," bringing us back to a stable position. Supported by this mainstay, we now become our new selves at this moment, and only by going through this self-transformation can we *live* the world of expression.[106]

In the 1970s, advocates of apparatus film theory maintained that the film viewer is destined to remain in a passive state. Even if he would feel that he attains an immanent and superior subjectivity when watching films, this subjectivity is nothing more than a false illusion set up by the visual function of the cinematic apparatus.[107] Though writing thirty years earlier, Nagae was able to reject such negative observations about film viewing by mobilizing Nishida's concept of "active intuition." As we have seen, the main purpose of active intuition was to foreground the noetic dimension of intuition. And because all the intentional actions generated through our corporeal experience encompass certain forms of productivity, the act of seeing in this concept can also be the act of making. Thus, whether it is voluntary or forced by the cinematic apparatus, our intentional act of seeing in the movie theater does not lose its singularity as a positive and productive experience. For Nagae, to see a film means to consciously delve into the world of expression and then to accept whatever we see there as a self-expression. In other words, by reflecting on our being-in-this-world in the form of visual images and sensory phenomena artificially bracketed from the objective existence of physical reality, we as the film viewer can become the "acting-self" (*kōi suru jiko*), or the genuine subject of self-transformation.[108]

In this world of filmic expression, things or objects in physical reality also transform their mode of existence. Nagae admits that the photographic image has a direct and existential connection with the objects it captures. But he also stresses that the same photographic image instantly loses its own materiality—or its spatial functions—once it begins to be projected on the screen with a temporal duration. As Nagae writes, "The *thing* that appears in the world of filmic expression retains its concrete *shape*, but it also transcends this *shape* by constantly presenting itself to us as a relation of meaning."[109] By radically shifting its status from matter (noumenon) to form (phenomenon), the filmed object enables a more direct and intimate correspondence with the viewer's sensory perception and intellectual understanding. Implied in this process of self-negation is the possibility for transfiguring the ways in which we speculate about the relationship between our own being-in-this-world and the being of the external world. Once captured into filmic expression, both human beings and things in physical reality mutually become a non-existential being living in the world of the senses and meaning. But to reiterate Nagae's point, this is not a passive escape to the kingdom of shadows but an active attempt to make a conscious return to the things themselves within a particular mediascape in the first half of the twentieth century.

The last remaining question for Nagae's inquiry is how film relates itself to the historical reality of his times. Nagae addresses this issue by looking further into film's own temporality. In Nagae's view, there are at least four different types of time involved with the filmic medium: diegetic time, running time, expressive time, and environmental time.[110] While the first two must be self-evident, the latter two require a brief explanation. Expressive time refers to visual markers of the transition or compression of time represented on screen, including the use of wipes, dissolves, flashbacks, slow-motion, and so on. Environmental time designates the particular historical moment in which each individual film is produced and consumed, encompassing cultural, political, and discursive contexts surrounding film practice as a whole. Nagae's discussion of environmental time is of particular interest because it helps understand the exteriority of Nagae's seemingly inward-looking philosophical perspective.

Repeatedly, Nagae argues that a moving image exists only in the here and now, regardless of the temporal distance between when it was actually filmed and the moment of projection. Thus, whenever or as long as it is projected on screen, each film acquires a new life, as if it is living in the eternal present. While this attribute effectively endorses the liveliness of objects or human characters represented in film, Nagae also admits that films of the past easily give us an impression of antiquity, creating a strong sense of nostalgia. Nagae thinks this is mostly due to the continuous addition of new technological features to the cinematic apparatus, not to mention a dynamic series of changes in film styles and stars.[111] Seen this way, film is no doubt vulnerable to the march of time. However, Nagae sees no negative implication in this temporal vulnerability because he believes that film situates itself within the ongoing process of creative evolution, within the eternal stream of becoming, as if it had its own *élan vital* or life force. As a concluding remark for *Cinema, Expression, Formation*, he writes as follows with great excitement:

> At present, our cinema is becoming an eye that sees solemn moments at which our soldiers are fighting at the risk of their lives. At the same time, it also becomes an eye that patiently observes the experiments by scientists. In these instances, the concept of cinema can no longer remain the same as that of the cinema of yesterday. Cinema is now becoming conscious of its own being. In doing so, the cinema of yesterday revitalizes itself as a new cinema. This awakening of cinema must be grounded on a self-awareness that it is neither a mere apparatus nor a form of industrial commerce, but rather a living form of expression that connects itself with human beings through their mutual corporeality. Cinema must become cinema by itself. Just as we Japanese are a people that have never overlooked language, we must never undervalue this particular form of expression called cinema in the present moment. In this sense, it is only today that we can acknowledge the being of cinema.[112]

As striking as it is paradoxical, this unabashed championing of the "cinema of today" (i.e., the cinema of 1942) tellingly reveals the pros and cons of Nagae's film theory. On the one hand, this statement encourages us to embrace the perpetual changes occurring to the medium as a necessary and constitutional feature of what we affectionately call "cinema." Keeping this ontological instability in mind, it becomes possible or even mandatory for us to positively examine the recent shift from celluloid film stock to digital media platforms in film production and exhibition, as well as the emergence of personalized viewing environments and interfaces. In other words, Nagae seems to compel us to embrace the proliferation of what Francesco Casetti calls the "kinetic" or "screenic" experiences in today's mediascape and in turn to stop lamenting the disappearance of the "filmic" or "cinematic" ones that used to be dominant in the "cinema of yesterday."[113]

However, Nagae's celebration of the mutual evolution of human beings and the world by means of the self-transformation of the cinematic apparatus also pushes us to read his argument in the specific discursive context of wartime Japan. This is not simply to say that both Nagae and Japanese war ideologues drew on Nishida's philosophy to develop their own theories. Rather, I would illuminate the unmistakable methodological affinities observed in their respective treatments of Japan and the cinema as particular examples of anti-dualistic entities. It is true that Nagae never prioritized "Japan" in his ontological account of the film experience in general. Nonetheless, he made an arbitrary historical break before and after Pearl Harbor, implicitly anticipating that Japan's victory over the Allies would be the precondition for cinema's self-transformation into a medium of non-capitalist modes of production and consumption. What is overlooked in this shared desire for overcoming Western capitalist modernity is that the coexistence of opposing dichotomies in one and the same entity, which Nagae and Japanese war ideologues saw as the particular property of either cinema or Japan, has already and always been inscribed in the very constitution of the West as a negative but superior image of the rest of the world.[114] As Thomas LaMarre's reminds us, "modernity is one *and* multiple" in itself, always dissolving and reproducing the same ontological contradictions that Nishida, Nagae, and supporters of Japanese fascism attempted to resolve in their own ways.

This critical remark, however, serves less to devalue the innovation and originality of Nagae's film theory than to remind us of the necessity to read it in its original historical context. It is no exaggeration to say that Nagae provides us with an informative point of reference that encourages us to rewrite the whole history of the lively and sustained interactions between phenomenology and film theory from a truly transnational, non-Eurocentric perspective. But at the same time, his writing equally brings us back to the basic assumption that I have repeatedly emphasized throughout this study. That is, a truly productive approach to the historicization of film theory is only possible by challenging the notion of theory as a universal and ahistorical account of a given object or phenomenon, and in turn by treating it as a living discourse mobilized at specific moments and situations in twentieth-century history.

One could affirm the validity of such a revisionist approach to film theory by considering the impact that Nagae's *Cinema, Expression, Formation* had—or failed to have—on its local readers. Despite its clarity and boldness, this monograph did not receive any serious critical attention except that it was mentioned in passing in the 1944 edition of *Philosophy Yearbook* (*Tetsugaku nennkan*) as a work that shows "the author's serious and self-reflexive attitude and rich intelligence."[115] Thereafter, Nagae's work fell into oblivion. When postwar theorists like Asanuma Keiji and Hara Masato reintroduced phenomenology to the field of Japanese film theory in the 1960s and 1970s, they completely neglected to mention Nagae's prior contribution and relied solely on the work of Merleau-Ponty and other French scholars associated with the *Filmologie* movement.[116] Having said that, it is possible to see the indirect legacy of Nagae's film theory in the discourse of the postwar Japanese avant-garde art and film movement. Hanada Kiyoteru, the most influential advocate of this movement in the 1950s, also developed an idiosyncratic theory of cinematic realism through his critical adoption of Nishida's concept of "the self-identity of absolute contradiction."

Epilogue
Hanada Kiyoteru and Postwar Debates

THE CONTINUITY OF DISCONTINUITY

On August 15, 1945, Emperor Hirohito announced through a radio broadcast the acceptance of the Potsdam Declaration and the unconditional surrender of Japan to the Allies. This event immediately led to the liberation of Taiwan, Korea, Manchuria, and all the other colonized territories in the Pacific and Southeast Asia that had been under Japan's militaristic rule. But it also marked the beginning of the Allied occupation of Japan, which lasted nearly seven years until the enforcement of the San Francisco Peace Treaty in April 1952. Although the occupation was officially initiated by the international council representing the United States, the Soviet Union, China, and Australia, it soon came under the single rule of the US government, with General Douglas MacArthur serving as Supreme Commander for the Allied Powers (SCAP).

Under MacArthur's guidance, the occupation government aimed to demilitarize and reconstruct the defeated nation through a democratic revolution from above. In addition to granting the Japanese rights for universal suffrage, agrarian reform, freedom of speech and assembly, the unionization of workers, and legalization of communist and socialist parties, the occupation officers also took the lead in drafting a new constitution that went into effect in May 1947. However problematic in its actual use and interpretation, Article 9 of the constitution renounced war as a legitimate means of solving international conflicts and thereby banned Japan from maintaining any armed forces. However, the dominant policy of the US occupation radically shifted from liberal to conservative during the second half of the seven-year period. In February 1947, Gen. MacArthur forcibly suppressed a planned general strike of four million government workers, in line with the rise of the Second

Red Scare (also known as "McCarthyism") in the United States. And when the Korean War broke out in 1950, the occupation government ordered the establishment of the National Police Reserve (*keisatsu yobitai*) with a light infantry force of seventy-five thousand. This ultimately led to the remilitarization of Japan, as the organization changed its name to the Japan Self-Defense Forces in 1954.

The Japanese film industry also went through a series of changes in the postwar period.[1] Japanese movie theaters began to show films on August 22, 1945, after only a weeklong hiatus. Although at this point no official policy on domestic film practice was as yet released from the Civil Information and Education Section (CIE) of the occupation government, three remaining Japanese film companies—Shōchiku, Tōhō, and Daiei—cautiously excluded from their programs films that supported or glorified Japan's war against the Allies. The notorious 1939 Film Law became invalid by December of the same year; accordingly, the distribution of raw film stock, the hiring of new personnel, and many other issues related to the management of film production became denationalized. To democratize the structure of the industry further, the CIE not only purged the CEOs of local film companies as war criminals but strongly encouraged workers in the industry to unionize themselves. As a result, the Japanese film industry in this period became dominated by those affiliated with the newly reestablished Japanese Communist Party (JCP), initiating a number of labor disputes that demanded the right of collective bargaining and protection from unjust dismissals.

Moreover, the occupation officers also took full advantage of film's affective attraction to implement their military, political, and social reforms. The state censorship of film by the Japanese Ministry of Internal Affairs was lifted in the first months of the occupation period, but it was soon replaced by the CIE's preproduction censorship and the Civil Censorship Department's (CCD) postproduction censorship. The main function of this dual censorship system was to check whether submitted or completed film projects met the criteria of their reeducation program for Japanese citizens. These criteria were presented through the list of subjects either forbidden or recommended for postwar Japanese film directors and companies to deal with. For instance, the famed theme of revenge frequently appearing in *jidaigeki* films was prohibited because it portrays "feudal loyalty or contempt of life as desirable and honorable."[2] At the same time, films featuring a young couple openly kissing each other in public or a group of young people condemning the deceits of the older generation were welcomed by the censors, as they supposedly demonstrated ideas of democracy, individual liberties, and fundamental human rights. In spite of these seemingly progressive regulations, any critique of the SCAP and other governmental authorities or institutions was strictly banned throughout the entire occupation period.

Under this circumstance, Japanese filmmakers embraced the unequivocal defeat of the nation as a golden opportunity for reclaiming their political and artistic emancipation. Having spent years in prison during the war for depicting war-weariness in films like *Fighting Soldiers* (*Tatakau heitai*, 1938), Kamei Fumio (1908–1987) became one of the most respected directors of the time. This was not only for his close ties with the JCP but also for his brave accusation of the emperor's war responsibilities in films such as *The Japanese Tragedy* (*Nihon no higeki*, 1945) and *War and Peace* (*Sensō to heiwa*, 1947).[3] In this period, old masters such as Mizoguchi and Ozu also dealt with social issues of postwar Japan, including prostitution, war orphans, and women's liberation.[4]

However, the Japanese filmgoers of the time most vividly felt the advent of a new era by watching the work of younger directors such as Kinoshita Keisuke (1912–1998) and Kurosawa Akira (1910–1998). Both Kinoshita and Kurosawa had made their directorial debuts before 1945, but they attained critical acclaim and wide recognition through a series of films they directed in the first ten years of the postwar period. While Kinoshita became the most beloved filmmaker among domestic viewers with films such as *Carmen Goes Home* (*Karumen kokyō ni kaeru*, 1952) and *Twenty-Four Eyes* (*Nijūshi no hitomi*, 1954), Kurosawa opened the way for exporting Japanese films abroad after his *Rashomon* (1950) won the Golden Lion at the Venice Film Festival in 1951 and an Academy Honorary Award in 1952. In the meantime, the importation of American films to the Japanese market restarted as early as February 1946, and it was soon followed by a wide variety of films from the United Kingdom, the Soviet Union, France, and Italy.

Despite these huge changes in film practice, film criticism in Japan largely remained unaffected by Japan's surrender. All but one film magazine, *Nihon eiga*, official organ of the Film Association of Greater Japan, had disappeared by the end of the war. And yet other major magazines such as *Kinema junpō* and Eiga hyōron succeeded in relaunching by the end of 1945, and the years that followed saw a mushrooming of third-rate and short-lived film periodicals as part of the postwar publishing boom that is generically known as *kasutori* or "dregs" magazines. This growing demand for both popular and critical writings on film did less to invite a new discourse than to protect the vested rights of already established local critics. Indeed, if you open any of those postwar film magazines and quickly scan its table of contents, you will find the familiar names of critics who had been writing on this medium since the 1920s, including Iijima Tadashi, Kitagawa Fuyuhiko, Hazumi Tsuneo, Futaba Jūzaburō, and Tsumura Hideo.

This situation inevitably led some Japanese critics to denounce local postwar film criticism for being outdated. In his 1948 article "The Responsibility of Film Critics" (*Eiga hihyōka no sekinin*), Iwasaki Akira (1903–1981) rightly points out that the reform of local film criticism requires critics' self-reflection on their past conduct.[5] Accordingly, Iwasaki does this first by confessing what he did during the war. Iwasaki started his career in the 1920s and became one of the most vocal theorists of the proletarian film movement in prewar Japan. But when it became impossible to write about film based on his Marxist perspective in the late 1930s, he found a position at the Tokyo branch of Man'ei, a state-funded film production company based in Changchun, capital city of Manchukuo, helping Japan's militaristic expansion from the home front. Iwasaki admits that he is equally responsible for Japan's war against China and the Allies, even though he did not write anything overtly supporting Japanese fascism due to the prohibition on writing. Iwasaki then exhorts his fellow critics to engage in self-criticism:

> The mentality of Japanese film critics has not changed at all for these ten years. Or else, they simply extend the same line of thought by inertia.... Film critics must be men of miracle if they go through this most profound experience in the history of our nation with no traces left on their skin. Or as human beings, they must be great fearless figures who are never interrupted by anything. I would respect them if they engaged in philosophical debates in a bamboo grove like the Seven Sages of ancient China. But I can never respect them as men of action who commit themselves to film criticism as part of today's journalism in this actual society.[6]

This statement, however, did not automatically exempt Iwasaki from his own accusation. On the contrary, Iwasaki's postwar writing was more often than not colored with an undeniable trace of repetition from the 1920 and 1930s.

The years around 1950 saw the revival of realism among Japanese filmmakers and critics. This was partly because they shared a consensus that it finally became possible to depict reality as it is after the abolishment of the heavy censorship of the militaristic government. But it was also because of the impact of Roberto Rossellini's *Paisan* (1946), which one local critic praised as a "monumental work" that "established a great realism by transforming documentary methods into a new form of creation."[7] Against this backdrop, Iwasaki developed his own account of the history of cinematic realism in Japan. Ozu and Mizoguchi, he maintained, played an important role in bringing a realistic approach into prewar Japanese cinema, but their works remained either a truthful depiction of everyday life or naturalism, lacking a more subjective and forceful criticism of the contradictions and injustices of capitalist society. Another remarkable event in Iwasaki's account was the advent of "tendency films" in the late 1920s. Although this genre was meaningful for its attempt to focus on the plights of the working class, it did not develop into a real "proletarian" movement, failing to fully incorporate Kurahara's concept of proletarian realism as its own method. Iwasaki went on to argue that there was no realism at all during the period between 1937 and 1945, due to Japanese cinema's total devotion to war propaganda and thought control.[8] With this sweeping denial in mind, Iwasaki declared that both the production and theorization of realism in and of film finally became possible after the war. As he wrote in 1949, "Unlike literature and theater, in which issues of realism have always been discussed theoretically, there is almost no study in film about the theory of its creative method. Seen from the level of actual filmmaking, film has just begun to stand at the threshold of realism. We have just started to realize the need for understanding what realism is. Japanese film people must and will accomplish this task by exploring both the praxis and theory of their own work."[9]

Obviously, Iwasaki treated the year 1945 as a significant historical rupture in the history of cinematic realism in Japan. But this marked emphasis on discontinuity paradoxically placed him within the continuous flow of the domestic discourse on realism. First, Iwasaki assumed the existence of a universal theory of realism—that is, proletarian realism—which can be applied to both literature and film on an equal basis. This attitude, most clearly represented by Kurahara and his followers, had already been the subject of local criticism by the mid-1930s, as it was not able to address the specificity of film as a medium and its particular relationship with the shifting notions of reality. For instance, the critic Tsuji Hisakazu pointed out in 1936 that there was no theoretical consensus as to "what realism is" in the twentieth-century. Tsuji's remark was more progressive than Iwasaki's in that it related issues of realism to the changing nature of the modern mediascape and the viewers' cognition process.[10] Lastly, most crucial here is Iwasaki's complete ignorance of everything that happened during the war. As we have seen, it was in the period after 1937 that the Japanese debates on cinematic realism became theoretically matured through their recourse to epistemology, phenomenology, and other philosophical and sociopolitical discourses. Depicting a history that lacked any serious and reflexive reference to this disturbing period inevitably ended up foregrounding less Japanese cinema's theoretical backwardness than Iwasaki's own nostalgia for the days of the proletarian movement.

Where, then, can we find a new theory of cinematic realism in postwar Japan? It is, I argue, in the work of Hanada Kiyoteru (1909–1974) that such a theory emerges, in particular with his concept of "sur-documentary" (*shuru-dokyumentarī*). In Japanese cultural history, Hanada is widely acclaimed as one of most influential advocates and theorists of the postwar avant-garde art movement. But what is of more interest for this present study is his persistent call for the historicization of film theory on both domestic and international fronts. Unlike Iwasaki's arbitrary disconnection of history, Hanada's innovation was always based on the critical inheritance and rearticulation of preexisting discourses.

In the 1950s, Hanada developed a theory of sur-documentary as his own contribution to postwar Japanese debates on cinematic realism. But writing twenty years after the initial introduction of the term *documentary* to Japan, Hanada did not simply praise documentary as the most legitimate genre for social justice or truth claims. Rather, Hanada presented his theory as a meta-critique of existing interpretations of the Griersonian concept of documentary by Japanese film theorists. Specifically, Hanada intended to deliver his intervention through a "negation of the negation," following the basic formula of Hegelian dialectics. And since

Hanada's argument encompassed Marxism, the 1920s avant-garde art movement, and the Kyoto School of Philosophy, it also allows us to reflect on how the legacy of prewar and wartime Japanese theorizations of cinematic realism merged with postwar film practice and discourse in the form of the continuity of discontinuity.

HANADA KIYOTERU: SUR-DOCUMENTARY

Born in 1909, Hanada studied literature at Kyoto Imperial University from 1929 to 1931. During his time at the college, he was totally absorbed in Nishida's philosophy, treating the latter's *Intuition and Reflection in Self-Consciousness* as his bible. Although he never concealed his intellectual indebtedness, Hanada was attentive enough to detect the deceptive nature of Nishida's transcendental stance even before the end of the war. "This author," wrote Hanada in 1938, "tactfully keeps alive our nation's feudalistic ideology by *criticizing* various European civil philosophies."[11] In Hanada's view, Nishida's philosophy proved problematic especially in its promotion of the "absolute dialectic" (*zettai benshōhō*). Though it is presented as a form of dialectics, this mode of thinking "quite carelessly integrates the opposites using quite absurd phrases such as 'the self-identity of absolute contradiction,' 'being qua nonbeing,' and 'one is many, many is one.'"[12] As a result, Nishida's philosophy gives the readers "an easy impression that they can directly achieve the integration or harmony of essential meanings without passing through the process of severe skepticism."[13] Contrary to Nishida's ahistorical adoption of the Leibnizian "pre-established harmony," Hanada followed Lenin's account of the law of dialectics and defined his own dialectic as always based on "the struggle of mutually exclusive opposites."[14]

During the war, Hanada worked as editor-in-chief of the opinion magazines *Tōtairiku* (*The Eastern Continent*) and *Bunka soshiki* (*Cultural Organization*), funded by the right-wing warmonger Nakano Seigō. The purpose of his writing in this period was to criticize the nativist logic of Japanese fascism from within, to appropriate a relatively relaxed discursive space given to the rightists as a cover for his protest. In particular, Hanada took issue with the law of noncontradiction (*jidōritsu*), which assures that the two propositions—"A is A" and "A is not A"—are mutually exclusive and thus impossible to be true at the same time. It is not difficult to see here influence from Nishida's lifelong struggle to overcome dualistic thinking in Western philosophy. However, Nishida challenged this law precisely because it could in turn serve as the main logic behind Japan's ultra-nationalism, which stressed the cultural, spiritual, and even historical discrepancies between Japan and the rest of the world. As he wrote in 1940:

> Why is it so hard [for Japanese nationalists] to be called reactionary? They must suffer from a social disease that one could call reaction-phobia. They must believe from the bottom of their heart the simple dynamic relation between action and reaction to

be the sole principle for movement.... [For this reason] they want to divide everything clearly into two categories. If one is progressive, the other is regressive. If one is an era of darkness, the other is an era of light. If men are intellectual, women are instinctive. These are nothing but typical examples of the formal logic.[15]

Thanks to this formal logic, Japanese war ideologues assured themselves that there is no unsolvable conflict or difference among the members of the allegedly self-contained category called Japan. But Hanada found it necessary to abolish such ethnocentric illusions through what he called "dialectical logic" (*benshōteki ronri*). According to Hanada, this alternative logic provides the only viable way to break through the stagnation of Japan's intellectual discourse in the early 1940s.[16] And it would do so by consciously and persistently adopting self-contradiction as its own method, expressed either as a formula that "A is at once A and not A" or in a more eye-catching phrase "to integrate opposites as opposites" (*tairitsubutsu wo tairitsu no mama tōitsu suru*).[17] One could perhaps read this dialectical logic as an implicit support for Japan's military expansion, a process through which non-Japanese citizens residing in Taiwan and Korea were forcibly registered, drafted, and exploited as if they were Japanese. But Hanada seemed to have evaded this expected criticism by applying his dialectical logic to the very existence of individual human beings. In other words, Hanada maintained that our own being is rife with countless pairs of mutually exclusive opposites and therefore is irreducible to a single view or standpoint, whether it be national and cultural essentialism or political and religious credos.

As an example of this split and self-contradictory mode of being, Hanada developed his concept of the "elliptical imagination" (*daen gensō*) in the years between 1941 and 1943. Hanada used this concept to explain the particular mentality of European thinkers and artists including Dante, Leonardo, Copernicus, Swift, Poe, and so on. Living in the transitional periods from the Middle Ages to the Renaissance, or from the Renaissance to modernity, these figures represented in their works the coexistence of opposing elements such as poetry and mathematics, science and alchemy, intuition and reason, vulgarity and piety, humanism and anti-humanism. Hanada then argued that the ellipse, a geomatic figure that appears when a point moving on a plane has constant distances from the two foci located inside that movement, is a more relevant form than Nishida's concentric circle to describe the existence of the world that human beings confronted with ongoing social and historical changes.

Hanada began his postwar activity by putting his concept of the elliptical imagination into practice. In 1949, Hanada founded a study group called The Night Society (*yoru no kai*) with writers and artists who became the forerunners of the postwar Japanese avant-garde art movement, including Okamoto Tarō, Haniya Yutaka, Sasaki Kiichi, Noma Hiroshi, and Abe Kōbō. Of these members, Okamoto served as a cofounder of the society and Hanada's foremost collaborator. Arguably the most iconic figure in the history of modern Japanese art, Okamoto stayed in France throughout the 1930s, creating abstract and surrealist paintings as a member of Abstraction-Création. When he met Hanada after the war, Okamoto advocated what he called "bipolarism" (*taikyoku shugi*). Okamoto argued that avant-garde art movements in 1920s Europe were composed mainly of two opposing currents—the rational and non-figurative expression of abstract painting, and the irrational but concrete expression of surrealism. The relationship between these two tendencies, he continued, should not be easily combined or integrated through eclecticism. Instead, postwar avant-garde artists like Okamoto must explore a new horizon of visual representation by consciously intensifying the conflict between the two as deeply as possible.[18] Hanada found a strong affinity between Okamoto's bipolarism and his own dialectical logic, and the theorization of the coexistence of concreteness (*gutai*) and abstraction (*chūshō*) in filmic representation became the central concern for Hanada's film theory.

In April 1950, Hanada became a coterie member of the film magazine *Eiga bunka* (*Film Culture*) along with Imamura Taihei, Iwasaki Akira, Nakai Masakazu, Sugiyama Heiichi, and Tsurumi Shunsuke. At this point, Hanada was still hesitant to write about film, and his first essay on this medium did not appear until October 1951. However, this does not mean that he paid no attention to the history of Japanese film theory. In his 1951 article, "Machine and Roses" ("Kikai to bara"), for instance, Hanada referred to the late 1920s disputes between Itagaki and Kurahara as a significant reference point for the Japanese reception of the machine aesthetic.[19] Moreover, it is Hanada who helped reestablish Imamura's fame as a pioneering theorist of animation and documentary among postwar readers. In his preface to the 1950 reprint of Imamura's *The Form of Film Art*, Hanada wrote: "Although there are so many film critics around us, only a few can think things cinematically. If [the poet] Nishiwaki Junzaburō's so-called pictorial thinking [*kaigateki shikō*] was peculiar to surrealists of the past, one could say that Imamura Taihei's cinematic thinking [*eigateki shikō*] stands at the forefront of our times."[20] Despite such a high accolade, Hanada's evaluation of Imamura was to become soured as Hanada developed his own theory of sur-documentary in subsequent years.

As mentioned above, Hanada presented his theory of sur-documentary as a meta-critique of existing Japanese interpretations of the Griersonian concept of documentary. I use the term *Griersonian* rather than call it "Grierson's" here, because the importation of the term *documentary* to Japan was unusual and indirect. In fact, it was neither Grierson's own writings nor the films he supervised at the EMB or the GPO film units that had palpable impacts on the Japanese film world. Instead, it was through the translation of Paul Rotha's 1935 monograph *Documentary Film* that the term *documentary* attained wide currency and stirred heated debates among Japanese readers. According to Markus Nornes, this book's popularity was so enormous that it went into third printings within the first months after its publication in September 1938. Moreover, as the book gradually earned a reputation as the "bible" for local documentary filmmakers, Rotha's name began to appear everywhere in the history of Japanese critical writings on cinema, achieving similar esteem to the likes of Balázs, Arnheim, and Eisenstein.[21]

In the Anglo-American context, Rotha is remembered solely for his relatively short and minor contribution to the British Documentary Film Movement.[22] But to understand his unexpected popularity in Japan, it is necessary to treat him as a theorist with a distinct political view rather than as a mere stand-in for Grierson. It cannot be denied that Rotha borrowed many examples in his argument from Grierson's preceding essays, such as "The Russian Example" and "First Principles of Documentary." But I argue that Rotha can still be distinguished from Grierson in his incorporation of dialectical thinking into the theoretical debates on documentary, which can be clearly observed in Rotha's replacement of Grierson's original definition of documentary ("the creative treatment of actuality") with his own ("the creative dramatization of actuality"). Accordingly, both wartime and postwar Japanese commentaries on Rotha came to revolve mostly around this author's definition of documentary as a dialectic of fiction (dramatization) and nonfiction (actuality).

In his discussion of sur-documentary, Hanada specifically refers to two distinct readings of Rotha by Japanese film theorists as the foothold of his counterargument. The first reading is provided by Tsumura Hideo, who in 1939 wrote a sixty-page treatise titled "A Critique of Paul Rotha's Film Theory: On His *Documentary Film*" ("Pōru Rūta no eigaron hihan: Sono cho 'Documentary Film' ni tsuite").[23] What drove Tsumura to write this piece was Rotha's relentless attack on fiction films as "an emotional catharsis" produced only to quench the demand of the present capitalist system of film production. "While praising the documentary that is based on materialist socialism as the most valuable future form of cinema," wrote Tsumura, "it in turn smashes fiction film into smithereens and verbally abuses it everywhere and as much as possible. Moreover, the way he assaults fiction film is totally reckless and idealistic, and I must confess that this is one of the reasons that gave me the impetus to present my criticism of Paul Rotha."[24]

For Tsumura, the generic distinction between fiction and nonfiction films was essential because they differ from each other not only in terms of how (form) but also of what (content) their filming processes demonstrate. To clarify this point, Tsumura strategically interpreted Rotha's definition of documentary as assigning two different domains of the world to each mode of filmmaking, namely, *actuality* to documentary and *reality* to fiction films. The distinction between actuality and reality was not visible to general readers of the Japanese translation of Rotha's book, for in its Japanese translation these two terms were identically translated into the same word, *genjitsu*. However, Tsumura shrewdly detected it by reading the English original. Furthermore, he also went on to give a philosophical account of the substantial difference between actuality and reality by using their German equivalents, *Wirklichkeit* and *Realität*.

According to Tsumura, actuality/*Wirklichkeit* emphasizes an immediate and external presence (*genzon*) of the world that is characterized by force and motion, whereas reality/*Realität* designates an objective being (*kyakkanteki sonzai*) of the world that will never be affected by anything but its essential determinants. In other words, actuality and reality should be distinguished for their differing modalities, which Tsumura described as "existence" (*sonzai*) and "essence" (*shinri*), respectively.[25] And if Rotha's notion of documentary aims to offer a purportedly materialist presentation of *actuality*, he continues, fiction film is remarkable for its idealistic and aesthetic exploration of *reality* through what the Germans called *Dichtung*, or "the most important human intuitions and sensibilities that make art possible."[26] Tsumura's undeniably romanticist stance here had some resonance with Grierson's own discussion of documentary, which also sought for the revelation of the essence of reality—or "the really real," to use Grierson's own words—through the creative *interpretation* of actuality.[27] But Rotha, at least in his monograph, seemed to be unaware of the philosophical distinction between actuality and reality, and therefore appeared to Tsumura as a "clichéd and dogmatic materialist" who invaded the well-maintained territory of fiction film with his self-congratulatory concept of documentary.[28]

On the other hand, Imamura Taihei's 1951 essay "Paul Rotha's *Documentary Film*" ("Pōru Rōza no *Kiroku Eigaron*") represents the second type of Japanese readings of Rotha.[29] Imamura began his argument by specifying how incorrectly his fellow Japanese critics had read and talked about Rotha's documentary theory. While Rotha seemed to be taking the position of a formalist who turned down all kinds of fiction films, Imamura reminded the reader that what Rotha really criticized in his book was not fiction film as a whole but the capitalist basis of the film industry that had privileged this genre as the most profitable mode of film practice. Similarly, Imamura spoke highly of Rotha's promotion of documentary as an effective tool for mass education. Rotha's writing, as he stated, "reflects [the author's] strong social consciousness ... and is based on the most urgent/real demand of the contemporary mass public." It thus should be respected above all for its unflinching aim to "enlighten the people politically, to turn their eyes to fundamental contradictions of the modern social system."[30]

Imamura's committed interpretation of Rotha, however, was motivated largely by his personal desire to promote the superiority of nonfiction film as a distinct genre. To put it differently, Imamura used Rotha as a mouthpiece to disseminate his own film theory. In addition to Tsumura's idealist distinction between reality and actuality, Imamura introduced the third term *fact* (*jijitsu*) as the foundation of his discussion. Although Imamura did not deny the creative intervention of filmmakers in the production of documentary, his theory always emphasized the factuality of filmic documentation guaranteed by its "photographic nature" (*shasinsei*).³¹ And as long as it makes use of this property properly, documentary—or what he deliberately called "the cinema of fact" (*jijitsu no eiga*)—must be placed higher than "the cinema of fiction" (*kakō no eiga*).³² Rotha himself repeatedly differentiated documentary from a purely descriptive or objective treatment of facts commonly found in educational or scientific films. Nevertheless, Imamura portrayed this British theorist as someone who "paid special attention to the film's recording ability and came to believe that the real beauty lies only in the documentation of the fact."³³

Hanada argues that these two seemingly opposing readings were equally problematic for their tendency to make clear-cut distinctions between reality and actuality, essence and existence, and fiction and nonfiction. He then asks his readers to go back again to Rotha's original definition of documentary because it meant not to separate but rather to dialectically integrate these given dichotomies through "the creative dramatization of actuality." Thus, what has been missing in previous Japanese discussions of documentary in general and of Rotha in particular, he continues, is a careful interpretation of this self-contradictory definition from a rigorous philosophical point of view.³⁴

Let us look first at how Hanada articulates the correlation between "actuality" (*akuchuaritī*) and "reality" (*riaritī*). Unlike Tsumura, Hanada does not treat these two terms as separate and independent domains. Hanada considers reality to be a mysterious, uncanny, and unknowable entity, an object that transcends human reasoning and empirical observation as in the case of "the thing-in-itself" in Kantian philosophy.³⁵ But he also stresses that we can never reach or at least get closer to reality unless we squarely deal with raw and urgent problems observed in the actuality of our own times. To illuminate the relevance of actuality as the subject of film practice, Hanada tells us that actuality is indeed replaceable with "contingency" (*gūzensei*), in part following Imamura's assertion that "documentary film is an art that reveals the necessary among the contingent."³⁶ Nevertheless, Hanada rejects Imamura's documentary theory as a whole precisely because Imamura pays no attention to the distinction between actuality and reality, given his naive trust in the factuality of the photographic image.

Hanada's equation of actuality and contingency also comes from Hegel, who defined contingency as "the shape in which actuality first presents itself to consciousness."³⁷ As an idealist philosopher, Hegel was rather critical of contingency for its indeterminate, transformative, and inessential nature. Nevertheless, Hanada finds more promising values in exactly what Hegel has negated. He argues that the purpose of film practice is to critically reflect on those transient and ephemeral phenomena that appear and exist for and through our perception. In this way, Hanada also relates his actuality-contingency dyad to "existence" (*jitsuzon*). And as if to recapitulate Sartre's famous proposition that "existence precedes essence," Hanada contends that the advantage of film practice is to enable us "to focus more

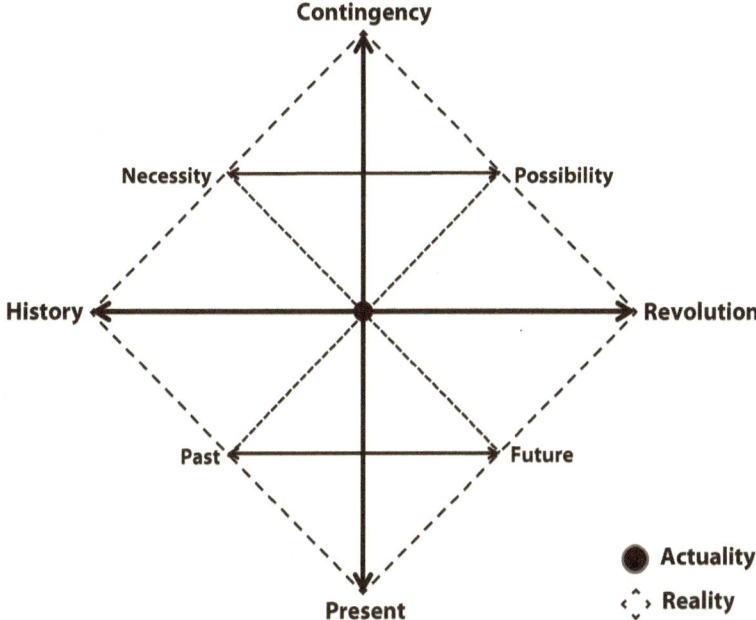

FIGURE 13. Hanada Kiyoteru's philosophical worldview.

on 'the individual thing' [*kobutsu*] as such than on its 'essence' [*honshitsu*] or 'universal meaning [*fuhenteki imi*].'"[38]

Hanada further addresses the importance of actuality by explicating its temporal dimension. Here Hanada refers to Kant's *Critique of Pure Reason* and delivers from it two other modal categories—necessity (*hitsuzensei*) and possibility (*kanōsei*)—to be coupled with contingency. He then states that each of these modalities corresponds to three different moments in temporal progression, namely, necessity to the past, possibility to the future, and contingency to the present. In Hanada's view, reality appears only in and through the complex web of these modalities. "Reality," he writes, "is that which sublates [*Aufhebung*] in itself the necessity of the past and the possibility of the future by using the contingency of the present as its stepping stone."[39] Hanada admits that this formula might seem "too Hegelian" in its schematic application of a dialectical process.[40]

But for the same reason, it is possible to understand Hanada's philosophical worldview using the same diagram I have employed in my discussion of Nishida and Nagae (see figure 13). Reflecting Hanada's sympathy with Marx and Lenin, the horizontal axis represents the ongoing historical progression toward world revolution. On the other hand, the vertical axis marks a specific moment in history and

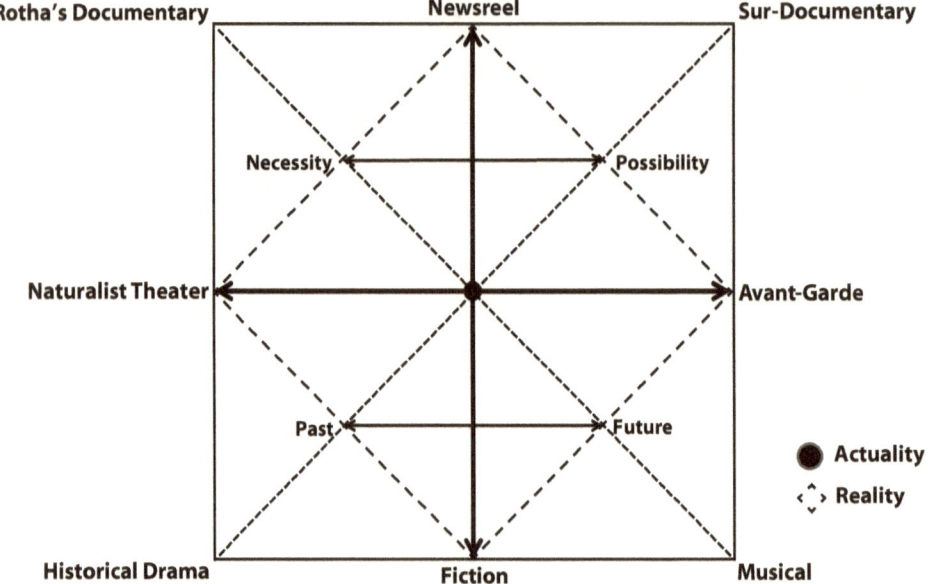

FIGURE 14. Hanada's cinematic worldview.

illustrates that contingency is the modality of the present. Actuality is located at the intersection of these coordinate axes, dialectically mediating two pairs of opposing categories of modality and temporality, necessity and possibility, and the past and the future. The diagram also tells us that alternative (vertical) combinations of these four categories indicate that both history and revolution are products of either the necessity-past dyad or the possibility-future dyad. Finally, reality is a transcendental place or precondition that makes possible all of these interactions and is therefore unknowable to us in its entirety.

What is remarkable, however, is that Hanada employs this worldview to explain the fundamental difference between Rotha's documentary theory and his own conception of sur-documentary. His argument here can also be explained through another diagram (figure 14). Above all, Hanada finds it problematic that Rotha aimed to enhance the dramatic quality of filmed events in accordance with conventions of theatrical realism developed since Ibsen. "What Rotha meant by the term *drama*," says Hanada, "was nothing but the highly rational drama of everyday life that is completely caught in the grips of causal relationships."[41] In this sense, Rotha's call for "the dramatization of actuality" appears to be a regressive return to the days of nineteenth-century naturalism, going against the ongoing historical progression toward revolution. Moreover, this criticism also applies to Imamura's defense of documentary as a way to distinguish necessity from contingency. In the 1950s, Imamura supported the emergence of a new genre called "semi-documentary." Beginning with Italian neorealists and then followed by contemporary directors such as Jules Dassin and René Clément, this genre stressed the increasing unity of fiction (the drama of causality, written scripts, credible characters) and nonfiction (actual events, location shooting, nonprofessional actors) for the sake of pragmatic necessity.[42] But for Hanada, both Rotha's documentary and Imamura's semi-documentary represent nothing more than "a mere artistic expression of social reformism" and thus must be rejected.[43]

On the contrary, Hanada's sur-documentary must advance in the opposite direction on the horizontal axis, aiming for the dialectical unity of avant-garde and non-fiction through the mediation of possibility. The French prefix "sur-" used here, of course, indicates this concept's indebtedness to surrealism. But it also denotes the self-negation of the traditional documentary method as a whole by consciously incorporating in itself the legacy of the 1920s avant-garde as both artistic and political movement. It is necessary to clarify what Hanada means by the term *avant-garde* in his film theory. Like Okamoto's bipolarism, Hanada first maintains that German absolute films and French dada/surrealist films embody not simply the two major directions in 1920s avant-garde film practice but the major conflict between abstraction and concreteness in twentieth-century art. However, he soon adds that such a clear-cut distinction between abstraction and concreteness cannot be seen as a real dialectic in film because filmmakers must always deal with the concrete objects that the camera captures and represents before them.[44] For this reason, avant-garde artists of the past mostly made use of this mechanical capacity of the film medium "to boldly visualize our internal world" under the banner of dream, unconsciousness, and absurdity. And in doing so, those artists often lost or underrated a direct contact with actuality.[45]

Thus, Hanada argues that the real dialectic in film practice should rather be placed between the documentary method and the avant-garde aesthetic. Far from accepting what the camera presents to us as a priori facts, creators of sur-documentary must start with a recognition that "concrete things in the external world are nothing but an incomprehensible and mysterious being."[46] One way of achieving such recognition is to completely abandon the objective treatment of actual events or phenomena that is commonly found in Rotha's documentary theory and Ibsen's theatrical realism. Just as surrealists in the 1920s have tried to give concrete expression to the uncanny and irrational structure of their internal world, sur-documentarists are obliged to present a totally subjective and imaginative treatment of the filmed objects to reveal the unknowability of the external world.

Another method to surmount our normal perception is to bring extraordinary events or spectacles into the space of everyday life or film screening. Here Hanada refers to Eisenstein's concept of "the montage of attractions" as a plausible example. As is well known, Eisenstein incorporated scenes of boxing and circus in the theatrical plays that he directed for *Proletkult*.[47] This famous attempt, according to

Hanada, was made to renovate the role of popular art and its political potentials. More specifically, it proved that "propaganda and agitation that makes use of an artistic means can provoke the masses to adopt actuality as a steppingstone to grasp reality."[48] Interestingly, Hanada finds musical films to be a more updated example of the montage of attractions. Contrary to supporters of traditional realism or fans of highbrow art cinema, Hanada sees this popular film genre as dialectically integrating the avant-garde sprit of revolutionary Russia and the total negation of the drama of causality within the realm of fiction films.[49]

The last remaining question is what kind of films will be counted as exemplary of sur-documentary. Like Imamura, Hanada speaks of Dassin's *The Naked City* (1948), Clément's *The Damned* (1947), and some Italian neorealist films. These films, he argues, partly share his existentialist attitude in that they focus less on the search for the general truth of reality than on the filmic presentation of the contingent status of concrete objects and social phenomena. He also praises Luis Buñuel's *The Young and the Damned* (1950) for its conscious attempt to look at the actuality of Mexican society through the eyes of a surrealist. These examples, however, still cannot be called genuine sur-documentary films that are able to reformulate the entire genre of documentary by negating its conventional choice and treatment of subject matter. As the most relevant and promising theme for sur-documentary, Hanada goes so far as to suggest the creative adoption of Japanese traditional stories about ghosts or supernatural creatures (*kaidan*) which have been a source for popular imagination for centuries. "Especially in stories of ghost cat incidents in the Arima and Nabeshima clans," he says, "surrealistic elements are merged into highly realistic elements. If it is to be possible for us to inherit and develop this tradition properly, then we must be able to create a documentary art that can prevail over surrealism—the finest of its kind with novelty and eccentricity."[50]

FROM SUR-DOCUMENTARY TO SOCIALIST REALISM

However eccentric, Hanada's theory of sur-documentary had a decisive impact on the formation of postwar Japanese avant-garde cinema. For instance, Teshigahara Hiroshi visualized seemingly unmemorable rural areas in Japan as "an incomprehensible and mysterious being" in films such as *Pitfall* (*Otoshiana*, 1962) and *Woman in the Dunes* (*Suna no onna*, 1964). In making these internationally acclaimed films, Teshigahara worked in close collaboration with the writer Abe Kōbō, the youngest and arguably most talented member of Hanada and Okamoto's Night Society. At the same time, Matsumoto Toshio aimed to deconstruct the conventional documentary method with his concept of "avant-garde documentary" (*zen'nei kiroku eiga*).[51] While in *The Weavers of Nishijin* (*Nishijin*, 1961) he made excessive use of extreme close-ups and refused to show the shape of the filmed object in its entirety, *The Song of Stone* (*Ishi no uta*, 1963) was entirely composed of still photographic images of a stone quarry previously taken by an American photojournalist. In one of his memoires, Matsumoto clearly expresses his indebtedness to Hanada's theory of sur-documentary: "Critical consciousness to challenge conventional thinking, uncompromising anti-authoritarianism, and an unflinching attitude to objectify both subject and object without being entrapped with sentimental emotions—these were the best things I learned from Mr. Hanada. His dynamic and flexible method that unifies the essential opponents as opponents had served as a practical guide for me for a long time."[52] Traces of Hanada's provocative propositions can also be found in the fields of literature, art criticism, and early TV production. It is thus no exaggeration to say that Hanada was the most persuasive forerunner (*sendōsha*) and agitator (*sendōsha*) of the postwar Japanese avant-garde movement and its theorization.

I have also argued that Hanada's theory of sur-documentary embodies the best reference point to see how wartime and postwar Japanese theorizations of cinema were dialectically connected to each other in the form of the continuity of discontinuity. This point becomes most obvious in light of Hanada's declaration that his theoretical intervention was intended to be his answer to long-lasting but still unsolved debates on realism. As he stressed, the purpose of his sur-documentary was to create a new realism through the negation of his fellow Japanese critics' preceding negation of Rotha's documentary theory. In this realism, oppositions between subject and object, interiority and exteriority, abstraction and concreteness, rationalism and irrationalism, and avant-garde and documentary are synthesized without dissolving their essential conflicts. In a film that adopts this realism, reality reveals itself momentarily and paradoxically through the logic of self-negation. The more fantastic or fictional elements it contains, the more realistic and contingent effects it produces. In other words, this realism seeks for the possibility of apprehending the truth in its eternal impossibility. Because it is logically impossible to integrate opposites as opposites, this realism ultimately designates the eternal and self-transformative movement between the two poles, as in the circumference of the ellipse. Hanada's realism, therefore, is at once realism and not realism.

Interestingly, Hanada also suggested that his realism be called "socialist realism" (*shakai shugi riarizumu*).[53] One may assume that Hanada did this to criticize the current state of socialist realism in the Soviet Union, which had officially ousted the legacy of 1920s avant-garde art as a product of bourgeois formalism. But I would maintain that Hanada seemed to trust in the potential of socialist realism as a legitimate method for postwar art and politics, precisely because of its self-contradictory nature. To put it in Hanada's paradoxical formula described above, socialist realism could present us with a glimpse of reality precisely because it is nothing but fiction.[54] Hanada also used a similar kind of oxymoron in his evaluation of Stalin. When the majority of Japanese leftists began following Nikita Khrushchev's critique of Stalin's cult of personality, Hanada defended Stalin by insisting that

"I believe that 'the critique of Stalin' was put into practice based on his own will."[55] This statement tellingly indicates the gradual detachment of Hanada from the actuality of late 1950s Japan, which was marked by the emergence of the New Left.

Hanada joined the Japanese Communist Party in 1949 and served as the editor-in-chief for *Shin Nihon bungaku* (*New Japanese Literature*), the party's official literary magazine, from 1952 to 1954. It is true that Hanada tried to diversify the JCP's official discourse on art and politics from within, frequently having conflicts with members of the central committee until he was purged from the party in 1961. Nevertheless, it is equally true that his popularity in the world of criticism during the 1950s would never have been possible without the privilege he gained through his commitment to party politics. Hanada's rhetorical defense of socialist realism and Stalin thus appeared as less a promising proposition for a new realism than a dogmatic justification of the Communist Party. Indeed, Haniya Yutaka, another member of the Night Society and Hanada's lifelong rival, made the most trenchant criticism on this matter. As a writer similarly challenging the law of noncontradiction in his unfinished magnum opus *Dead Souls* (*Shirei*), Haniya fully recognized the theoretical value of Hanada's concept of the elliptical imagination. However, Haniya criticized Hanada for lacking any critical reflection on the party as a modern instrument for totalization, as well as for his being an anti-revolutionary authoritarianist.[56] Despite his celebration of self-contradiction, Hanada's own political stance led him to integrate the opposites as a result of his active participation in party politics.

This final episode gives us another incentive to treat Japanese film theory not as a universal and ahistorical account of the given object but as a living and self-transformative discourse on actual historical moments in the twentieth century. At the same time, it also encourages us to understand the history of postwar Japanese cinema in the form of the continuity of discontinuity. As manifested in Matsumoto's "theory of avant-garde documentary" and Yoshida Kijū's "logic of self-negation" (*jiko hitei no ronri*), filmmakers of the Japanese New Wave from the late 1950s onward undoubtedly inherited in their own writings the legacy of Hanada's film theory.[57] However, what rendered their works "new" in the context of Japanese film history was their conscious and collective commitment to the burgeoning New Left movement. Amid the upsurge of mass protests against the enforcement in June 1960 of the Security Treaty between the United States and Japan, student radicals formed the Communist League (*kyōsan shugisha dōmei*, also known as Bund) as a united front consisting of three thousand members either purged from or antagonistic to the JCP. As a sympathizer of this new political organization, Ōshima Nagisa directed *Night and Fog in Japan* (*Nihon no yoru to kiri*, 1960), depicting the internal struggle among members of the JCP from the perspective of the younger generation. And from the works of these younger directors emerged a new movement called the Japanese New Wave.

This mounting conflict between Old and New Lefts in postwar Japan, however, once again leads us to situate Japanese cinema and its theorizations after 1960 within an international history of art and politics toward May 1968 and beyond. This is why future studies of Japanese film and media theories must be at once local and global, critically treating the geographical modifier "Japanese" as a sign of its ontological non-Japaneseness. Or as Akira Lippit puts it, the history of Japanese film and media theories must be seen as reciprocal movements between intensity and extensity: "As intensity, these lines move from without to within Japan; as extensities, from within to without. In this matrix of media praxis and thought, Japan itself becomes a medium, an interface of multiple lines of practice and thought bound by the charges that animate the nation as a temporary and finite media state."[58] If I have chosen to focus on realism throughout my study, it is precisely because Japanese film theorists from the first half of the twentieth century have employed this specific concept as the best means to articulate their lived experience of film and Japan as media.

NOTES

INTRODUCTION

1. Leo Braudy and Marshal Cohen, eds., *Film Theory and Criticism*, 7th ed. (New York: Oxford University Press, 2009); Bill Nichols, ed., *Movies and Methods*, 2 vols. (Berkeley: University of California Press, 1976, 1985); Dudley Andrew, *The Major Film Theories* (New York: Oxford University Press, 1976); Toby Miller and Robert Stam, eds., *A Companion to Film Theory* (Malden, MA: Wiley Blackwell, 2004); Marc Furstenau, ed., *The Film Theory Reader: Debates and Arguments* (New York and London: Routledge, 2010).

2. Noël Burch, *To the Distant Observer: Form and Meaning in the Japanese Cinema*, rev. and ed. Annette Michelson (Berkeley: University of California Press, 1979), 83.

3. See Hugo Münsterberg, *Eigageki: Sono shinrigaku to bigaku* [*The Photoplay: A Psychological Study*], trans. Kuze Kōtarō (Tokyo: Ōmura Shoten, 1924); Jean Epstein, "Eiga nōteki yōso" [an abridged translation of "Le cinématographe vue de l'Etna"], trans. Okada Shinkichi, *Eiga ōrai* 24 (December 1926): 34–37; Béla Balázs, *Eiga bigaku to eiga shakaigaku* [*Der Geist des Films*], trans. Sasaki Norio (Tokyo: Ōraisha, 1932); Rudolf Arnheim, *Geijutsu to shite no eiga* [*Film als Kunst*], trans. Sasaki Norio (Tokyo: Ōraisha, 1933); V. I. Pudovkin, *Eiga kantoku to eiga kyakuhonron* [translated from *Film regie und Filmmanuskript*, 1928], trans. Sasaki Norio (Tokyo: Ōraisha, 1930); Pudovkin, *Eiga haiyūron*, trans. Magami Gitarō (Tokyo: Naukasha, 1935); Pudovkin, *Eiga sōsakuron* [translated from *Film Technique*, exp. ed., 1933], trans. Sasaki Norio (Tokyo: Eiga Hyōronsha, 1936); Dziga Vertov, "Verutofu no eigaron" [retranslated from the German translation of "From Kino-Eye to Radio-Eye" published on *Die Forms*], trans. Itagaki Takao, *Shinkō geijutsu*, November 1929, reprinted in Itagaki's *Kikai to geijutsu to no kōryū* (Tokyo: Iwanami Shoten, 1929), 153–169; Sergei Eisenstein, "Yojigen no eiga," trans. Fukuro Ippei, *Kinema junpō*, October 1, 1929; Eisenstein, "Nihon bunka to montāju," trans. Fukuro Ippei, *Kinema junpō*, January 11, 1930–February 21, 1930, reprinted in Fukuro Ippei, ed. and trans., *Eizenshutain eigaron* (Kyoto: Daiichi Geibunsha, 1940), 46–61

and 9–45; Eisenstein, *Eiga no benshōhō* [*Dialectics of Cinema*, an original anthology of Eisenstein's writings], trans. Sasaki Norio (Tokyo: Ōraisha, 1932); Lev Kuleshov, "Kureshofu eiga geijutsuron," trans. Magami Gitarō, *Eigageijutsu kenkyū* 2–9, June 1933–July 1934; Kuleshov, *Eiga kantokuron*, trans. Magami Gitarō (Tokyo: Eiga Hyōronsha, 1937).

4. Abé Mark Nornes, *Japanese Documentary Film: The Meiji Era through Hiroshima* (Minneapolis: University of Minnesota Press, 2003), xviii.

5. Teshome H. Gabriel, "Colonialism and 'Law and Order' Criticism," *Screen* 27, nos. 3–4 (May–August, 1986): 140–148; Homi K. Bhabha, "The Commitment to Theory," in *Questions of Third Cinema*, ed. Jim Pines and Paul Willemen (London: BFI, 1989), 111–132; Mitsuhiro Yoshimoto, "The Difficulty of Being Radical." Yoshimoto provided an enlarged version of this essay under the new title "Japanese Cinema in Search of a Discipline," in *Kurosawa: Film Studies and Japanese Cinema* (Durham, NC: Duke University Press, 2000), 7–50

6. See David Bordwell, "A Case for Cognitivism," *Iris* 9 (1989): 11–40; Bordwell, "Contemporary Film Studies and the Vicissitudes of Grand Theory," in *Post-Theory: Reconstructing Film Studies*, ed. David Bordwell and Noël Carroll (Madison: University of Wisconsin Press, 1996), 3–36; Noël Carroll, "The Power of Movies," *Daedalus*, 114, no. 4 (Fall, 1985): 79–103; Carroll, "Prospects for Film Theory: A Personal Assessment," in *Post-Theory*, 37–68.

7. Bordwell, "Contemporary Film Studies," 27, 29.

8. For more on this, see my "Soviet Montage Theory and Japanese Film Criticism," in *The Japanese Cinema Book*, ed., Hideaki Fujiki and Alastair Philips (London and New York: Bloomsbury, Bloomsbury, 2020), 68–80.

9. Aaron Gerow, ed., "Decentering Theory: Reconsidering the History of Japanese Film Theory," special issue, *Review of Japanese Culture and Society* 22 (December 2010); Yuriko Furuhata, *Cinema of Actuality: Japanese Avant-Garde Filmmaking in the Season of Image Politics* (Durham, NC: Duke University Press, 2013); Victor Fan, *Cinema Approaching Reality: Locating Chinese Film Theory* (Minneapolis: University of Minnesota Press, 2015); Jessica Ka Yee Chan, *Chinese Revolutionary Cinema: Propaganda, Aesthetics, and Internationalism, 1949–1966* (London: I.B. Tauris, 2019).

10. D. N. Rodowick, "An Elegy for Theory," *October* 122 (Fall 2007): 94.

11. See Alan Langdale, ed., *Hugo Münsterberg on Film: The Photoplay: A Psychological Study and Other Writings* (New York: Routledge, 2001); Béla Balázs, *Béla Balázs: Early Film Theory, "Visible Man" and "The Spirit of Film,"* ed. Erica Carter (New York: Berghahn Books, 2011); Sarah Keller and Jason N. Paul, eds., *Jean Epstein: Critical Essays and New Translations* (Amsterdam: Amsterdam University Press, 2012); Miriam Bratu Hansen, *Cinema and Experience: Siegfried Kracauer, Walter Benjamin, and Theodor W. Adorno* (Cambridge, MA: Harvard University Press, 2011); Dudley Andrew and Hervé Jourbert-Laurencin, eds., *Opening Bazin: Postwar Film Theory and Its Afterlife* (New York: Oxford University Press, 2011). We can also add to this list Anton Kaes, Nicholas Baer, and Michael Cowan, eds., *The Promise of Cinema: German Film Theory, 1907–1933* (Oakland: University of California Press, 2016).

12. Marc Steinberg and Alexander Zahlten, "Introduction," in *Media Theory in Japan*, ed. Marc Steinberg and Alexander Zahlten (Durham, NC: Duke University Press, 2017), 1–29.

13. Shu-mei Shih and François Lionnet, "The Creolization of Theory," in *The Creolization of Theory*, ed. Françoise Lionnet and Shu-mei Shih (Durham, NC: Duke University Press, 2011), 23.

14. Steinberg and Zahlten, "Introduction," 11.
15. Ibid., 6.
16. D. N. Rodowick, *Elegy for Theory* (Cambridge: Harvard University Press, 2014), 54-80.
17. Gavin Walker, "Filmic Materiality and Historical Materialism: Tosaka Jun and the Prosthetics of Sensation," in *Tosaka Jun: A Critical Reader*, ed. Ken C. Kawashima, Fabien Schäfer, and Robert Stolz (Ithaca, NY: Cornell University Press, 2013), 220.
18. Ibid., 235–236.
19. Susan Buck-Morss, "The Cinema as Prosthesis of Perception: A Historical Account," in *The Senses Still: Perception and Memory as Material Culture in Modernity*, ed. C. Nadia Seremetakis (Chicago: University of Chicago Press, 1996), 50; Alan Badiou, "Philosophy and Cinema," in *Infinite Thought: Truth and the Return of Philosophy*, trans. Oliver Feltham and Justin Clemens (London: Continuum, 2005), 111.
20. Shih and Lionnet, "The Creolization of Theory," 23.
21. Rey Chow, *The Age of the World Target: Self-Referentiality in War, Theory, and Comparative Work* (Durham, NC: Duke University Press, 2006), 80.
22. Ibid., 76.
23. Ibid., 85.
24. Ibid., 86. Emphasis in original.
25. Aaron Gerow, "Introduction: The Theory Complex," *Review of Japanese Culture and Society* 22 (December 2010):3.
26. Itami Mansaku, "Tenpo to iu koto ni tsuite," in *Itami Mansaku zenshū* (Tokyo: Chikuma Shobō, 1961), 2:8.
27. Kurata Fumindo, *Shinarioron* (Kyoto: Daiichi Geibunsha, 1940).
28. Itami Mansaku, "*Shinarioron* no naka no shomondai," in *Itami Mansaku zenshū*, 2:79.
29. Ibid.
30. Sato Tadao, "Does Theory Exist in Japan?" trans. Joanne Bernardi, *Review of Japanese Culture and Society* 22 (December 2010): 21, 14.
31. Ibid., 21–22.
32. Austin C. Lescarboura, *Eiga geijutsu kenkyū* [abbreviated translation of *Behind the Motion-Picture Screen*], trans. Kawazoe Toshimoto (Tokyo: Shūhōkaku, 1924); Gilbert Seldes, *Tōki to eiga geijutsu* [*The Movies and the Talkies*], trans. Takahara Fujirō (Tokyo: Eiga Hyōronsha, 1930); V. O. Freeburg, *Eigabi ron: Sukurīn jō no bi ni tsuite* [*Pictorial Beauty on the Screen*], trans. Kawazoe Toshimoto (Tokyo: Naigaisha, 1932); Eric Elliot, *Eiga gijustu to eiga geijutsu* [*The Anatomy of Motion Picture Art*], trans. Kishi Matsuo (Tokyo: Ōraisha, 1932); and Fedor Stepun, *Junsui geijutsu toshite no eiga* [*Theater und kino*], trans. Sasaki Norio (Tokyo: Geijutsusha, 1935).
33. "Henshū kōki," *Eiga kikan* no. 1 (November 1948): 116.
34. Gerow, "Introduction: The Theory Complex," 6.
35. D. N. Rodowick, *The Crisis of Political Modernism: Criticism and Ideology in Contemporary Film Criticism*, rev. ed. (Berkeley: University of California Press, 1995). For critical accounts of film theory in this period, see also Constance Penley, "Feminism, Film Theory, and the Bachelor Machines," in *The Future of An Illusion: Film, Feminism, and Psychoanalysis* (Minneapolis: University of Minnesota Press, 1989), 56–80; Philp Rosen, "Screen and 1970s Film Theory," in *Inventing Film Studies*, ed. Lee Grieveson and Haidee Wasson (Durham, NC: Duke, 2008), 264–297.

36. Trenchant critiques of Bazin's realist theory can be found in Peter Wollen, "'Ontology' and 'Materialism' in Film," *Screen* 17, no. 1 (Spring 1976): 7–23; Jean-Louis Comolli, "Technique and Ideology: Camera, Perspective, Depth of Field," trans. Diana Matias, in Nichols, *Movies and Methods*, 2:40–57.

37. See, for instance, Jean-Louis Baudry, "Ideological Effects of the Basic Cinematographic Apparatus," trans. Alan Williams, *Film Quarterly* 28, no. 2 (Winter 1974–1975): 39–47; Laura Mulvey, "Visual Pleasure and Narrative Cinema," *Screen* 16, no. 3 (Autumn 1975): 6–18.

38. Colin MacCabe, "Realism and the Cinema: Notes on Some Brechtian Theses," *Screen* 15, no. 2 (Summer 1974): 7–27.

39. Dudley Andrew, *Concepts in Film Theory* (New York: Oxford University Press, 1984), 37–56; Philip Rosen, "History of Image, Image of History: Subject and Ontology in Bazin," *Wide Angle* 9, no. 4 (Winter 1987/88): 7–34.

40. Andrew, *The Major Film Theories*, 142.

41. David Bordwell, *Narration in the Fiction Film* (Madison: University of Wisconsin Press, 1985), 26.

42. See, for example, Ivone Margulies, ed., *Rites of Realism: Essays on Corporeal Cinema* (Durham, NC: Duke University Press, 2002); Lúcia Nagib, *World Cinema and the Ethics of Realism* (New York: Continuum, 2011); Tiago de Luca, *Realism in the Senses in World Cinema: The Experience of Physical Reality* (London: I.B. Tauris, 2013).

43. Lúcia Nagib and Cecília Mello, "Introduction," in *Realism and the Audiovisual Media*, ed. Lúcia Nagib and Cecília Mello (New York: Palgrave, 2009), xxi.

44. Ibid.

45. For this distinction, see André Bazin, "The Evolution of the Language of Cinema" in *What Is Cinema?* trans. Hugh Gray (Berkeley: University of California Press, 1967), 1:23–40; Siegfried Kracauer, "Basic Concepts," in *Theory of Film: The Redemption of Physical Reality* (New York: Oxford University Press, 1960), 27–40.

46. André Bazin, "The Ontology of the Photographic Image," in *What Is Cinema?* 1:12.

47. Ibid., 11.

48. Ibid., 13.

49. Raymond Williams, "Realism," in *Keywords: A Vocabulary of Culture and Society*, new ed. (New York: Oxford University Press, 2015), 198.

50. Ibid., 199.

51. Fredric Jameson, "The Existence of Italy," in *Signature of Realism*, new ed. (New York: Routledge, 2007), 217.

52. Ibid., 223–224.

53. Ibid., 215–217.

54. I discuss this debate later in this introduction with regards to Harry Harootunian's work.

55. Yokomitsu Riichi, "Kankaku katsudō," *Bungei jidai* 2, no. 2 (February 1925): 7.

56. Roman Jakobson, "On Realism in Art," in *Language in Literature*, ed. Krystina Pomorska and Stephen Rudy (Cambridge, MA: Harvard University Press, 1987), 24.

57. Ibid., 20.

58. Ibid., 21.

59. Tsuji Hisakazu, "Eiga no riarizumu," *Eiga hyōron* 124 (July 1936): 96.

60. Dilip Parameshwar Gaonkar, "On Alternative Modernities," in *Alternative Modernities*, ed. Dilip Parameshwar Gaonkar (Durham, NC: Duke University Press, 2001), 1.
61. Ibid., 14.
62. Ibid., 17–18.
63. Ibid., 15.
64. Ibid., 17.
65. Harry Harootunian, "Ghostly Comparisons," in *Impacts of Modernities*, ed. Thomas Lamarre and Kang Nae-hui (Hong Kong: Hong Kong University Press, 2004), 44.
66. This symposium was published as Chiteki kyōryoku kaigi, ed., *Kindai no chōkoku* (Tokyo: Sōgensha, 1943). For more on this symposium, see Sun Ge, "In Search of the Modern: Tracing Japanese Thought on 'Overcoming Modernity,'" in Lamarre and Kang, *Impacts of Modernities*, 53–75; Harry Harootunian, *Overcome by Modernity: History, Culture, and Community in Interwar Japan* (Princeton, NJ: Princeton University Press, 2000), especially chapter 2.
67. Thomas Lamarre, "Introduction: Impacts of Modernities," in Lamarre and Kang, *Impacts of Modernities*, 12.
68. Ibid., 14.
69. Ibid., 15.
70. Ibid., 34.
71. Karl Marx, *Capital: A Critique of Political Economy*, trans. Ben Fowkes, repr. (Penguin Books: London, 1990), 1:198.
72. Hanada Kiyoteru, "Daen gensō—Viyon," in *Hanada Kiyoteru zenshū* (Tokyo, Kōdansha, 1977–1980), 2:395.
73. Ōsawa Masachi, "Daen gensō—Shihon shugi no seishin to tenkeiki no seishin," in *Shihon shugi no paradokkus*, new ed. (Tokyo: Chikuma Shobō, 2008), 113–118.
74. Hanada Kiyoteru, "Tentaizu—Koperunikusu," in *Hanada Kityoteru zenshū*, 2:267.
75. Vladimir I. Lenin, "On the Question of Dialectics," in *The Lenin Anthology*, ed. Robert C. Tucker (New York: W. W. Norton, 1975), 649.
76. Hanada Kiyoteru, "Yūmoresuku," in *Hanada Kiyoteru zenshū*, 4:14.

CHAPTER 1

1. Satō Tadao, "Tōkī jidai: Nihon eigashi 3," in *Tōkī no jidai*, vol. 3 of *Kōza Nihon eiga*, ed. Imamura Shōhei, Satō Tadao et al. (Tokyo: Iwanami Shoten, 1986), 30.
2. Ibid.
3. Yoda Yoshikata, *Mizoguchi Kenji no hito to geijutsu*, quoted in Satō, "Tōkī jidai," 31.
4. Joseph L. Anderson and Donald Richie, *The Japanese Film: Art and Industry*, exp ed. (Princeton, NJ: Princeton University Press, 1982), 45.
5. Chiba Nobuo, "*Sei no kagayaki* kara *Orochi* made," in *Nihon eigashi: Jissha kara seichō konmei no jidai made*, ed. Yamamoto Kikuo et al. (Tokyo: Kinema Junpōsha, 1976), 29.
6. Hereafter, I call him by his first name "Shōyō" following a convention in Japanese literary studies.
7. Tsubouchi Shōyō, "Shōsetsu shinzui," in *Seiji shōsetsu, Tsubouchi Shōyō, Futabatei Shimei shū*, vol. 1 of *Gendai Nihon bungaku taikei* (Tokyo: Chikuma Shobō, 1971), 195.
8. Ibid., 194.

9. For more detailed accounts of this essay, see Tomi Suzuki, *Narrating the Self: Fiction of Japanese Modernity* (Stanford, CA: Stanford University Press, 1996); Atsuko Ueda, *Concealment of Politics, Politics of Concealment: The Production of "Literature" in Meiji Japan* (Stanford, CA: Stanford University Press, 2007).

10. Futabatei Shimei, "Shōsetsu sōron," in *Seiji Shōsetsu, Tsubouchi Shōyō, Futabatei Shimei shū*, 371.

11. Ibid. Besides his own translation of the term *realism* (*shujitsu shugi*), Futabatei also added its transliteration (*riarizumu*) for the sake of clarity.

12. Ibid.

13. Futabatei Shimei, "Yoga honyaku no hyōjun," in *Seiji Shōsetsu, Tsubouchi Shōyō, Futabatei Shimei shū*, 374.

14. Cited in Donald Keene, *Dawn to the West: Japanese Literature of the Modern Era, Fiction* (New York: Holt, Rinehart and Winston, 1984), 226. In this case, the "poet" refers to any type of creative writers.

15. Hasegawa Tenkei, "Genmetsu jidai no geijutsu," in *Shizenshugi* (Tokyo: Hakubunkan, 1908), 1–18.

16. Hasegawa Tenkei, "Kinji shōsetsudan no keikō," in *Shizen shugi*, 110.

17. Shimamura Hōgetsu, "Bungei jō no Shizen Shugi," in *Kindai bungaku hyōron taikei*, ed. Yoshida Seiichi et al. (Tokyo: Kadokawa Shoten, 1971–1975), 3:101–102.

18. Sōma Gyofū, "Bungei jō shukyaku ryōtai no yūkai," in *Kindai bungaku hyōron taikei*, 3:61.

19. Ishikawa Takuboku, "Jidai heisoku no genjō," in *Kindai bungaku hyōron taikei*, 3:334.

20. Gonda Yasunosuke, *Gonda Yasunosuke chosakushū* (Tokyo: Bunwa Shobō, 1974–1975), 1:311.

21. Aaron Gerow, *Visions of Japanese Modernity: Articulation of Cinema, Nation, and Spectatorship, 1895–1925* (Berkeley: University of California Press, 2010), 80.

22. Aaron Gerow, "Gonda Yasunosuke ga sozō shita eigabunmei gensetsu," in *Gonda Yasunosuke, Katsudō shashin no genre oyobi ōyō*, reprinted as vol. 24 of *Nihon eigaron gensetsu taikei*, ed. Makino Mamoru (Tokyo: Yumani Shobō, 2006), Appendix 16.

23. Gonda, Yasunosuke, *Katsudō shashin no genri oyobi ōyō* (Tokyo: Uchida Rōkakuho, 1916), 400.

24. Hugo Münsterberg, *Photoplay: A Psychological Study* (New York: D. Appleton, 1916), 144.

25. Gonda, *Katsudō shashi*, 444.

26. William James, *Saikin shichō jissai shugi: Genmei puragumatizumu* [Pragmatism: A New Name for Some Old Ways of Thinking], trans. Kiatazawa Sadakichi et al. (Tokyo: Kōdōkan, 1910).

27. Ōsugi Sakae, "Rōdō mondai to puragumatizumu," in *Hangyaku no seishin: Ōsugi Sakae hyōronshū* (Tokyo: Heibonsha, 2011), 170–182.

28. William James, *Pragmatism: A New Name for Some Old Ways of Thinking* (New York: Longmans, 1907), 3–40.

29. Gonda, *Katsudō shashin*, 344.

30. Ibid., 305.

31. Ibid., 446.

32. Ibid.

33. Ibid., 404–406.
34. Ibid., 400–401.
35. Henri Bergson, *An Introduction to Metaphysics*, trans. T. E. Hulme (New York and London: G. P. Putnam's Sons, 1912), 7.
36. Ibid., 36.
37. Gonda, *Katsudō shahsin*, 412.
38. Ibid., 415.
39. Ibid., 397.
40. Ibid., 410.
41. Ibid., 454.
42. Ibid., 453.
43. Ibid., 452–453.
44. Béla Balázs, *Béla Balázs: Early Film Theory*, 14.
45. Gonda, *Katsudō shashin*, 11.
46. Ibid., 12–13.
47. Gerow, *Visions of Japanese Modernity*, 73.
48. These monographs are all reprinted as vols. 1 and 2 of *Gonda Yasunosuke chosakushū*.
49. For a detailed analysis of this first regulation, see Hase Masato, "Ken'estu no tanjō: Taishō-ki no keisatsu to katsudō shashin," *Eizōgaku* 53 (1994): 124–138; Gerow, *Visons of Japanese Modernity*, 174–221.
50. See Gerow, *Visons of Japanese Modernity*, 1–2.
51. Nakagi Sadakazu, "Katsudō shashin no geijutsuteki kachi: Gaimenteki keshikiron," *Katsudō gahō* 5, no. 5 (May 1921): 25.
52. Katano Hakuro, "Nihon eiga to gaikoku eiga no hikaku kenkyū," *Katsudō gahō* 3, no. 3 (March 1919): 165.
53. See my "Where Did the Bluebird of Happiness Fly? Bluebird Photoplays and the Reception of American Film in 1910s Japan," *Iconics* 10 (2010): 143–166.
54. Balázs, *Béla Balázs: Early Film Theory*, 59.
55. Kaeriyama Norimasa, *Katsudō shashingeki no sōsaku to satsueihō* (Tokyo: Hikōsha, 1917). Its expanded edition (1921) is reprinted as vol. 25 of *Nihon eigaron gensetsu taikei*, ed. Makino Mamoru (Tokyo: Yumani Shobō, 2006). Hereafter citations are from this reprinted version.
56. Kaeriyama, *Katsudō shashingeki*, 110.
57. Ibid, 107–108.
58. Ibid., 120.
59. Ogawa Seiji, "Sen'nendo no katsudō shashinkai zakkan," *Kinema rekōdo*, no. 6 (January 1914): 9–10.
60. Kaeriyama, *Katsudō shashingeki*, 21–22.
61. Münsterberg, *Photoplay*, 173.
62. Together with Sessue Hayakawa and Tsuru Aoki, Kurihara had worked for a while as an actor at Thomas Ince's Oriental Production before his return to Japan in 1918.
63. See, for instance, Chiba Nobuo, *Eiga to Tanizaki* (Tokyo: Seiabō, 1989); Thomas LaMarre, *Shadows on the Screen: Tanizaki Jun'ichirō on Cinema and "Oriental" Aesthetics* (Ann Arbor: University of Michigan Center for Japanese Studies, 2005).

64. Tanizaki Jun'ichirō, "Asakusa kōen," in *Tanizaki Jun'ichirō zenshū* (Tokyo: Chūō Kōronsha, 1981–1983), 22:60.
65. Georg von Lukács, "Thoughts toward an Aesthetic of the Cinema," trans. Janelle Blankenship, *Polygraph* 13 (2001): 14.
66. Tanizaki Jun'ichirō, "The Present and Future of Moving Pictures," trans. Thomas LaMarre, in LaMarre, *Shadows on the Screen*, 68–69.
67. Tanizaki, "The Present and Future," 67–68, 70.
68. Tanizaki Jun'ichirō, "Nikkai," in *Tanizaki Jun'ichirō zenshū*, 9:40–44. Translation of this passage is taken from Joanne Bernardi, *Writing in Light: The Silent Scenario and the Japanese Pure Film Movement* (Detroit: Wayne State university Press, 2001), 147–148.
69. LaMarre, *Shadows on the Screen*, 1–4.
70. Ibid., 9.
71. Tanizaki Jun'ichirō, "Sōshun zakkan," in *Tanizaki Jun'ichirō zenshū*, 22:66–68.
72. LaMarre, *Shadows on the Screen*, 5.
73. Tanizaki, "The Present and Future," 69.
74. Ibid., 67.
75. Tanizaki, "Sōshun zakkan," 68.
76. Ibid., 69.
77. Tanizaki Jun'ichirō, "*Karigari hakase* wo miru," in *Tanizaki Jun'ichirō zenshū*, 22:112.
78. Murata Mironu, "Hyōgenha no eiga no kanshō: Hyogenha to wa nanika," *Katsudō no sekai* 4, no. 10 (October 1922): 63.
79. Midorikawa Harunosuke, "Eigageki gūkan," *Katsudō kurabu* 4, no. 8 (August 1921): 41.
80. Mitsuse Sueo, "Futatsu no izumu," *Kinema junpō* 181 (January 1, 1925): 65.
81. Raymond Williams, "When Was Modernism?" *New Left Review* 1, no. 175 (May–June 1989): 49.
82. Mitsuse, "Futatsu no izumu," 66.

CHAPTER 2

1. Kudō Shin'nosuke, *Hyōgenha no eiga* (Tokyo: Chūō Bijutsusha, 1923), 4.
2. Ibid., 5.
3. Tanizaki Junichirō, "*Karigari hakase* wo miru," 110.
4. Jean Epstein, "The Senses I (b)," trans. Tom Milne, in *French Film Theory and Criticism*, ed. Richard Abel, (Princeton, NJ: Princeton University Press), 1:244.
5. Béla Balázs, *Béla Balázs: Early Film Theory*, 38.
6. Dziga Vertov, "Kinoks: A Revolution," in *Kino-Eye: The Writings of Dziga Vertov*, ed. Annette Michelson, trans. Kevin O'Brien (Berkeley: University of California Press, 1984), 14–15.
7. Francesco Casetti, *Eye of the Century: Film, Experience, Modernity* (New York: Columbia University Press, 2008), 8.
8. Malcolm Turvey, *Doubting Vision: Film and the Revelationist Tradition* (New York: Oxford University Press, 2008), 3.
9. Ibid., 49–78.
10. Dudley Andrew et al., "Roundtable on the Return to Classical Film Theory," *October* 148 (Spring 2014): 15.

11. Ibid., 15–16.
12. Itagaki Takao, *Kikai to geijutsu to no kōryū* (Tokyo: Iwanami Shoten, 1929).
13. Iijima Tadashi, "Eiga shōron," in *Shinema no ABC* (Tokyo: Kōseikaku Shoten, 1928), 5.
14. F. T. Marinetti, "Miraishugi no sengen," trans. Mori Ōgai, *Subaru* (May 1909).
15. More detailed accounts of the Japanese reception of twentieth-century avant-garde art can be found in Omuka Toshiharu, *Nihon no avangyarudo geijutsu: "Mavo" to sono jidai* (Tokyo: Seidosha, 2001); Wada Hirofumi, ed., *Nihon no avangyarudo* (Kyoto: Sekai Shisōsha, 2005).
16. For Murayama's activities in Berlin and Tokyo, see Murayama Tomoyoshi, *Engekiteki jijyoden*, 4 vols. (Tokyo: Tōhō Shuppansha, 1970–1977); Omuka Toshiharu, "Murayama Tomoyoshi no ishikiteki kōseishugi: 'Subete no boku ga futtō suru tameni,'" in *Nihon no avangyarudo geijutsu*, 49–65.
17. Yokomitsu Riichi, "Kaisetsu ni kaete (1)," in *Teihon Yokomitsu Riichi zenshū*, 13:584.
18. Gennifer Weisenfeld, "Designing after Disaster: Barrack Decoration and the Great Kantō Earthquake," *Japanese Studies* 18, no. 3 (1998): 229–246.
19. Quoted in William O. Gardner, *Advertising Tower: Japanese Modernism and Modernity in the 1920s* (Cambridge, MA: Harvard University Asia Center, 2006), 36.
20. Yokomitsu Riichi, "Kankaku katsudō," 7.
21. Seiji M. Lippit, *Topographies of Japanese Modernism* (New York: Columbia University Press, 2002), 78.
22. Yokomitsu Riichi, "Shinkankaku bungaku no kenkyū," *Teihon Yokomitsu Riichi zenshū*, 14:312.
23. Gregory Golley, *When Our Eyes No Longer See: Realism, Science, and Ecology in Japanese Literary Modernism* (Cambridge, MA: Harvard University Asia Center, 2008), 17.
24. Ibid., 20.
25. Itagaki Takao, "Gendai geijutsu kōsatsusha no shuki," *Shinkō geijutsu kenkyū* 1 (February 1931): 208–209.
26. For the historical significance of *shinkō shashin*, see Takeba Joe, "The Age of Modernism: From Visualization to Socialization," in *The History of Japanese Photography*, ed. Anne Wilkes Tucker et al. (New Haven, CT: Yale University Press, 2003), 142–183.
27. Horino Masao, *Kamera, me x Tetsu, kōsei* (Tokyo: Mokuseosha Shoin, 1932).
28. Itagaki Takao and Horino Masao, "Dai-Tokyo no seikaku," *Chūō kōron* 46, no. 10 (October 1931): appendixes 1–20. Moholy-Nagy's "Dynamics of the Metropolis," in *Painting Photography Film*, trans. Janet Seligman (Cambridge, MA: MIT Press, 1969), 124–137.
29. It seems that Lu Xun had a keen interest in the writings of Itagaki and his colleagues at *Shinkō geijutsu*. In addition to Iwasaki's article, Lu Xun translated Itagaki's 1927 book *Minzokuteki shikisai o shu to suru kindai bijutsushichō ron* under the title "'Yi minzu secai' weizhude jindai meishushichao lun." This translation is included in vol. 15 of *Lu Xun quanji* (Shanghai: Shanghai Lu Xun Quanji Chubanshe, 1938).
30. "Hakkan no ji," quoted in Makino Mamoru, "*Shinkō geijutsu* to *Shinkō geijutsu kenkyū* no jidai," in *Shinkō Geijutsu*, vol. 3 of *Nihon modanizumu no kōryū*, ed. Makino Mamoru. (Tokyo: Yumani shobō, 1990), 163.
31. Hirano Ken, *Shōwa bungakushi* (Tokyo: Chikuma Shobō, 1963).
32. Itagaki Takao, "Kikai bunmei to gendai bijutsu," in *Kikai to geijutsu to no kōryū*, 40–41.

33. Ibid., 44. Le Corbusier's dictum was first introduced in his 1923 book *Ver une architecture*, translated as *Toward an Architecture*, ed. Jean-Louis Cohen, trans. John Goodman (Los Angeles: Getty Research Institute, 2007).

34. Itagaki, "Kikai bunmei to gendai bijutsu," 44–50.

35. Ibid., 63. In contrast, Itagaki repeatedly criticized Fritz Lang's *Metropolis* (1925) as an example of what he called "machine romanticism." As a caption for stills from the film, he wrote: "It is impossible to interpret the 'machine' more anachronistically than this!" in *Kikai to geijutsu to no kōryū*, 2.

36. Itagaki Takao, "Kikai to geijutsu to no kōryū," in *Kikai to geijutsu to no kōryū*, 97–98.

37. I discuss the Japanese reception of Soviet montage theory in more detail in chapter 3.

38. According to Itagaki, the German translation of Vertov's manifesto appeared in the July 1929 issue of *Die Form*. In addition to this, Itagaki also obtained information from other German magazines such as *Das Kunstblatt* and *Das neue Frankfurt*.

39. Dziga Vertov, "From Kino-Eye to Radio-Eye," in *Kino-Eye*, 87–88.

40. Itagaki Takao, "Kikai no riarizumu e no michi," in *Kikai to geijutsu to no kōryū*, 150.

41. Itagaki, "Kikai to geijutsu to no kōryū," 73.

42. Ibid., 71–72.

43. Itagaki Takao, "Kikaibi no tanjō," in *Kikai geijutsuron*, ed. Itagaki Takao (Tokyo: Tenjinsha, 1930), 2–3.

44. Mats Karlson, "Kurahara Korehito's Road to Proletarian Realism," *Japan Review* 20 (2008): 236. Needless to say, this view has also been shared by many Japanese literary scholars including Yamada Seisaburō, Miyamoto Kenji, Hirano Ken, Sobue Shōji, and Kobayashi Shigeo.

45. Kurahara Korehito, "Saikin no Sowēt eigakai (1)" *Kinema junpō* 254 (March 1, 1927): 24; "Saikin no Sowēto eigakai (2)," *Kinema junpō* 257 (April 1, 1927): 30.

46. V. I. Lenin, "Declaration of the Editorial Board of Iskra," in *Collected Works* (Moscow: Foreign Language Publishing House, 1960–70), 4:354.

47. Kurahara, "Proretaria rearizumu e no michi," in *Kurahara Korehito shū*, vol. 4 of *Nihon puroretaria bungaku hyōronshū* (Tokyo: Shin Nihon Shuppansha, 1990), 118.

48. Ibid.

49. Ibid., 122–123.

50. Sobue Shōji, "Puroretaria bungaku I," in *Kindai puroretaria bungaku*, vol. 13 of *Iwanami kōza: Nihon bungakushi*, ed. Subue Shōji and Takeuchi Yoshimi (Tokyo: Iwanami Shoten, 1959), 3–55.

51. Komiyama Akitoshi, "Puroretaria bungaku no gendankai: Soshite sorewa ikanaru hōkō e susumu beki dearu ka," in *Kōki puroretaria bungaku hyōronshū 2*, vol. 7 of *Nihon Puroretaria bungaku hyōronshū* (Tokyo: Shin Nihon Shuppansha, 1990), 190.

52. Ibid.

53. Kurahara Korehito, "Shin-geijutsu keishiki no tankyū e: Puroretaria geijutsu tōmen no mondai ni tsuite," in *Kurahara Korehito shū*, 237.

54. Kobayashi Takiji, "Kikai no kaikyūsei' ni tsuite" in *Kōki puroretaria bungaku hyōronshū 2*, vol. 7 of *Nihon Puroretaria bungaku hyōronshū* (Tokyo: Shin Nihon Shuppansha, 1990), 68–69.

55. Kimura Toshimi, "Kikai to geijutsu kakumei," in *Kikai to geijutsu kakumei*, ed. and trans. Kimura Toshimi (Tokyo: Hakuyōsha, 1930), 255–256.

56. Itagaki Takao, "Gendai geijutsu kōsatsusha no shuki," 227.
57. Kimura Toshimi, "Hashigaki," in Kimura, *Kikai to geijutsu kakumei*, 7. The *X*'s in this passage, usually called *fuseji*, indicate a word censored by the government. But because the rule for this concealment was not that complicated, it is easy to retrieve the original words according to the contexts.
58. Wadayama Shigeru, "*Korega Roshia da*," *Kinema junpō* 431 (April 1, 1932): 43.
59. Kiuchi Tsuguo, "*Korega Roshia da*," *Eiga hyōron* 11, no. 4 (April 1932): 139.
60. Kamo Kyōji, "*Korega Roshia da*," *Purokino* 1, no. 1 (May 1932): 75
61. Tomioka Shō, "Tōkī geijutsu no rearizumu e no michi," *Eiga hyōron* 14, no. 5 (May 1933): 69.
62. Ibid., 73.

CHAPTER 3

1. See, for instance, Ōtsuka Kyōichi, "*Sono yoru no onna*," *Eiga hyōron* 16, no. 12 (December 1934): 153–154.
2. Anderson and Richie, *The Japanese Film*, 96.
3. A detailed review of *Constellations on the Earth* is found in Ōtsuka Kyōichi, "Eiga jihyō: Tōkī no konponsaku o juritsu seyo," *Eiga hyōron* 17, no. 1 (July 1934): 23. Like *The Woman That Night*, this film no longer exists today.
4. Ikeda Terukatsu and Tomoda Jun'ichirō, "1934-nendo gyōkai sōkessan," *Kinema junpō* 527 (January 1, 1935): 278.
5. Tsuji Hisakazu, "Shimazu Yasujirō: Tōkī igo," *Eiga hyōron* 108 (March 1935): 31.
6. Henshūbu, "Shuyō Nihon eiga hihyō: *Sono yoru no onna*," *Kinema junpō* 523 (November 11, 1934): 101.
7. Ōtsuka, "*Sono yoru no onna*," 153.
8. Hazumi Tsuneo, "Eiga riarizumu no teishō," *Kinema junpō* 560 (December 1, 1935): 75.
9. André Bazin, "The Evolution of the Language of Cinema," in *What Is Cinema?* 1:24.
10. Sekino Yoshio, "Tōkī: Shinema geijutsu no aratanarau tenkai," *Bigaku kenkyū*, no. 2 (April 1930): 260.
11. Thomas Elsaesser and Malte Hagener, *Film Theory: An Introduction through the Senses* (New York: Routledge, 2010), 22.
12. Rudolf Arnheim, *Geijutsu to shite no eiga* [Film als Kunst], trans. Sasaki Norio (Tokyo: Ōraisha, 1933).
13. Nakagawa Shigeaki, *Keiji shin'in shokuhai bigaku* (Tokyo: Hakubunka, 1911), 154.
14. Kawazoe Toshimoto, *Eigageki gairon: Eizōgeki e no "daiichi no mon"* (Tokyo: Sun'nansha, 1927), 158–159. His translation of *Pictorial Beauty on the Screen* was published under the title *Eigabiron: Skurīn jō no bi ni tsuite* (Tokyo: Naigaisha, 1932).
15. Sergei Eisenstein, "Beyond the Shot," in *Sergei Eisenstein: Selected Works, vol. 1, Writings, 1922–34*, ed. Richard Taylor (London and New York: I.B. Tauris, 2010), 138–150.
16. See my "Soviet Montage Theory and Japanese Film Criticism."
17. Satō Tadao, "Does Film Theory Exist in Japan?" 16.
18. Ibid., 19.
19. Shimizu Hikaru, "Eiga to kikai," in *Kikai geijutsuron*, ed. Itagaki Takao (Tokyo: Tenjinsha, 1930), 67.

20. Ibid., 64.

21. Hirabayashi Hatsunosuke, "Geijutsu no keishiki to shite no shōsetsu to eiga," in *Hirabayashi Hatsynosuke ikōshū*, ed. Hirabayashi Komako (Tokyo: Heibonsha, 1932), 121.

22. Sawamura Tsutomu, *Eiga no hyōgen* (Tokyo: Suga Shoten, 1942), 231–232. According to Sawamura, this essay was originally written in 1937 but remained unpublished until 1942.

23. Saitō Kōji, ed., "Sakusha betsu eiga-ka sareta bungei, taishjū, shōsetsu, gikyoku," *Eiga hyōron* 107 (February 1935): 65–82.

24. Tosaka Jun, "Nihon ideologīron: Gendai Nihon ni okeru Nihon shugi, fashizumu, jiyū shugi, shisō no hihan," in *Tosaka Jun zenshū* (Tokyo: Keisō Shobō, 1966–1967), 2:368.

25. Eiga bungaku kenkyūkai, "1936-nen bungei eiga no oboegaki," *Eiga shūdan* 8 (January 1937): 51.

26. Andrew, *Concepts in Film Theory*, 100.

27. Eiga bungaku kenkyūkai, "1936-nen bungei eiga no oboegaki," 51.

28. Cited in Kishi Matsuo, *Nihon eiga yōshikikō* (Tokyo: Kawade Shobō, 1937), 145.

29. The print of *Unending Advance* is preserved at the National Film Archive in Tokyo, but this version was heavily reedited when it was redistributed in the immediate postwar period. To reduce the film's tragic tone, this version abruptly ends in the middle where the protagonist's "happy" dreams all come true.

30. Although this was what local critics of the time believed to be the case, Shōchiku had already begun by this time to offer Nikkatsu a financial support in an attempt to buy it out.

31. Ozu Yasujirō (original story), Yagi Yasutarō (adaptation), "Shinario: Tanoshiki kana Yasukichi-kun," *Shinchō* 34, no. 8 (August 1937): 201–245.

32. Nanbu Keinosuke, Hazumi Tsuneo et al., "Kagirinaki zenshin wo megutte," *Kinema junpō* 628 (November 11, 1937): 12.

33. Ozu and Yagi, "Shinario: Tanoshiki kana Yasukichi-kun," 244.

34. Murakami Tadahisa, *Nihon eiga sakkaron* (Tokyo: Ōraisha, 1936); Ōtsuka Kyōichi, *Nihon eiga kantokuron* (Tokyo: Eiga Hyōronsha, 1937).

35. Kitagawa Fuyuhiko, "Bungei eiga sakuhin shoken sonota," *Kinema junpō* 529 (January 21, 1935): 59–60.

36. Iijima Tadashi, "Shinario bungakuron josetsu," in *Shinario taikei*, vol. 1 of *Shinario bungaku zenshū*, ed. Iijima Tadashi et al. (Tokyo: Kawade Shobō, 1937), 6.

37. Ibid., 19–23.

38. For Kamei's activity in the Soviet Union, see Anastasia Fedorova, *Riarizumu no gensō: Nisso eiga koryūshi, 1925–1955* (Tokyo: Shinwasha, 2018).

39. Kamei Fumio, "Kiroku eiga shinario: Pekin," *Eiga hyōron* 147 (June 1938), 73.

40. For a detailed account of the production history of the film, see Saeki Tomonori et al., eds., *FC 90: Uchida Tomu kantoku tokushū* (Tokyo: Tokyo Kokuritsu Kindai Bijutsukan Firumu Sentā, 1992), 37–41.

41. See my "Tōkī rirarizumu e no michi," in *Eigashi o yominaosu*, ed. Komatsu Hiroshi et al., vol. 2 of *Nihon eiga wa ikiteiru*, ed. Yomota Inuhiko et al. (Tokyo: Iwanami Shoten, 2010), 211–259.

42. Darrell W. Davis, *Picturing Japaneseness: Monumental Style, National Identity, Japanese Film* (New York: Columbia University Press, 1996), 69.

43. For more on the historical shift from *kyūha* to *jidaigeki*, see Kyōto eigasai jikkō iinkai, ed., *Jidaigeki eiga to wa nani ka: Nyū firumu stadīzu* (Kyoto: Jinbun Shoin, 1997).

44. Although the film itself is not extant today, *Before Dawn* is said to have featured a montage of the ceremonial procession of a feudal lord and rituals practiced at the Buddhist temple in reference to a similar montage of the religious procession of peasants and rituals practiced at the Orthodox Church in Eisenstein's *Old and New* (1929).

45. For the Japanese interwar culture known as *ero guro nansensu*, see Miriam Silverberg, *Erotic Grotesque Nonsense: The Mass Culture of Japanese Modern Times* (Berkeley: University of California Press, 2006).

46. Anderson and Richie, *The Japanese Film*, 95.

47. Tsumura Hideo, "Kinugasa Teinosuke-shi e no tegami: Rekishi eiga no teishō," in *Eiga to hihyō* (Tokyo: Koyama Shoten, 1939), 115–128.

48. As a historical event, the summer battle of Osaka took place from April to May 1615, ending with the final victory of the Tokugawa Shogunate over the Toyotomi clan.

49. Tsumura, "Kinugasa Teinosuke-shi e no tegami," 118.

50. Ibid., 126.

51. Mori Ōgai, "Rekishi sono mama to rekishi banare," in *Mori Ōgai zenshū* (Tokyo: Iwanami Shoten, 1951–1956), 23:506.

52. Ibid.

53. Tsumura, "Kinugasa Teinosuke-shi e no tegami," 126.

54. Kumagai Hisatora, "*Abe ichizoku* no eiga-ka," *Nihon eiga* 3, no. 2 (February 1938): 59.

55. Sawamura Tsutomu, "*Abe ichizoku o megutte*," *Eiga hyōron* 146 (April 1938): 61–66.

56. Tsumura, "Rekishi eiga ni tsuite," in *Eiga to hihyō*, 144.

57. See Fujimoto Chizuko, "Ōgai *Abe ichizoku* no hassō: Sakuhin to jittaiken," *Kindai bungaku shiron* 14 (October 1975): 10–18; Yamamoto Hirofumi, *Junshi no kōzō* (Tokyo: Kōbundō, 1994), 14–36.

58. James Schamus, "Dreyer's Textual Realism," in Margulies, *Rites of Realism*, 315–324.

59. Tsumura Hideo, "Eiga geijutsu e no dansō," in *Eiga to hihyō*, 9.

60. Ibid., 10–11.

61. Tsumura, "Rekishi eiga ni tsuite," 136.

62. Hasegawa Nyozekan, "Rekishi eiga no geijutsuteki seikaku," in *Nihon eigaron* (Tokyo: Dai-Nippon Eiga Kyōkai, 1943), 120.

63. Mizoguchi Kenji, "Genroku chūshingura no konpon taido," in *Mizoguchi Kenji chosakushū*, ed. Sasō Tsutomu (Tokyo: Kinema Junpōsha, 2015), 249.

64. Ibid., 250.

65. Tsumura Hideo, *Eiga seisakuron* (Tokyo: Chūō Koronsha, 1943); Tsumura, *Eigasen* (Tokyo: Asahi Shinbunsha, 1944).

CHAPTER 4

1. Hazumi Tsuneo, *Eiga 50 nenshi* (Tokyo: Masu Shobō, 1942), quoted in Peter B. High, *The Imperial Screen: Japanese Film Culture in the Fifteen Years' War, 1931–1945* (Madison: University of Wisconsin Press, 2003), 95.

2. For more details about these films, see Nornes, *Japanese Documentary Film*, 72–92.

3. Quoted in Nornes, *Japanese Documentary Film*, 63.

4. Indeed, Atsugi Taka, the Japanese translator of Rotha's *Documentary Film*, gave the title *Bunka eigaron* (On Culture Film) to the first edition of her translation and changed it

back to "dokyumentari eiga" (Documentary Film) in a revised edition published after World War II.

5. For these debates, see Fujii Jinshi, "Films That Do Culture: A Discursive Analysis of Bunka Eiga, 1935–1945," trans. Lori Hitchcock, *Iconics* 6 (2002): 51–68.

6. See my "Soviet Montage Theory and Japanese Film Criticism."

7. See Terada Torahiko, "Eiga no sekaizō," in *Terada Torahiko zuihitsushū*, ed. Komiya Toyotaka (Tokyo: Iwanami Shoten, 1947–1948), 3:133–141; Terada, "Eiga geijutsu," in *Terada Torahiko zuihitsushū*, 3:201–238.

8. Terada Torahiko, "Nyūsu eiga to shinbun kiji," in *Terada Torahiko zenshū* (Tokyo: Iwanami Shoten, 1960–1962), 7:49–53.

9. Ibid., 52.

10. Ibid., 53.

11. Nornes, *Japanese Documentary Film*, 55.

12. For Tosaka's personal ties with members of the Kyoto School, see Tanabe Hajime et al., *Kaisō no Tosaka Jun* (Tokyo: Keisō Shobō, 1976); Kozai Yoshishige, *Senjika no yuibutsuronja tachi* (Tokyo: Aoki Shoten, 1982); and Yamada Kō, *Tosaka Jun to sono jidai* (Tokyo: Kadensha, 1990).

13. Quoted in Yamada, *Tosaka Jun*, 75.

14. According to Nornes, of thirty-seven colleagues associated with the magazine, twenty-two were ex-members of Prokino. See his *Japanese Documentary Film*, 132.

15. Makino Mamoru, "Kiroku eiga no riroteki dōkō o otte 16," *Uni tsūshin* (3 March 1977), quoted in Nornes, *Japanese Documentary Film*, 132.

16. Harry Harootunian, *Overcome by Modernity*, 118.

17. Tosaka Jun, "Shisō to fūzoku," in *Tosaka Jun zenshū*, 4:274.

18. Tosaka Jun, "Eiga no shajitsuteki tokusei to fūzokusei oyobi taishūsei," in *Tosaka Jun zenshū*, 4:285–286. This article was originally published in *Eiga sōzō* 1, no. 1 (May 1936) as "Eiga no shajitsuteki tokusei to taishūsei."

19. Ibid., 289.

20. Ibid., 285.

21. Tosaka Jun, "Eiga no ninshikironteki kachi to fūzoku byōsha," *Nihon eiga* 2, no. 6 (June 1937): 14.

22. Walter Benjamin, "The Work of Art in the Age of Its Technological Reproducibility (Second Version)," trans. Edmund Jephcott and Harry Zohn, in *The Work of Art in the Age of Its Technological Reproducibility and Other Writings on Media*, ed. Michael W. Jennings, Brigid Doherty, and Thomas Y. Levin (Cambridge, MA: Belknap and Harvard University Press, 2008), 37.

23. Thomas Y. Levin, "Film," in Benjamin, *The Work of Art*, 316.

24. Benjamin, "The Work of Art," 23.

25. Tosaka Jun, "Eiga geijutsu to eiga: Abusutorakushon no sayō e," in *Tosaka Jun zenshū*, 4:465.

26. Ibid., 466.

27. Ibid., 469.

28. Tosaka Jun, "Ninshikiron to wa nani ka," in *Tosaka Jun zenshū*, 3:444.

29. Tosaka, "Eiga geijutsu to eiga," 468–469.

30. André Bazin, "The Ontology of the Photographic Image," 16.

31. Ueno Kōzō, "Geijutsuteki ninshiki ni tsuite," in *Eiga no ninshiki* (Kyoto: Daiichi Geibunsha, 1940), 22–46.

32. Following Ueno's essay, Tosaka wrote a brief comment about Ueno, criticizing the latter's inability to grasp basic assumptions of epistemology. See Tosaka Jun, "Ueno Kōzō-shi ni taisu," in *Tosaka Jun zenshu: Bekkan* (Tokyo: Keisō Shobō, 1979), 303–305.

33. Kozai Yoshishige, "Tosaka Jun to yuibutsuron," in Tanabe et al., *Kaisō no Tosaka Jun*, 164–165.

34. Nakai Masakazu, "Tosaka-kun no tsuioku," in Tanabe et al., *Kaisō no Tosaka Jun*, 97–98.

35. For Nakai's commitment to the Popular Front movement, see Banba Toshiaki, *Nakai Masakazu densetsu: Nijūichi no shōzō ni yoru yūwaku* (Tokyo: Potto Shuppan, 2009), 103–225. For a more general account of the Japanese reception of the Popular Front, see Richard Torrance, "The People's Library: The Spirit of Prose Literature versus Fascism," in *The Culture of Japanese Fascism*, ed. Alan Tansman (Durham, NC: Duke University Press, 2009), 56–79.

36. Nakai even experimented with color films in amateur filmmaking. See Nakai Masakazu, "Shikisai eiga no omoide," in *Nakai Masakazu zenshū*, ed. Kuno Osamu (Tokyo: Bijutsu Shuppansha, 1981), 3:232–235. His films are also discussed in Nornes, *Japanese Documentary Film*, 143–147.

37. Nakai Masakazu, "Kontinuitī no ronrisei," in *Nakai Masakazu zenshū*, 3:164–165.

38. Nakai Masakazu, "Gendai bigaku no kiki to eiga riron," in *Nakai Masakazu zenshū*, 3:191.

39. Nakai Masakazu, "Kabe," in Nojima Kōzō et al., *Kōga kessakushū* (Tokyo: Kokusho Kankōkai, 2005), 31.

40. Ibid., 31

41. Nakai Masakazu, "Utsusu," in *Kōga kessakushū*, 40–43.

42. Ibid., 44.

43. Both Shimizu and Nagae graduated from Kyoto University and published essays on Soviet montage theory in their own magazine *Eiga genjitsu* (*Film Actuality*). Though circulated only among a small number of readers residing in Kyoto, this magazine was notable for providing Japanese translations of Vertov's film theory in addition to Itagaki's retranslation of it from German.

44. Leon Mousinnac, *Sovieto Roshiya no eiga, shinema no tanjō, eiga gijutsu no mirai*, trans. Iijima Tadashi (Tokyo: Ōraisha, 1930). As the title suggests, this book also contains an abridged translation of Moussinac's earlier book, *Naissance du cinéma* (1925).

45. Moussinac, *Sovieto Roshiya no eiga*, 121.

46. Nakai Masakazu, "*Haru no kontinuitī*," in *Nakai Masakazu zenshū*, 3:149–150.

47. Nakai Masakazu, "Kontinuitī no ronrisei," 170.

48. Ibid., 171.

49. Nakai Masakazu, "Bigaku nyūmon," in *Nakai Masakazu zenshū*, 3:134.

50. Nakai Masakazu, "Shisōteki kiki ni okeru geijutsu narabi ni sono dōkō," in *Nakai Masakazu zenshū*, 2:48.

51. Ibid., 48–49.

52. Ibid., 56.
53. Ibid., 56–57.
54. Ibid., 58.
55. Ibid., 58–59.
56. Nakai Masakazu, "Iinkai no ronri: Hitotsu no sōkō to shite," in *Nakai Masakazu zenshū*, 1:46–108.
57. Nakai Masakazu, "Kantanshi no aru shisō," in *Nakai Masakazu hyōronshū*, ed. Nagata Hiroshi (Tokyo: Iwanami Shoten, 1995), 212. For Nakai's political conversion (*tenkō*), see Kinoshita Nagahiro, *Nakai Masakazu: Atarashii "bigaku" no kokoromi*, rev. ed. (Tokyo: Heibonsha, 2002).
58. Imamura Taihei, "Kaisetsu," in *Nakai Masakazu zenshū*, 3:323–324.
59. Ōkuma Nobuyuki, "Batsu," in Imamura Taihei, *Eiga geijutsu no keishiki* (Tokyo: Ōshio Shorin, 1938), 411.
60. Satō, "Does Film Theory Exist in Japan?" 14.
61. Imamura Taihei, *Eiga geijutsu no keishiki*; *Eiga to bunka* (Kyoto: Daiichi Geibunsha, 1940); *Kiroku eigaron* (Kyoro: Daiichi Geibunsha, 1940); *Manga eigaron* (Kyoto: Daiichi Geibunsha, 1941); and *Sensō to eiga* (Kyoto: Daiichi Geibunsha, 1942). These monographs are all reprinted under the title *Imamura Taihei eizō hyōron* (Tokyo: Yumani Shobō, 1991).
62. Imamura Taihei, "Japanese Art and the Animated Cartoon," trans. Tsuruoka Furuichi, *Quarterly Review of Film, Radio and Television* 7, no. 3 (September 1953): 217–222. Imamura was also the only Japanese theorist whose text was included in Iwamoto Kenji, ed., *Eiga riron shūsei* (Tokyo: Firumu Ātsha, 1982), an anthology of film theory widely used in film studies programs at Japanese universities.
63. See Mark Driscoll, "From Kino-Eye to *Anime*-eye/ai: The Filmed and the Animated in Imamura Taihei's Media Theory," *Japan Forum* 14, no. 2 (2002): 269–296; Yuriko Furuhata, "Rethinking Plasticity: The Politics and Production of the Animated Image," *Animation: An Interdisciplinary Journal* 6, no. 1 (2011): 25–38; Thomas Lamarre, "Cartoon Film Theory: Imamura Taihei on Animation, Documentary, and Photography," in *Animating Film Theory*, ed. Karen Beckman (Durham, NC: Duke University Press, 2014), 221–251.
64. For Imamura's reading of Friche, see Makino Mamoru, "*Eiga shūdan ni tsuite*," in *Eiga shūdan: Jō*, vol. 9 of *Senzen eizō riron zasshi shūsei*, ed. Makino Mamoru (Tokyo: Yumani shobō, 1989), 1–9. It is Kurahara who translated Friche's *The Sociology of Art* into Japanese. See V. M. Friche, *Geijutsu shakaigaku no hōhōron*, trans. Kurahara Korehito (Tokyo: Sōbunkaku, 1930).
65. Imamura Taihei, "Eiga geijutsu no seikaku: Geijutsu no kodokusei no hitei," in *Eiga geijutsu no seikaku*, 2. Imamura often referred to *The Country Cousin* (1936, dir. Wilfred Jackson) as his favorite example of the photography-based animated film.
66. Imamura Taihei, "Monogatari keishiki kara kiroku keishiki e," in *Eiga geijutsu no keishiki*, 269.
67. Imamura Taihei, "A Theory of the Animated Sound Film," trans. Michael Baskett, *Review of Japanese Culture and Society* 22: 48.
68. Imamura, "Geijutsu keishiki to shite no eiga," in *Eiga geijutsu no keishiki*, 152.
69. Benjamin, "The Work of Art," 33. Emphasis in original.
70. Imamura Taihei, "Kiroku eigaron," in *Kiroku eigaron*, 36–39.

71. Alexandre Astruc, "The Birth of a New Avant-Garde: La Caméra Stylo," in *The New Wave: Critical Landmarks*, ed. Peter Graham (Garden City, NY: Doubleday, 1968), 17–23.
72. Imamura Taihei, "Doramatsurugī to shinematsurugī," in *Eiga geijutsu no keishiki*, 238–239.
73. Imamura, "Kiroku eigaron," 26.
74. Imamura Taihei, "Eiga kirokuron," in *Kiroku eigaron*, 92.
75. Ibid., 86–87.
76. Imamura, "Kiroku eigaron," 47.
77. Imamura Taihei, "*Minzoku no saiten*," quoted in Satō, *Nihon eiga rironshi*, 202.
78. Ibid., 201.
79. Nornes, *Japanese Documentary Film*, 99.
80. Imamura Taihei, "Nyūsu eiga to seiji," in *Sensō to eiga* (Kyoto: Daiichi Geibunsha, 1942), 41.
81. Ibid., 44–45.
82. Imamura Taihei, "Eiga no sendenryoku," in *Sensō to eiga*, 1–15.
83. Aikawa Haruki, "Bunka eiga e no rohyō," in *Bunka eigaron* (Tokyo: Kasumigaseki shobō, 1944), 67. Aikawa was a member of Tosaka's Yuiken before writing this book.
84. In Aikawa's view, the definition of *bunka eiga* was "to stage the truth as a 'narrative' by using faithful documents of the society and facts." Ibid., 53. Of course, this was no more than one of the many definitions posed by Japanese critics of the time. Imamura, for instance, always insisted that *bunka eiga* should only mean nonfiction films with educational or scientific purposes, as in UFA's original *Kulturfilm*.
85. Imamura Taihei, "*Sensō eigaron*," *Sensō to eiga*, 135–136.
86. Fujita Motohiko, "Bunka to kiroku no aida: Kamei Fumio to sono rekishikan," in *Nihon eiga gendaishi: Showa 10-nendai* (Tokyo: Kashinsha, 1977), 60.

CHAPTER 5

1. Indeed, the years between 1941 and 1945 saw the publication of books with disturbing titles. See Hazumi Tsuneo, *Eiga to minzoku* (Tokyo: Eiga Nihonsha, 1942); Ichikawa Sai, *Eiga shintaiseiron* (Tokyo: Kokusai Eiga Tsūshinsha); Okada Shinkichi, *Eiga to kokka* (Tokyo: Seikatsusha, 1943).
2. Sugiyama Heiichi, *Eiga hyōronshū* (Kyoto: Daiichi Geibunsha, 1941); Nagae Michitarō, *Eiga, hyōgen, keisei* (Kyoto: Kyōiku Tosho, 1942).
3. Gilles Deleuze, *Cinema 1: The Movement-Image*, trans. Hugh Tomlinson and Barbara Habberjam (Minneapolis: University of Minnesota Press, 1986), 1.
4. Ibid., 3.
5. Jean Epstein, "Magnification and Other Writings," trans. Stuart Liebman, *October* 3 (Spring 1977): 23.
6. André Bazin, "A Bergsonian Film: 'The Picasso Mystery,'" trans. Bert Cardullo, *Journal of Aesthetic Education* 35, no. 2 (Summer 2001): 3.
7. Dudley Andrew, "The Neglected Tradition of Phenomenology in Film Theory," in Nichols, *Movies and Methods*, 2: 626–632.
8. Vivian Sobchack, *The Address of the Eye: A Phenomenology of Film Experience* (Princeton, NJ: Princeton University Press, 1992). For more on current scholarship on film

and phenomenology in the Anglo-American context, see Allan Casebier, *Film and Phenomenology: Towards a Realist Representation of Cinematic Representation* (Cambridge: Cambridge University Press, 1991); Malin Wahlberg, *Documentary Time: Film and Phenomenology* (Minneapolis: University of Minnesota Press, 2008); Thomas Elsaesser and Malte Hagener, "Cinema as Skin and Touch," in *Film Theory*, 108–128.

9. Sobchack, *The Address of the Eye*, 15, 36.
10. Ibid., xviii.
11. Ibid., 3.
12. Tosaka Jun, "Testugaku hyōron," in *Tosaka Jun Zenshū*, 3:173.
13. James W. Heisig, Thomas P. Kasulis, and John C. Maraldo, eds., *Japanese Philosophy: A Source Book* (Honolulu: University of Hawai'i Press, 2011), 565.
14. Ibid.
15. Inoue Enryō, "Tetsugaku issekiwa," quoted in Heisig et al., *Japanese Philosophy*, 561.
16. Inoue Enryō, "Buddhism and Philosophy," trans. Gerard Clinton Godart, in Heisig et al., *Japanese Philosophy*, 623.
17. Inoue Tetsujirō "Fragments of a World View," trans. Gerard Clinton Godart, in Heisig et al., *Japanese Philosophy*, 613.
18. Nishida Kitarō, *An Inquiry into the Good*, trans. Masao Abe and Christopher Ives (New Haven, CT: Yale University Press, 1992).
19. For instance, the philosopher Takahashi Satomi wrote as early as 1912: "Something makes this work really seem philosophical in comparison to others. Is it not the first book and only philosophical work in post-Meiji Japan?" See Takahashi, "Ishiki genshō no jijitsu to sono imi: Nishida-shi *Zen no kenkū* wo yomu," quoted in *Japanese Philosophy*, 574.
20. James, *Pragmatism*, 3–40.
21. Bergson, *An Introduction to Metaphysics*, 36.
22. Tanabe Hajime, "Genshōgaku ni okeru atrashiki tenkō: Haideggā no sei no genshōgaku," in *Tanabe Hajime zenshū* (Tokyo: Chikuma Shobō, 1963–1964), 4:19–34.
23. Ibid., 29.
24. Mutai Risaku, "Edomundo Husseru" in *Mutai Risaku Chosakushū*, ed. Furuta Hikaru, et al. (Tokyo: Kobushi Shobō, 2000–2002), 3:225.
25. Heidegger talked extensively about Kuki in his interview with a Japanese scholar visiting him after World War II. See Martin Heidegger, "A Dialogue on Language: Between a Japanese and an Inquirer," in *On the Way to Language*, trans. Peter D. Hertz (New York: Harper and Row, 1971), 1–56.
26. Kuki Shūzo, *Jituzon no tetsugaku* (Tokyo: Iwanami Shoten, 1933).
27. For an English translation of this text, see Hiroshi Nara, *The Structure of Detachment: The Aesthetic Vision of Kuki Shūzō with a Translation of "Iki no kōzō"* (Honolulu: University of Hawai'i Press, 2005). For Kuki's work and life, see Leslie Pincus, *Authenticating Culture in Imperial Japan: Kuki Shūzō and the Rise of National Aesthetics* (Berkeley: University of California Press, 1996); Michael F. Marra, "A Dialogue on Language between a Japanese and an Inquirer: Kuki Shūzō's Version," in *Essays on Japan: Between Aesthetics and Literature* (Leiden: Brill, 2010), 167–185.
28. Kuki Shūzō, "Bergson au Japon," in *Kuki Shūzō zenshū*, ed. Amano Teiyū, Omodaka Hisayuki, and Satō Akio (Tokyo: Iwanami Shoten, 1980–82), 1:260.
29. Ibid., 259.

30. Naoki Sakai, "Resistance to Conclusion: The Kyoto School of Philosophy under the Pax Americana," in *Re-politicizing The Kyoto School as Philosophy*, ed. Christopher Goto-Jones (London: Routledge, 2008), 189. Emphasis in original.

31. Ibid.

32. Mutai Risaku, "Hyōgen no ronri," in *Mutai Risaku chosakushū*, 3:7–229; Kimura Motomori, *Keiseiteki jikaku* (Tokyo: Kōbundō, 1941).

33. For Sugiyama's activity as a poet, see Sugiyama Heiichi, *Sugiyama Heiichi zenshishū*, 2 vols. (Tokyo: Henshū Kōbō Noa, 1997); Sako Yūji, *Shijin Sugiyama Heiichi ron: Hoshi to eiga to ningen'ai to* (Kyoto: Chikurinkan, 2002).

34. For Sugiyama's career as a film critic, see Makino Mamoru, "Imamura Taihei: Kokō dokusō no eiga hyōronka to chosha Sugiyama Heiichi no isō," *Eizōgaku* 45 (1991): 59–84.

35. Sugiyama Heiichi, "Bungaku e no sekkin no mondai," *Eiga shūdan* 4 (December 1935): 9.

36. Ibid.

37. Sugiyama Heiichi, "Junbungaku eigaka no hitei," *Eiga shūdan* 1 (July 1935): 7–8.

38. Sugiyama Heiichi, "Kyamera no soshitsu to shite no shajitsu," *Eiga hyōron* 18, no. 7 (July 1936): 71.

39. Sugiyama Heiichi, "Eiga ni okeru fun'iki no mondai," *Eiga shūdan* 3 (October 1935): 10–11

40. Ibid., 11.

41. Sugiyama, *Eiga hyōronshū*, i–ii.

42. Ibid., 1–2.

43. Ibid., 5–6.

44. Vsevolod Pudovkin, *Eiga kantoku to kyakuhonron*, trans. Sasaki Norio (Tokyo: Ōraisha, 1930).

45. Vsevolod Pudovkin, *Film Technique and Film Acting*, rev. ed., trans. and ed. Ivor Montagu (New York: Grove Press, 1970), 95.

46. Sugiyama, *Eiga hyōronshū*, 9–10.

47. For Uchida's use of the long take in his "realist" masterpiece *Earth* (1939), see my "Tōkī riarizumu e no michi," 230.

48. Sugiyama, *Eiga hyōronshū*, 9. For Metz's argument on a shot as a sentence, see Christian Metz, "The Cinema: Language or Language System?" in *Film Language: A Semiotics of the Cinema*, trans. Michael Taylor (New York: Oxford University Press, 1974), 31–91.

49. Sugiyama, *Eiga hyōronshū*, 17–18.

50. Ibid., 17.

51. Ibid. Though Sugiyama did not mention this, his reference to Yamanaka as a pioneer of deep focus can be historically proven. Mimura "Harry" Akira, the cinematographer of Yamanaka's last film *Humanity and Paper Balloons* (*Ninjō kamifūsen*, 1938), had worked in Hollywood for five years under the tutelage of George Burns, Alvin Wyckoff, and, most importantly, Gregg Toland, prior to his return to Japan in 1934.

52. Ibid., 51.

53. André Bazin, "The Ontology of the Photographic Image," 9–16.

54. André Bazin, "Theater and Cinema—Part Two," in *What Is Cinema?* 1:95–124.

55. André Bazin, "The Virtues and Limitation of Montage," in *What Is Cinema?* 1:41–52.

56. André Bazin, "The Evolution of the Language of Cinema," in *What Is Cinema?* 1:23–40.
57. Dudley Andrew, *The Major Film Theories*, 136.
58. Sugiyma, *Eiga hyōronshu*, 33.
59. Ibid.
60. Ibid., 38
61. Immanuel Kant, *Critique of Pure Reason*, trans. and ed. Paul Guyer and Allen W. Wood (Cambridge: Cambridge University Press, 1998), 272.
62. Sugiyama, *Eiga hyōronshū*, 38.
63. Ibid., 29.
64. Ibid., 30.
65. Ibid., 12.
66. Ibid., 41.
67. Ibid., 11.
68. Sugiyama, *Eiga hyōronshū*, 63.
69. Tanaka Masasumi, "Eiga hyōronka to shite no Sugiyama Heiichi," in Sugiyamana Heiichi and Tanigawa Testuzō, *Eiga Hyōronshū, Geijutsu shōronshū: Shōroku*, vol. 7 of *Nihon eigaron gensetsu taikei*, ed. Makino Manoru (Tokyo: Yumani Shobō, 2003), 341.
70. For instance, Satō only mentions Nagae's book title in passing in his *History of Japanese Film Theory*. See Satō, *Nihon eigarironshi*, 8.
71. Nagae Michitarō, *Eiga hyōgen, keisei*, reprinted as vol. 4 of *Nihon eigaron gensetsu taikei*, ed. Makino Mamoru (Tokyo: Yumani Shobō, 2003).
72. Makino, "Nagae Michitarō," 335.
73. See, "Eiga hihyōka oyobi kenkyūka retsuden," *Eiga hyōron* 16, no. 2 (February 1934): 163.
74. Murayama Tomoyoshi, "Eiga no genkaisei," *Kinema junpō* 507 (June 1, 1934): 67–68. Sugiyama also brought forward a counterargument against this essay. See his "Murayama-shi no 'eiga no genkaisei' kara," *Kinema junpō* 509 (June 21, 1934): 66–67.
75. Murayama, "Eiga no genkaisei," 67.
76. Nagae Michitarō, "Kino: Dai-isshō: Murayama Tomoyoshi 'Eiga no genkaisei' o kien to shite," *Eiga hyōron* 16, no. 9 (September 1934): 66.
77. Balázs, *Belá Balázs: Early Film Theory*, 14.
78. Nagae, "Kino: Dai-isshō," 67.
79. Ibid.
80. Nagae Michitarō, "Hyōgen no ronri: Dai-ishhō," *Eiga hyōron* 18, no. 7 (July 1936): 30–31.
81. Ibid., 32.
82. Ibid.
83. Nishiida Kitarō, "Testugaku no konpon mondai," in *Nishida Kitarō zenshū*, ed. Takeda Atsushi, et al. (Tokyo: Iwanami Shoten, 2002–2009), 7:141. For a detailed annotation of Nishida's late philosophy, see Miki Kiyoshi, *Testugaku nyūmon* (Tokyo: Iwanami Shoten, 1940); Kosaka Kunitsugu, *Nishida Kitarō: Sono shisō to gendai* (Kyoto: Mineruva Shobō, 1995).
84. See, for instance, Nishida Kitarō, "The Standpoint of Active Intuition," in *Ontology of Production: Three Essays*, trans. and intr. William Haver (Durham, NC: Duke University Press, 2012), 64–143.

85. Nishida Kitarō, "Human Being," in *Ontology of Production*, 147.
86. Nishida Kitarō, "Testugaku ronbunshū 2," in *Nishida Kitarō zenshū*, 8: 399.
87. Nishida, "Human Being," 144.
88. Nishida Kitarō, "Zettai mujunteki jikodōitsu," in *Jikaku ni tsuite, hoka 4 hen*, vol. 3 of *Nishida Kitarō tetsugaku ronshū*, ed. Ueda Shizuteru (Tokyo: Iwanami Shoten, 1989), 36.
89. Nishida Kitarō, "Watashi to nanji," in *Nishida Kitarō zenshū*, 6:356.
90. Kōsaka Masaaki et al., *Sekaishiteki tachiba to Nihon* (Tokyo: Chūō kōronsha, 1943), 128.
91. Tosaka, "Testugaku hyōron," 171–174.
92. Nagae, *Eiga, hyōgen, keisei*, 8–9.
93. Ibid., 9–14.
94. Ibid., 24–29.
95. Ibid., 57.
96. Ibid., 33.
97. Ibid., 70.
98. Ibid., 126–127.
99. Ibid., 142.
100. Ibid., 144.
101. Ibid., 161–170.
102. For instance, Epstein wrote in 1935 that film complements "man's physiological inability to master the notion of space-time" because "the specific quality of this new projected world is to make another perspective of matter evident, that of time." See Jean Epstein, "*Photogénie* and the Imponderable," in Abel, *French Film Theory and Criticism*, 189. Similarly, Dulac defined film as "an art of movement" and paid special attention to "a slow-motion study of the blooming of flowers." See Germaine Dulac, "The Essence of Cinema: The Visual Idea," in *The Avant-Garde Film: A Reader of Theory and Criticism*, ed. P. Adams Sitney, trans. Robert Lamberton (New York: New York University Press, 1978), 36–42.
103. Nagae, *Eiga, hyōgen, keisei*, 132–134.
104. Ibid., 231. Emphasis in original.
105. In 1949, Bazin made a similar remark on the dialectics regarding De Sica's *Bicycle Thieves*: "De Sica's supreme achievement, which others have so far only approached with a varying degree of success or failure, is to have succeeded in discovering the cinematographic dialectic capable of transcending the contradiction between the action of a 'spectacle' and of an event. For this reason, *Ladri di Biciclette* is one of the first examples of pure cinema. No more actors, no more story, no more sets, which is to say that in the perfect aesthetic illusion of reality there is no more cinema." See his "Bicycle Thief," in *What Is Cinema?* 2:60.
106. Nagae, *Eiga, hyōgen, keisei*, 214–215.
107. See, for instance, Jean-Louis Baudry, "Ideological Effects of the Basic Cinematographic Apparatus," trans. Alan Williams; Baudry, "The Apparatus: Metapsychological Approaches to the Impression of Reality in Cinema," trans. Jean Andrews and Bertrand Augst, in *Narrative, Apparatus, Ideology: A Film Theory Reader*, ed. Phil Rosen (New York: Columbia University Press, 1986), 286–298, 299–318.
108. Nagae, *Eiga, hyōgen, keisei*, 217.
109. Ibid., 232.
110. Ibid., 260–261.

111. Ibid., 287–291.

112. Ibid., 308–309.

113. Francesco Casetti, *The Lumière Galaxy: Seven Keywords for the Cinema to Come* (New York: Columbia University Press, 2015), 114.

114. See, for instance, Naoki Sakai, "Modernity and Its Critique: The Problem of Universalism and Particularism," in *Postmodernism and Japan*, ed. Masao Miyoshi and H. D. Harootunian (Durham, NC: Duke University Press, 1989), 93–122.

115. Usui Jishō, et al. eds., *Tetsugaku nennkan* (Osaka: Seibunsha, 1944), 300.

116. See Asanuma Keiji, *Eiga bugaku nyūmon* (Tokyo: Bijutsu shuppansha, 1963), and Hara Masato, *Mitai eiga no koto dake o* (Osaka: Yūbunsha, 1977).

EPILOGUE

1. For more on this topic, see Tanaka Jun'ichirō, *Nihon eiga hattatsushi* (Chūō Kōronsha, 1980), 3:214–417; Kyoko Hirano, *Mr. Smith Goes to Tokyo: Japanese Cinema under the American Occupation, 1945–1952* (Washington, DC: Smithsonian Institution Press, 1992).

2. Cited in Hirano, *Mr. Smith Goes to Tokyo*, 44–45.

3. For more on Kamei's *The Japanese Tragedy*, see Nornes, *Japanese Documentary Film*, 183–190.

4. Mizoguchi dealt with the liberation of women and prostitution problems in films such as *Victory of Women* (*Josei no shōri*, 1946), *The Love of the Actress Sumako* (*Joyū Sumako no koi*, 1947), and *Women of the Night* (*Yoru no onnatachi*, 1948); Ozu addressed the issue of war orphans in *The Record of a Tenement Gentleman* (*Nagaya shinshiroku*, 1947) and portrayed a wife who turns to prostitution before her husband's repatriation in *A Hen in the Wind* (*Kaze no naka no mendori*, 1948).

5. Iwasaki Akira, "Eiga hihyōka no sekinin," in *Gendai Nihon eigaron taikei*, ed. Ogawa Tōru et al. (Tokyo: Tōjusha, 1970–72), 1:181–190.

6. Ibid., 182.

7. Baba Eitarō, "Riarizumuron no yukue," in *Gendai Nihon eigaron taikei*, 1:412.

8. Iwasaki Akita, "Eiga riarizumu e no tenbō," in *Riarizumu kenkyū*, ed. Kozai Yoshishige and Kurahara Korehito (Tokyo: Hakuyōsha, 1949), 277–287.

9. Ibid., 280.

10. Tsuji, "Eiga no riarizum," 96.

11. Hanada Kiyoteru, "Hata," in *Hanada Kityoteru zenshū* (Tokyo: Kōdansha, 1977–1980), 2:13–14.

12. Hanada Kiyoteru, "Geijutsuka no seifuku," in *Hanada Kityoteru zenshū*, 4:26.

13. Ibid.

14. Lenin, "On the Question of Dialectics," 649.

15. Hanada Kiyoteru, "Ōgon bunkatsu," in *Hanada Kityoteru zenshū*, 2:84–86.

16. Hanada Kiyoteru, "Higeki ni tsuite," in *Hanada Kityoteru zenshū*, 2:115.

17. Hanada Kiyoteru, "Tentaizu—Koperunikusu," in *Hanada Kityoteru zenshū*, 2:267.

18. Okamoto Tarō, "Taikyoku shugi," in *Taikyoku to bakuhatsu*, vol. 1 of *Okamoto Tarō no uchū*, ed., Yamashita Yūji, Sawaragi Noi, and Hirano Akiomi (Tokyo: Chikuma shobō, 2011), 409–412. See also Ōtani Shōgo, "Okamoto Tarō no 'Taikyokushugi' no seiritsu wo meggute," *Tokyo kokuritsu kindai bijutsukan kenkyū kiyō* 13 (2009): 18–36.

19. Hanada Kiyoteru, "Kikai to bara," in *Hanada Kiyoteru zenshū*, 4:163–172.

20. Hanada Kiyoteru, "Imamura Taihei," in *Hanada Kityoteru zenshū*, 4:431.

21. Abé Mark Nornes, "'Pôru Rûta'/Paul Rotha and the Politics of Translation," *Cinema Journal* 38, no. 3 (Spring 1999): 94.

22. That said, several attempts are made to change this negative view of Rotha. See, for instance, Duncan Petrie and Robert Kruger, eds., *A Paul Rotha Reader* (Exeter, UK: University of Exeter Press, 1999).

23. Tsumura Hideo, "Pōru Rūta no eigaron hihan—Sono cho *Documentary Film* ni tsuite," in *Zoku eiga to hihyō* (Tokyo: Koyama shoten, 1940), 107–168.

24. Ibid., 111.

25. Ibid., 144–145.

26. Ibid., 133.

27. John Grierson, "Untitled Lecture on Documentary (1927–33)," in *The Documentary Film Movement: An Anthology*, ed. and intro. Ian Aitken (Edinburgh: Edinburgh University Press, 1998), 76–77. In his introduction to this anthology, Aitken offers a detailed account of Grierson's idealist background, arguing, "Grierson's first definition of documentary film was based on the revelation of the real through the manipulation of documentary footage by formative editing technique." Aitken, *Documentary Film Movement*, 40.

28. Tsumura, "Pōru Rūta," 132.

29. Imamura Taihei, "Pōru Rōza no 'Kiroku eigaron,'" in *Eiga riron nyūmon* (Tokyo: Itagaki Shoten, 1952), 150–176.

30. Ibid., 153–154.

31. Imamura Taihei, "Eiga no tokushitsu," in *Gendai eigaron* (Tokyo: Heibonsha, 1957), 97.

32. Imamura Taihei, "Kiroku eiga no hatten to eikyō," in *Gendai eigaron*, 137.

33. Imamura, "Pōru Rōza no 'Kiroku eigaron,'" 155.

34. Hanada Kiyoteru, "Waraineko," in *Hanada Kiyoteru zenshū*, 4:244.

35. Hanada Kiyoteru, "Kikai to bara," 170.

36. Hanada Kiyoteru, "Gūzen no mondai," in *Hanada Kiyoteru zenshū*, 6:367. Imamura's definition of documentary as the revelation of necessity among the contingent appears in his "Watakushi no eiga no kangaekata," in *Eiga nyūmon* (Tokyo: Shakai Shisō Kenkyūkai, 1955), 107.

37. G. W. F. Hegel, *The Encyclopaedia Logic, with the Zusätze*, trans. and intro. T. F. Geraets et al. (Indianapolis: Hackett Publishing, 1991), 218.

38. Hanada, "Gūzen no mondai," 373.

39. Ibid., 367.

40. See Sasaki Kiichi, Hanada Kiyoteru et al., "Eiga riron no hihan to sōzō," *Shin-Nihon bungaku* 11, no. 12 (December 1956): 151.

41. Hanada Kiyoteru, "Shukumei wo megutte," in *Hanada Kiyoteru zenshū*, 8:163.

42. Imamura Taihei, "Semi dokyumentarī ron," in *Gendai eigaron*, 25–42.

43. Hanada Kiyoteru, "Shuru-dokyumentarizumu ni kansuru ichi kōsatsu," in *Hanada Kiyoteru zenshū*, 8:157.

44. Hanada Kiyoteru, "20-nendai no 'avangyarudo,'" in *Hanada Kyoteru zenshū* 4:214–215.

45. Hanada, "Kikai to bara," 164.

46. Ibid., 170.
47. See Sergei Eisenstein, "The Montage of Attractions," in *S. M. Eisenstein Selected Works, Vol. 1*, 33–38.
48. Hanada Kiyoteru, "Gūzen no mondai," 374.
49. Hanada Kiyoteru, "Mūzikarusu to avangyarudo," in *Hanada Kyoteru zenshū*, 7:256–261.
50. Hanada Kiyoteru, "Waraineko," 234.
51. Matsumoto Toshio, "A Theory of Avant-Garde Documentary," trans. Michael Raine, *Cinema Journal* 51, no. 4 (Summer 2012): 148–154.
52. Matsumoto Toshio, "Hanada-san to eiga hihyō," *Hanada Kiyoteru zenshū*, 7:appendix 10.
53. Hanada, "Kikai to bara," 171.
54. Hanada Kiyoteru, "Akuchuaritī to riaritī," in *Hanada Kiyoteru zenshū*, 6:353.
55. Hanada, "Gūzen no mondai," 368.
56. Haniya Yutaka, "Eikyū kakumeisha no hiai," in *Haniya Yutaka zenshū* (Tokyo: Kōnsha, 1998–2001), 4–43. Haniya also developed his own theorization of the self-contradictory nature of the film experience. See my "Anbako kara no tōshi: Haniya Yutaka no sonzaironteki eigaron ni tsuite," in *Tenkeiki no mediorogī: 1950-nendai Nihon no geijutsu to media no saihensei*, ed. Toba Kōji and Yamamoto Naoki (Tokyo: Shinwasha, 2019), 105-130.
57. Yoshida Kijū, *Jikohitei no ronri, sōzōryoku ni yoru henshin* (Tokyo: San'ichi Shobō, 1970).
58. Akira Lippit, "Preface (Interface)," in *Media Theory in Japan*, xiii.

SELECTED BIBLIOGRAPHY

JOURNALS

Kinema Record (1913–1917)
Kinema junpō (*Movie Times*, 1919–1940, 1946–1950, 1950–)
Eiga hyōron (*Film Criticism*, 1926–1940, 1941–1943, 1944–1975)
Shinkō geijutsu / Shinkō geijutsu kenkyū (*New Art / Studies of New Art*, 1929–1931)
Yibutsuron kenkyū (*Studies of Materialism*, 1932–1938)
Eiga shūdan (*Film Collective*, 1935–1938)
Eiga sōzō (*Film Creation*, 1936–1937)
Nihon eiga (*Japanese Cinema*, 1936–1945)
Bunka eiga (*Culture Film*, 1938–1940, 1941–1943)
Bunka eiga kenkyū (*Studies of Culture Film*, 1943–1940)
Eiga kikan (*Film Quarterly*, 1948–1950)

BOOKS AND ARTICLES

Abel, Richard, ed. *French Film Theory and Criticism: A History/Anthology, 1907–1937.* 2 vols. Princeton, NJ: Princeton University Press, 1988.
Aikawa Haruki. *Bunka eigaron* [On Culture Film]. Tokyo: Kasumigaseki Shobō, 1944.
Aitken, Ian, ed. *The Documentary Film Movement: An Anthology.* Edinburgh: Edinburgh University Press, 1998.
———. *Realist Film Theory and Cinema: The Nineteenth-Century Luckácsian and Intuitionist Realist Traditions.* Manchester: Manchester University Press, 2006.
Anderson, Joseph, and Donald Richie. *The Japanese Film: Art and Industry.* Expanded ed. Princeton, NJ: Princeton University Press, 1982.
Andrew, Dudley. *Concepts in Film Theory.* New York: Oxford University Press, 1984.
———. *The Major Film Theories: An Introduction.* New York: Oxford University Press, 1975.

———. "The Neglected Tradition of Phenomenology in Film Theory." In *Movies and Methods: An Anthology*, edited by Bill Nichols, 2:625–632. Berkeley: University of California Press, 1985.

Andrew, Dudley, and Hervé Jourbert-Laurencin, eds. *Opening Bazin: Postwar Film Theory and Its Afterlife*. New York: Oxford University Press, 2011.

Andrew, Dudley, and Anton Keas, Sarah Keller, Stuart Liebman, Annette Michelson, and Malcolm Turvey. "Roundtable on the Return to Classical Film Theory." *October* 148 (Spring 2014): 5–26.

Arnheim, Rudolf. *Film as Art*. 50th Anniversary ed. Berkeley: University of California Press, 2006.

Bhabha, Homi K. "The Commitment to Theory." In *Questions of Third Cinema*, edited by Jim Pines and Paul Willemen, 111–132. London: BFI, 1989.

Balázs, Béla. *Béla Balázs: Early Film Theory: "Visible Man" and "The Sprit of Film."* Edited by Erica Carter. Translated by Rodney Livingstone. New York: Berghahn Books, 2010.

Banba Toshiaki. *Nakai Masakazu densetsu: Nijūichi no shōzō ni yoru yūwaku* [Nakai Masakazu's Legend: Temptations by Twenty-One Portraits]. Tokyo: Potto Shuppan, 2009.

Baskett, Michael. *The Attractive Empire: Transnational Film Culture in Imperial Japan*. Honolulu: University of Hawai'i Press, 2008.

Bazin, André. "A Bergsonian Film: *The Picasso Mystery*." In *Bazin at Work: Major Essays and Reviews from the Forties and Fifties*. Translated by Alain Piette and Bert Cardullo, edited by Bert Cardullo, 211–220. New York: Routledge, 1997.

———. *What Is Cinema?* 2 vols. Selected and translated by Hugh Gray. Berkeley: University of California Press, 1967–1971.

Benjamin, Walter. *Walter Benjamin: Selected Writings*. 3 vols. Translated by Edmund Jephcott, Howard Eiland, and others. Edited by Howard Eiland and Michael W. Jennings. Cambridge, MA: Harvard University Press, 2002.

———. *The Work of Art in the Age of Its Technological Reproducibility and Other Writings on Media*. Edited by Michael W. Jennings et al. Cambridge, MA: Harvard University Press, 2008.

Bergson, Henri. *Creative Evolution*. Translated by Arthur Mitchell. New York: Henry Holt, 1926.

———. *An Introduction to Metaphysics*. Translated by T. E. Hulme. New York: G. P. Putnam's Sons, 1912.

———. *Matter and Memory*. Translated by N. M. Paul and W. S. Palmer. New York: Zone, 1988.

Bernardi, Joanne. *Writing in Light: The Silent Scenario and the Japanese Pure Film Movement*. Detroit: Wayne State University Press, 2001.

Bordwell, David. "A Case for Cognitivism." *Iris* 9 (1989): 11–40.

———. "Contemporary Film Studies and the Vicissitudes of Grand Theory." In *Post-Theory: Reconstructing Film Studies*, edited by David Bordwell and Noël Carroll, 3–36. Madison: University of Wisconsin Press, 1996.

———. *Narration in the Fiction Film*. Madison: University of Wisconsin Press, 1985.

Braudy, Leo, and Marshal Cohen, eds. *Film Theory and Criticism*. 7th ed. New York: Oxford University Press, 2009.

Burch, Noël. *To the Distant Observer: Form and Meaning in the Japanese Cinema*. Revised and edited by Annette Michelson. Berkeley: University of California Press, 1979.

Carroll, Noël. "The Power of Movies." *Daedalus*, 114, no. 4 (Fall 1985): 79–103.

———. "Prospects for Film Theory: A Personal Assessment." in *Post-Theory: Reconstructing Film Studies*, edited by David Bordwell and Noël Carroll, 37–68. Madison: University of Wisconsin Press, 1996.

Casebier, Allan. *Film and Phenomenology: Towards a Realist Theory of Cinematic Representation*. New York: Cambridge University Press, 1991.

Casetti, Francesco. *Eye of the Century: Film, Experience, Modernity*. Translated by Erin Larkin with Jennifer Pranolo. New York: Columbia University Press, 2008.

———. *The Lumière Galaxy: Seven Keywords for the Cinema to Come*. New York: Columbia University Press, 2015.

———. *Theories of Cinema: 1945–1995*. Translated by Francesca Chiostri and Elizabeth Gard Bertolini-Salimbeni, with Thomas Kelso. Austin: University of Texas Press, 1999.

Cazdyn, Eric. *The Flash of Capital: Film and Geopolitics in Japan*. Durham, NC: Duke University Press, 2002.

Chan, Jessica Ka Yee. *Chinese Revolutionary Cinema: Propaganda, Aesthetics, and Internationalism, 1949–1966*. London: I.B. Tauris, 2019.

Chiba Nobuo. *Eiga to Tanizaki* [Film and Tanizaki]. Tokyo: Seiabō, 1989.

———. "*Sei no kagayaki* kara *Orochi* made" [From *The Glow of Life* to *Orochi*]. In *Nihon eigashi: Jissha kara seichō konmei no jidai made*, edited by Yamamoto Kikuo et al, 22–37. Tokyo: Kinema Junpōsha, 1976.

Chow, Rey. *The Age of the World Target: Self-Referentiality in War, Theory, and Comparative Work*. Durham, NC, Duke University Press, 2006.

Le Corbusier. *Toward an Architecture*. Edited by Jean-Louis Cohen. Translated by John Goodman. Los Angeles: Getty Research Institute, 2007.

Davis, Darrell W. *Picturing Japaneseness: Monumental Style, National Identity, Japanese Film*. New York: Columbia University Press, 1996.

Deleuze, Gilles. *Cinema 1: The Movement-Image*. Translated by Hugh Tomlinson and Barbara Habberjam. Minneapolis: University of Minnesota Press, 1986.

———. *Cinema 2: The Time-Image*. Translated by Hugh Tomlinson and Robert Galeta. Minneapolis: University of Minnesota Press, 1989.

Doane, Mary Ann. *The Emergence of Cinematic Time: Modernity, Contingency, The Archive*. Cambridge, MA: Harvard University Press, 2002.

Driscoll, Mark. "From Kino-Eye to *Anime*-eye/ai: The Filmed and the Animated in Imamura Taihei's Media Theory." *Japan Forum* 14, no. 2 (2002): 269–296.

Elsaesser, Thomas, and Malte Hagener. *Film Theory: An Introduction through the Senses*. New York: Routledge, 2010.

Epstein, Jean. "Magnification and Other Writings." Translated by Stuart Liebman. *October* 3 (1977): 9–31.

———. "The Senses I (b)." Translated by Tom Milne, In *French Film Theory and Criticism*, edited by Richard Abel, 1:241–246. Princeton, NJ: Princeton University Press, 1988.

Fan, Victor. *Cinema Approaching Reality: Locating Chinese Film Theory*. Minneapolis: University of Minnesota Press, 2015.

Fedorova, Anastasia. *Riarizumu no gensō: Nisso eiga koryūshi, 1925–1955* [An Illusion of Realism: The History of Filmic Exchanges between Japan and the Soviet Union, 1925–1955]. Tokyo: Shinwasha, 2018.

Firumu Raiburarī Kyōgikai, ed. *Shiryō Nihon hassei eiga no sōseiki: "Reimei" kara "Madamu to nyōbō" made* [Documents of the Initial Period of Japanese Sound Film: From *Dawn* to *Neighbor's Wife and Mine*]. Vol. 10 of *Nihon eigashi sokō*. Tokyo: Firumu Raiburarī Kyōgikai, 1973.

Fujii, Jinshi. "Film That Cultures: Analyzing the Discourse of Culture Film in the Shōwa Teens." Translated by Loli Hitchcock. *Iconics* 6 (2002): 51–68.

Fujimoto Chizuko. "Ōgai *Abe ichizoku* no hassō: Sakuhin to jittaiken" [The Origin of Ōgai's *The Abe Family*: The Work and Actual Experience]. *Kindai bungaku shiron* 14 (October 1975): 10–18

Fujita Motohiko. *Nihon eiga gendaishi: Shōwa 10 nen-dai* [Contemporary History of Japanese Cinema: The Shōwa Teens]. Tokyo: Kashinsha, 1977.

Furstenau, Marc, ed. *The Film Theory Reader: Debates and Arguments*. New York: Routledge, 2010.

Furuhata, Yuriko. *Cinema of Actuality: Japanese Avant-Garde Filmmaking in the Season of Image Politics*. Durham, NC: Duke University Press, 2013.

———. "Rethinking Plasticity: The Politics and Production of the Animated Image," *Animation: An Interdisciplinary Journal* 6, no. 1 (2011): 25–38.

Futabatei Shimei. "Shōsetsu sōron" [General remarks on the novel]. In *Seiji Shōsetsu, Tsubouchi Shōyō, Futabatei Shimei shū*. Vol. 1 of Gendai Nihon bungaku taikei [A Series on Contemporary Japanese Literature], 370–372. Tokyo: Chikuma Shobō, 1971.

———. "Yoga honyaku no hyōjun." [The Standard of My Translation]. In *Seiji Shōsetsu, Tsubouchi Shōyō, Futabatei Shimei shū*.Vol. 1 of *Gendai Nihon bungaku taikei*, 372–375. Tokyo: Chikuma Shobō, 1971.

Gabriel, Teshome H. "Colonialism and 'Law and Order' Criticism." *Screen* 27, nos. 3–4 (May–August, 1986): 140–148.

Gaonkar, Dilip Parameshwar, ed. *Alternative Modernities*. Durham, NC: Duke University Press, 2001.

Gerow, Aaron, ed. "Decentering Theory: Reconsidering the History of Japanese Film Theory." Special Issue, *Review of Japanese Culture and Society* 22 (December 2010).

———. "Introduction: The Theory Complex." *Review of Japanese Culture and Society* 22 (December 2010): 1–13.

———. *A Page of Madness: Cinema and Modernity in 1920s Japan*. Ann Arbor: Center for Japanese Studies, University of Michigan, 2008.

———. *Visions of Japanese Modernity: Articulations of Cinema, Nation, and Spectatorship, 1895–1925*. Berkeley: University of California Press, 2010.

Golley, Gregory. *When Our Eyes No Longer See: Realism, Science, and Ecology in Japanese Literary Modernism*. Cambridge, MA: Harvard University Asia Center, 2008.

Gonda Yasunosuke. *Gonda Yasunosuke chosakushū*. 4 vols. Tokyo: Bunwa Shobō, 1974–1975.

———. *Katsudō shashin no genri oyobi ōyō* [Principles and Applications of the Moving Pictures]. Tokyo: Uchida Rokakuho, 1914.

Hanada Kiyoteru. *Hanada Kiyoteru zenshū* [Complete Works of Hanada Kiyoteru]. 15 vols. Tokyo: Kōdansha, 1977–1979.
Hansen, Miriam Bratu. *Cinema and Experience: Siegfried Kracauer, Walter Benjamin, and Theodor W. Adorno.* Cambridge, MA: Harvard University Press, 2011.
Harootunian, Harry. "Ghostly Comparisons." in *Impacts of Modernities*, edited by Thomas Lamarre and Kang Nae-hui, 39–52. Hong Kong: Hong Kong University Press, 2004.
———. *Overcome by Modernity: History, Culture, and Community in Interwar Japan.* Princeton, NJ: Princeton University Press, 2000.
Hase, Masato. "Nihon eiga no zentai shugi: Tsumura Hideo no eiga hihyō wo meggute [Japanese film and Totalitarianism: On Tsumra Hideo's Film Criticism]." In *Nihon eiga to nashonarizumu 1931–1945* [Japanese Film and nationalism 1931–1945], edited by Iwamoto Kenji, 273–294. Tokyo: Shinwasha, 2004.
Hasegawa Nyozekan. *Nihon eigaron* [On Japanese Cinema]. Tokyo: Dai-Nippon Eiga Kyōkai, 1943.
Hasegawa Tenkei. *Shizen shugi* [Naturalism]. Tokyo: Hakubunkan, 1908.
Hazumi Tsuneo. "Eiga riarizumu no teishō" [Proposal for Cinematic Realism]. *Kinema junpō* 560 (December 1, 1935): 75–76.
Heidegger, Martin. "A Dialogue on Language: Between a Japanese and an Inquirer." In *On the Way to Language*, translated by Peter D. Hertz. New York: Harper and Row, 1971.
Heisig, James W., Thomas P. Kasulis, and John C. Maraldo, eds. *Japanese Philosophy: A Source Book.* Honolulu: University of Hawai'i Press, 2011.
High, Peter B. *The Imperial Screen: Japanese Film Culture in the Fifteen Years' War, 1931–1945.* Madison: University of Wisconsin Press, 2003.
Hirabayashi Hatsunosuke. *Hirabayashi Hatsunosuke ikōshu* [Posthumous Collection of Hirabayashi Hatsunosuke]. Edited by Hirabayashi Komako. Tokyo: Heibonsha, 1932.
Hirano Ken. *Bungaku, Showa 10-nen zengo* [Literature around 1935]. Tokyo: Bungei Shunjūsha, 1972.
Hirano, Kyoko. *Mr. Smith Goes to Tokyo: Japanese Cinema under the American Occupation, 1945–1952.* Washington, DC: Smithsonian Institution Press, 1992.
Horino Masao. *Kamera, me x Tetsu, kōsei* [Camera, Eye x Steel, Construction]. Tokyo: Mokuseosha Shoin, 1932.
Igarashi Toshiharu, ed. *Itagaki Takao: Kurashikku to modan* [Itagaki Takao: Classic and Modern]. Tokyo: Shinwasha, 2010.
Iijima Tadashi. "Shinario bungakuron josetsu" [Introduction to the Theory of Scenario Literature]. In *Shinario taikei*. Vol. 1 of *Shinario bungaku zenshū*, edited by Iijima Tadashi, Uchida Kisao, Kishi Matsuo, and Hazumi Tsuneo, 1–26. Tokyo: Kawade Shobō, 1937.
———. *Shinema no ABC* [ABC of Cinema]. Tokyo: Kōseikaku Shoten, 1928.
Iizawa Kōtarō and Kaneko Ryūichi, eds. *Kōga kessakushū* [Masterpieces of *Kōga*]. Tokyo: Kokusho Kankōkai, 2005.
Imamura Taihei. *Eiga geijutsu no keishiki* [Forms of Film Art]. Tokyo: Ōshio Shorin, 1938.
———. *Eiga riron nyūmon* [An Introduction to Film Theory]. Tokyo: Itagaki Shoten, 1952.
———. *Gendai eigaron* [On Contemporary Cinema]. Tokyo: Heibonsha, 1957.
———. "Japanese Art and the Animated Cartoon." Translated by Tsuruoka Furuichi. *The Quarterly Review of Film, Radio and Television* 7 no. 3 (September 1953): 217–222

---. *Kiroku eigaron* [On Documentary Film]. Kyoto: Daiichi Geibunsha, 1940.
---. *Sensō to eiga* [War and Film]. Kyoto: Daiichi Geibunsha, 1942.
Itagaki Takao. "Gendai geijutsu kōsatsusha no shuki" [Memoirs of an Observer of Contemporary Art]. *Shinkō geijutsu kenkyū* 1 (February 1931): 208–209.
---. *Kansō no gangu* [Playthings of Contemplation]. Tokyo: Ōhata Shoten, 1933.
--- ed. *Kikai geijutsuron* [On Machine Art]. Tokyo: Tenjinsha, 1930.
---. *Kikai to geijutsu to no kōryū* [Exchanges between Art and Machine]. Tokyo: Iwanami Shoten, 1929.
Itagaki Takao and Horino Masao. "Dai-Tokyo no seikaku" [Characteristics of Greater Tokyo]. *Chūō kōron* 46, no. 10 (October 1931): appendixes 1–20.
Itami Mansaku. *Itami Mansaku zenshū*. 3 vols. Tokyo: Chikuma Shobō, 1961.
Iwamoto Kenji. "Itagaki Takao to Terada Torahiko: Eiga no sekaizō wo meguru futari no tachiba" [Itagaki Takao and Terada Torahiko: Their Attitudes toward the Image of the Cinematic World]. *Nihon daigaku geijutsu gakubu kiyō* 53 (2011): 111–118.
---, ed. *Nihon eiga to modanizumu* [Japanese Cinema and Modernism]. Tokyo: Ributopōto, 1991.
---. "Nihon ni okeru montāju riron no shōkai" [Introduction of Montage Theory to Japan]. *Hikaku bungaku nenshi* 10 (1974): 67–85.
Iwasaki Akira. "Eiga hihyōka no sekinin" [Film Critics' Responsibility]. In *Gendai Nihon eigaron taikei* [A Series on Contemporary Japanese Film Criticism], edited by Ogawa Tōru et al., 1:181–190. Tokyo: Tōjusha, 1970–72.
---. "Eiga riarizumu e no tenbō" [A Prospect of Cinematic Realism]. In *Riarizumu kenkyū* [A Study of Realism], edited by Kozai Yoshishige and Kurahara Korehito, 257–300. Tokyo: Hakuyōsha, 1949.
---. *Eiga to shihon shugi* [Film and Capitalism]. Tokyo: Ōraisha, 1931.
Jakobson, Roman. "On Realism in Art." In *Language in Literature*, edited by Krystina Pomorska and Stephen Rudy, 19–27. Cambridge, MA: Harvard University Press, 1987.
James, William. *Pragmatism: A New Name for Some Old Ways of Thinking*. New York: Longmans, 1907.
Jameson, Fredric. *Signatures of the Visible*. New York: Routledge, 1992.
Kaeriyama Norimasa. "Eigageki to haiyū dōsa (1)" [The Photoplay and Acting (1)]. *Katsudō gahō* 3, no. 7 (July 1919): 5.
---. *Katsudō shashingeki no sōsaku to satsueihō* [The Production and Photography of Moving Picture Drama], exp. ed. Tokyo: Seikōsha, 1921.
Kaes, Anton, Nicholas Baer, and Michael Cowan, eds. *The Promise of Cinema: German Film Theory, 1907–1933*. Oakland: University of California Press, 2016.
Kamei Fumio. "Kiroku eiga shinario: *Pekin*." [Documentary Script: *Peking*]. *Eiga hyōron* 147 (June 1938): 67–74.
Kamo Kyōji, "*Korega Roshia da*" [*This Is Russia*]. *Prokino* 1, no. 1 (May 1932): 74–76.
Kant, Immanuel. *Critique of Pure Reason*. Translated and edited by Paul Guyer and Allen W. Wood. Cambridge: Cambridge University Press, 1998.
Karlson, Mats. "Kurahara Korehito's Road to Proletarian Realism." *Japan Review* 20 (2008): 231–273.
Kawazoe Toshimoto. *Eigageki gairon: Eizōgeki e no "daiichi no mon"* [An Introduction to the Photoplay: The First Gate to Image Dramas]. Tokyo: Sun'nansha, 1927.

Keene, Donald. *Dawn to the West: Japanese Literature of the Modern Era, Fiction*. New York: Holt, Rinehart and Winston, 1984.
Keller, Sarah, and Jason N. Paul, eds. *Jean Epstein: Critical Essays and New Translations*. Amsterdam: Amsterdam University Press, 2012.
Kimura Motomori. *Keiseiteki jikaku* [Formational Self-Awareness]. Tokyo: Kōbundō, 1941.
Kimura Toshimi, ed. *Kikai to geijutsu kakume*i [Machine and the Revolution of Art]. Tokyo: Hakuyōsha, 1930.
Kishi Matsuo. *Nihon eiga yōshikikō* [A Study in the Style of Japanese Films]. Tokyo: Kawade Shobō, 1937.
Kitagawa Fuyuhiko. "Bungei eiga sakuhin shoken sonota" [Brief View on Literary Films and Others]. *Kinema junpō* 529 (January 21, 1935): 59–60.
———. *Gendai eigaron* [On Contemporary Film]. Tokyo: Mikasa Shobō, 1941.
———. *Sanbun eigaron* [On Prosaic Film]. Tokyo: Sakuhinsha, 1940.
Kiuchi Tsuguo. "*Korega Roshia da*" [*This Is Russia*]. *Eiga hyōron* 11, no. 4 (April 1932): 138–139.
Kobayashi Takiji. "'Kikai no kaikyūsei' ni tsuite" [On the "Class Aspect of the Machine"]. In *Kōki puroretaria bungaku hyōronshū* 2 [Late Proletarian Literary Criticism 2], 62–66. Vol. 7 of *Nihon Puroretaria bungaku hyōronshū*, Tokyo: Shin Nihon Shuppansha, 1990).
Komatsu Hiroshi. "Shinematogurafu to wa nan datta no ka: Ideorogī sōchi to shite no eiga." [What Was the Cinématograph? Film as an Ideological Apparatus]. In *Eiga denrai: Shinematografu to Meiji no Nihon*, edited by Yoshida Yoshishige et al., 103–123. Tokyo: Iwanami Shoten, 1995.
———. "Transformation in Film as Reality (Part 1): Questions Regarding the Genesis of Nonfiction Film." Translated by A. A. Gerow. *Documentary Box* 5 (15 October 1994): 1–5.
Komiyama Akitoshi. "Puroretaria rearizumu no gendankai: Soshite sorewa ikanaru hōkō e susumu beki dearu ka" [The Current Stage of Proletarian Realism: To What Direction Should It Advance?]. In *Kōki puroretaria bungaku hyōronshū* 2, 189–195. Vol. 7 of *Nihon Puroretaria bungaku hyōronshū*, 189–195. Tokyo: Shin Nihon Shuppansha, 1990.
Kosaka Kunitsugu. *Nishida Kitarō: Sono shisō to gendai* [Nishida Kitarō: His Thought and the Present]. Kyoto: Mineruva Shobō, 1995.
Kōsaka Masaaki, Nishitani Keiji, Takayama Iwao, and Suzuki Shigetaka. *Sekaishiteki tachiba to Nihon* [The Standpoint of World History and Japan]. Tokyo: Chūō Kōronsha, 1943.
Kozai Yoshishige. *Senjika no yuibutsuronja tachi* [Materialists during the Wartime Period]. Tokyo: Aoki shoten, 1982.
Kracauer, Siegfried. *Theory of Film: The Redemption of Physical Reality*. New York: Oxford University Press, 1960.
Kudō Shin'nosuke. *Hyōgenha no eiga* [Expressionist Film]. Tokyo: Chūō Bijutsusha, 1923.
Kuki Shūzō. "Bergson au Japon." In *Kuki Shūzō zenshū* [Completed Works of Kuki Shūzō], edited by Amano Teiyū et al., 1:257–261. Tokyo: Iwanami Shoten, 1980.
———. *Jituzon no tetsugaku* [Existentialist Philosophy]. Tokyo: Iwanami Shoten, 1933.
Kumagai Hisatora. "*Abe ichizoku* no eiga-ka" [Adaptation of *The Abe Family*]. *Nihon eiga* 3, no. 2 (February 1938): 59–61.
Kurahara Korehito. *Kurahara Korehito shū*. Vol. 4 of *Nihon puroretaria bungaku hyōronshū* [Collections of Japanese Proletarian Literary Criticism], 116–124. Tokyo: Shin-Nippon Shuppansha, 1990.

———. "Saikin no Sowēt eigakai (1)" [Recent Soviet Cinema (1)]. *Kinema junpō* 254 (March 1, 1927): 24.
———. "Saikin no Sowēt eigakai (2)" [Recent Soviet Cinema (2)]. *Kinema junpō* 257 (April 1, 1927): 30.
Kurata Fumindo. *Shinarioron* [On Film Script]. Kyoto: Daiichi Geibunsha, 1940.
Kurushima, Yukio. "Eiga to riarizumu: Eiga riron no hatten o mezashite [Film and Realism: Toward the Development of Film Theory]." *Eiga hyōron* 18, no. 7 (July 1936): 48–51.
Kyōto Eigasai Jikkō Iinkai, ed. *Jidaigeki eiga to wa nani ka: Nyū firumu stadīzu* [What Are Period Films? New Cinema Studies]. Kyoto: Jinbun Shoin, 1997.
LaMarre, Thomas. *Shadows on the Screen: Tanizaki Jun'ichirō on Cinema and "Oriental" Aesthetics*. Ann Arbor: Center for Japanese Studies, University of Michigan, 2005.
Lamarre, Thomas, and Kang Nae-hui, eds. *Impacts of Modernities*. Hong Kong: Hong Kong University Press, 2004.
Langdale, Alan, ed. *Hugo Münsterberg on Film: The Photoplay: A Psychological Study and Other Writings*. New York: Routledge, 2001.
Lionnet, Françoise, and Shu-mei Shih, eds. *The Creolization of Theory*. Durham, NC: Duke University Press, 2011.
Lippit, Akira. "Preface (Interface)." In *Media Theory in Japan*, edited by Marc Steinberg and Alexander Zahlten, xi–xv. Durham, NC: Duke University Press, 2017.
Lippit, Seiji M. *Topographies of Japanese Modernism*. New York: Columbia University Press, 2002.
Lukács, Georg. *Essays on Realism*. Translated by David Frenbach. Edited and introduced by Rodney Livingston. London: Lawrence and Wishart, 1980.
———. "Narrate or Describe?" Translated by Arthur D. Kahn. In *Writer and Critic and Other Essays*, 110–148. New York: Grosset and Dunlap, 1970.
———. "Thoughts toward an Aesthetic of the Cinema." Translated by Janelle Blankenship. *Polygraph* 13 (2001): 13–18.
MacCabe, Colin. "Realism and Cinema: Notes on Some Brechtian Theses." *Screen* 15, no. 2 (Summer 1974): 7–27.
Makino Mamoru. "*Eiga shūdan* ni tsuite" [On *Eiga shūdan*]. In *Eiga shūdan: Jō*, edited by Makino Mamoru, 1–9. Vol. 9 of *Senzen eizō riron zasshi shūsei* [Collection of Prewar Film Theory Magazines]. Tokyo: Yumani shobō, 1989.
———. "'Imamura Taihei: Kokō dokusō no eiga hihyōka' to chosha Sugiyama Heiichi no isō [Imamura Taihei: A Solitary and Innovative Critic of the Moving Image and the Position of Its Author Sugiyama Heiichi]." *Eizōgaku* 45 (October 1991): 59–84.
———. "Nagae Michitarō eiga riron kenkyū shōryō" [Preliminary Research on Nagae Michitarō's Film Theory]. In Nagae Michitarō, *Eiga, hyōgen, keisei* [Cinema, Expression, Formation], 335–337. Vol. 4 of *Nihon eigaron gensetsu taikei* [Japanese Film Theory and Discourse], edited by Makino Mamoru. Tokyo: Yumani Shobō, 2003.
———. "Shinkō geijutsu to Shinkō geijutsu kenkyū no jidai" [The Period of Shinkō geijutsu and Shinkō geijutsu kenkyū]. In *Shinkō Geijutsu*, edited by Makino Mamoru, 157–205. Vol. 3 of *Nihon modanizumu no kōryū* [Upsurge of Japanese Modernism]. Tokyo: Yumani shobō, 1990.

Margulies, Ivone, ed. *Rites of Realism: Essays on Corporeal Cinema*. Durham, NC: Duke University Press, 2003.
Marra, Michael F. "A Dialogue on Language between a Japanese and an Inquirer: Kuki Shūzō's Version." In *Essays on Japan: Between Aesthetics and Literature*, 167–185. Leiden: Brill, 2010.
Metz, Christian. *Film Language: Essays on the Semiotics of the Cinema*. Translated by Michael Taylor. New York: Oxford University Press, 1974.
Miki Kiyoshi. *Testugaku nyūmon* [An Introduction to Philosophy]. Tokyo: Iwanami Shoten, 1940.
Miller, Toby, and Robert Stam, eds. *A Companion to Film Theory*. Malden, MA: Wiley-Blackwell, 2004.
Mitsuse Sueo "Futatsu no izumu" [Two Isms]. *Kinema junpō* 181 (January 1, 1925): 65–66.
Miyao, Daisuke, ed. *The Oxford Handbook of Japanese Cinema*. Oxford: Oxford University Press, 2014.
Mizoguchi Kenji. *Mizoguchi Kenji chosakushū* [Collected Writings of Mizoguchi Kenji], edited by Sasō Tsutomu. Tokyo: Kinema Junpōsha, 2015.
Mizumachi Seiji. "*Kagirinaki zenshin*" [*Unending Advance*]. *Kinema junpō* 628 (November 11, 1937): 96
Moholy-Nagy, László. *Painting, Photography, Film*. Translated by Janet Seligman. Cambridge, MA: The MIT Press, 1969.
Mori Ōgai. "Rekishi sono mama to rekishi banare" [History as It Is and the Detachment from History]. In *Mori Ōgai zenshū*, 23:505–510. Tokyo: Iwanami Shoten, 1951.
Moussinac, Léon. *Le cinéma soviétique*. Paris: Gallimard, 1928.
Münsterberg, Hugo. *Photoplay: A Psychological Study*. New York: D. Appleton, 1916.
Murata Mironu. "Hyōgenha no eiga no kanshō: Hyogenha to wa nanika" [Watching an Expressionist Film: What Is Expressionism?]. *Katsudō no sekai* 4, no. 10 (October 1922): 62–63.
Murayama Tomoyoshi. "Eiga no genkaisei" [The Limits of Cinema]. *Kinema junpō* 507 (June 1, 1934): 67–68.
———. *Engekiteki jijoden* [Theatrical Autobiography]. 4 vols. Tokyo: Tōhō shuppansha, 1970–1977.
Mutai Risaku. *Hyōgenteki sekai no ronri* [The Logic of the Expressive World]. Vol. 3 of *Mutai Risaku Chosakushū* [Collective Works of Mutai Risaku], edited by Furuta Hikaru et al. Tokyo: Kobushi Shobō, 2001.
Nagae, Michitarō. *Eiga, hyōgen, keisei* [Film, Expression, Formation]. Kyoto: Kyōiku Tosho, 1942.
———. "Hyōgen no ronri: Daiisshō [Logic of Expression: Chapter 1]." *Eiga hyōron* 18, no. 7 (July 1936): 29–37.
———. "Kino: Dai-isshō: Murayama Tomoyoshi 'Eiga no genkaisei' o kien to shite" [Kino, Chapter 1: A Response to Murayama Tomoyoshi's "The Limits of Cinema"]. *Eiga hyōron* 16, no. 9 (September 1934): 59–70.
Nagib, Lúcia, and Cecília Mello, eds. *Realism and the Audiovisual Media*. New York: Palgrave, 2009.
Nakagawa Shigeaki. *Keiji shinin shokuhai bigaku* [An Aesthetics of Detached Contact]. Tokyo: Hakubunkan, 1911.

Nakagi Sadakazu. "Katsudō shashin no geijutsuteki kachi: Gaimenteki keishikiron" [Artistic Values of the Moving Picture: On External Forms]. *Katsudō gahō* 5, no. 5 (May 1921): 24–25.

Nakai Masakazu. *Ikiteiru kūkan: Shutaiteki eiga geijutsuron* [Living Space: Subjective Essays on Film Art]. Edited by Tsujibe Seitarō. Tokyo: Tenbinsha, 1971.

———. *Nakai Masakazu hyōronshū* [Collected Essays of Nakai Masakazu], edited by Nagata Hiroshi. Tokyo: Iwanami Shoten, 1995.

———. *Nakai Masakazu zenshū* [Complete Works of Nakai Masakazu]. Edited by Kuno Osamu. 4 vols. Tokyo: Bijutsu shuppansha, 1964–1981.

Nakamura Mitsuo. *Fūzoku shōsetsuron* [On the Social Custom Novel]. Tokyo: Kawade shobō, 1950.

———. "Shizen shugi bungaku gaisetsu" [A Survey on Naturalist Literature]. In *Nakamura Mitsuo zenshū*, 3:513–540. Tokyo: Chikuma Shobō, 1972.

Namiki Shinsaku. *Nihon puroretaria eiga dōmei (purokino) zenshi* [A Comprehensive History of The Proletarian Film League in Japan (prokino)]. Tokyo: Gōdō Shuppan, 1986.

Nara, Hiroshi. *The Structure of Detachment: The Aesthetic Vision of Kuki Shūzō with a Translation of "Iki no kōzō."* Honolulu: University of Hawai'i Press, 2005.

Nichols, Bill, ed. *Movies and Methods*. 2 vols. Berkeley: University of California Press, 1976–1985.

Nishida Kitarō. *An Inquiry into the Good*. Translated by Masao Abe and Christopher Ives. New Haven, CT: Yale University Press, 1992.

———. *Nishida Kitarō zenshū* [Complete Works of Nishida Kitarō]. 3rd ed. 24 vols. Edited by Takeda Atsushi et al. Tokyo: Iwanami Shoten, 2002–2009.

———. *Ontology of Production: Three Essays*. Translated and Introduction by William Haver. Durham, NC: Duke University Press, 2012.

Nornes, Abé Mark. *Cinema Babel: Translating Global Cinema*. Minneapolis: University of Minnesota Press, 2007.

———. *Japanese Documentary Film: The Meiji Era through Hiroshima*. Minneapolis: University of Minnesota Press, 2003.

Okada Shinkichi. *Eiga to kokka* [Film and Nation]. Tokyo: Seikatsusha, 1943.

Omuka Toshiharu. *Nihon no avangyarudo geijutsu: "Mavo" to sono jidai* [The Japanese Avant-Garde Art: "Mavo" and Its Times]. Tokyo: Seidosha, 2001.

Ōno Takeo. "Eigageki wa kanarazu shizenteki nare" [The Photoplay Must Be Natural]. *Katsudō gahō* 6, no. 8 (August 1922): 100–101.

Ōsawa Masachi. *Shihon shugi no paradokkusu* [The Paradox of Capitalism]. New ed. Tokyo: Chikuma Shobō, 2008.

Ōsugi Sakae. "Rōdō mondai to puragumatizumu." [Labor Issues and Pragmatism]. In *Hangyaku no seishin: Ōsugi Sakae hyōronshū* [A Rebellious Spirit: Critical Writings of Ōsugi Sakae], 170–182. Tokyo: Heibonsha, 2011.

Ōtsuka Kyōichi. "Sono yoru no onna" [The Woman That Night]. *Eiga hyōron* 16, no. 12 (December 1934): 153–154.

Overbey, David, ed. *Springtime in Italy: A Reader on Neorealism*. Hamden, CT: Archon Books, 1979.

Ozu Yasujirō and Yagi Yasutarō. "Shinario: Tanoshiki kana Yasukichi-kun" [Scenario: What a Cheerful Guy, Mr. Yasukichi]. *Shinchō* 34, no. 8 (August 1937): 201–245.

Pincus, Leslie. *Authenticating Culture in Imperial Japan: Kuki Shūzō and the Rise of National Aesthetics.* Berkeley: University of California Press, 1996.
Poulton, M. Cody. "The Rhetoric of the Real." In *Modern Japanese Theatre and Performance.* edited by David Jortner et al., 17–31. Lanham, MD: Lexington Books, 2006.
Pudovkin, Vsevolod. *Film Technique and Film Acting.* Revised ed. Translated and edited by Ivor Montagu. New York: Grove Press, 1970.
Rodowick, D. N. "An Elegy for Theory." *October* 122 (Fall 2007): 91–109.
———. *Elegy for Theory.* Cambridge, MA: Harvard University Press, 2015.
———. *The Crisis of Political Modernism: Criticism and Ideology in Contemporary Film Criticism.* Revised ed. Berkeley: University of California Press, 1995.
Rosen, Philip. *Change Mummified: Cinema, Historicity, Theory.* Minneapolis: University of Minnesota Press, 2001.
———. "History of Image, Image of History: Subject and Ontology in Bazin." *Wide Angle* 9, no. 4 (Winter 1987/88): 7–34.
———. ed. *Narrative, Apparatus, Ideology: A Film Theory Reader.* New York: Columbia University Press, 1986.
Rotha, Paul. *Documentary Film.* London: Farber and Farber, 1936.
Saeki Tomori and Sazaki Yoriaki, eds. *FC 90: Uchida Tomu kantoku tokushū* [FC 90: Special Issue on the Director Uchida Tomu]. Tokyo: Kokuritsu kindai bijutsukan firumu sentā, 1992.
Sakai, Naoki. "Modernity and Its Critique: The Problem of Universalism and Particularism." *South Atlantic Quarterly* 87, no. 3 (Summer 1988): 475–504.
———. "Resistance to Conclusion: The Kyoto School of Philosophy under the Pax Americana." In *Re-politicizing The Kyoto School as Philosophy*, edited by Christopher Goto-Jones, 183–198. London: Routledge, 2008.
Sasa Genjū. "Gangu/Buki—Satsueiki" [Camera—Toy/Weapon]. *Senki* 1, no. 2 (June 1928): 29–33.
Sato Tadao. "Does Theory Exist in Japan?" Translated by Joanne Bernardi. *Review of Japanese Culture and Society* 22 (December 2010): 14–23.
———. *Nihon eiga rironshi* [History of Japanese Film Theory]. Tokyo: San'ichi Shobō, 1977.
———. "Tōkī jidai: Nihon eigashi 3" [The Talkie Era: Japanese Film History 3]. In *Tōkī no jidai* [The Era of the Talkie], edited by Imamura Shōhei et al., 2–63. Vol. 3 of *Kōza Nihon eiga* [Lectures on Japanese Cinema]. Tokyo: Iwanami Shoten, 1986.
Sawamura Tsutomu. "*Abe ichizoku wo megutte*" [On *The Abe Family*]. *Eiga hyōron* 146 (April 1938): 61–66.
———. *Eiga no hyōgen* [Film Expression]. Tokyo: Suga Shoten, 1942.
———. "Tokushū eiga hihan: *Kagirinaki zenshin*" [Special Film Criticism: *Unending Advance*]. *Eiga hyōron* 142 (December 1937): 106–109.
Schamus, James. "Dreyer's Textual Realism." In *Rites of Realism: Essays on Corporeal Cinema*, edited by Ivone Margulies, 315–324. Durham, NC: Duke University Press, 2003.
Sekino Yoshio. "Tōkī no ikubeki michi" [The Direction of the Talkie]. *Eiga hyōron* 8, no. 1 (January 1930): 22–30.
———. "Tōkī no ikubeki michi (3)" [The Direction of the Talkie (3)]. *Eiga hyōron* 8, no. 5 (May 1930): 56–61.

Shimizu Hikaru. "Eiga to kikai" [Film and Machine]. In *Kikai geijutsuron*, edited by Itagaki Takao, 45–68. Tokyo: Tenjinsha, 1930.

Silverberg, Miriam. *Erotic Grotesque Nonsense: The Mass Culture of Japanese Modern Times*. Berkeley: University of California Press, 2006.

Sobchack, Vivian. *The Address of the Eye: A Phenomenology of Film Experience*. Princeton, NJ: Princeton University Press, 1992.

Steinberg, Marc, and Alexander Zahlten, eds. *Media Theory in Japan*. Durham, NC: Duke University Press, 2017.

Sugiyama Heiichi. "Bungaku e no sekkin no mondai" [Problems in Film's Approaches to Literature]. *Eiga shūdan* 4 (December 1935): 7–10.

———. *Eiga hyōronshū* [Essays on Film]. Kyoto: Daiichi Geibunsha. 1941.

———. *Imamura Taihei: Kokō dokusō no eizō hyōronka* [Imamura Taihei: A Solitary and Innovative Critic of the Moving Image]. Tokyo: Riburopōto, 1990.

———. "Kyamera no soshitsu to shite no shajitsu" [Realism as the Potential of the Camera]. *Eiga hyōron* 18, no. 7 (July 1936): 70–72.

Suzuki, Tomi. *Narrating the Self: Fictions of Japanese Modernity*. Stanford, CA: Stanford University Press, 1996.

Takeba, Joe. "The Age of Modernism: From Visualization to Socialization." In *The History of Japanese Photography*, edited by Anne Wilkes Tucker et al., 142–183. New Haven, CT: Yale University Press, 2003.

Tanabe Hajime, "Genshōgaku ni okeru atarashiki tenkō: Haideggā no sei no genshōgaku" [A New Turn in Phenomenology: Heidegger's Phenomenology of Life]. In *Tanabe Hajime zenshū*, edited by Nishitani Keiji et al., 4:19–34. Tokyo: Chikuma Shobō, 1963.

Tanabe Hajime, Kozai Yoshishige, Nakai Masakazu, et al. *Kaisō no Tosaka Jun* [Remembrances of Tosaka Jun]. Tokyo: San'ichi Shobō, 1948.

Tanaka Jun'ichirō. *Nihon eiga hattatsushi* [History of the Development of Japanese Cinema]. 5 vols. Tokyo: Chūō kōronsha, 1975–1976.

Tanaka Masasumi, "Eiga hyōronka to shite no Sugiyama Heiichi" [Sugiyama Heiichi as a Film Critic]. In Sugiyama Heiichi and Tanikawa Tetsuzō, *Eiga hyōronshū, Geijutsu shōronshū: Shōroku* [Essays on Film, A Small Collection of Essays on Art: Excerpt] 331–342. Vol. 7 of *Nihon eigaron gensetsu taikei* [Japanese Film Theory and Discourse], edited by Makino Mamoru. Tokyo: Yumani Shobō, 2003.

Tanizaki Jun'ichirō. "The Present and Future of Moving Pictures." Translated by Thomas LaMarre. In Thomas LaMarre, *Shadows on the Screen: Tanizaki Jun'ichirō on Cinema & "Oriental" Aesthetics*, 65–74. Ann Arbor: Center for Japanese Studies, University of Michigan, 2005.

———. *Tanizaki Jun'ichirō zenshū* [Complete Works of Tanizaki Jun'ichirō]. 28 vols. Tokyo: Chūō Kōronsha, 1966–70.

Terada Torahiko. "Eiga geijutsu." In *Terada Torahiko zuihitsushū*, edited by Komiya Toyotaka, 3:201–238. Tokyo: Iwanami Shoten, 1948.

———. "Eiga no sekaizō." In *Terada Torahiko zuihitsushū*, edited by Komiya Toyotaka, 3:133–141. Tokyo: Iwanami Shoten, 1948.

———. "Nyūsu eiga to shinbun kiji" [New Film and Newspaper Article]. In *Terada Torahiko zenshū*, edited by Komiya Toyotaka, 7:49–53. Tokyo: Iwanami Shoten, 1961.

Togata Sachio. "*Jinsei gekijō*: Sutairu ni tsuite" [*Theater of Life*: On Style]. *Eiga hyōron* 119 (February 1936): 140–144.
Tomioka Shō. "Tōkī geijutsu no rearizumu e no michi" [A Road to Realism in Talkie Art]. *Eiga hyōron* 14, no. 5 (May 1933): 66–73.
Torrance, Richard. "The People's Library: The Spirit of Prose Literature versus Fascism." In *The Culture of Japanese Fascism*, edited by Alan Tansman, 56–79. Durham, NC: Duke University Press, 2009.
Tosaka Jun. "Eiga no shajitsuteki tokusei to taishūsei [Cinema's Realistic Property and Popularity]." *Eiga sōzō* 1, no. 1 (May 1936): 6–16.
———. "Eiga no ninshikironteki kachi to fūzoku byōsha [Cinema's Epistemological Value and Its Depiction of Social Customs]." *Nihon eiga* 2, no. 6 (June 1937): 13–19.
———. "Eiga geijutsu to eiga: Abusutorakushon no hō e [Film Art and Film: Toward the Operation of Abstraction]." *Eiga sōzō* 3, no. 1 (January 1938): 6–13.
———. *Tosaka Jun zenshū* [Complete Works of Tosaka Jun]. 5 vols. Tokyo: Keisō Shobō, 1966–1967.
———. *Tosaka Jun zenshu: Bekkan* [Complete Works of Tosaka Jun: A Supplement]. Tokyo: Keisō Shobō, 1979.
Toyoda Shirō. "Shimazu kantoku ni tsuite no jakkan no kansatsu" [A Few Observations on the Director Shimazu]. *Eiga hyōron* 108 (March 1935): 36–43.
Tsuji Hisakazu "Eiga no riarizumu" [Realism in Cinema] *Eiga hyōron* 18, no. 7 (July 1936): 95–108.
———. "Shimazu Yasujirō: Tōkī igo" [Shimazu Yasujirō: After the Talkie]. *Eiga hyōron* 108 (March 1935): 31–35.
Tsukada Yoshinobu. *Nihon eigashi no kenkyū: Katsudō shashin torai zengo no jijō* [A Study of Japanese Film History: The Situation of the Arrival of the Motion Pictures]. Tokyo: Gendai Shokan, 1980.
Tsumura Hideo. *Eiga to hihyō* [Film and Criticism]. Tokyo: Koyama Shoten, 1939.
———. *Eiga to kanshō* [Film and Appreciation]. Tokyo: Sōgensha, 1941.
———. *Eigasen* [Film War]. Tokyo: Asahi Shinbunsha, 1944.
———. *Zoku eiga to hihyō* [Film and Criticism: Continued]. Tokyo: Koyama Shoten, 1940.
Tsubouchi Shōyō. "Shōsetsu shinzui" [The Essence of the Novel]. In *Seiji shōsetsu, Tsubouchi Shōyō, Futabatei Shimei shū*, 182–235. Vol. 1 of *Gendai Nihon bungaku taikei* [A Series on Contemporary Japanese Literature]. Tokyo: Chikuma Shobō, 1971.
Turvey, Malcolm. *Doubting Vision: Film and the Revelationist Tradition*. New York: Oxford University Press, 2008.
Ueno Kōzō. *Eiga no ninshiki* [Cognition in Film]. Kyoto: Daiichi Geibunsha, 1940.
Vertov, Dziga. *Kino-Eye: The Writings of Dziga Vertov*. Edited by Annette Michelson. Translated by Kevin O'Brien. Berkeley: University of California Press, 1984.
Wada Hirofumi, ed. *Nihon no avangyarudo* [Avant-Garde in Japan]. Kyoto: Sekai Shisōsha, 2005.
Wada-Marciano, Mitsuyo. *Nippon Modern: Japanese Cinema of the 1920s and the 1930s*. Honolulu: University of Hawai'i Press, 2008.
Wada Shūzō. *Kindai bungaku sōseiki no kenkyū: Riarizumu no seisei* [Studies in the Formative Period of Modern Literature: The Creation of Realism]. Tokyo: Ōfūsha, 1973.

Wadayama Shigeru. "*Korega Roshia da*" [*This Is Russia*]. *Kinema Junpō*, 431 (April 1, 1932): 43–44.

Walker, Gavin. "Filmic Materiality and Historical Materialism: Tosaka Jun and the Prosthetics of Sensation." In *Tosaka Jun: A Critical Reader*, edited by Ken C. Kawashima, Fabien Schäfer, and Robert Stolz, 218–254. Ithaca, NY: Cornell University Press, 2013.

Walton, Kendall L. *Mimesis as Make-Believe: On the Foundations of the Representational Arts*. Cambridge, MA: Harvard University Press, 1990.

Weisenfeld, Gennifer. *Mavo: Japanese Artists and the Avant-garde, 1905–1931*. Berkeley: University of California Press, 2002.

Willemen, Paul. "On Realism in the Cinema." *Screen* 13, no. 1 (Spring 1972): 37–44.

Williams, Raymond. *Keywords: A Vocabulary of Culture and Society*. New ed. New York: Oxford University Press, 2015.

———. "A Lecture on Realism." *Screen* 18, no. 1 (Spring 1977): 61–74.

———. "When Was Modernism?" *New Left Review* 1, no. 175 (May–June 1989): 48–52.

Wollen, Peter. "'Ontology' and 'Materialism' in Film." *Screen* 17, no. 1 (Spring 1976): 7–23.

Yamada Kō. *Tosaka Jun to sono jidai*. Tokyo: Kadensha, 1990.

Yamamoto Kikuo. *Nihon eiga ni okeru gaikoku eiga no eikyō: Hikaku eigashi kenkyū* [The Influence of Foreign Cinema on Japanese Films: A Study in Comparative Film History]. Tokyo: Waseda Daigaku Shuppanbu, 1983.

Yamamoto Hirofumi. *Junshi no kōzō* [The Structure of the Ritual Suicide]. Tokyo: Kōbundō, 1994.

Yamamoto, Naoki. "Anbako kara no tōshi: Haniya Yutaka no sonzaironteki eigaron ni tsuite" [As Seen from the Camera Obscura: On Haniya Yutaka's Ontological Film Theory]. In *Tenkeiki no mediorogī: 1950-nendai Nihon no geijutsu to media no saihensei* [Mediology in a Transformative Period: Reconfigurations of Art and Media in 1950s Japan], edited by Toba Kōji and Yamamoto Naoki, 105–130. Tokyo: Shinwasha, 2019.

———. "Experiencing the World through Cinema: Nagae Michitarō and the Bergsonian Approach to Film in Wartime Japan." In *Dall'inizio, alla fine: Teorie del cinema in prospettiva*, edited by Francesco Casetti et al., 571–576. Udine: Forum Editrice Universitaria Udinese, 2010.

———. "Fūkei no saihakken: Itami Mansaku to *Atarashiki Tsuchi* [Re-discovery of Landscape: Itami Mansaku and The New Earth]." In *Nihon eiga to nashonarizumu, 1931–1945* [Japanese Film and Nationalism, 1931–1945], edited by Iwamoto Kenji, 63–102. Tokyo: Shinwasha, 2004.

———. "Soviet Montage Theory and Japanese Film Criticism." In *The Japanese Cinema Book*, edited by Hideaki Fujiki and Alastair Philips, 68–80. London: Bloomsbury, 2020.

———. "Tōkī rirarizumu e no michi" [A Road to Talkie Realism]. In *Eigashi o yominaosu*, edited by Komatsu Hiroshi et al., 211–259. Vol. 2 of *Nihon eiga wa ikiteiru*, edited by Yomota Inuhiko et al. Tokyo: Iwanami Shoten, 2010.

———. "Where Did the Bluebird of Happiness Fly? Bluebird Photoplays and the Reception of American Film in 1910s Japan." *Iconics* 10 (2010): 143–166.

Yoda Yoshitaka, *Mizoguchi Kenji no hito to geijutsu*. Tokyo: Eiga Geijutsusha, 1964.

Yokomitsu Riichi. *"Love" and Other Stories of Yokomitsu Riichi*. Translated by Denis Keen. Tokyo: Japan Foundation, 1974.

———. *Teihon Yokomitsu Riichi zenshū* [Complete Works of Yokomitsu Riichi]. 16 vols. Tokyo: Kawade Shobō Shinsha, 1981–1987.

Yoshida Seiichi, Asai Kiyoshi, Inagaki Tatsurō, Satō Masaru, and Wada Kingo, eds. *Meijiki* [The Meiji Period]. Vols 1–3 of *Kindai bungaku hyōron taikei* [A Series on Modern Japanese Literary Criticism]. Tokyo: Kadokawa Shoten, 1971–1972.

Yoshida Yoshishige, Yamaguchi Masao, and Kinoshita Naoyuki, eds. *Eiga denrai: Shinematografu to Meiji no Nihon* [The Introduction of Film: The Cinématograph and "Meiji Japan"]. Tokyo: Iwanami Shoten, 1995.

Yoshimoto, Mitsuhiro. *Kurosawa: Film Studies and Japanese Cinema*. Durham, NC: Duke University Press, 2000.

INDEX

47 Ronin, The (1941–42), 100

Abe Family, The (1938), 92–93, 97*fig.*, 98, 100
Abe Isoo, 30
Abe Kōbō, 172, 180
Address of the Eye, The: A Phenomenology of Film Experience (Sobchack), 135
aesthetics, 8, 31, 34, 36–39, 60, 63, 100, 109, 113–14, 118–20, 126, 140–41, 148–49, 175; aestheticization of the documentary method, 125–28; avant-garde, 58, 179; and epistemology, 12–13, 65; film, 25, 43, 46, 49, 80–81, 128–29; montage, 106; and realism, 11–12, 15, 21, 91. *See also* machine aesthetic
Agel, Henri, 135
Age of the World Target, The (Chow), 7
Aikawa Haruki, 130, 201n84
Aitken, Ian, 207n27
All Japan Federation of Proletarian Arts (NAPF), 68
Alternative Modernities (Gaonkar), 16
Anderson, Joseph L., 25, 94
Andrew, Dudley, xi, 1, 10, 86, 135, 146, 185n1, 186n11,
And Yet They Go On (1931), 25
Anthology of Scenario Literature (Kitagawa et al), 90
anti-dualism, 136–41
apparatus theory, 3, 162

Archipenki, Alexander, 57
architecture, 64–65
Arnheim, Rudolf, 2, 6, 81–82, 159, 174, 185n1
Atsugi Taka, 197–98n4
avant-garde art movement, 54, 56, 172–73, 179–80; in 1920s Japan, 56–60; in postwar Japan, 4, 165, 170–82; impact of the Great Kantō Earthquake on, 58
Ayfre, Amedee, 135
Azuma Hiroki, 5

Badiou, Alain, 6
Balázs, Béla, 2, 6, 37, 43, 47, 53, 54, 65, 151, 159, 174, 186n11, 188n45
Battleship Potemkin (1925), 66, 68
Bay of Death, The (1926), 68
Bazin, André, 3, 6, 21, 80, 112, 135, 141, 146, 148, 186n11, 188n45; definition of realism, 10–12; "shot in depth" technique of, 146
Before Dawn (1931), 93, 95, 197n44
Being and Time (Heidegger), 139
Benjamin, Walter, 6, 47, 109–10, 119, 125
Bergson, Henri, 21, 23, 26, 32, 34–35, 39, 134–135, 139–141, 155, 161; and the concept of pure duration, 146–47
Berlin: Symphony of a Great City (Ruttmann), 65
Best Years of Our Lives, The (1946), 145
Bhabha, Homi K., 3
Bicycle Thieves (De Sica), 205n105

225

Bordwell, David, 3, 10
British Documentary Film Movement, 24, 81, 174
Buck-Morss, Susan, 6
Bukharin, Nikolai, 69
Buñuel, Luis, 180
Burch, Noël, 2, 10
Burliuk, David, 57

Cabinet of Dr. Caligari, The (1921), 52, 53
Capital (Marx), 30
capitalism, 10, 19, 20, 74, 85, 119, 121, 125, 127, 141
Capricious Young Man (1936), 94
Carmen Goes Home (1952), 168
Carroll, Noël, 3
Casetti, Francesco, xi, xiii, 54, 164
Chan, Jessica Ka Yee, 4
Chaplin, Charlie, 74
Characteristics of Greater Tokyo (Itagaki and Horino), 62, 62*fig.*
Chiba Nobuo, 25
Chinese Revolutionary Cinema: Propaganda, Aesthetics, and Internationalism, 1949–1966 (Chan), 4
Chow, Ray, 7
Cinema 1 and 2 (Deleuze), 134
Cinema of Actuality: Japanese Avant-Garde Filmmaking in the Season of Image Politics (Furuhata), 4
Cinema Approaching Reality: Locating Chinese Film Theory (Fan), 4
Cinema, Expression, Formation (Naga), 134, 141, 149, 152, 159–165
Citizen Kane (1941), 145
Civil Censorship Department (CCD), 167
Civil Information and Education Section (CIE), 167
Clément, René, 179, 180
Cohen-Séat, Gilbert, 135
collectivism, logic of, 113–22
Communist International (Comintern), 69, 71
comparative literature, 7; and the "grid of intelligibility," 7, 9, 13
computer-generated imagery (CGI), 10–11
Constellations on the Earth (1934), 77–78
Contemporary History of Japanese Cinema, A (Fujita), 132
"Continuity of *In Spring*, The" (Nakai), 116, 117*fig.*
Creative Evolution (Bergson), 134, 155
"Critique of Paul Rotha's Film Theory, A: On His *Documentary Film*" (Tsumura), 174–75
Critique of Pure Reason (Kant), 177
Crossroads (1928), 57, 95

Crown of Life, The (1936), 87
cubism, 14, 26, 34, 49, 59
"Current Stage of Proletarian Realism, The" (Komiyama), 72

dada, 14, 57, 59, 179
Damned, The (1947), 180
Dassin, Jules, 179, 180
Davis, Darrell W., 92–93, 100–101
Day of Wrath (1941), 98–99
Dead Souls (Haniya), 182
"Decentering Theory: Reconsidering the History of Japanese Film Theory" (Gerow), 4
Deleuze, Gilles, 6, 134–135
dialectics, 67; dialectical materialism, 112; dialectical montage, 82–83; Hegelian dialectics, 170, 177; of Lenin, 20, 171; natural dialectics, 118; social dialectics, 118; without synthesis, 20–21
Documentary Film (Rotha), 173–74
Dreyer, Carl, 98–99, 143
Driscol, Mark, 122
"Dynamics of the Metropolis" (Moholy-Nagy), 62

Earth (1939), 91
Edison, Thomas, 159
Edo Period (1603–1868), 26, 93, 94, 96, 140
Eiga bunka (*Film Culture*), 173
Eiga hyōron (*Film Criticism*), 9, 15, 150, 168
Eiga kikan (*Film Quarterly*), 9
Eiga sōzō (*Film Creation*), 108, 198n14
Eisenstein, Sergei, 66, 82, 116, 174, 185n3; on "the montage of attractions," 179–80; on Japan, 82, 106
Elliot, Eric, 9
"elliptical imagination," 19–20, 23, 172, 182
Elsaesser, Thomas, 81, 202n8
empiricism, 30, 32–35, 52, 139
Epstein, Jean, 2, 6, 47, 53, 55, 54, 65, 135, 161, 185n1; on film and the notion of space-time, 205n102
Ermler, Fridrikh, 91
Essays on Film (Sugiyama), 134, 141, 143–49
"Essence of the Novel, The" (Shōyō), 26
Eucken, Rudolf, 32
Exchanges between Machine and Art (Itagaki), 55, 55*fig.*, 63
existentialism, 10, 140
expressionism, 26; German; 14, 52–53
Expressionist Cinema (Kudō), 53

Fan, Victor, xii, 4
Fanon, Frantz, 17

INDEX   227

Fedorova, Anastasia, 196n38
Fenollosa, Ernest, 137
fiction/nonfiction, integration of, 128–32
Fighting Soldiers (1939), 91, 168
Film Collective (*Eiga shūdan*), 141–42
Film Law (*eigahō*, 1939), 22, 80, 90, 104, 127, 133, 167,
"Film as a Means of Agitprop" (Iwasaki), 63
film studies, 1; institutionalization of, 4
film theory, 1–2, 11, 53; "auteurist" approach to, 9, 25, 79, 84–92; classical, 1–10, 23, 31, 37, 54, 68, 135; film semiotics, 145; "formative tradition," 11, 151, 161, ; and "Grand Theory," 3–4; Japanese translations of, 2, 9, 82, 104, 116, 174–76, 185n3, 187n32; "phenomenological" approach to, 10, 23, 133–136; "realist tradition," 10–13, 151, 161
Flaherty, Robert, 11
Flaubert, Gustave, 70
Formative Self-Awareness (Kimura), 141
Form of Film Art, The (Imamura), 122, 173
Fourier, Charles, 113
Four Seasons School (Shikiha), 141
Freeburg, V. O., 9, 82
"From Kino-Eye to Radio-Eye" (Vertov), 66
From Morning 'til Midnight (Kaiser), 58
Fujifilm, 81
Fujimoto Chizuko, 98
Fujita Motohiko, 132
Fukada Yasukazu, 113
Fukumoto Kazuo, 69
Furuhata, Yuriko, xii, 4, 122
Futaba Jūzaburō, 168
Futabatei Shimei, 27–28
Futurism, 26, 49; Italian, 64

Gabriel, Teshome H., 3
Gance, Abel, 82
Gaonkar, Dilip Parameshwar, 16–19
"General Account of the Novel, A" (Futabatei), 27
General, Staff, and Soldiers (1942), 130–31, 131*fig*.
Gerow, Aaron, xi, 4, 7, 9, 31, 39
globalization, 11
Glow of Life, The (1918), 42, 42*fig*.
Golley, Gregory, 59–60
Goncourt, Edmond and Jules de, 70
Gonda Yaunosuke, 30, 50, 52, 149; on the aesthetic potential of cinema, 36–37; on art, 31–32; on the development of technological inventions, 33; on the different viewing environments of traditional theaters and movie theaters, 35–36; on philosophy, 32; and theorizing of the cinematic intuition, 30–40; on the universality of film culture, 37–38
Great Kantō Earthquake (1923), 50, 58, 93
Greater East Asian Co-Prosperity Sphere, 101, 105, 128, 132, 157, 168,
Grierson, John, 173–74, 207n27
Griffith, D. W., 44
Gropius, Walter, 64
Guattari, Félix, 6
Guimarães, César, 6

Hagener, Malte, 81
Hagiwara Kyōjirō, 57
Hall, Stuart, 18
Hanada Kiyoteru, 19–20, 68, 165; on actuality and contingency, 176–77; application of Hegelian dialectic by, 177; cinematic worldview of, 177–79; 178*fig*.; and the concept of "elliptical imagination," 172–73; and the concept of the "sur-documentary," 170–80; and the correlation between "actuality" and "reality," 175; defense of Stalin, 181–82; as forerunner of the postwar Japanese avant-garde, 181; as a member of the Japanese Communist Party (JCP), 182; philosophical worldview of, 176–78, 177*fig*.; on Rotha, 174–179; and socialist realism, 181–83
Hanayagi Harumi, 42
Haniya Yutaka, 172, 208n56
Hara Masato, 165
Harootunian, Harry, 17, 108
Hasegawa Nyozekan, 93, 100
Hasegawa Shin, 84
Hasegawa Tenkei, 28–29
Hauptmann, Gerhart, 42
Hayashi Fubō, 84, 94
Hazumi Tsuneo, 79, 88–89, 168
Hegel, G. W. F., 21, 32, 114, 137, 176; Hegelian dialectics, 170, 177
Heidegger, Martin, 23, 114, 136, 139–140; phenomenology of, 139, 140
Hijikata Yoshi, 58
Hirano Ken, 63
Hirato Renkichi, 57
History (1940), 100
History and Class Consciousness (Lukács), 69
History of Japanese Film Theory, The (Satō), 8, 122
Hollywood cinema, 2, 10, 24, 38, 40, 45, 84, 93, 124–125, 129, 145; animated films, 123–124; post–World War I influx of Hollywood films into Japan, 42–45; newsreels, 126

Horino Masao, 61–62, 62*fig.*
Hori Tatsuo, 141
Hugo, Victor, 94
humanism, 49, 172; anti-humanism, 29, 172; "idealist humanism," 85, 89
Humanity and Paper Balloons (1937), 94, 203n51
Hume, David, 32
Husserl, Edmund, 23, 136, 139, 140, 153; bracketing, 157; noesis and noema, 153–157

Ibsen, Henrik, 42
Idealism, 12, 19, 32, 35, 85, 137
identity, law of, 19
Iijima Tadashi, 55, 168
Iketani Shinzaburō, 57
Imamura Taihei, 9, 22, 76, 128–30, 133, 141–42, 173, 200n62; and the documentation of the war effort, 122–25, 127–28; magazines launched by, 123; published monographs of, 122; on Rotha, 175–176; on "semi-documentary," 178–179
imperialism, 9, 85
impressionism, 34; French impressionism, 14
Inagaki Hiroshi, 93, 100
Ince, Thomas, 43–44
individualism, 70, 119
Inoue Enryō, 137–38
Inoue Tetsujirō, 137–38
Inquiry into the Good, An (Nishida), 138–39, 141
Intelligence of the Machine, The (Epstein), 135
intuition, 34–35, 52; as the solution to the opposition between empiricism and rationalism, 35; and Gonda, 30–40; and Nishida, 137, 153–158; and Sugiyama, 147
Ishikawa Takuboku, 30
Itagaki Takao, 14, 51, 55–56, 73–74, 149, 194n35; assessment of his contribution to film theory, 67–68; avant-garde journals started by, 62–63; collaboration with Horino Masao, 61–62, 62*fig.*; on the gaze of the camera, 65; on the internal logic of the machine, 64; on the "International Style," 64–65; and machine realism, 22–23, 56, 60–68, 72–75, 109
Italian neorealism, 11, 24, 77
Itami Mansaku, 8, 90, 94–95
Itō Daisuke, 90, 93
Iwasaki Akira, 62, 108, 168–170, 173

Jakobson, Roman, 14–15
James, William, 32, 138–139, 141; on intuition as the solution to the opposition between empiricism and rationalism, 35
Jameson, Fredric, 12–13

Japanese, The (1913), 44
Japanese Communist Party (JCP), 69, 123, 150, 167, 182
Japanese Film, The: Art and Industry (Anderson and Richie), 25
Japanese Philosophy: A Source Book (Heisig et al), 136–37
Japanese Tragedy, The (1945), 168
Japanese writing system; reform of (*genbun itchi*), 27–28, 48, 152
Junghans, Wolfram, 116

kabuki, 2, 36, 82; actors; 93–94; cinema, 14, 40, 41*fig.*, 44–45; theater, 35–36, 93
Kaeriyama Norimasa, 40–45, 93
Kamei Fumio, 91, 168
Kamo Kyōji, 75
Kant, Immanuel, 32, 114, 137, 147, 177; the Copernican turn, 83; neo-Kantianism, 61, 113, 139–140
Karlson, Mats, 68
Katano Hakuro, 41
Kaufman, Mikhail, 116
Kawaguchi Masakazu, 91
Kawakami Sadayakko, 42
Kawarasaki Chōjūrō, 94
Kawatake Mokuami, 94
Kawazoe Toshimoto, 82
Kean (1924), 82
Keywords (Williams), 12
Khrushchev, Nikita, 181
Kikuchi Kan, 84
Kikuchi Yūhō, 43
Kimura Motomori, 141
Kimura Toshimi, 73, 74
Kinema Junpō (*Movie Times*), 9, 40, 78*fig.*, 79, 141, 168; best films list of, 81, 84, 87, 123
Kinema Record, 40, 43–44
kino-eye, 65–66; anxiety concerning, 72–76; Vertov's concept of, 115–16, 159–60
Kinoshita Keisuke, 25, 90, 168
Kinugasa Teinosuke, 57, 93, 96–97
Kitagawa Fuyuhiko, 90–91, 168
Kōchiyama Sōshun (1936), 94
Komiyama Akitoshi, 72
Kondō Iyokichi, 42
Kosugi Tengai, 28
Kōtoku Shūsui, 30
Kozintsev, Grigori, 91
Kracauer, Siegfried, 6, 54, 119, 186n11, 188n45
Kuki Shūzō, 139–40
Kurahara Korehito, 14, 51, 56, 60, 79, 112; arrest of, 69; definition of proletarian realism,

INDEX 229

70–71; on nineteenth-century French realist novelists, 70; and proletarian realism, 68–72
Kuleshov, Lev, 82
Kulturfilm, 104, 116
Kumagai Hisatora, 84, 86, 92, 96–98, 100, 130
Kurata Fumindo, 8
Kurihara, Thomas, 45
Kurosawa Akira, 1, 90, 94, 168
Kyoto School of Philosophy, 23, 107, 113, 136, 139–141, 171
Kyōya Collar Shop, The (1922), 25

Lamarre, Thomas, xi, 18–19, 47, 122, 165
Lang, Fritz, 194n35
La Roue (1923), 82
Last Days of Edo, The (1941), 100
L'Atlantide (1932), 143
Le cinéma soviétique (Moussinac), 115–16
Le Corbusier, 56, 64
Leibniz, G. W., 156, 171
Lescarboura, Austin, 9
"Letter to Mr. Kinugasa Teinosuke, A: A Proposal for Historical Film" (Tsumura), 95
Levin, Thomas Y., 109–10
Lionnet, Françoise, 5, 7, 17
Lippit, Akira, 183
literary adaptation, 84–92; and "the renaissance of literary art" (*bungei fukkō*), 85
Living Corpse, The (1918), 43
Locke, John, 32
Logic of Expression, The (Mutai), 141
Lower depths, The (1936), 97
Lukács, Georg, 46, 69
Lumière, Auguste, 11
Lumière, Louis, 11
Lump of Flesh, A (Tanizaki), 47
Lu Xun, 63, 193n29

MacArthur, Douglas, 166–67
MacCabe, Colin, 10
machine aesthetic, 14, 22, 23, 54–56, 67–68; and collectivism, 120; Japanese reception of, 39; second generation machine aesthetic, 64–65; and twentieth-century modernity, 63–64
Machine and the Revolution of Art, The (Kimura), 73
"Machine and Roses" (Hanada), 173
Maeterlinck, Maurice, 42
Maiden in the Storm (1932), 78
Major Currents in Western Art (Itagaki), 61
Makino Masahiro, 93
Man'ei, 169

Man-Slashing, Horse-Piercing Sword (1929), 93
Man With a Movie Camera (Vertov), 66, 75, 116
Marco Polo Bridge Incident (1937), 103
Marey, Étienne-Jules, 159
Marinetti, F. T., 56, 57
Marx, Karl, 19–20, 67, 177
Marxism, 23, 31, 85, 107, 112, 113, 121, 171; Althusserian Marxism, 3
materialism, 12, 19, 32, 35, 85, 137, 157; dialectical, 112–113, "society for," 107
Matsui Sumako, 42
Matsumoto Toshio, 180–81
Matter and Memory (Bergson), 134
Maupassant, Guy de, 70
Mavo, 57, 58; manifesto of, 59
media theory, 4–5; in Japan, 5–6; and non-Theoretical media theories, 5–6
Media Theory in Japan (Steinberg and Zahlten), 4–5
Medium (*baizai*), 118–19
Meiji Restoration (1868), 14, 27, 28, 41
Meiji period (1868–1912), 27, 57, 94; emperor, 92
Méliès, Georges, 11
Mello, Cecília, 11
Mimetic depiction, 21, 25, 40, 53, 66, 78–79, 81, 111; ambivalence of, 26–30
Merleau-Ponty, Maurice, 135, 136, 165
metaphysics, 32, 35, 107, 139, 153, 157
Metropolis (1925), 194n35
Metz, Christian, 3, 145, 203n48,
Midorikawa Harunosuke, 49
Minamoto no Yoshitsune, 34
Mistress of a Foreigner (1930), 25
Mitsuhiro Yoshimoto, 3, 186n5
Mittel (*baizai*), 118–119
Mitsuse Sueo, 49–50, 50–51
Miyazawa Kenji, 59
Miyoshi Tatsuji, 141
Mizoguchi Kenji, 1, 24–25, 94–95, 100–101, 145, 168–169, 206n4
modernism, 13; distinction between realism and modernism, 14; literary modernism, 59–60; "political modernism," 10; realism within modernism, 52–56. *See also* postmodernism
modernity, 165; alternative modernities, 16–21; as both one and multiple, 19; criticism of alternative modernities, 17–18; deconstructive approach to, 18; the "end of modernity," 16; non-Western, 7, 18, 19; "overcoming modernity," 13, 17–18; pluralizing of, 18; twentieth-century modernity and the machine aesthetic, 63–64; Western, 16, 17, 19

modernization, 18; of Japan, 19; of Japan in the 1920s, 58–59; "modernization theory," 20. *See also* realism, within Japanese modernization
Modern Times (1936), 74
Moholy-Nagy, László, 22, 56, 62, 64–65
montage, 59, 80–84, 118, 126, 134, 144, 151, 159; of attractions, 179–180, Nakai's theorization of, 115–121; "photomontage," 62. *See also* Soviet montage theory
Mori Ōgai, 56, 92, 96–98, 100–101; novels of, 96
Mother (1926), 66, 68
Moussinac, Leon, 115–16
Mukden Incident (1931), 103–5
Münsterberg, Hugo, 2, 6, 31, 159, 185n3, 186n11
Murakami Tadahisa, 89
Murata Minoru, 42, 43, 49, 58
Murayama Tomoyoshi, 57–58, 150
Mutai Risaku, 141
Muybridge, Eadweard, 159

Nagae Michitarō, 23, 39, 115, 134, 136, 141, 149–152, 157–159, 199n43; *Cinema, Expression, Formation*, 159–65; cinematic world view of, 158*fig.*
Nagai Kafū, 28, 85
Nagatsuka Takashi, 91
Nagib, Lúcia, 11
Nakagawa Shigeaki, 82
Nakagi Sadakazu, 41
Nakai Masakazu, 22, 76, 105, 113–122, 123–125, 150, 158, 161, 173
Nakamura Kan'emon, 94
Nakano Seigō, 171
Naked City, The (1948), 180
Naked Town, A (1937), 87
Nana (Zola), 28
Naoki Sanjūgo, 84
Naomi (Tanizaki), 46
Naruse Mikio, 25
nationalism, 101; ultra-nationalism in Japan, 171–72
National Mobilization Law (*kokka sōdōinhō*, 1938), 133
Natsume Sōseki, 106
naturalism, 14, 24–26, 96, 169; impact of on Japanese literary discourse, 26–30, 41; critique of, 45–49, 60, 66–67, 70–71; Japanese naturalism, 26–30, 31; literary naturalism, 14, 21, 70; localization of, 29–30; and the Pure Film Movement, 40–45; revival of, 78–79, 85.
New Art school (Shinkō geijutsuha), 63
New Drama (*shingeki*) Movement, 25, 41–43, 45, 78, 93

New Sensation School (Shinkankakuha), 14, 57, 59, 63, 152
"News Film and Newspaper Article" (Terada), 106
Night and Fog in Japan (1960), 182
Night Society, The (Yoru no kai), 172, 180, 182
Nikkatsu, 42–43, 86, 196n30
Nishi Aamane, 136
Nishida Kitarō, 23, 107, 136, 138–39, 140, 149; critique of Western dualism, 158–59; philosophical worldview of, 155*fig.*, 156*fig.*; theory of the self-identity of absolute contradiction, 153–59
Nishiwaki Junzaburō, 57, 173
Noda Kōgo, 49
Noh, 2, 36
Noma Hirosi, 172
Nomura Hōtei, 77–78, 93
Nornes, Abé Mark, xi, 3, 106, 128, 173–74

O Fragrant Stoker (Nishiwaki), 57
Oguri Fūyō, 28
Ōishi Kuranosuke, 34
Oka Kunio, 107
Okamoto Tarō, 172; and the concept of "bipolarism," 173, 179
One's Own Sin (1919), 43
Onoe Matusunosuke, 41*fig.*, 93
"On Realism in Art" (Jakobson), 14–15
"Ontology of the Photographic Image, The" (Bazin), 11–12, 112
Osanai Kaoru, 25, 40, 42, 43, 78
Ōsawa Masachi, 20
Ōshima Nagisa, 182
Ōsugi Sakae, 30, 32
Ōtsuka Eiji, 5
Ōtsuka Kyōichi, 89
Ōtsuka Yasuji, 60
Our Neighbor Miss Yae (1934), 78
"Overcoming Modernity" symposium (1942), 17–18, 189n66
Owen, Robert, 113
Ozaki Shirō, 86, 87
Ozu Yasujirō, 1, 24–25, 49, 88–89, 90, 143, 168, 169

Pabst, G. W., 143
Page of Madness, A (1926), 57
Palmov, Victor, 57
Passion of Joan of Arc, The (1928), 98–99
"Paul Rotha's *Documentary Film*" (Imamura), 175–76

INDEX   231

Peace Preservation Law (*chian ijihō*, 1925), 69, 112, 121
Percival, Arthur, 129
Pitfall (1962), 180
phenomenology, 10, 23, 134, 136, 170; existential, 135; of Heidegger, 139–140; of Husserl, 139–140, 153; phenomenological approaches to film experience and theory, 11, 133–136, 159–165; transcendental, 136, 139
Phenomenology of Perception (Merleau-Ponty), 136
Photoplay (Münsterberg), 45
Plekhanov, Georgi, 69
Popular Song (Kosugi), 28
positivism, 16, 60, 74; logical, 54
postmodernism, 13
Power of Plants, The (2013), 161
pragmatism, 21, 26, 32
Pragmatism: A New Name for Some Old Ways of Thinking (James), 32
"Present and Future of Moving Pictures, The" (Tanizaki), 46
Principles and Applications of the Moving Picture (Gonda), 30, 31, 39
Production and Photography of Moving Picture Drama, The (Kaeriyama), 43
Progressive Theater (Zenshinza), 94
Proletarian Film League of Japan (Prokino), 75, 105, 108, 112, 125
psychoanalysis, Lacanian, 3
Pudovkin, Vsevolod, 66, 82, 83, 115, 144–145, 185n3
Pure Film Movement (*jun'eigageki undō*), 40–45, 93

Quilt, The (Katai), 29

Rancière, Jacques, 6
Rashomon (1950), 168
rationalism, 32, 35, 181
realism, 2, 19, 27, 28, 49, 51; aesthetic realism, 11; "American realism," 43; in art, 14–15; Bazin's definition of, 11–12; cinematic realism, 15–16, 21, 96, 170–71; distinction between realism and modernism, 14; "epistemological realism," 101–2; etymological account of, 12; French poetic realism, 24, 81; Jameson's definition of, 12–13; "machine realism," 22–23, 56, 60–68, 72–73, 74–75, 102, 109; "naturalist realism," 25; neorealism, 77–80; Nippon realism, 24–26, 51; paradox of, 10–13; persistence of in local Japanese discourse, 14, 15; "proletarian" realism, 22, 56, 60, 68–72, 79, 85, 169; psychological realism, 11; socialist realism, 180–83; textual realism and historical film, 92–102; within Japanese modernization, 13–16; within modernism, 52–56
Renoir, Jean, 97, 146
"Responsibility of Film Critics, The" (Iwasaki), 168–69
Richie, Donald, 25, 77, 94
Riefenstahl, Leni, 127
"Road to Machine Realism, The" (Itagaki), 65, 68
"Road to Proletarian Realism, The" (Kurahara), 68, 69–70
Rodowick, D. N., 4, 5
romanticism, 34, 49, 73, 96, 119, ; neo-, 49
Room, Abram, 68
Rosen, Philip, xii, 10
Rotha, Paul, 76, 104, 173–76, 181
Russo-Japanese War (1904–5), 28, 103, 130
Ruttmann, Walter, 65

Saigusa Hiroto, 107
Saint-Simon, Henri de, 113
Sakai, Naoki, 140–41
Sakakura Junzō, 62
San Francisco Peace treaty (1951), 166
Sanshō the Bailiff (1954), 100
Sanyūtei Enchō, 27
Sargent, E. W., 43
Sartre, Jean-Paul, 10, 176
Sasaki Kiichi, 172
Satō Tadao, 8, 24–25, 51, 83, 122
Sawamura Tsutomu, 84, 196n22
Scenario Literature Movement (*shinario bungaku undō*), 76, 90–92, 142, 150
Second Sino-Japanese War (1937), 89
Seldes, Gilbert, 9
self-negation, 45, 153–54, 160, 163, 170; logic of, 181, 182
Shanghai (1938), 91
Shiga Naoya, 85, 94
Shimamura Hōgestu, 28, 29, 42
Shimazaki Tōson, 29
Shimazu Yasujirō, 25, 77–78, 90
Shimizu Hikaru, 83
Shimizu Hiroshi, 25, 90
Shimizu Jirochō (1922), 93
Shinkō geikutsu (*The New Art*), 62–63
Shinkō geijutsu kenkyū (*Studies of the New Art*), 62–63
Shōchiku, 25, 43, 77–79, 88, 90, 93, 150, 167, 196n30

Shōwa period (1926–1989), 57; emperor, 166
Shu-mei Shih, 5, 7, 17
silent film, 37, 150; and narration provided for by *benshi* performers, 38, 40, 41, 80
Sobchack, Vivian, 135, 136
Social Darwinism, 70
socialism, 30, 31, 74; utopian, 113, 121
Sōma Gyofū, 29
Song of Stone, The (1963), 180–81
Souls on the Road (1921), 43, 49
Soviet montage theory, 2, 11, 63, 75, 80, 93, 96, 106, 150, 199n43; critique of, 8, 145–146, impact of on Japanese film criticism, 82–84; introduction of to Japan, 66, 82
Spring on Leper's Island (1940), 130
Stalin, Joseph, 69, 130, 181–82
Steinberg, Marc, xii, 4–5
Stepun, Fedor, 9
subjectivity, 26, 34–35, 74, 76, 100, 118, 162; non-human, 65, 67
Sugiyama Heiichi, 39, 134, 141–49, 161, 173; *Essays on Film*, 143–149; on film as "a mirror" and film as "a window," 143–44
Summer battle of Osaka, The (1937), 95, 197n48
Sun, The (1926), 58, 95
Supreme Commander for the Allied Powers (SCAP), 166–67
surrealism, 173, 179–80
Survey of Photoplay, A (Kawazoe), 82
Svilova, Yelizavata, 75

Taikatsu, 45
Taishō period (1912–1926), 57
Takahashi Satomi, 202n19
Tale of a Giant, The (1938), 94
Tanabe Hajime, 139
Tanaka Eizō, 25, 42–43
Tanaka Kinuyo, 77
Tanaka Masasumi, 149
Tange Sazen (1927–1935), 94
Tanizaki Jun'ichirō, 40, 45–51, 52, 53, 59, 149; and the "cinematization of the world," 47–51; intervention in domestic film practice, 45–46; and the mobility of the film medium, 46–47; suggestions of for novels that could be made in to films, 48
Tasaka Tomotaka, 84, 86, 130
Tayama Katai, 29
Terada Torahiko, 106–7
Teshigahara Hiroshi, 180
Theater of Life (1936), 86–87, 97–98
Thought and Custom (Tosaka), 108

"Thoughts toward an Aesthetic of the Cinema" (Lukács), 46
"Three Encounters" (Turgenev), 27
To the Distant Observer: Form and meaning in the Japanese Cinema (Burch), 2
Tokuda Shūsei, 29
Toland, Gregg, 145
"To Project/Reflect" (Nakai), 115
Tosaka Jun, 6–7, 22, 76, 85, 101, 113–14, 122–23, 126, 132, 157; and social epistemology, 106–13; on Nishida Kitarō, 136, 157
totalitarianism, 74, 85, 105, 121–22, 141
Tsubouchi Shōyō, 26–27, 36, 42
Tsuji Hisakazu, 15, 170
Tsumura Hideo, 94–96, 96–100, 133, 168, 174–75; on "historical film," 92–102; on Rotha, 174–175
Tsurumi Shunsuke, 173
Turgenev, Ivan, 27–28
Turvey, Malcolm, 54
Twenty-Four Eyes (1954), 168

Uchida Tomu, 86–87, 90, 91–92, 97–98, 100; use of the "long take" by, 145
Ueno Kōzō, 112, 199n32
Unending Advance (1937), 87–89, 88*fig.*, 196n29

Vampyr (1932), 143
van der Rohe, Ludwig Mies, 64
Vertov, Dziga, 53, 54, 56, 64, 66, 75–76; and the concept of the "kino-eye," 115–16, 159–60
Virilio, Paul, 6
Visible Man (Balázs), 43
Volkoff, Alexander, 82
von Koeber, Raphael, 137
von Sternberg, Josef, 11
von Stroheim, Erich, 11

Wadachi Tomoo, 57
Walker, Gavin, 6–7
"Wall, The" (Nakai), 114
War Comrade's Song (1939), 131
War and Peace (1947), 168
Weavers of Nishijin, The (1961), 180
Weisenfeld, Gennifer, 58
Wells, Orson, 145, 146
White Burch School (Shirakabaha), 29
Williams, Raymond, 12, 50
Wittgenstein, Ludwig, 54
Woman in the Dunes (1964), 180
Woman and the Pirate, The (1923), 93
Woman That Night, The (1931), 77–78, 78*fig.*

"Work of Art in the Age of Its Technological Reproducibility, The" (Benjamin), 109–10
Wyler, William, 145, 146

Yagi Yasutarō, 88–89
Yamakawa Hitoshi, 69
Yamamoto Hirofumi, 98
Yamanaka Sadao, 94–95, 146, 203n51
Yangtze River Fleet (1938), 131
Yellow Race, The (1913), 44
Yoda Yoshikata, 25

Yokomitsu Riichi, 14, 59, 95, 152
Yoshida Kijū, 182
Yoshikawa Eiji, 94
Yoshikawa Shizuo, 62–63
Yoshimura Kōzaburō, 25
Yoshiya Nobuko, 84
Young and the Damned, The (1950), 180
Yutkevich, Sergei, 91

Zahlten, Alexander, xii, 4–5
Zeno's paradox, 135
Zola, Émile, 28, 30, 70

Founded in 1893,
UNIVERSITY OF CALIFORNIA PRESS
publishes bold, progressive books and journals
on topics in the arts, humanities, social sciences,
and natural sciences—with a focus on social
justice issues—that inspire thought and action
among readers worldwide.

The UC PRESS FOUNDATION
raises funds to uphold the press's vital role
as an independent, nonprofit publisher, and
receives philanthropic support from a wide
range of individuals and institutions—and from
committed readers like you. To learn more, visit
ucpress.edu/supportus.

www.ingramcontent.com/pod-product-compliance
Lightning Source LLC
Chambersburg PA
CBHW030539230426
43665CB00010B/960